The Heart of
Confederate Appalachia

CIVIL WAR AMERICA · *Gary W. Gallagher, editor*

The University of North Carolina Press

Chapel Hill & London

John C. Inscoe & Gordon B. McKinney

The Heart of
Confederate Appalachia

Western North Carolina in the Civil War

© 2000 The University of North Carolina Press
Manufactured in the United States of America

Designed by Heidi Perov
Set in Bulmer and Miehle Classic Condensed
by Keystone Typesetting, Inc.

The paper in this book meets the guidelines for permanence and
durability of the Committee on Production Guidelines for
Book Longevity of the Council on Library Resources.

Library of Congress Cataloging-in-Publication Data
Inscoe, John C., 1951–
The heart of Confederate Appalachia :
western North Carolina in the Civil War /
John C. Inscoe and Gordon B. McKinney.
p.   cm. — (Civil War America)
Includes bibliographical references and index.
ISBN 0-8078-2544-1 (cloth: alk. paper)
1. North Carolina—History—Civil War, 1861–1865.
2. North Carolina—History—Civil War, 1861–1865—Social aspects.
3. United States—History—Civil War, 1861–1865—Social aspects.
4. Appalachian Region, Southern—History, Military—19th century.
5. Appalachian Region, Southern—Social conditions—19th century.
I. McKinney, Gordon B., 1943–   .   II. Title.   III. Series.
E524.I54 2000
973.7′456—dc21   99-056658

04 03 02 01 00   5 4 3 2 1

Contents

Acknowledgments ix

Introduction 5

1 · Antebellum Western North Carolina
A Population So Widely Diversified 12

2 · Secession
To Stand with Either Honor or Safety 30

3 · Mobilization
The Mountains Are Pouring Forth Their Brave Sons 59

4 · Unionists
Lincolnite Proclivities—Matters of General Notoriety 83

5 · Guerrilla Warfare
Rule by Bushwhackers, Tories, and Yankees 105

6 · Political Dissent
We Are Tired of This Desolating, Ruinous War 139

7 · Economic Strain
Laboring under Grate Disadvantage 166

8 · Women at War
Assuming All the Duties of the Sterner Sex 187

9 · Slavery
Many Negro Buyers in This Part of the Country 208

10 · Military Incursion and Collapse
Oh! This Is a Cruel World and Cruel People in It 232

11 · Aftermath
A Peace We Little Expected and Did Not Want 266

Notes 287

Bibliography 329

Index 359

ILLUSTRATIONS AND MAPS

ILLUSTRATIONS

Asheville in 1851 24

Advertisement soliciting slave labor
for railroad construction 28

Thomas Clingman 33

William Waightstill Avery 39

Zebulon B. Vance, ca. 1860 66

William Holland Thomas 67

"Union Bushwhackers Attacking Rebel Cavalry" 116

"Rebel Mode of Capturing Escaped Prisoners" 130

William Woods Holden 148

Malinda Blalock, alias "Sam" Blalock 190

"Meeting with Deserters" 192

"The Escaped Correspondents
Enjoying the Negro's Hospitality" 227

General George Stoneman 245

Confederate prison in Salisbury 249

Troops moving along the French Broad River 256

Zebulon B. Vance, 1866 268

Blacks registering to vote in Asheville 273

MAPS

Western North Carolina in 1860 2

Western North Carolina in 1861 3

Secession vote in western North Carolina, February 1861 54

Stoneman's raid through western
North Carolina, March–April 1865 246

Acknowledgments

W
E have both benefited tremendously from the camaraderie and collabora-
tions of our friends and colleagues who are also examining the Civil War
in the mountain South: Ralph Mann, Tracy McKenzie, Todd Groce,
Richard Melvin, Martin Crawford, and Ken Noe. We're especially grateful to
Martin, who has shared with us so much of his extraordinarily rich work on one
of *our* counties—Ashe, and to Ken, who has edited pieces of our work and
provided an astute and very useful critique of this whole manuscript.

We are equally grateful to other Appalachian scholars who we count as good
friends and whose work has significantly enriched our own: Durwood Dunn,
Altina Waller, David Hsiung, Dwight Billings, Ron Lewis, Paul Salstrom, Mary
Anglin, Wilma Dunaway, John Williams, Ron Eller, Mary Beth Pudup, Curtis
Wood, and Tyler Blethen, all of whom have made nineteenth-century Appalachia such a fascinating place to be. The Appalachian Studies Association
and its annual conferences have long provided us all with an invaluable venue
for exchanging and testing ideas, sharing work, developing friendships, and
much enhancing our understanding of the complexities of the region and
constantly reminding us of the broad and complex whole, of which we are
exploring only a small piece and a short time.

Beyond Appalachia, we are grateful to other colleagues who have supported
our efforts and influenced our work in significant ways: Paul Escott, Daniel
Sutherland, Steve Ash, Dan Crofts, Thomas Jeffrey, Michael Fellman, and Bill
Harris. Richard Melvin of Franklin, North Carolina, has generously shared his
considerable knowledge of the war in that part of the state and of the troops that
served from that area.

Archivists and librarians have been of tremendous help to us. In addition to
the staffs of the Southern Historical Collection, Duke, and North Carolina State
Archives, we owe a particular debt to Dick Shrader at the Southern Historical
Collection, Michael Musick at the National Archives, Lewis Buck at Ashe-
ville's Pack Memorial Library, Fred Hay at Appalachian State's Appalachian
Collection, and especially to George Frizzell at Western Carolina's Hunter
Library for locating and passing along to us a number of hidden jewels in that
rich collection.

We feel privileged to be in the capable and caring hands of UNC Press. We are particularly grateful to David Perry for his sustained interest in and support of this project over a far longer period than he ever thought he would have to endure, and to Mary Caviness, whose good, sharp editing has much improved our prose. We appreciate the staffs of Cartographic Services and Photographic Services at the University of Georgia for all their good work in producing our maps and so many of our illustrations.

John C. Inscoe and Gordon B. McKinney

My initial involvement in this project came through a suggestion from Jeff Crow of the North Carolina Department of Archives and History that I consider continuing the Zebulon B. Vance Papers project. A grant from the National Historical Publication and Records Commission allowed me to complete a microfilm edition of the papers with my co-editor Richard McMurry—a former colleague at Valdosta State University. Our work on the Vance project was greatly facilitated by Carolyn Wallace at the Southern Historical Collection at the University of North Carolina and David Olson and Ed Morris at the State Archives. A very good friend, Stan Godbold of Mississippi State University, shared his extensive knowledge of William Holland Thomas that included a memorable tour of the original Thomas homestead. I was also able to discuss ideas with a graduate school classmate, Mike Fellman of Simon Fraser University, who shared his insights about the Civil War in the border regions. I deeply appreciated the willingness of my former colleagues at Western Carolina University, including Max Williams, Tyler Blethen, Curtis Wood, Theda Perdue, Bill Anderson, and the late Alice Mathews, to share their ideas about the Civil War and Appalachia with me. Several friends and fellow professionals at Berea College, including David Nelson, Warren Lambert, Gerald Roberts, and Shannon Wilson, have provided information and an active dialogue that all scholars need. More importantly, I have been able to continue to work on this project over a long period of time because of the constant support of my wife, Martha. Her personal sacrifices that led to her intellectual renewal and professional growth have been a stimulus for my own work, and her good humor and enthusiasm have been a constant source of energy and support.

Gordon B. McKinney

It is a pleasure to be part of a history department in which so many colleagues share an interest in *the war*, even as we study it from such different angles.

Emory Thomas, Bill McFeely, Lee Kennett, Nash Boney, Tom Dyer, and Jean Friedman have inspired me and informed my thinking about the conflict and those caught up in it in numerous direct and indirect ways. I'm grateful to these good friends, all, but the latter two have been especially helpful: Jean, for all I've learned from her in how I've come to think of the intricacies of community, particularly through the team-taught seminars we've done together; and Tom, who not only fed my fascination for his Atlanta Unionists throughout that most fascinating of his projects, and in so doing, greatly shaped my understanding of our mountain Unionists, but also for all of the many other ways in which he encourages and supports me in all that I do. I much appreciate the support of three department heads—John Morrow, David Roberts, and Jim Cobb— throughout the duration of this process, and that of other colleagues, new and old, too numerous to name, who make LeConte Hall at the University of Georgia such an interesting and stimulating place in which to work, even if, for some odd reason, they *don't* all write about the Civil War.

I've learned much from the often extraordinary work of several of our graduate students, past and present, on either the war or Appalachia, or both, and appreciate all they've shared and continue to share with me from their findings: David McGee, Jonathan Sarris, Craig Brashear, Mark Huddle, Brian Wills, Jonathan Bryant, Lesley Gordon, Rod Andrew, Denise Wright, Keith Bohannon, Jennifer Gross, Glenda Bridges, and Wally Warren.

I'm always grateful to John David Smith for his close friendship and support, and particularly in this case, for his having first taught me how much fun it is to work with a co-author. Catherine Clinton, Jane Censer, John Boles, Bob Kenzer, and Warren Rogers are among the other valued friends whose support and interest in this and other projects have been especially meaningful and whose own work has much informed mine.

Sheree Dendy puts up with incredible chaos and confusion that I create but sails through it all with great patience and calm, keeping the *Georgia Historical Quarterly*'s operation far more efficient and timely than it ever would be if left in my hands alone. Finally, a terrific family—wife, children, parents, brothers, and in-laws—have always enriched whatever I try to do. Those three with whom I live, Jane, Meg, and Clay, also put up with my disorder—mental and physical— but manage to do so with a great deal of love, tolerance, and good humor.

John C. Inscoe

The Heart of
Confederate Appalachia

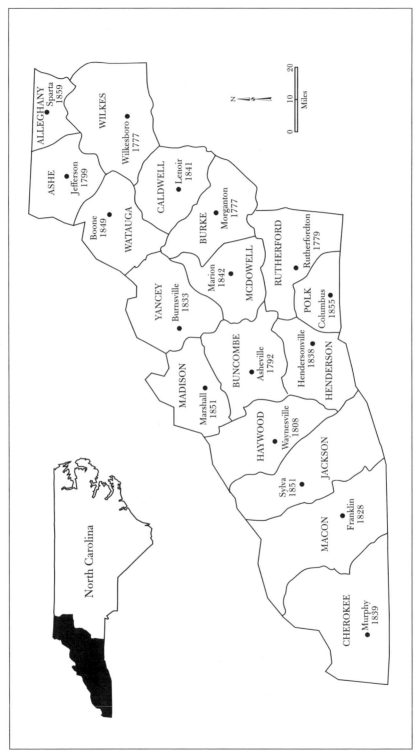

Western North Carolina counties in 1860 (including county seats and years established) (University of Georgia Cartographic Services)

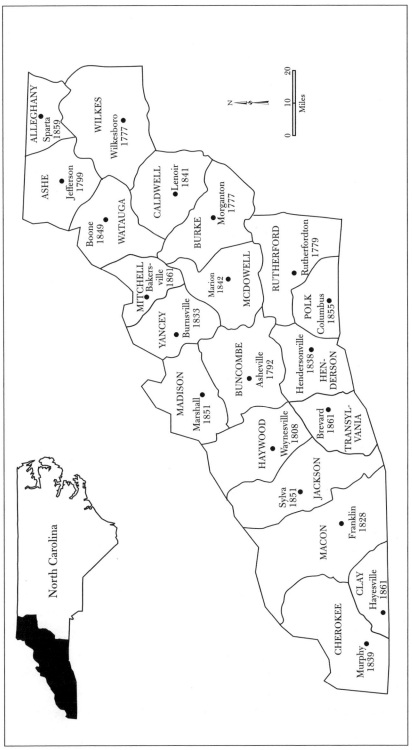

Western North Carolina counties in 1861 (including county seats and years established) (University of Georgia Cartographic Services)

INTRODUCTION

O N a number of occasions throughout the Civil War, both residents of and
visitors to western North Carolina commented on the seeming calm that
prevailed in the midst of the storm that raged elsewhere in the South. In
July 1862 Sarah Lenoir in Morganton informed her cousin in nearby Caldwell
County that "Morganton must be the *safest* place in the whole Confederacy . . .
but then again, you're even more remote than we are."[1] Nearly a year later,
another young woman, Katherine Polk, sought refuge with her family in a
rented house in Asheville, which her father, Leonidas Polk, "considered a safe,
retired place" after Union troops plundered their Mississippi plantation. In
moving up the French Broad River to their new highland quarters in the spring
of 1863, she noted that "peace & plenty ruled everywhere; the country was so
shut in from the world, it seemed almost impossible for the desolations of war to
reach the happy homes along the route."[2]

Even more prominent Confederate figures saw the Carolina mountains as an eagerly sought refuge far from the turmoil of the war elsewhere. Just after the conflict began, Mary Chesnut mused that the destinations of fashionable southern travelers, "hitherto . . . Newport, Saratoga, Europe—& must now be Flat Rock, Buncombe, White Sulphur, &c, &c.," all highland retreats in North Carolina. On several occasions thereafter, the South Carolina diarist yearned for the tranquility offered by her family's summer resort home at Flat Rock. Yet another South Carolinian who had long summered at the home he maintained at that same resort was Christopher Memminger, the Confederacy's secretary of the treasury. Shortly after resigning from that position, he urged Jefferson Davis to move his government to Henderson County, insisting that its remoteness made it far more defensible against Union assault than Richmond.[3]

These responses to the war were not necessarily typical of Carolina highlanders, but they serve as reminders that mountain residents, like Southerners elsewhere, experienced the war at different times and in different ways. What makes this commentary particularly striking, however, is that it reflects a situation far different from that anticipated for western North Carolina on the eve of war in early 1861. A number of residents and outside observers, North and South, had predicted a much more central role for the southern highlands in the new Confederacy. A Henderson County visitor reported that residents of that "mountain kingdom" anticipated that the "capital city of the Southern Confederacy" might be placed in their midst, where it would "have its seat of government within 100 miles of the capitals of six other states."[4]

William Holland Thomas, the most prominent businessman and political leader in the state's southwestern corner, had an even grander vision of the impact of secession on his region. "The mountains of Western North Carolina would be the centre of the Confederacy," he stated, and "we shall then have one of the most prosperous countries in the world . . . the centre of manufacturing for the Southern market, the place where Southern people will spend their money, educate their children and very probably make laws for the nation."[5] A Minnesota journalist, on the other hand, speculated that Southern Appalachia, including the North Carolina mountains, would provide a military key to defeating the Confederacy; he reasoned that the absence of slavery and lack of sympathy for it among highlanders could, with proper encouragement and aid, lead them to instigate a counterrevolution against their fellow Southerners. Even President Lincoln saw the region as vital to putting down the Southern insurrection, and he offered assurances "that a military highway will be opened between the loyal regions of East Tennessee and Western North Carolina, and other faithful parts of the Union."[6]

But neither scenario—Confederate capital nor bastion of loyalist resistance—ever materialized in the Carolina mountains as the war and its seats of power moved off in directions far from that corner of Appalachia. Thus, in some obvious respects and compared to other parts of the South, the mountain region of North Carolina was indeed relatively untouched by the war until its closing days. Certainly it never witnessed the full-scale military conflict that tore apart other parts of Southern Appalachia, such as the campaigns through Virginia's Shenandoah Valley and northwest Georgia, the guerrilla warfare that plagued eastern Kentucky, and the combination of both that made battle-grounds of Chattanooga, Knoxville, and other parts of East Tennessee.

But the calm that by comparison seemed to characterize North Carolina's mountains is deceptive and belies the extent to which western North Carolina experienced the traumas and hardships of war—in fact, as fully as any other part of the Confederate home front. This book is an attempt to come to terms with the variety of means at a variety of levels in which the Civil War impinged upon this particular segment of Appalachian society and the extent to which that society responded to such impingements.

This study is in a sense a merger of two historiographic trends currently in full swing. One is a new appreciation of community studies as a means of understanding the dynamics of the Civil War's course and on its long- and short-term impact on civilians, North and South. The second is a new and more sophisticated examination of preindustrial Appalachia and the recognition that it embraced a far wider and more complex range of experiences and degrees of development than were ever recognized or accounted for in the long-standing stereotypes of the mountain South.

In 1989, Maris Vinovskis asked in the *Journal of American History*: "Have social historians lost the Civil War?" He bemoaned the fact that despite the vast outpouring of scholarship on the war, we know very little about its effects on everyday life in the United States. "Very little has been published on civilian life in the North or the South during the war years," he stated, and accused social historians of the nineteenth century of having "ignored the Civil War altogether."[7] While perhaps this is an overstatement, other scholars have also acknowledged such a void. Daniel Sutherland, in a 1990 essay titled "Getting the 'Real War' into the Books," echoed the need for coming to grips with the home front. "No war," he wrote, "and particularly no civil war, can be understood

without considering the civilian population." He suggested that the most prom-
ising means of doing so is through local history, "a reconstruction of the stories
of individual communities and their inhabitants[.] . . . [T]o understand the real
war, one must stay put. One must watch, weigh, measure, evaluate the consequences of war as they affected a single concentrated area and the people,
soldiers and civilians, who occupied it."[8]

There have been significant studies of Southern communities during the war,
but until very recently, most have focused on locales, particularly cities, in
which the military struggle was center stage.[9] By contrast, what are now beginning to emerge are studies of communities that were not so crucial or strate-
gically central as battlegrounds but were, rather, truly home fronts in the sense
that they experienced the war far removed from any front lines. In examining
these more typical Confederate locales and their residents, historians are reaching new conclusions regarding not only the war's impact on civilian life but also
how civilian life and morale shaped the course of Confederate efforts in waging
the war.[10]

If any common thread runs through this profusion of new work on the Civil
War, it is the realization of how differently Americans experienced it. Women
experienced it differently from men, Southerners differently from Northerners,
generals from privates, Union troops from Confederate troops. On the Confederate home front alone, we are more aware than ever of the extent to which
planters often endured the war very differently from yeomen; urban residents
from rural; slaves from free blacks; Georgians from Alabamians or Texans; and,
of course, highlanders from lowlanders. Yet, as the recent explosion of scholarship on the Civil War in Appalachia is demonstrating, even within the southern
highlands, the war played out in very different ways for western North Carolinians than it did for East Tennesseans or north Georgians or western Virginians
or eastern Kentuckians.

As part of the mountain region of a single state, western North Carolinians
shared much in common with one another. But they were also part of a network
of communities, which in themselves exhibited significant variations in geographical situation, socio-economic makeup, political sentiments, and citizenry,
individually and collectively. The region's county seats alone reflect the wide
discrepancies in rates of development, degrees of isolation, and character of
residents. As the vibrant hub of the region's economic activity, Asheville was
very different from the remote, semisecluded Shelton Laurel, in an adjacent
county. Morganton, Lenoir, and Wilkesboro shared a past and a planter base

that was foreign to the much more recently settled frontier communities of Marshall, Franklin, or Burnsville. Hendersonville, Flat Rock, and Waynesville hosted summer lowland elites and their slaves who rarely frequented more secluded outposts such as Boone, Jefferson, or Sylva. The vast majority of Carolina highlanders did not live in or even near these towns, villages, or crossroads, yet they, too, found themselves in greatly varied situations—from the broad river valleys of the French Broad or Catawba to remote, nearly inaccessible hollows high in the Blue Ridge or Great Smokies. The way in which western North Carolinians experienced the Civil War had as much to do with the communities of which they were a part, and the variables that rendered those communities such different entities, as did more obvious factors such as gender, race, or class identities.

One of our primary goals in this study is to explore these issues among the multiple communities that made up western North Carolina. Despite the perceptions of Sarah Lenoir and Katherine Polk as to their insulation from the war (and both would endure personal experiences that would change their minds soon after recording those impressions), the war imposed tremendous upheaval on residents of their communities in Burke and Buncombe Counties, as well as the other fifteen counties on which this study focuses. (Those seventeen counties in 1860 had become twenty counties with the establishment of three new mountain counties in 1861.) Although relatively minor militarily, incursions by both Union and Confederate troops, particularly from East Tennessee, where their presence was of much more vital military significance, disrupted life and threatened the social stability of several of those counties at different times and in different ways. Even more disruptive were the internal divisions among western Carolinians themselves that emerged as early as the secession crisis and intensified as the war progressed. Differing ideologies turned into opposing loyalties, and those divisions eventually proved as disruptive as anything imposed by outside armies in certain areas. As the mountains came to serve as refuges and hiding places for deserters, draft dodgers, escaped slaves, and escaped prisoners of war, the conflict became even more localized and internalized, and at the same time became far messier, less rational, and more mean-spirited, vindictive, and personal. How and why the war came to evolve in those terms tells us much about the social, economic, and political complexities of mid-nineteenth-century Appalachian society.

Another goal of this study is to set western North Carolina's war experience within the context of the current debate among Appalachian scholars as to when, how, and to what extent the region was transformed from a preindustrial to an industrial society. Although there remains substantial disagreement over whether Southern Appalachia ever underwent so definitive a transformation, and if so, whether it was a long-term evolution rooted in the antebellum period or a more sudden postbellum shift, a vital, and rather obvious question is what role, if any, the Civil War played in that process. A number of recent studies have viewed the conflict as a crucial factor in altering the course of local or regional development, though there seems to be little consensus as to how and why it wrought the changes it did, or even whether such impact was positive or negative in its effects.[11]

In her study of the impact of the Revolutionary War on Charles County, Maryland, Jean Lee observed: "Wars are flash points that provide unusual access to past communities. They throw into graphic relief the contours of the societies involved: their resilience and fragility, their capacity both to endure and to change."[12] The Civil War has long served as such a flash point, particularly for historians of the South. This examination of western North Carolina's home front addresses the capacity of its society both to endure and to change; it demonstrates the extent to which the dynamics of the war reflected mountain society's sources of resilience and its sources of fragility.

Finally, it is important to remember a basic fact of Appalachian geography. As John C. Campbell once noted, the southern highlands make up "the backyard of several southern states."[13] Rather than treat Appalachia as a single region, it is crucial—particularly in explaining why highlanders experienced the sectional crisis and the war itself in such different ways—to think of it as several substate sections that were inextricably bound (if to varying degrees) to the allegiances and identities of different states, which in all but one instance were more nonmountainous than mountainous in character. Western North Carolina happened to be part of the Confederate state in which dissent during the war proved most intense, or, as one historian recently put it, Tar Heels were "perhaps the most ornery population of any Confederate state." And although scholarly scrutiny of that dissent has been and continues to be abundant, only in very recent years has such scrutiny come to be applied to the mountain South.[14] Yet there is considerable evidence that the war was in many respects experienced with more intensity in the mountains than elsewhere in the state.

This book, then, is an attempt to examine the variety of ways in which a very particular populace, and the several communities among which it was distributed, confronted the Civil War in economic, social, and political terms. Did it represent a step forward, if even temporarily, in highlanders' integration into the rest of Southern society, or was it a step backward? In what ways was the balance of social and political power in mountain society upset by the conflict? Did the new political issues raised by the war and by the new nation loosen or tighten the reins of local and regional authority? Did economic hardship and deprivation imposed by the war fan the flames of internal class tensions or intrastate sectional rivalries, and what form did such dissension take? What role did slavery and its demise play in reshaping the power structure within and beyond the region? There are no easy answers to any of these questions, but as Southerners, as Confederate citizens, as North Carolinians, and as mountaineers, highlanders faced them all at some point during the four years over which the military struggle was played out largely elsewhere. Like all Southerners, their lives and their situations were different in 1865 from what they had been in 1860, whether at a personal, a community, or a regional level. Our aim is to determine the extent of those differences and the extent to which their mountain environment shaped the particular direction and degree of the change they experienced.

ANTEBELLUM WESTERN NORTH CAROLINA

A Population So Widely Diversified

O NLY a few contemporary observers of mid-nineteenth-century Southern Appalachia recognized the socio-economic diversity of mountain life. In 1866, soon after moving to Rutherford County, Randolph Shotwell wrote of western North Carolina that "probably no section of the state contains a population so widely diversified in politics, wealth, morals and general intelligence." He elaborated by describing the rich farms along the rivers and creeks inhabited by "many families that in culture, education, gentility, and staunch adherence to right principles may compare with the best classes of the South" and noted that they were "generally slave-holders." Although there may have been several hundred of "this intelligent class," the vast majority of the region's populace, according to Shotwell, were "neither intelligent, . . . nor particularly respectable." They were mainly "poor tenants of small farms, or parts of farms or still ruder mountaineers, dwelling in squalid log huts, and living by fishing, by occasional days' work in the gold mines, by illicit distilling, roguery of all sorts and other invisible means of support. Hundreds of these cabin dwellers are scattered in every mountain cove."[1]

Somewhat less sensitive to the gradations of class among Carolina high-landers, a New York journalist traveling through the Yadkin River valley in 1868 concluded that the community there was "divided into two entirely separate and distinct classes. The one occupying the fertile lands adjacent to the Yadkin River and its tributaries is educated and intelligent, and the other, living on the spurs and ridges of the mountains, is ignorant, poor and depraved."[2]

Although still guilty of the same stereotyping already in vogue in descriptions of mountain life, both of these observers at least acknowledged what few others had about the Carolina highlands—that the socio-economic range among its residents was nearly as great as that anywhere in the antebellum South. These social distinctions had been inherent since the region's earliest settlement in the mid-eighteenth century and merely intensified as slavery, if not the plantation system, established itself soon thereafter.

The Appalachian chain rises to its highest elevations in North Carolina and, as it crosses into Tennessee, spreads to its greatest width. North Carolina's mountains consist of an area of approximately 10,000 square miles, which stretch in a diagonal band almost 250 miles long and from 70 to 150 miles wide across the state's westernmost fifth. The Blue Ridge on the eastern side and the Great Smokies farther south and west are the predominant ranges in terms of area, and are linked by a variety of smaller transverse ranges, often of greater elevations, including the Balsams, the Unakas, and the Black Mountains.[3]

Settlement and traffic patterns were determined by the contours of these ranges and even more so by the river valleys that cut through them. As the eastern continental divide, the Blue Ridge determines the ultimate direction of the many headwaters that originate in the Carolina highlands. Often beginning their routes through narrow, rugged gorges, several of these rivers expand into the broad fertile valleys that proved so attractive to early settlers. East of the Blue Ridge, the Catawba and Yadkin River valleys were among the first lands claimed by mid-eighteenth-century migrants; during and after the Revolutionary War, equally rich land was claimed by those pushing farther westward to the French Broad, the Swannanoa, the Toe, the Pigeon, and the New River valleys. Although still within what was designated as Cherokee Indian territory, even the Tuckaseigee, the Hiawassee, the Oconaluftee, and the Nantahala Rivers in the state's southwestern corner saw frontier settlement before 1800.[4] Across this rugged landscape throughout the antebellum period a steady influx of frontiersmen, farmers, and opportunists settled themselves at a rate exceeding the population growth of any other part of the state. Yet western North Carolina remained the most sparsely inhabited section of the state in 1860, when its 130,000 residents made up only 13 percent of the state's population.[5] But throughout its century or so of growth before the Civil War, all elements of Randolph Shotwell's varied mountain populace were represented.

The earliest claimants to large tracts of bottomland in the Catawba, Yadkin, and French Broad Valleys were men of means whose investments in that land allowed their sons and grandsons to emerge as not only the region's largest slaveholders and wealthiest men but also its political and social elite. It is perhaps worthy of note that the first white settler west of the Blue Ridge, Samuel Davidson, was accompanied by a wife, a baby, and a slave when he moved through the Swannanoa Gap and settled in the Swannanoa River valley in 1784. Samuel was killed by Cherokee hunters soon afterward, but his twin brother, William, moved into the same area three years later and established what became a thriving community, whose descendants would remain some of the most prominent political and slaveholding families in the region.[6]

The antebellum leadership of Burke, Caldwell, Wilkes, Buncombe, and Haywood Counties was also characterized by multigenerational kinship networks that accounted for the prominence of the Avery, Erwin, Jones, Lenoir, McDowell, Baird, Patterson, Gwyn, and Love families. But settlers of more modest means were close behind. They, too, often as multihousehold units, moved into these same rich, wide, and accessible river valleys; then, as those prime claims became more scarce by the 1820s and 1830s, they pushed on into the numerous coves and creekbeds of higher elevation and less accessibility. The more severe topographical and economic limitations imposed on these later settlers meant that they and their descendants generally had to settle for smaller farms and often less fertile lands. In the westernmost counties, still the most sparsely settled by 1860, a mere 10 percent of owned acreage was cultivated, compared with an average of over 29 percent statewide.[7] This was due not only to the more rugged terrain on which mountain farming took place but also to the amount of land mountain farmers devoted to livestock, which foraged freely for most of the year on their owners' vast woodlands. In many respects, livestock, particularly hogs and cattle, and in some areas sheep, formed the backbone of the agricultural economy of the highlands, and the distribution of land usage reflected that preeminence.[8]

Antebellum observers exploring the Carolina highlands noted the remoteness and the crudity of the farms they encountered, but more often than not, they were impressed with the abundance produced on these valley homesteads. As early as 1811, a visitor to "mountaineous and Hilley" Ashe County commented that it was nevertheless blessed with "extremely rich" soil, which yielded "in abundance wheat Rye oats Barley & Buck wheat and every other vegetable equal to any cold country on Earth." He went on to note the "Great numbers of cattle and sheep" raised in the county, "which brings much wealth to the farmer."[9] British journalist Charles Lanman described a farm he encountered when he was moving through the Nantahala Valley in 1847 as "a miserable log hovel . . . which a respectable member of the swine family would hardly deign to occupy," but he went on to note that its rich soil and abundant yield made the property very much in demand and its owner a "wealthy man."[10]

Frederick Law Olmsted also took note of highland yeomen in his 1854 tour of the Southern Appalachians. The New York journalist observed far fewer instances of real poverty in the mountains than elsewhere in the South and claimed that small farmers in western North Carolina were better off than their lowland counterparts. "Compared with the non-slaveholders of the slaveholding districts," he wrote, farmers in the mountains were "more hopeful, more ambitious, more intelligent, more provident, and more comfortable."[11] Much of this contemporary evidence confirmed, indeed helped create, the traditional view of Southern Appalachia as an egalitarian society made up of small, family-operated independent farms, and scholars have long perpetuated that basic assumption.[12] Only recent studies have begun to recognize a far more complex social structure in antebellum highland society prior to the Civil War, a complexity based on the presence of a significant number of whites at either end of the socio-economic spectrum.[13]

Not all of the small farmers in antebellum western North Carolina were white, however. It is important to remember that the oldest residents of the region, the Cherokee Indians, were still a significant presence in the southwestern corner of the state in the decades following the forced removal of most of their number in 1838. In 1840, just over a thousand Cherokees lived in what were then only Cherokee and Macon Counties, according to figures submitted to the census bureau by William Holland Thomas, the white merchant, slaveholder, and self-appointed legal guardian of the Indians who remained in the area. The majority, some seven hundred Cherokees, lived in and around Thomas's own base of operations, called Quallatown; the rest were scattered along the Hiwassee, Cheoah, and Valley Rivers.[14]

These Cherokees consisted of a diverse mix in terms of their racial makeup, degrees of acculturation, and relationship to this particular area; some had always lived there, while others moved into the area as removal refugees from Georgia, or even postremoval returnees from the Indian Territory in Oklahoma. In their farming methods, religious practices, local governance, and even their legal status, the Cherokees who endured in these relatively remote valleys of the Smoky Mountains maintained what John Finger has called a "cultural syncretism," an uneven and often fluid mix of Indian and white practices and traditions. Thanks largely to the purchasing power and legal guardianship of Thomas, most Indian families owned the land that they farmed and, again thanks to Thomas, maintained good relations with the white settlers who moved into the area. North Carolina's Eastern Band thrived economically, socially, and demographically throughout the rest of the antebellum period, having grown to around 1,500 in number by 1860.[15] A traveling correspondent in 1860 commented on the multicultural nature of the remote society he stumbled upon during "a week in the Great Smoky Mountains." Describing an evening meal with his host, a Mr. Enloe of Quallatown, he wrote that he "sat down to table with several Indians, and two of Mr. E's negroes waited on us. The ends of the earth seemed to have met around that table—Europe, America, Africa were all there!—the children of Japhet, of Shem, and of Ham."[16]

The most elusive element in antebellum North Carolina's mountain society was its nonlandholding whites. Recent studies have demonstrated what contemporary observers rarely acknowledged: the widespread presence in antebellum Appalachia of tenant farmers and other landless laborers. Durwood Dunn discovered that in the Cades Cove community, on the Tennessee side of the Great Smokies, over half of farm households did not own the land they worked.[17] The most thorough study of antebellum tenancy focuses on Georgia and indicates that the highest concentration of tenant farmers were in the north Georgia mountains, where 40 percent of farms were operated by tenants. In the fullest study of Appalachia's landless populace, Wilma Dunaway calculates that nearly two-fifths of the region's labor force worked farmland that they did not own.[18] Studies of Jackson and Haywood Counties confirm the prevalence of tenantry in western North Carolina as well, as do the 1850 and 1860 censuses of other selected counties.[19]

What is not clear from these studies or from the census is the form such landless labor arrangements took. In North Carolina's mountains, tenants or day laborers yielded the most flexible form of farm labor, often in combination with slavery. Landholders in Jackson County's rich Tuckaseigee Valley utilized white and occasionally Cherokee tenants, most often as sharecroppers, far more often than slave labor. Alfred W. Bell, in neighboring Macon County, owned no slaves in 1860 but both rented out a part of his acreage to a local landless farmer and hired another white man on short-term contracts to help him and his wife farm their own tract. He also hired two slaves, a man and a woman, on annual contracts.[20] Census figures for Burke, Buncombe, and Wilkes Counties in 1860 indicate a substantial number of "day labourers." Unlike tenant farmers, most workers in this category were young—in their late teens and early twenties—and were concentrated in the towns of Morganton, Asheville, and Wilkesboro, which suggests that nonagricultural enterprises were dependent on and offered opportunities to young men who did not have the resources to buy property or to go into business for themselves.[21]

Slaveholders themselves, many of whom owned multiple tracts of land throughout the mountains, often supplemented their labor force with white tenants, who farmed those tracts under terms established by their absentee landlords. Calvin J. Cowles, a Wilkesboro merchant and slaveholder, and one of the region's largest landholders, operated two of his three farms and several smaller tracts in Wilkes, Caldwell, and Ashe Counties with annual renters, some of whom were even granted the use of several of his slaves on their rented acreage. He employed at least one of his tenants for occasional carpentry jobs.[22] For close to four decades, Thomas and William Lenoir of Caldwell County used hired hands, renters, and sharecroppers, along with their slaves, to man their vast Haywood County holdings to the west.[23] In perhaps the most unusual variation on landless labor arrangements, Barnett Moore of Burke County owned seventeen slaves but no land. He and his black workforce moved about working the Linville River farms of relatives and friends.[24] In this highland situation in which agricultural options could be considered limited, the adaptability—short and long term—of white tenants allowed slaveholders and even some yeomen to maintain larger and more distant landholdings than would have been possible with either family or slave labor alone. At the same time, such labor demands provided much needed employment to a group that one upcountry South Carolinian labeled "poor people who can neither buy nor move away."[25]

The prevalence of tenantry in the mountains can be explained by both the relatively small slave presence in the region as well as the abundance of land available at low cost throughout much of the region. Low costs allowed those with capital to buy up far more land than they or their families, or even in some cases their slaves, could work themselves. Hiring the slaves of others was one means of meeting the labor demands in situations where direct supervision was available, but many of these larger holdings, such as those of Calvin Cowles or the Lenoir family, were widely scattered and called for more stable and more responsible management, which the landowners felt only white tenants could provide.

Finally, as was the case throughout the Old South, the hierarchical order of mountain society was capped by its slaveholders. Both they and their black property made up a considerably smaller proportion of the populace than was true for most of the South, but their dominance of that society, its economy, and its politics was as hegemonic as that of any Southern planter elite, and had been since the initial settlement of the region's rich river valleys in the late eighteenth century.[26] In the state's seventeen westernmost counties in 1860, only 10.3 percent of all heads of households owned slaves, while (by uncanny coincidence) slaves themselves made up 10.2 percent of the region's total population. Those proportions varied considerably from county to county, and the correlations of owners to owned were not so precise. For example, almost a third (31.6 percent) of Burke County's residents were black bondsmen in 1860, but they were owned by about a sixth (16.6 percent) of the county's white heads of households.[27] At the other extreme were the four northwesternmost counties bordering Tennessee, where less than 4 percent of residents were slaveholders, and blacks made up only from 3 to 6 percent of the populations.[28]

This distribution of property among mountain masters indicates that they owned far fewer slaves than was true of the South as a whole. Only four men in the region owned more than one hundred slaves in 1860, and the 50 largest slaveholders—out of a total of 1,877 owners in 1860—each had more than thirty slaves. Almost 40 percent of slaveholders owned only one or two slaves, and 83 percent owned fewer than ten.[29] The number of slaves increased dramatically in certain mountain communities during the spring and summer months, as planters from Charleston and elsewhere in coastal South Carolina moved up into the Carolina highlands. Nearly all of these "summer people" were large slaveholders, and although they left the vast majority of their labor force at home under the supervision of overseers or kinsmen, they often brought several slaves to serve their families and maintain their households. Flat Rock and Hendersonville emerged as especially affluent resort communities, the former actually referred to as "the little Charleston of the mountains." Warm Springs, Waynesville, and Asheville also attracted numerous summer visitors with black and white entourages that shifted, for at least a few months a year, both the racial complexion and the social dynamics of these communities.[30]

Yet the limitations of mountain agriculture would neither have justified nor supported even this small African American labor force. Perhaps the most distinctive characteristic of slavery in western North Carolina was that within a society as rural as any part of the antebellum South, the largest slaveholders were actively engaged in nonagricultural pursuits. Frederick Law Olmsted recognized this during his 1854 trip through the region, where he observed: "Of the people who get their living entirely by agriculture, few own negroes; the slaveholders being chiefly professional men, shop-keepers, and men in office, who are also land owners, and give a divided attention to farming."[31] Indeed, two-thirds of the ten largest slaveholders in each of five sample counties were merchants; another third were either lawyers or doctors. Only 3 percent of that sample engaged in no commercial or professional pursuit other than agriculture.[32]

These enterprises not only provided owners with the capital to invest in slave property, they also allowed these entrepreneurial masters to utilize their slaves in a wide variety of nonagricultural activity. Slaves worked in their owners' stores, their mines, their mills, and increasingly by mid-century, their hotels and resorts, the owners and operators of which were some of the region's largest slaveholders.[33] Since most of these men owned and cultivated farmland as well, their slaves by no means escaped the more traditional rigors of field work. This diversity and flexibility in the application of a black labor force insured both slavery's profitability for those who invested in it and its steady expansion within the region up until the eve of the Civil War.[34]

Equally vital to slavery's economic viability in this mountain environment was the extent to which slave hiring was practiced. Slaveowners who rented out the labor of their bondsmen on either short- or long-term bases not only often earned considerable income, they also enabled a large segment of the region's nonslaveholding or very small slaveholding populace to benefit directly from the available black labor source. The region's extensive gold and copper mining operations from the late 1820s on and railroad construction by the late 1850s both depended heavily on slave labor, much of which was supplied on monthly, annual, or semiannual terms by local owners.[35]

Perhaps the most significant facet of the extensive tenant and hired slave labor force in western North Carolina was the degree of mutual dependency it imposed upon all levels of white mountain society. The transactions between both slaveholding and nonslaveholding landowners in the exchange of slave labor and landholding and nonlandholding whites in tenant relationships suggests a social and economic structure far more complex than that traditionally attributed to Appalachia. This interclass interaction extended well beyond labor relations. The interdependency of all elements of mountain society—elite, yeomen, landless, and slave—highlights what historians have only recently come to acknowledge about preindustrial Appalachia: the centrality of community. Although mountaineers were for so long stereotyped as "rugged individualists" and celebrated for their independence and self-reliance, they were not as isolated from each other or from the world beyond them as was once assumed.[36]

Recent studies have refuted such notions by demonstrating the extent to which, as both concept and reality, community penetrated antebellum Appalachia and was not negated by the remoteness or sparsity of highland homesteads.[37] Jean Friedman's observation of the antebellum rural South in general, that "the isolation and expanse of southern settlements made 'community' less a village of proximate neighbors than an understanding of the heart among distant kinfolk and neighbors," is even more applicable to its highland regions.[38] The fact that homesteads were often widely dispersed along broad valleys or more remote creekbeds did not indicate individual or single-family migration into such an area. Studies of the settlement of the Yadkin River's "Happy Valley" and the Catawba River valley east of the Blue Ridge and of the Shelton Laurel, Rocky Creek, Toe River, and Tuckaseigee valleys west of the Blue Ridge indicate that multiple units of one or more extended families moved into the area together or in stages over a brief period of time. They remained in close contact with each other and identified themselves as distinct communities, with kinship bonds strengthened through intermarriage over several generations.[39]

Highlanders' mutual dependence was grounded as much in economic terms as social. Although highland farmers were never completely a part of a market economy either before or after the Civil War, neither were they nearly as self-sufficient as once assumed. The debate among historians over the nature of

small farms and their role in the local and regional transformations to a capitalist
economy has moved, after years of analysis of the colonial Northeast, to the
nonplantation South of the nineteenth century.[40] These studies have led to
a new awareness that the small independent family farm was never as self-
sufficient as once assumed, with differences of opinion emerging most often
over the degree and rate of its participation in a broader market network.

Two of the most important of those studies, those by Steven Hahn and Lacy
Ford on upcountry Georgia and South Carolina, respectively, have been based
on the assumption that yeomen's transition from a self-sufficient to market-
based orientation was tied to their conversion to cotton cultivation and access to
railroads.[41] Yet for at least two reasons, the situation in Appalachia was not
comparable to these models of agricultural commercialization either north or
south. The most obvious is that Southern Appalachia never experienced this
agricultural transformation during the nineteenth century in any widespread
form; in fact, farmers in many highland areas moved against the national trend
by reverting from commercial to more subsistent farming during the century's
middle decades.[42]

Second, unlike the situation in either South Carolina or Georgia, the market
economy in the mountains was dependent on neither staple crop production
nor access to railroads. It only took a small surplus on relatively small farms to
allow participation in—indeed dependency on—ever expanding trade outlets.
Robert Mitchell's study of the early Shenandoah Valley, *Commercialism and
Frontier*, was the first of several that offered convincing evidence of the variety
of ways in which, from the earliest settlement on, Virginia Appalachians engaged in trade well beyond their own farms or neighborhoods. Other studies
have indicated even more flexibility and variety in the ways and degrees to
which highland farmers moved beyond subsistence to commercialization, and
indeed combined both.[43]

Such was the case in the Carolina highlands as well. Merchants were often
among the first to settle in some of the more remote sections of western North
Carolina, where their stores or trading posts provided a core around which
subsequent settlement centered. James Patton at Wilkesboro and later Asheville, Joseph Cathey at Forks of the Pigeon, Jesse Siler at Franklin, Jordan
Councill at Boone, William Holland Thomas and Archibald Hunter at Quallatown, and James Harper at Lenoir were all examples of businessmen who were
pioneers in terms of moving very early into remote and as yet unsettled areas.
Some of their operations remained no more than crossroad outposts in this

sparsely settled agricultural society. But a number of them formed the core of villages and towns that encouraged even further intercourse with markets and provided access to them.[44]

The merchants in these communities provided yeomen in their areas with basic supplies and services, such as milling, tanning, and blacksmithing. But they were equally important as local conduits for outgoing commodities as well. Beginning in the late eighteenth century and to a steadily growing degree throughout the antebellum period, these and other store owners actively engaged, on their own behalf and as agents for local farmers, in trade with either plantation or urban markets to their north and south. Although several merchants in the northwestern corner of the state looked toward Baltimore, Philadelphia, and New York as the major outlets for their trade, most western North Carolina merchants made annual or semiannual trips to Greenville, Spartanburg, Columbia, and Charleston in South Carolina or Augusta, Athens, and Savannah in Georgia, transporting wagon loads of mountain products and produce, ranging from honey, ginseng, and other roots and herbs, to apples, peaches, and their liquid byproducts, to smoked game, furs, and tanned hides. But by far the greatest highland export was livestock. From late summer through the fall of every year, cattle, some sheep, ducks, and turkeys all joined the particularly vast hog traffic that poured out of the mountains as the Upper South came to supply more and more of the sustenance of the cotton South.[45]

Mountain merchants sold or bartered this agricultural excess in order to restock their own shelves for the year ahead with staples, hardware, and other manufactured goods to meet the demands of their customers. A number of farmers engaged in these treks themselves without the benefit of mercantile intermediaries. Although not all Carolina highlanders participated in this market network, either directly or indirectly, very few were too remotely situated by the 1860s to be denied access to the services and products of these ubiquitous merchants if they desired such outlets.

Mercantile operations often formed the core of mountain towns and villages, but their commercial functions were only one of several ways in which these concentrated highland communities shaped the character of western North Carolina before the Civil War. Whether they originated as commercial centers, county seats, or summer resorts, such towns were not only the clearest manifestations of the economic and social viability and diversity of its antebellum society; they also provided the strongest sense of community identity to their own residents as well as to the vast rural populace for whom they provided vital links to the world beyond.

Settlers in several areas of western North Carolina managed to do without any village or town for a number of years after their arrival. Often the creation of new counties spurred the need for a courthouse and a surrounding seat. But once established they proved indispensable to farmers in the vicinity in terms of the services and supplies they made available. The towns themselves attracted enterprising men of varied training and backgrounds. The governmental and judicial function of the county seats made lawyers, judges, clerks, and other officeholders prominent among the earliest residents. They and their families created a need for other professionals such as doctors, ministers, and teachers, who soon followed in their wake as either permanent or seasonal residents or as circuit riders who served several such communities. Even when stores or trading posts were not the initial nuclei around which these towns emerged, merchants and artisans, tavern keepers and innkeepers were never far behind in establishing their operations as the economic cores that ensured the viability of these communities as local market centers.[46]

But despite the fact that communities in western North Carolina had certain features in common, there were also significant variations in their character and patterns of development. The older, more established towns that quickly emerged in the foothills east of the Blue Ridge—Morganton, Lenoir, Wilkesboro, and Rutherfordton—were shaped by the relatively affluent planters and professionals who staked their claims early along the rich river valleys in which those towns were built. These towns' thriving commerce was based on their positions as gateways into the highlands from the rest of the state and out of them, and that position, along with their function as county seats, provided them with as diverse and as prosperous a residential base as any small town in the antebellum South.

Across the Blue Ridge, forty to sixty miles farther west, even more affluent communities took root. In addition to having the same economic bases of the foothills communities, Asheville, Hendersonville, Flat Rock, and to a lesser extent Waynesville and Warm Springs owed their growth to the tourists and seasonal residents who flocked to the mountains in the late spring and summer to enjoy their scenic beauty, cool climate, and in some cases, healing mineral springs. Much of the influx to these "charming refuges from the hot plains of the lowlands" was from the cities and plantations of South Carolina and

Asheville in 1851 (North Carolina Division of Archives and History)

Georgia.[47] This seasonal wealth endowed these highland resorts with vast and often opulent summer estates and numerous hotels at the same time that they provided yet another vital economic and social link between the Carolina highlands and the plantation South.

Of these towns, Asheville was in a class by itself. From its establishment in 1795, it served as the hub of western North Carolina commerce. Situated at the juncture of two of the widest river valleys west of the Blue Ridge, the French Broad and the Swannanoa, it was, as native son Thomas Wolfe later described it, "of all that mountain district of the west, 'the place.'" Although its population was only 1,100 permanent residents by 1860, that figure was twice what it had been twenty years earlier, and its growth showed no signs of abating. By the late antebellum period, Ashevillians were some of the region's ablest and most ambitious citizens, who had built and supported over twenty stores or businesses, a courthouse, a jail, three churches, three large hotels, several schools, and a female college.[48] In addition to being a solid base as the market center for the region, it also supported—and was supported by—a large influx of seasonal residents and more transient tourists.

Finally, north and west of Asheville, in the latest and most sparsely settled sections of North Carolina's mountains, were a series of county seats that remained small, crude, frontierlike villages. In sharp contrast to the older, more refined resorts, they seemed to evoke disdain from the visitors who ventured through their somewhat less accessible vicinities. They rarely had more than a hundred residents, who operated only one or two stores and hotels situated around a courthouse. Franklin, Murphy, Marshall, Boone, and Burnsville all fit this description, and observers consistently described them as dirty, primitive, and poor, inhabited by residents prone to drunken and disorderly behavior.[49]

With the emergence of these various communities, access to and from them became vital to western North Carolina's participation in the Southern market economy. The issue of internal improvements thus proved to be an ever more important priority of mountain residents throughout the antebellum period. The location of these early regional thoroughfares was based on topographical features, with broad river valleys and gaps in mountain ridges determining major routes, many of which grew from rough trails or Indian paths. The French Broad River valley was the earliest and remained the most important artery through the Carolina highlands. Cutting through the heart of the region on a north-south axis that linked Asheville, Marshall, Flat Rock, and Hendersonville with Greenville, South Carolina, and Greenville, Tennessee, the original 1790 road was improved and expanded to become the Buncombe Turnpike in 1828. It soon carried a phenomenal amount of commercial and tourist traffic into and out of the mountains. It invigorated the livestock trade from Tennessee and Kentucky to the plantation markets of South Carolina and Georgia and provided opportunities not only for western Carolinians to join more readily that southward flow, but also for those along that route to profit—through taverns, way stations, and corn sales—from the traffic, both two- and four-legged, that swept through the area.[50]

The Buncombe Turnpike's success generated a clamor throughout the region for other roads, many of which directly or indirectly fed into the Buncombe Turnpike at some point along its hundred-mile section in North Carolina. The effect of this and other roads, such as those through the Hickory Nut Gap, the Saluda Gap, and the Ocunaluftee and Chattahoochee valleys, was that they linked western North Carolina far more easily to South Carolina and Georgia to the south and Tennessee and Kentucky to the northwest than to the rest of North Carolina to the east. The implications of those ties would be significant during the war years, as would the intrastate sectionalism that characterized western efforts to win support for internal improvements from an unsympathetic and often uncooperative state government.[51]

The intensity with which these campaigns for roads, turnpikes, and, ultimately, railroads were waged by mountain leaders testified to both the strong entrepreneurial spirit in the region and the fallacy that isolation was central to the character of the Appalachian frontier. As elsewhere in rural America, such efforts were initiated and perpetuated by the region's planter and commercial interests. Where western North Carolinians differed perhaps from other Southerners was in the broad-based support they gave to such developments, thus avoiding the class conflict those measures engendered elsewhere.[52]

These issues were foremost among the goals of a number of men within and beyond the region who recognized the tremendous potential the natural resources of western North Carolina offered. Thomas Clingman, Calvin Cowles, William Holland Thomas, and others actively promoted their own corners of the region as ripe for commercial agricultural opportunities—from raising livestock and producing dairy products to growing peaches and apples and making wine, and mining operations for the mountains' bounty—from copper and iron ore to marble. "This is a Mineral Kingdom," exclaimed S. R. Mount of Murphy in 1853 in terms typical of fellow visionaries in the southwestern corner of the state, "and it only wants energy upon the part of its inhabitants to unbed the precious Mettles, Gold, Silver, Led, Copper."[53] In broader terms, a newspaper editor from Franklin bemoaned the highlands' untapped potential in the state agricultural journal and was quick to pass blame: "Our unsurpassed water power and sites for manufacturing establishments, our inexhaustible forests of furniture timber . . . our rich mountains, pure water and mineral springs of Haywood, Macon, and Cherokee [Counties] must all remain unappreciated and unvisited by the capital and enterprise of our own state unless the auspices of a brighter day should dawn upon us, and a more liberal and just sentiment possesses North Carolina legislators."[54] Some eastern North Carolinians were equally eager to see these western resources exploited, from University of North Carolina geologist Elisha Mitchell, who compared the Carolina highlands to "ancient Arcadia—the country of herdsmen and shepherds," to Governor John Motley Morehead, who complained that eastern North Carolinians were so rarely the beneficiaries of "the vast productions of the fertile West," which went instead to South Carolina and Georgia.[55]

But, even with a governor's urging, state support for such projects proved difficult to obtain. In the face of barriers from the eastern planter-dominated legislature, highlanders looked increasingly to private resources in neighboring states, particularly regarding railroads. Early schemes usually involved laying tracks across western North Carolina as a means of linking coastal ports with interior cities, such as an 1835 proposal, initiated by South Carolinians, for a line from Charleston to Knoxville, and an 1850 plan to link Charleston and Columbia to Cincinnati. Both of these lines would have had to move through North Carolina's mountains, the first through Asheville and Hendersonville, the latter farther west through Franklin, and both were widely embraced by those along their proposed routes. But for a variety of reasons, both political and financial, neither materialized.[56]

A state-sponsored project, driven by party politics in the mid-1850s, gave western Carolinians their greatest hope of being linked by rail to the lowland markets they so craved. A statewide railroad was the central issue of the 1854 gubernatorial campaign, and western voters, traditionally far more of a Whig base of strength, swept Democrat Thomas Bragg into the governor's seat and reelected him two years later on the basis of his initiative in making that dream a reality. In 1855, the legislature chartered the Western North Carolina Railroad but without the full appropriation of public funds to make its construction more than piecemeal. Thus it was only in the last months before the Civil War broke out that tracks for the Western North Carolina Railroad finally made their way into the region, extending from Salisbury westward toward Morganton. In May 1861, construction halted for the war's duration with only ten miles of track laid in Burke County.[57]

In many ways, western North Carolina on the eve of the Civil War was a society on the rise led by men on the make. The reality—or near reality—of railroad access was merely the latest indication of the economic development that mountain residents had witnessed, indeed had instigated and endorsed, throughout the antebellum period. But the rate of that development was by no means uniform throughout the region. There was considerable variation among the state's seventeen westernmost counties in terms of agricultural production, slaveholdings, urban influences, accessibility, and per capita wealth. With these differences came ideological differences in terms of future economic development and the political implications for the region, for communities within the region, and for individuals within those communities.

In an influential article on the mind-set of early rural America, James Henretta has argued that farmers valued the preservation of family and community more than their own individual aggrandizement and profit.[58] Although the

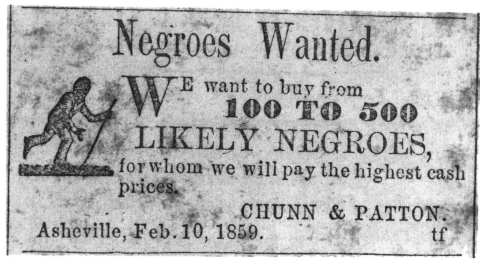

Advertisement soliciting slave labor for railroad construction
(Asheville News, February 10, 1859)

more traditional values of family and community preservation were certainly evident among western North Carolina's antebellum yeomanry as well, the two sets of values were not mutually exclusive. By 1860, there was growing evidence that many Carolina highlanders embraced the tradition without abandoning their commitment to progress.

The large number of yeomen scattered across this sparsely populated mountain landscape and the crudity of their lifestyle led both contemporary observers and historians since to conclude that antebellum Appalachia remained locked in a frontier state of development. But recent scholarship on the region suggests a far more complex rate of growth that challenges such generalizations and stereotypes. Paul Salstrom has provided a model of three subregions within the southern highlands based on when and how each evolved from frontier status, with internal variables such as topography, economics, and demographics all vital to the differences among the three, with different parts of western North Carolina falling into both his "older" and his "intermediate" phases of development.[59]

Other historians have affirmed these variables, though they have categorized them in different terms and recognized that developmental differences could coexist within the same areas of the region. For Robert Mitchell, antebellum Appalachia can best be viewed as "a series of frontiers." No longer, he insists, can we view southern highlanders as "isolated and unchanging, waiting pas-

sively for an external economic stimulus to carry them into the modern age."
More precisely, Mitchell's characterization of preindustrial Appalachia's evolution as "a complex process of differential change that left some places at basic
subsistence and other places deeply involved in market operations" is particularly apt for antebellum western North Carolina.[60]

The contrast was obvious to outside observers. Journalist David Hunter
Strother (under the pseudonym Porte Crayon) described the wide range of
development he found existing side by side within Tennessee mountain society
in 1858, a juxtaposition that he could have observed just as easily across the
state line in North Carolina: "In these days one may see a great many queer
sights in Tennessee. He may discern the print of the deer-skin moccasin and the
French kid slipper side by side. Overlooking the mud-chinked cabin of the
pioneer, carefully imitated from the handiwork of Daniel Boone, he may see the
elegant villa from the design by Downing or Vaux. Strangely contrasting with
the simple garb and manner of the olden time, he meets every where the luxury
and polish of modern refinement."[61]

Indeed a wide spectrum of economic development and cultural advancement
separated southern highlanders by the late antebellum era. But regardless of
where on that spectrum western North Carolinians found themselves, community ties remained strong. It was through interaction with the various components of their communities across class lines that mountain residents responded to the Civil War. External forces, of course, determined how and to
what extent the conflict disrupted mountain life, but individual relationships at
the local level—between patron and client, merchant and customer, landlord
and tenant, master and slave, slaveholder and nonslaveholder, and neighbor
and neighbor—had much to do with how mountain residents responded to that
disruption.

SECESSION

To Stand with Either Honor or Safety

W HEN the sectional crisis came to a head in 1860, western North Carolinians
were by no means caught off guard by either the issues or the stakes it
involved. Perhaps more than most North Carolinians, and certainly more
than southern highlanders in other states, they were fully attuned to the sectional tensions that had characterized the previous decade. Ever since the
territorial gains of the Mexican War had infused new life into the only slightly
dormant questions of slavery and its expansion westward, Carolina highlanders
found their congressional representative at the center of the ensuing debates
that raged in Washington and throughout the nation over the next decade.
Thomas Clingman was the most "ultra-Southern" member of North Carolina's
congressional delegation, and his defense of slavery and Southern interests
made him a prominent player throughout the sectional crisis as it developed
over the course of the 1850s. The way in which that role was shaped by and

conveyed to his highland constituents tells us much about their own concerns on these matters.

Clingman emerged politically at the height of the second party system. Despite the personal popularity of Andrew Jackson among western Carolinians, the Whig Party clearly established its preeminence over the Democratic Party by the end of the 1830s, as it had in North Carolina as a whole. For a variety of reasons—from its role as the party of reform and champion of internal improvements to the popularity of Henry Clay and the organizational strength of local leaders—the Whigs established so strong a majority among mountain voters that by 1842 the *Raleigh Register* referred to the highlands as "the Gibraltar of Whig principles" and Whig leaders came to put stock in what they referred to as "our glorious Western Reserve."[1]

Yet the mountains were never a single-party stronghold, and Democrats remained viable opponents in several areas. Yancey County consistently voted Democratic, and to a slightly less extent, so did Ashe. In Burke, Buncombe, Henderson, and Haywood Counties, Democrats beat Whigs in several legislative contests and ran close races in others.[2] Clouding party distinctions during much of the late antebellum period was the fact that divisions over most of the issues debated fell more along regional than partisan lines. Statewide issues such as free suffrage in the late 1840s (whether or not voting rights should be tied to ownership of property) and ad valorem taxation in the late 1850s (whether taxes on slaves and other property would replace poll taxes as the basic source of state revenue) were generally debated in terms of their effects on the mountain region as opposed to other sections of the state.[3]

Far more significant to western Carolinians than either free suffrage or ad valorem taxation in both popularity and long-term impact were internal improvements. The Whigs' strong endorsement of government funding and sponsorship of various transportation projects led the majority of mountain voters into the party in the late 1830s and kept them loyal to the party throughout the 1840s. Highland Democrats soon realized that they could not afford not to support internal improvements themselves, and Democratic leaders became as aggressive as their Whig opponents in championing such projects. Highland representatives focused much of their legislative efforts in Raleigh and their campaign energies within the region on securing authorization and funding for various road and turnpike projects in the 1830s and 1840s and railroad schemes in the 1850s. A variety of setbacks, both financial and political, stalled plans for railroad construction for nearly a decade. It was not until late in 1860 that the

Western North Carolina Railroad's long-anticipated extension from Salisbury to Asheville and beyond finally crossed into Burke County.

These issues remained central to antebellum politics in Appalachian North Carolina and had much to do with the formation of a regional consciousness. But just as mountain residents came to think of themselves politically as westerners within their state, more momentous developments forced them to think of themselves as Southerners within the nation as well. Since both Whigs and Democrats were dependent on both Northern and Southern memberships, the second party system remained viable only as long as sectional issues were kept at bay. Once slavery thrust its way back into national politics in the late 1840s, the bisectional party system was doomed to break down. Democrats proved quicker and more assertive in championing Southern interests, a fact not lost on Thomas Clingman.

A native of Surry County, in the northeastern foothills of North Carolina's Blue Ridge, Clingman practiced law there and represented it in the state legislature until 1834, when he moved west to Asheville. Buncombe County's seat, already the political and economic hub of the expanding mountain region, offered far more opportunity to the ambitious twenty-two-year-old lawyer. Once he established himself as part of its legal elite, Clingman ran for Congress as a Whig. He lost his first bid in 1841, but he won two years later; and except for a single two-year lapse in the mid-1840s, he served in Washington until North Carolina's secession from the Union in May 1861.[4]

The Asheville-based Whig wasted no time in jumping into the new sectional fray. Clingman's ultra-Southern voice in Congress, which first emerged in the late 1840s, both reflected the sentiments of his highland constituents and heightened their awareness of the volatile issues that would eventually lead them to war. But taking sides on sectional issues meant distancing himself from a Whig stance that still sought to maintain neutrality on issues of slavery or Southern rights, a stance he recognized would sooner or later mean the party's deterioration, at least in the South. Clingman managed to stay a step ahead of his party's demise, which was complete by 1855. His deft conversion from Whig to Democrat over the course of three odd-year election campaigns (leading one historian to label him a "political hermaphrodite") positioned him not only to survive as the longest-serving congressman in antebellum North Carolina, but also to move from the House of Representatives to the U.S. Senate in 1858. Throughout the conversion process, he articulated a position that would have won him as much support in the Deep South as in western North Carolina.

*Thomas Clingman (North Carolina Collection,
Pack Memorial Public Library, Asheville, N.C.)*

Clingman's self-assertiveness, his impassioned and accomplished oratory, and his popularity among his fellow highlanders made him a particularly visible and influential participant in the sectional battles of the 1850s. As early as 1847, he delivered a strong attack on the Wilmot Proviso, which would have banned slavery from any new territory acquired from Mexico, and on the Northern abolitionists behind the measure. During the debate over California's admission to the Union three years later, he gave a speech in Congress titled "In Defence of the South against the Aggressive Movement of the North," in which he warned that recent events were rapidly weakening Southerners' once-strong commitment to the Union. "Do us justice," he proclaimed to his Northern colleagues, "and we continue to stand with you; attempt to trample on us, and we separate."[5]

This was the most blatantly secessionist statement made yet in Congress, and Clingman soon found himself embraced by Southern Democrats. He also won a strong mandate from mountain voters a year later, when he first ran without a Whig label. If Clingman dominated sectional politics in western North Carolina for most of the final prewar decade, he rarely went unchallenged. He maintained his strong, proslavery, states' rights stance on a national stage at the same time that more cautious and moderate voices also rose to prominence in his home district.

The most significant spokesman for this moderate stance during the latter part of the decade and continuing through the war years was Zebulon B. Vance. Vance first emerged before a regionwide electorate in 1857 when he challenged Clingman for his congressional seat. A Buncombe County native who returned to Asheville after receiving a Chapel Hill education, Vance had already established his credentials as an ardent Unionist as assistant editor of the *Asheville Spectator*. Through its pages, he launched a full-scale attack on Clingman, calling him "a liar and a scoundrel," whose radical rhetoric and secessionist bent seriously threatened the Union. But Clingman proved invincible to the challenge posed by Vance and the "Opposition," as the remnants of the state's Whig Party came to be called. He won reelection by so great a majority that a Wilmington newspaper observed that "those transmontane fellows . . . will cling to Clingman with a pernacity only equalled by the love a Loco has for the spoils of office."[6] Vance did not have to wait long for another shot at the same seat, however. When Clingman won the appointment to a vacated Senate seat in May 1858, Vance ran again for his House seat and won a decisive victory over William Waightstill Avery, a Democrat whose ultra-Southern views were second only to Clingman's in intensity, and a prominent member of one of Burke County's most elite families.[7]

Thus by the time that John Brown's raid so dramatically intensified the sectional crisis and infused the presidential election that followed with ominous new implications, two of western North Carolina's ablest leaders—one at the climax of his political career, the other emerging—presented to their shared constituency a range of responses. And it was those approaches that formed the bases of debate that would continue until North Carolina actually left the Union nearly a year and a half later.

In November 1859, the Appalachians became the focus of the most dramatic development yet in the ever escalating sectional crisis. John Brown's raid on Harpers Ferry in the heart of northern Virginia's Allegheny Mountains and the scheme behind it revealed southern highlanders' strong commitment to slavery.[8] And yet North Carolina highlanders reacted to Brown's raid far less as mountain residents than as Southerners. Very much like most white residents of the South, they viewed Brown's fanatical scheme in terms of what it suggested about the vulnerabilities of slavery to abolitionist aggressions. The *Asheville News* set the tone for regional reactions and conveyed the significance of the presidential election a year away when, in December, it condemned the "Black Republicans" that had instigated the raid, and warned its readers that "when we see the feast of blood to which they will invite the South, we have but to be ready with measures firm, quiet and decided, when the popular majority of the North shall evince their approbation of it."[9]

Both Vance and Clingman echoed the alarmism so apparent among their mountain constituents. In a circular addressed to Eighth District voters in February 1860, Vance articulated their fears. Observing "good and true men of the North" turned into "aliens, acknowledging no longer any constitutional obligations or brotherly regard for us," he asked, "what restraint is there upon the furious and bloodthirsty fanaticism which led John Brown, bristling with arms, into a sleeping southern city?" Clingman was even more militant in his response. In a January address on the Senate floor, he noted that the admiration and sympathy expressed toward Brown and his actions in the North suggested that "any crime committed against our section [would be] applauded there," a fact that "ought to have united the whole South for its common defense."[10]

But perhaps more significant in terms of the new level of intensity to which John Brown's raid raised the stakes of the sectional crisis was the reaction at grassroots levels. For the first time ever, communities mobilized: they held public forums, formed committees, issued resolutions, raised militia units, and organized boycotts. Mountain residents, like their counterparts throughout the South, joined forces locally in response to what they rightly perceived to be a national crisis.[11] Such dynamics would continue to operate throughout the secession crisis and to a large extent throughout the war years themselves.

At least five mountain counties—Buncombe, Caldwell, Henderson, Madison, and Yancey—held public meetings before the end of 1859 and formed vigilante committees. The first three, given their more substantial slave populace, both permanent and transient, seemed particularly intent on monitoring and controlling slaves' activity.[12] In a letter to North Carolina governor John B. Ellis, *Asheville News* editor Marcus Erwin referred to Ellis's Virginia counterpart when he wrote: "Abolition emissaries, either native or foreign, will meet with as little favor in this region as they would in the household of Governor [Henry A.] Wise himself."[13]

These and other western counties formed militia companies in order to respond to such threats. Their stated purpose, according to one decree, was "to put down insurrection, quell rebellion, or resist invasion at home" while making their services available to other parts of the state, or even other "sister Southern states" that may be threatened by Northern aggression. In the *Asheville News*, the Buncombe Rifles urged local citizens, "Arm! Arm! . . . to prepare against the evil day." Editor Erwin informed Governor Ellis that "the military spirit is fully aroused here & I am satisfied that upon any collision or any immediate prospect of one in or out of Congress, I could raise a thousand men in this country."[14]

Of perhaps even broader import was the economic response of mountain residents. Although they were in an area often assumed to be less market-oriented and more self-sufficient than other parts of the South, mountain residents felt the need to challenge what they saw as their growing dependency as consumers on the manufacturing North. As early as 1857, the *Asheville News* had called for a suspension of trade with the North, maintaining that "the only way to stop the infernal whining of Northern Abolitionists is to cut of[f] the supplies on which they grow fat. Let us trade at home and drink at home, travel for business and pleasure in the South; learn to supply each other's wants and to rely on ourselves."[15]

Such sentiments intensified in the wake of Harpers Ferry. In January 1860, Asheville leaders addressed a gathering of local women, urging them "to take active part in the movement now so general, the encouragement of Southern enterprise." Nicholas Woodfin called for a return to home manufactures, bemoaning the fact that "twenty years ago, there were looms to be found in every farmhouse—now it is hard to get a good piece of homemade jeans." In this meeting and others like it, Buncombe County residents supported resolutions declaring that, for the next three years, they would not purchase men's clothing or farm implements manufactured outside the region, and that local merchants should limit their merchandise to products either made in the South or imported directly into Southern ports.[16] So pervasive was the county's resolve during the early months of 1860 that even the moderate Zebulon Vance conceded in March that the South would have to develop its own "manufactures and mechanic arts" if abolitionist activity continued unabated.[17]

The move toward greater self-sufficiency was not limited to the region's commercial hub. Residents of more remote counties followed Buncombe's lead and drew up resolutions of their own. Farmers in Macon County, in the state's southwesternmost corner, formed an agricultural society "for the encouragement of home manufactures," which by "increasing our resources and wealth, will contribute to the independence and prosperity of the South." An "ardent friend of the South and southern independence" urged in the Franklin newspaper that "farmers, merchants, mechanics and all who are interested in the county's prosperity" follow suit in neighboring Jackson County.[18]

There is little indication of how earnestly Carolina highlanders attempted to implement their goals of economic independence in the final prewar months. But their rhetoric alone reflects their astute self-consciousness of the extent to which they were tied to far greater market forces than they felt they should have been. That realization would become even more pronounced during the war years. The conflict would force western North Carolinians, like Southerners elsewhere, to resort to means of self-sufficiency and economic independence to which they had voluntarily adapted only a few months earlier. Their efforts to draw on local and regional resources to fill needs formerly supplied by markets elsewhere proved to be one of the heaviest strains mountain society faced during the war.

The political implications of these moves toward both military preparedness and economic self-sufficiency were not lost on regional spokesmen. While moderates such as Zebulon Vance claimed that such measures merely would increase Southern bargaining power within the Union, more radical voices suggested that secession was the logical next step. Marcus Erwin made this argument most succinctly in an *Asheville News* editorial as early as December

1859. He noted: "[A]s far as we know the sentiment of the people of this section of the State, a large majority of them are in favor of a perpetual non-intercourse with the North. If they had their choice they would never again buy a dollar's worth of goods in any Northern state." That fact, coupled with the fact that North Carolinians and other Southerners had formed vigilante committees and militia groups with which to guard against "our *brethren* of the North," led Erwin to conclude: "If this be so, and it is, is not the Union already virtually dissolved? Why continue it longer, if we can only remain in it with arms in our hands?"[19]

Few people in the area other than his close ally Thomas Clingman would have endorsed the logic of Erwin's extremist conclusions at this point; nevertheless, through the efforts of both men, Erwin's position enjoyed a widespread hearing throughout the mountains in the winter and spring of 1860. A gubernatorial election and the issue of ad valorem taxation provided a temporary reprieve from this larger sectional debate, but 1860 was a presidential election year as well, and the parties' nominating conventions were taking place that spring and summer, which meant that those diversions were short-lived.

A Burke County Democrat was at the center of the Democratic debacle in Charleston, where in April the party's convention first split over sectional issues. William Waightstill Avery headed the committee that drafted the party's platform. As the son of one of the region's largest slaveholders, Avery made congressional protection of slavery in the territories a central part of the platform, defiantly claiming, "We regard this principle as more important in its ultimate effects than any principle ever discussed before in the South."[20] As he and other committee members must have known, any platform with such a blatantly sectional stipulation could not garner a majority of convention votes, and when it failed to do so, most Lower South delegates walked out of the convention. When the remaining delegates abandoned Charleston in failure and met two months later in Baltimore, they refused to readmit those who had walked out, thus leading other Southerners, including Avery and most of the North Carolina delegation, to walk out themselves. Stephen A. Douglas of Illinois emerged as the party's presidential nominee, while the breakaway Democrats held their own convention and named Kentucky senator John C. Breckinridge as its candidate, with Joseph Lane of Oregon (a Buncombe County native) as his vice presidential running mate. Sensing the self-inflicted disaster Democrats had set in motion, Southern remnants of the Whig Party organized

*William Waightstill Avery (North Carolina Division
of Archives and History)*

their own Baltimore convention in May and named former senator John Bell of
Tennessee as the nominee of the newly dubbed Constitutional Union Party.

In the campaign that followed, North Carolina's political leaders, like their
counterparts throughout the South, found themselves debating which of these
three candidates stood the best chance of thwarting that most dreaded of
possibilities, a victory by the Republican candidate, Abraham Lincoln. Even
before Douglas and Breckinridge, or even Lincoln himself, emerged as nomi-
nees, some sensed the Charleston debacle spelled doom for Southern interests.
Nicholas Woodfin of Asheville confided in May that "under existing circum-

stances I suppose a Black Republican must be elected if any one by the people."
He all too accurately foresaw the failure of what he called the "Secession
democracy" to join forces with any one or any party, even if it meant destroying
the Union.[21]

Even as most voters came to acknowledge the validity of Woodfin's dire
prediction, they could not agree as to who best could prevent the inevitable. Thomas Clingman, despite his secessionist tendencies, bitterly denounced
those ultra-Southernists in Charleston whose lack of foresight had created a
three-way split for Southern votes. Calling their action "unsurpassed in its
insanity and wickedness," he compared it to that of "a man about to do battle
for his life, who should, as a preparatory step, cut off one arm and one leg, in
order that he might march and strike with more efficiency." He saw Stephen
Douglas as the only electable alternative to "the Abolition candidate," arguing
that he alone could draw the intersectional support necessary to defeat Lincoln.
A rally was organized for Douglas in Buncombe County in July—one of only
three held in North Carolina—but few westerners gave him much hope. In a
rare split with Clingman, Marcus Erwin warned *Asheville News* readers that
"the only effect of Douglas' running is to divide and weaken the Democratic
party," and he urged party members to unite behind Breckinridge. By early fall,
when Douglas himself seemed to equivocate on supporting Southern interests,
what little enthusiasm mountain residents, including Clingman, had mustered
for him rapidly waned.[22]

The campaign evolved into a more traditional two-way race between John
Bell and John Breckinridge, though each man represented variants of the much
damaged Whig and Democratic Parties. Both received strong support in western North Carolina, with debate centered largely on their electability and their
commitment to Southern rights. Mountain Democrats stressed the fact that
Breckinridge's was the only platform that "fairly and squarely recognized the
rights of the South and the equality of the States," and that he alone "in the
Presidential chair will stand by and defend the rights of Southern men against
the aggressions of Northern fanatics." They also emphasized the Asheville
origins of his running mate, Lane.[23]

John Bell's supporters sought to portray Breckinridge as an extremist, a
position they insisted had no place in such volatile times. Moderation, for many
mountain residents, seemed to lie only in the Constitutional Union platform
and its candidate. In early June, even before the Democratic candidates had
been named, Rev. John Buxton of Asheville articulated the fears of fellow

conservatives in the area. "A sectionalized politician on the slavery question pro or con is my abomination, object of my implacable disgust," he wrote to his brother. "We want breadth, patriotism, moderation, honesty, and my opinion is that we won't find any of these things at large in either the Democratic or Republican parties."[24] The final slate of presidential contenders did nothing to assuage such fears, and support for Bell grew steadily among westerners, leading the *Iredell Express* in Statesville to report on October 5: "Our mountain friends are being thoroughly aroused in behalf of the Union, the Constitution, and the enforcement of laws."[25]

Despite such optimistic claims by partisan newspapers, the inevitability of a Republican victory dampened the enthusiasm of both camps throughout the fall. Local debate came to focus on the postelection responses to that all but certain outcome, and public rallies in support of the Union were held throughout the mountain counties. Only four days before the election, nearly five thousand people were reported to have gathered in Wilkesboro, the region's most united Unionist stronghold, to hear Zebulon Vance and others affirm the need for no rash action in response to Lincoln's victory.[26]

But such sentiments did not go unchallenged. At a rally for Bell in Asheville late in October, Burgess Gaither, a Morganton Whig, unabashedly called himself an "unconditional Unionist" and insisted that not only would he oppose North Carolina's secession from the Union, but he would also refuse aid to any other seceded state "that Lincoln might attempt to whip into submission." His claims evoked a surprisingly strong response. Gaither's opponents saw his "neutrality" as aloofness and quickly condemned his lack of allegiance to either his own state or the South. The *Asheville News* warned Gaither: "If the struggle should come, and it is not improbable, the South will say in the language of holy writ: 'He that is not with me is against me'; and your 'neutral' ground might prove unhealthy."[27]

Such discord merely accentuated the futility of attempting to defeat Lincoln. Sallie Lenoir's comments to her husband summed up the tensions that beset the mountains and much of the South in that final week before the election. "Great excitement now about the coming election," she wrote of the mood in Caldwell County. "Dick says that Lincoln will be elected and there seems to be a gloom over nearly every heart. How dark the future!"[28]

This sense of impending doom, combined with the frustration of knowing that none of the three names appearing on their ballots had much chance of defeating the one name that did not, kept many western Carolinians away from the polls on election day. The election proved to be a close one statewide, though, as Southern voters had long surmised, close only for second and third places nationally. Only 848 votes separated Bell and Breckinridge's North Carolina totals, with the latter taking 50.3 percent of the vote and thus its full electoral slate. In the mountains, Bell prevailed. The vote there followed traditional patterns of Whig and Democratic strength. Bell carried two-thirds of mountain counties, but his margin over Breckinridge was substantial only in the Whig-dominated northwestern counties. Breckinridge carried the five more-Democratic counties, but in sufficient numbers to keep Bell's total margin of victory in the mountains to 55 percent. Stephen Douglas won only 97 votes in the region, 49 of which came from Buncombe and were likely a residue of Clingman's earlier enthusiasm.[29]

Given voting patterns in the mountains over the preceding decade, the 1860 presidential returns were hardly surprising. Western voters conveyed a slightly greater commitment to the Union than did voters elsewhere in North Carolina, but as the strong response to Burgess Gaither's "unconditional Unionist" stance a week earlier indicated, Bell's supporters were not so conciliatory as to submerge Southern interests merely for the sake of unity. By the same token, Breckinridge's considerable support in the mountains did not result from the dis-Unionist label with which he was saddled. His strong defense of Southern rights appealed enough to voters that they were willing to risk, or in some cases overlook, the more radical implications of his stance. But equally unsurprising to western Carolinians was that nothing they or any other Southerners did at ballot boxes on November 6 had any effect on the national outcome. (Even the combined votes for Bell and Breckinridge would not have been enough to overcome the electoral majority the Republicans enjoyed.) Abraham Lincoln was to become president in four months, and western Carolinians' concerns quickly turned to how they should deal with that harsh reality.

As in the aftermath of John Brown's raid on Harpers Ferry, highlanders found public meetings to be useful means of discussing, confirming, and solidifying their responses to the election and to the secession of South Carolina, a fait accompli by December 20. Although the full range of Unionist and secessionist arguments were put forward right away and both sides of the issue were hotly debated, public assemblies usually gave voice to Unionist appeals while secessionism was expressed more through the print media and private correspondence.

Despite his uncharacteristically cautious tone prior to the election, once the results confirmed his worst fears, Clingman quickly resumed his role as the most forceful advocate of secessionism in the region. "It is not that a dangerous man has been elected to the Presidency of the United States," he said of Lincoln. "I assert that the President-elect has been elected *because he was known to be a dangerous man.* . . . [H]e declares that it is the purpose of the North to make war upon my section until its social system is destroyed, and for that he was taken up and elected. It is that great, remarkable and dangerous fact that has filled my section with alarm and dread for the future."[30]

Even before South Carolina seceded, Clingman joined with William Waightstill Avery in urging North Carolinians to hold a convention that would call for Lincoln to promise no interference with Southern rights and no forceful action against any Southern state that did secede. Only with such assurances, according to their proposal, would the Old North State remain in the Union. Once South Carolina's course of action became apparent and the creation of a separate nation seemed to be a reality, other western Carolinians became converts. A sense of history inspired some. It was perhaps fitting that in Burke, the region's oldest county, descendants of its earliest settlers analyzed the crisis in historical terms, finding apt parallels in the Revolution to bolster their changing sentiments. Isaac Avery (who was far more conservative than his son, William Waightstill) mused in mid-November that Lincoln's election had spurred "talk of a second declaration of independence," and he seemed resigned to the fact that it would take a war to uphold this declaration as it had the first. "If the conflict must come, perhaps it is as well now as any time," he wrote. "I hope for the best, but if furious Fanatics, after violating the compact of Union, drive us to the wall, Ramseurs, the Cowpens, and Kings Mountain may all have to be fought over again."[31]

By the end of the year, Edward Jones Erwin, who was of equally old and distinguished lineage in Burke, had abandoned his earlier caution and expressed outright disapproval of those who had still not made the conversion he had: "I am now for immediate secession as I have lost hope of the Union. The time is fast approaching to the situation that those [who] now advocated submission & renounce the South will be looked upon as Tories [were] in 1776." He berated those who still hoped for a less radical solution to the crisis, "when any man of common sense not warped by prejudice can't but see the Union is gone forever."[32] William Holland Thomas used an analogy to the Revolutionary War to make the same point in the state senate, where in a December debate he called those not bold enough to take decisive action "submissionists" and reminded his fellow legislators "that the Tories of the revolution had counselled submission to George the Third."[33]

Yet despite the force of these messages and the prominence and widespread respect commanded by their messengers, the vast majority of western Carolinians had not yet "lost hope of the Union." Few found Lincoln's election alone sufficient cause for leaving the Union and were quite content to adopt a "watch and wait" policy. Congressman Vance best articulated these sentiments as he traveled throughout his district, assuring his constituents that "we have everything to gain and nothing on earth to lose by delay, but by too hasty action we may take a fatal step we can never retrace—may lose a heritage that we can never recover." David W. Siler of Macon County echoed the flexibility that came with caution: "My policy is to hold on to the Union, until every remedy has been tried and if that fails it will be time enough then to get out."[34]

In at least six mountain counties, public meetings in December and January produced resolutions that reinforced such sentiments and condemned the rashness of those people ready to abandon alternatives to disunion. Unionists in Polk and Rutherford Counties met jointly in January and declared that "it would be unwise and suicidal to the best interests of North Carolina to secede from the Union for any cause now existing." At a Madison County meeting three days later, local leaders took more direct aim at those proposing secession, calling them "demagogues and broken down politicians" who sought to "erase civil rights, political and religious liberty, and set up a monarchy." In one of the more original rationales for adherence to the Union, they argued that the South within the Union could be far more effective in counteracting Northern abolitionists than it could ever be outside the nation.[35]

If flexibility and open options were central themes in Unionist rhetoric, its conditionalism was equally apparent from the beginning. Nearly all such proclamations issued from county meetings stressed the conditional nature of their commitment to the Union, including those from Caldwell County, which held one of the region's most intensely Unionist concentrations. Meeting in Lenoir on December 22, residents recognized the right of secession in the face of "an intermeddling spirit of many persons in the non-slaveholding South." If attempts at a peaceful and constitutional settlement failed, they believed, "the South must demand, and if necessary, force, a separation of the two sections."[36] Macon County citizens also affirmed the wisdom of patience but defined the limits of their tolerance. They stated after a December 11 meeting: "We will give

[Lincoln] a trial, until some overt or unconstitutional act of his administration against the South shall make it our duty to resist."[37]

Individuals, too, felt the necessity of qualifying their loyalties. In a circular of a speech made before the legislature in Raleigh, Thomas Crumpler reminded his fellow Ashe County residents that all parties in North Carolina had pledged loyalty to the Union in the past election. Nevertheless he insisted that he was not a "submissionist" (a label secessionists had been quick to apply to Unionists), but that he would hold on to his national heritage "until all hopes of any honorable settlement were gone." "If war comes," he declared, "I will yield to no man in devotion to the rights and honor of my State."[38]

Other mountain residents expressed just as much reluctance to leave the Union but readily maintained that loyalties to the South, rather than to North Carolina, were by no means compromised by a "watch and wait" policy. J. P. Eller, a Baptist minister in Madison County, assured Zebulon Vance of his area's support for the Union, which he qualified in closing: "This people is As true to the south As Any people that ever trod the soil But Let it [secession] be The Last Resort." W. W. Lenoir expressed his abhorrence for those "busy destroying the constitution and the Union," calling their actions "the greatest crime that has been done in the world since the temptation of Eve." But he, too, qualified the point at which he would endorse that "crime": "I stand out as stout as any Southern man ought for full justice from the north as an indispensable condition to union with the north."[39]

Most of the arguments employed by both Unionists and secessionists in the mountains drew on the same reasoning expounded by their counterparts throughout the Upper South.[40] But both factions often adapted their arguments to their own particular situation as western Carolinians and as mountaineers. It is those custom-made rationales behind what their own region had to gain or to lose by separating themselves from the Union that prove most revealing in terms of how Carolina highlanders would respond to the war itself over its four-year duration.

Geography remained a central factor in shaping debate in western North Carolina. Living in the only section of North Carolina that bordered all four of the state's neighbors, mountain residents were particularly sensitized to developments in those neighboring states. Tennessee made up the longest of those borders, and as the most entrenched of Unionist strongholds in the South, East Tennessee no doubt served to bolster pro-Union sentiments in the Carolina mountains. William "Parson" Brownlow's weekly newspaper, the *Knoxville Whig*, was among Unionism's most unrelenting and pervasive voices, and it enjoyed enough of a circulation in some areas of westernmost North Carolina to have, according to one observer, "quite an influence with the old Whig element."[41] Yet while East Tennesseans served to supplement and reinforce anti-secessionist arguments in the mountains to their east, political developments in Tennessee seemed of relatively little concern and warranted little discussion among western Carolinians. Most likely this was due to the fact that, given the solidity of its Unionism and the one-sidedness of the rhetoric emanating from its leaders, East Tennessee was the one neighbor whose allegiance and course of action they felt could be taken for granted.[42] Developments along their northern and southern borders preoccupied western North Carolinians far more.

South Carolina's rashness, in particular, generated much debate in the mountains. Like other North Carolinians, highland Unionists were disdainful of their southern neighbor's recklessness in declaring independence. They resented the added pressure such a move put on their own course of action but remained determined not to let it sway them. "It is deeply humiliating (or ought to be)," declared Calvin C. Jones of Lenoir, "to any citizen of a border state if they allow these arrogant Cotton Oligarchies south of them to dragoon them into their service." According to a story much repeated at the time, one mountaineer at a local gathering grew so impatient at the seemingly endless discussion of South Carolina's bold action that he jumped up and shouted, "For God's sake! Let South Carolina nullify, revolute, secede, and BE DAMNED!"[43]

Others, though, were intent on defending the principle upon which South Carolina had acted, and they based the conditionalism of their Unionism specifically on the federal government's noninterference in their state's declared independence. The day after the Palmetto State made its secession official but before the news reached the mountains, a Franklin man characterized sentiment in his area. "The Southern feeling is more strongly evident in Macon [County] and it is a general feeling that if our sister states should secede that coercion or an attempt to coerce on the part of the north will be a signal for to 'Strike' one and all for our rights & our lives."[44] Two weeks later, by which time South Carolina's official independence was much on the minds of western North Carolinians, William Holland Thomas in neighboring Cherokee County laid out the options that action dictated for his own state: "North Carolina cannot remain much longer stationary; she must write her destiny either under the flag of Mr. Lincoln and aid to coerce the south or unite with the south to resist and defend their rights."[45]

When Georgia followed South Carolina's lead a month later, it was again those in North Carolina's southwestern counties, the only ones to share a border with it, who were quick to note its significance. Thomas, the area's most ambitious entrepreneur, was concerned about the economic disadvantages of not joining them. Pointing out that residents in that corner of the state were closer to South Carolina, Georgia, and Tennessee than they were to Asheville, he expressed alarm at the prospect of being hemmed in by Confederate territory. The highlands would face economic ruin if North Carolina did not secede, for they "would be surrounded by foreign territory into which her citizens could not go without passports and with which she could not trade except through customhouses."[46]

But Thomas and others were also aware of the geographical advantages of joining the Confederacy. Local manufacturing efforts, so widely discussed during the previous year, would blossom under the added impetus of necessity. Independence would lead to long-term diversity and prosperity for the mountain economy. It would also divert Southern planters away from the Northern "watering holes" that many vacationers frequented and allow them to discover North Carolina's highland resorts, already well known to Charlestonians. The fact that several prominent Southern officials already frequented the area, including Confederate treasury secretary Christopher G. Memminger, who had a summer home in Flat Rock, led to speculation that the new government might establish its base there. "In this mountain kingdom," wrote a Henderson County visitor, "it is contemplated to place the capital city of the Southern Confederacy, having its seat of government within 100 miles of the capitals of six other states."[47]

Thomas envisioned even more grandiose possibilities, though he entertained them in the privacy of his correspondence with his wife. "The mountains of Western North Carolina would be the centre of the Confederacy," he enthused on the first of January, revealing his long-standing regional ambitions. "We shall then have one of the most prosperous countries in the world. It will become connected with every part of the South by railroad. It will then become the centre of manufacturing for the Southern market. The place where the southern people will spend their money, educate their children and very probably make laws for the nation."[48]

Yet other individuals, with equal entrepreneurial ambitions, found far less reason to support joining the Confederacy as long as Virginia seemed unlikely to do so. Merchants and other community leaders in the northwestern corner of the state, especially in Wilkes, Ashe, and Caldwell Counties, were much more dependent on commercial ties with Richmond, Baltimore, and other mid-Atlantic markets than with the plantation markets of South Carolina and Georgia. Motivated in large part by the trade barriers secession might impose between them and those markets, these men remained staunchly Unionist. They realized, too, that Virginia's decision regarding secession was at least as important as North Carolina's in determining their course. As much as they feared the vulnerability to Federal attack that they would face if Virginia remained in the Union and North Carolina seceded, thus putting them on the Confederacy's northernmost border, they also realized that if Virginia left the Union, they would have little choice but to do likewise. A Caldwell County man confided that awareness to Vance: "The Action of Virginia will decide the fate of North Carolina if she goes out of the Union[.] I fear N C must follow her very soon." No doubt he spoke for most of his neighbors when he said, "We look to the course and action of Va with great interest, and as far as I am Concerned with serious misgivings."[49] When Virginians elected a largely Unionist slate of delegates to their Richmond convention on February 4, most northwestern Carolinians confirmed their own commitment to the Union as well.[50]

Despite the strong trade ties between western North Carolina and markets in South Carolina and Georgia, some western North Carolinians were quick to question just how much the mountains shared economically with the Deep South. A Unionist broadside circulated in Buncombe County stressed that the "cotton monopoly is at the bottom of the revolution," a fact they claimed secessionists had "concealed from the people of Western North Carolina, because cotton is not raised here." It went on to argue that policies beneficial to "the rich cotton, sugar, and rice planters of the Cotton States," such as free trade and direct taxation, would not be in the best interests of highlanders and might, in fact, prove "oppressive and ruinous to the poor farmer and mechanic." It concluded by predicting that the Deep South states "are to reap golden rewards, while the middle States . . . are to be 'hewers of wood and drawers of water' for King Cotton."[51]

Yet it is significant that in neither this broadside nor other such political rhetoric was slavery itself ever cited as a distinguishing feature of the Lower South. In fact, the institution and its fate remained a central feature of debates in the mountains throughout the crisis, as both Unionists and secessionists claimed that its future was a high priority for them. While most of the region's political leaders were slaveholders and had a direct financial stake in the impact of the crisis on the "peculiar institution," they were also very much aware that the vast majority of those they sought to sway owned no slaves, and they shaped their public rhetoric accordingly.

Unionists argued that slavery was far safer within the Union and protected by constitutional guarantees than it would be if such guarantees were abandoned by secession, particularly if armed conflict ensued. William J. Brown, a Buncombe County Unionist, reasoned that if the North and South went to war, the very ownership of slaves would put Southerners at a decided disadvantage. The North, he explained to his son, "can do awful damage & destruction by and through our slaves. Once arouse them to insurrection & they will carry murder, Rape & arson into the midst of our firesides." If Southerners could convert their human property into funds, he concluded, they might survive the struggle intact. But, as long as they kept their slaves, they should do all they could to preserve the Union and avoid war.[52]

Secessionists used the same scenario to their advantage. Clingman argued that Republicans saw that the most effective means of subjugating the South "would be to liberate the slaves and leave them as free negros in those communities." He was appealing to the Negrophobia of his largely nonslaveholding constituency when he asserted that the "most dreaded" and "greatest evil" resulting from such emancipation would not be the property loss to slaveowners but rather "the social destruction of society by infusing into it a large free negro population." In a circular they jointly composed, W. W. Avery and Marcus Erwin even more explicitly played on white fears of slave emancipation by Republican coercion: "In addition to the terrible calamity of having three hundred thousand idle, vagabond free negroes turned loose upon you with all the privileges of white men—voting with you; sitting on juries with you; going to school with our children; and intermarrying with the white race . . . wages of all kinds of labor will be diminished; the price of agricultural productions of all kinds will fall so low that our farmers will be ruined."[53]

It is no coincidence that the authors of such dire warnings lived in Burke and Buncombe, counties that had relatively large numbers of slaves (nearly a third of Burke's populace; over a fifth of Buncombe's). But residents in counties with few slaves were reminded that the loosening of slavery's bonds would allow blacks to roam freely into their areas as well. Governor Joseph E. Brown of Georgia had very effectively made that argument in urging north Georgians to

support secession. "So soon as the slaves were at liberty," he warned, "thousands of them would leave the cotton and rice fields in the lower part of our
State, and make their way to the healthier climate in the mountain region. We
should have them plundering and stealing, robbing, and killing; in all the lovely
vallies [*sic*] of the mountains."[54] Western North Carolinians had already proven
themselves susceptible to such fears. The seasonal influx of lowland owners and
their slaves to highland resorts had often increased racial paranoia in the area,
particularly in the wake of tensions elsewhere, from Nat Turner's insurrection to
John Brown's raid.[55] The scenario Joe Brown described for Georgians must
have crossed the minds of many Carolina highlanders.

Although such fears were exploited by both secessionists and Unionists, the
latter made it quite clear that the crux of their conditionalism was whether or
not slave property was threatened under the new Republican regime. Tennessee's most outspoken Unionist, William "Parson" Brownlow of Knoxville,
spoke for most of his counterparts in western North Carolina (and was widely
quoted by them) in making that case. After reiterating that Lincoln's election
was an inadequate reason to leave the Union, he stated: "But, if we were once
convinced that the Administration in Washington . . . contemplated the subjugation of the South or the abolishing of Slavery, there would not be a Union
man among us in twenty-four hours."[56] In Macon County, legislator David W.
Siler echoed Brownlow in a circular that stated bluntly: "There are persons at
the North who profess to believe that they commit a sin against the Almighty in
supporting a Constitution that guarantees to the people of the South the right to
hold slaves; whenever . . . the Government must be controlled by those who
entertain this opinion, we must separate."[57]

It was not until the end of January, with six states already out of the Union,
that North Carolina's state legislature made provisions for a statewide forum on
the crisis. It approved a measure calling for a vote on February 28 on whether or
not to hold a convention to consider secession and to elect delegates to the
convention should a majority want it to take place. This development intensified the ongoing debates throughout the mountain counties and led their
leaders to speculate more intensely on popular opinion. Calvin Cowles's observation of Wilkes County in December, that "public sentiment here amongst the
rank & file is decidedly averse to extreme measures," still applied to most of the
region in early February. A Madison County man confirmed to Vance: "All the
Countys West of the Blue Ridge is union By a large majority. . . . Demagogs is a

trying to so the seed of Discord thruout this Country But they have faild."[58] Yet Calvin Jones of Lenoir provided a cautionary note. Acknowledging that "North Carolina and especially Caldwell and Wilkes are deeply attached to the Union," he qualified his appraisal with the reminder that "the nature of the Southern people is impulsive and sectional feeling contagious."[59]

Other Unionists were bitter that secessionist efforts produced so much uncertainty about the election's outcome. Tod R. Caldwell in Morganton claimed that Burke County voters, "if they were permitted to go to the polls and vote their own sentiments without interference on the part of leaders, would give a large anti-secession vote." "But," he continued, "we have a large floating vote in this County, and many active, unscrupulous, men amongst the democratic leaders . . . who will resort to any means, no matter how base, to carry their point."[60] A fellow Burke County Unionist echoed Caldwell's distress: "[T]he great misfortune is, there are so few who will stand firm, and stem the current of misrule in wild and revolutionary times like the present."[61]

Despite, or perhaps because of, the fluidity and unpredictability of popular sentiment, activists throughout the region speculated on the outcome. Voting patterns in the past proved to be only slight indicators of current trends. Although somewhat exaggerated, an observation made by a Madison County man, that the crisis "has split Whig & Democracy all into h—l," suggested the uncertainties many felt. Party leaders Clingman and Vance worked hard to keep supporters in their respective camps. Yet several prominent Clingman supporters, particularly in Buncombe and Polk Counties, strongly supported the Union, and many of Vance's former Whig supporters had become secessionists.[62]

The campaign was hard fought and nearly led to violence in some areas. David Coleman, a leading secessionist in Buncombe County, was nearly tarred and feathered when he carried his message into Madison County, according to a resident who described the incident as "a hot time." Yancey County secessionists, who attempted to equate Vance's Unionism with abolitionism, burned him in effigy at the Burnsville courthouse.[63] A Unionist minister elsewhere in Yancey incurred the wrath of three secessionists in his Baptist congregation at Cane Creek, who vowed to make him either "pray for Jeff Davis and the Confederacy, or ride him on a rail." Only when another minister took over his congregation was a violent confrontation averted.[64]

On the eve of the convention vote, Unionists remained confident that voters were not yet ready to secede. The momentum for secession created by the rapid succession of Deep South state withdrawals had somewhat abated, and hopes for a peaceful resolution to the crisis were revived. While Congress reconsidered the Crittenden Compromise proposal, a peace conference took place in Washington, and both Virginia and Tennessee rejected secession in statewide forums. Western Carolinians took note of all of these developments, and Unionists used the news of each effectively, giving Union sentiment within their own region "a chance to jell."[65]

By the slimmest of margins (50.3 percent of the vote) North Carolinians rejected the call for a convention on February 28. The turnout in the mountain counties was almost one and a half times as great as it had been in the presidential election three months earlier, which was a reflection of how much voters felt was at stake. This time, there were no foregone conclusions, as Lincoln's victory had been in November. In the mountains, results on the convention referendum were mixed. Seven of the seventeen counties included in this study (Burke, Rutherford, Polk, MacDowell, Buncombe, Haywood, and Jackson) voted for a convention by margins of over 60 percent. Three counties (Henderson, Macon, and Yancey) voted down a convention by relatively close margins, and the remaining seven (the five northwestern counties—Ashe, Alleghany, Wilkes, Watauga, and Caldwell, and two others bordering Tennessee—Madison and Cherokee) opposed it by more substantial majorities.[66]

The only surprise was the extent of proconvention support in the region, but it is important to note that such support was not necessarily prosecession. Only five of seventeen delegates elected from the region were disunionists, suggesting that while nearly half of the region's voters favored a convention, most were not yet ready to cast their own and their state's fate with the new Confederacy. The wide discrepancy here suggests that Unionists recognized the other functions a convention could serve. For some, definitive action of any sort was seen as preferable to remaining adrift. Samuel F. Patterson of Caldwell County confided in his son that he had voted for a convention: "I could not see under the circumstances then existing how we could get along without one—as most of the slave states yet in the Union were either holding or proposing to hold conventions. I could not see how N.C. could stand still with either honor or safety."[67]

Others bought into the logic of spokesmen like Vance, who had pointed out the leverage such a forum could provide North Carolina. A convention could serve as an effective means of making collective demands on the North, he argued, which, "if they are refused, then for making our voice heard with the Southern States." Even more importantly, Vance was politically astute enough to portray a convention as the only democratic means by which a people should commit themselves to war. "Though some of our Southern sisters have contemptuously refused to consult the wishes of 180,000 fighting men, over whose dead bodies an invading host, treading through the ashes, must reach them," he stated, "yet there are others who anxiously seek general and fraternal counsel, and they we should regard."[68]

The convention vote and the rationales behind it indicate that the spectrum of political opinion remained far wider in the mountains than was true of the state's central piedmont, where a large turnout and a far more solidly anticonvention vote provided the narrow margin of victory statewide for Unionist forces.[69] It is also important to acknowledge that sentiments in the western part of the state remained fluid, with outside factors altering the collective mood from week to week. Given the narrow margin by which a convention was voted down, a different verdict might well have resulted had the referendum been scheduled a month earlier or later.

By early March, in fact, opinions were already shifting, and any relief Unionists felt over the February 28 vote proved to be short-lived. The Washington Peace Conference, on which so many had placed much hope, had dissolved in failure a day earlier, and news reached western Carolinians within a week of their convention vote. That setback alone resigned some Unionists to the inevitability of their separation from the Union and war. James Gwyn of Wilkes County was disgusted that "it has adjourned & done nothing or that which amounts to nothing. . . . [T]here seems to be very little hope now of any settlement of the national difficulties." Nicholas Woodfin of Asheville claimed that had news of the conference's failure arrived sooner, it would have altered the convention vote. "The cause of the South is gaining here most decidedly," he informed an eastern Carolinian. "The failure of the vote here was in a great measure owing to the deception in regard to the passing of the compromise measures. The people here were made to believe all would be made all right with the South."[70]

Almost as unsettling as the failed conference was Lincoln's inaugural address on March 4. This first public pronouncement on the crisis by the man whose election had precipitated it was much anticipated. Of particular interest was what stand the president-elect would take toward those states already out of the

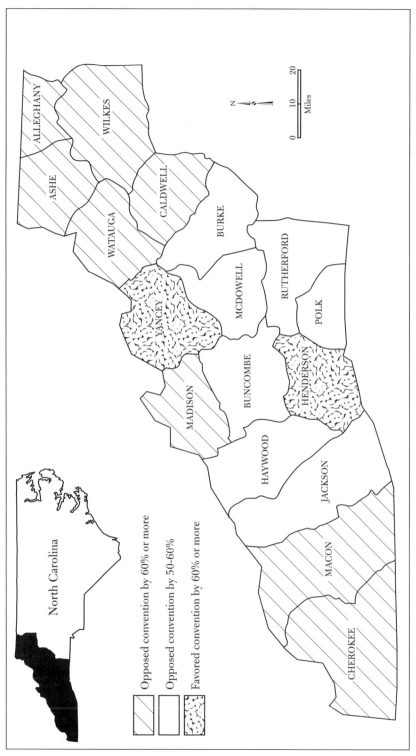

Secession convention vote in western North Carolina, February 1861 (University of Georgia Cartographic Services)

Union. The term "coercion" had become so central to both secession opposition and Unionist conditionalism in the mountains that any indication that the new president had such intentions toward their neighbors to the South could have reversed their ballot box decision a week earlier. Yet the text of his message remained ambiguous enough for Unionists to label it conciliatory and secessionists to call it belligerent. Unionists had hoped for more definitive assurances from the new president and became increasingly discouraged as to the possibility of peaceful resolution to the crisis at hand. They found themselves on the defensive, criticized by Thomas Clingman, William Holland Thomas, and others who claimed that a more united front by Southerners would have forced the president to make peace with the new nation rather than to hold out for the continued possibility of war. James Gwyn bemoaned the effect of the recent vacillation: "I think if all the Southern States had acted promptly & together that we might have had a peaceable separation, which would have been greatly preferable in my opinion to the Condition we shall be in for a year or two perhaps."[71]

Clingman continued to call for decisive statewide action, claiming that if Lincoln "intends to use the power in his hands," as he had implied in his inaugural address, then "we must have war." Further indecisiveness in the Upper South merely allowed the president time to take control of and prepare "the military arm of the Government."[72] David Siler countered Clingman, asserting that in waiting for a more justified provocation, a more solid South was assured. In another circular to his Macon County constituents, he argued that "the unanimity at the South, that an unquestioned, righteous cause must have produced, would abundantly compensate for any loss in the munitions of war."[73]

Well before the decisive events of mid-April, then, mountain residents, like other North Carolinians, were resigning themselves to the probability of their state's secession and of war. An Asheville man reflected the discouragement of many when he wrote on March 22 to his brother, who was abroad: "We are fast realizing the predictions of the monarchs of Europe that man is unfit to govern himself. You will have learned long before this shall reach you that our Government is on the verge of extinction."[74] Unionists should have been encouraged by the February election results, but their efforts over the next month seemed relatively subdued and defensive. Secessionists, on the other hand, became more and more outspoken and confident that their cause would ultimately prevail. Quite a few highlanders had probably progressed to the point reached by Sarah Tate, who confided to her brother William Lenoir that as of April 6, she had become "a *slight* secessionist."[75]

The attack on Fort Sumter by Confederate forces on April 12, 1861, did not come as a great surprise to western Carolinians, since the possibility of a clash there had been openly discussed for several weeks.[76] But it was Lincoln's response three days later that ended any complacency or reluctance on the part of the vast majority of conditional Unionists in the region. On April 15 the president called for 75,000 troops, including two regiments from North Carolina, to put down the rebellion South Carolina had instigated. With the well-entrenched conviction that "coercion" on the part of the Republican chief executive was the point at which tolerance toward him was no longer an option, western Carolinians united behind what David Siler had called "an unquestioned, righteous cause."[77]

Virginia's withdrawal from the Union on April 17 ended any lingering doubts as to the state's course. Charles Manly's description of the state as a whole—"All are unanimous. Even those who were loudest in denouncing secession are now hottest & loudest the other way"—applied to most of its western counties as well.[78] The most ardent Unionists described their conversion experiences as sudden and dramatic. Zebulon Vance, for example, wrote of his transformation: "I was canvassing for the Union with all my strength; I was addressing a large and excited crowd . . . and literally had my arm upward in pleading for peace and the Union of our Fathers, when the telegraphic news was announced of the firing on Sumter and the President's call for seventy-five thousand volunteers. When my hand came down from the impassioned gesticulation, it fell slowly and sadly by the side of a Secessionist. I immediately, with altered voice and manner, called upon the assembled multitude to volunteer, not to fight against but for South Carolina."[79]

Likewise, Josiah Cowles explained his own change of heart to his brother Calvin, Wilkes County's most committed Unionist. "I was as strong a union man as any in the state up to the time [of] Lincoln's proclamation calling for 75,000 volunteers. I then saw that the South had either to submit to abject vassallage or assert her rights at the point of a sword." Though with somewhat less than his uncle's conviction, Calvin Cowles resigned himself to the inevitability of his state's withdrawal from the Union. Early in May he wrote a friend in New York: "Congress should be assembled as quickly as possible and should recognize the Confederate States as an independent nation. I think the good sense of the North will quickly see the folly of the effort to coerce 15 states (for it amounts to that and nothing less) and give it up."[80]

The remarkable haste with which this new surge of secession sentiment was translated into action suggests that to a majority of western North Carolinians the events of mid-April did not so much lead to dramatic conversions as it confirmed expectations and triggered a conditioned reflex action for which they had already actively, even eagerly, prepared. It was over a month before North Carolina made its secession official. On May 13 voters elected delegates to a convention that would take place in Raleigh a week later.

The brief campaign for delegates reflected, for the most part, the unanimity of spirit that by then seemed so obvious throughout the mountains, as it did elsewhere in the state. Most candidates ran unopposed, and in what few two-man races were run, debate centered primarily on which of the two candidates was and had been the most committed secessionist throughout the crisis. In Buncombe County, for example, Nicholas Woodfin reminded voters that he had warned all along that Lincoln could not be trusted and that a united South had offered the safest recourse to Northern aggression. His opponent, Montreville Patton, like Vance and others, spoke of his dramatic conversion from Unionist to disunionist and claimed that he was now as staunch a supporter of a Southern confederacy as his opponent. But Woodfin harped unmercifully on Patton's former leanings and on how poor his judgment had been. "I need not remind you," he told voters, "how fearfully my worst fears have been realized, and how entirely all of his predictions have been falsified."[81] Woodfin easily won the election, as did other long-term secessionists wherever they ran. Former conditional Unionists who were now committed to secession won only when they ran unopposed.[82] Only two Unionists who still opposed secession, Tod R. Caldwell of Burke County and Alexander H. Jones of Henderson County, made any effort to run, though support for both was virtually nonexistent.[83]

Thus the mountain region joined in common cause, as its delegates joined with those from across the state to vote unanimously on May 20 to leave the Union and join the Confederacy. For a brief period, western Carolinians presented a united front—not only among themselves but in concert with the rest of their state and region. They were quick, and some quite explicit, in acknowledging the new identities imposed on them by recent events. An Asheville man informed his brother late in May, "I am becoming reconciled to aspire to nothing higher for the rest of my life than the place of a citizen of a Southern

Confederacy." Reflecting back on the events, a Mitchell County man made much the same point even more succinctly: "When the war come, I felt awful southern."[84]

By late April 1861, mountain residents were reveling in their new Southern citizenship; many even relished the prospect of a war. Circumstances would sustain and even bolster that mood for several weeks to come, and yet, there were from the beginning indications that the region's euphoria and clear sense of purpose would soon give way to a more complex and confusing reality.

MOBILIZATION

The Mountains Are Pouring Forth Their Brave Sons

A s early as January 8, 1861, teenage Mary Bryan in Rutherfordton giddily wrote to a cousin in Happy Valley: "We are all anticipating war here; we girls are reading all the stories we can find about the women of the Revolution, so that we'll know how to act bravely and magnanimously in time of war." She went on to confide that she had been practicing shooting. At first it "frightened me almost out of my wits, but then the thought of war, & those abominable Yankees and abolitionists sweeping upon us gave me renewed strength and courage sufficient to fire a pistol." By mid-April, the trend had spread elsewhere in the region. Sixteen-year-old Amelia Gwyn in McDowell County told her older sister that several local girls were buying pistols and practicing shooting. "You ought to hear us girls talk about fighting," she reported. "I believe we have all concluded to fight to the last and die before we'll give up to a Yankee."[1]

Even before news of Fort Sumter reached western North Carolinians, a "martial spirit" had so seeped into the region that even impressionable young girls were caught up in it. They were perhaps a little ahead of most of their elders in conveying their excitement in such belligerent tones. But once news of Sumter's fall and Lincoln's subsequent call for troops reached North Carolina highlanders, the defiance toward those "abominable Yankees and abolitionists" quickly became the dominant sentiment throughout the region.

The prospects of war had always been a central part of the secession debate, particularly after South Carolina left the Union. Mountain Unionists in particular had depicted the onerous effects of armed conflict to urge against rash action that might bring it on. At the same time, though, they insisted that the government's use, or even the threat, of military force was foremost among the conditions that would lead them to abandon their devotion to the Union.

As a result, the general mood in the mountains suggested as much relief as excitement that the die had, at long last, been cast. The mere sense of resolution after the months of vacillation and uncertainty was in itself cause for satisfaction for some, and at least resignation for many others. For some former Unionists, the sense of betrayal led to a particularly strong conversion. A week after Lincoln's call for troops, the *Carolina Watchman* in Salisbury described attitudes throughout the state, including those of many mountain men. For "old lifelong conservative men," an April 23 editorial stated, "the miserable duplicity of Lincoln stung them to the quick; one and all are freely bringing their sons and their treasures to offer on the altar of liberty."[2]

James Gentry, an Ashe County merchant, confirmed this widespread change of heart among those in his area and even admitted that their former caution had been a mistake. "We are all now for an independent southern Confederacy," he informed his father-in-law in Tennessee early in May. "We watch and wait men are out now. We have great reasons to fall out with Lincoln than you secessionists. While we were watching & waiting he was undermining for our subjugation, but now we are for separation and against all sorts of compromise. Death or victory is our motto."[3] But the vast majority of mountain residents never seemed to look back; they were caught up instead in the contagious mood of anticipation and determination. In particular, they focused on the task of sending forth an army to defend their new nation.

The mobilization of troops in the mountains proved to be one of the smoothest aspects of the transition into war, since the need had been widely anticipated and preparations had begun well before North Carolina's place in the Confederacy was assured. Much of that initiative at the state level had come from westerners. In a study of the organization of militias in North Carolina on the eve of the war, Raymond Heath notes that such movements in the 1850s were far stronger in the western part of the state than in the east.[4] Perhaps because the institution remained a more deeply embedded tradition in the more sparsely settled, frontierlike regions of the west, mountain leaders were more sensitized to the need for military preparedness once the possibility of war became apparent. And it is obvious from who was involved in these efforts that secessionists saw militias as far more of a priority than did Unionists.

In the aftermath of John Brown's raid on Harpers Ferry, Marcus Erwin, editor of the *Asheville News* and Thomas Clingman's staunchest ally, wrote Governor Ellis to express his concern over "the woefully disorganized and unprepared state here as well as elsewhere." He was among several who in late 1859 and early 1860 urged the governor to call a special session of the legislature to consider means for reorganizing and refortifying the state's militia system.[5]

Nothing came of those efforts, but in the wake of Lincoln's election, these concerns became more widespread. The necessity of armed readiness was the one prerogative that seemed to cut across Unionist and secessionist divisions in the public forums held throughout the mountains after the election. Polk County's resolution of November 18 was typical of many passed in mountain communities. At the end of a document that expressed the conditional nature of their Unionism, Polk County citizens added a far less equivocal resolve: "That the State of North Carolina should at once be placed in a condition of efficient and complete armed defence." From Raleigh, legislator David Siler assured his wavering constituents in Macon County that the state, "torn as it is between the fanaticism of the North and the fallacy of secession in the Deep South, [should] be armed for any emergency."[6]

With such mandates from their own counties, mountain leaders in the legislature were again at the forefront in pushing for state military preparedness. William Waightstill Avery of Burke introduced the first such legislation following the presidential election. On November 26 he proposed a bill appropriating $300,000 for the governor to use in organizing, arming, and equipping a volunteer military force of 10,000 men, and an additional $500,000 for the use of militias throughout the state, whenever the governor felt the situation warranted their mobilization.[7] A month later Marcus Erwin proposed that the governor be granted an additional $300,000 above that provided in Avery's bill to be spent on armaments alone, an action that provoked Unionist Jonathan

Worth to note, "The evident tendency of things here is to precipitate us into the arms of S.C.—it is getting pretty certain that conservative Democrats are falling into the hand of Avary [*sic*] and Erwin—10,000 volunteers will soon be armed—men love war—and the danger is in our attempt to frighten, we shall find ourselves in anarchy and civil war."[8] Nevertheless, by January 8, 1861, both proposals had been enacted.

Avery and Erwin were not the only mountain Democrats in the legislature championing preparedness. On December 4, Augustus Merrimon, also of Asheville, raised the issue of armament production in North Carolina, proposing before the House the model provided by the Tredegar Iron Works in Richmond.[9] Later that month, John A. Fagg of Madison County, as the chairman of the House Committee on Military Affairs, offered yet another bill to reorganize and strengthen the state militia system. Appropriately enough, once the measure passed in the House, it was Marcus Erwin who sponsored it in the Senate. Unlike his similar proposal after Brown's raid a year earlier, this one passed and became law in February 1861.[10]

With these measures well in place before the dramatic events of mid-April, North Carolinians were ready to move quickly once it became apparent that war was inevitable. On April 17, the day after he received Lincoln's call for federal troops, Governor Ellis called a special session of the legislature, and for the first two weeks in May it concerned itself largely with the raising of an army. Also on April 17, the governor issued his own call for 30,000 troops to fill North Carolina's Confederate ranks. Enlistees who responded to that call prior to legislative action in May signed on for six months' service, an indication of how quickly many thought a war could be won. Edmund W. Jones's comments no doubt reflected the assumptions of many of those men and boys who made up the first surge of enlistments. "I have not brought myself to believe that there will be much fighting," he wrote on May 20. "The courage of the North will evaporate after awhile, and the Southern States permitted to go in peace."[11]

Nevertheless, once the General Assembly convened, it authorized the governor to enlist, organize, equip, and train 20,000 to 50,000 volunteers, who would serve twelve-month terms, and another 10,000 who would volunteer to serve for the shorter of three years or the war's duration, thus suggesting that some legislators were already thinking more realistically about how long the conflict might last.[12] Yet these acts seemed to have little immediate impact on the rate of recruitment across the state. The momentum of enlistment was well under way by the time the legislature had established the policies that would define it and the finances that would support it.

Both the raising of these companies and their ultimate departures (usually to Raleigh) were very much public events, particularly during the rest of the spring and early summer. The first such gatherings reflected the celebratory mood and sense of purpose that so infused the post-Sumter weeks throughout the South. Less than a week after the Charleston fort fell, three days after Lincoln's proclamation, and two days after Governor Ellis's call for Confederate troops to report to Raleigh, both Burke and Buncombe Counties had assembled companies ready to do so. The Burke Rifles were enrolled into active service on April 18, arrived in Raleigh on April 25, and were mustered into state service as Company G of the 1st North Carolina Regiment on May 13, still a week before North Carolina officially seceded.[13]

We know much more about the departure of their counterparts from Asheville. The Buncombe Riflemen had been one of the companies established in December 1859 in response to the Harpers Ferry raid. It was one of the fourteen militia units more formally incorporated by the state in February 1861 as a result of Avery's legislative initiatives. They were thus fully organized and prepared to be the first to report for duty.[14] Their departure from Asheville for the state capital on April 18 served as a rallying point for their community, as would so many other send-offs soon to follow. According to the *Asheville News*, "The town was perfectly alive with people who had come to witness the departure of these brave volunteers. The scene was one of thrilling interest and well calculated to melt the stoutest heart to sympathy and tears." Impressed with how promptly this company had mobilized, calling it a demonstration of "their willingness to immediately engage in the services of the State and the South," the newspaper went on to assure its readers that the company was ready for whatever faced it. "The Buncombe Riflemen are composed of first rate material and if they get into any engagement will reflect honor upon themselves and their native section. . . . They are pure metal, no mistake, and will contest every inch of ground with the enemy."[15]

These occasions allowed political leaders to take advantage of local unanimity and enthusiasm heretofore unknown in most communities and sometimes to jockey for position. Nicholas Woodfin would soon be engaged in the election for Buncombe's representative to the state convention and saw no better opportunity than the Riflemen's send-off to remind voters of his stance. A sixteen-year-old member of the new company later remembered that Woodfin delivered "a parting address very feelingly and appropriate in which was some whole-some advice." But more than any words spoken, what the teenager recalled most vividly about Woodfin's "especially stimulating" speech was the tangible linkage he made to mountain men's last great clash in defense of their liberty, the Revolutionary War battle of King's Mountain. He held up two tea cups and saucers that Colonel Joseph McDowell, an ancestor both of Mrs. Woodfin and of the Riflemen's commander, Captain William W. McDowell, had captured during the battle from the mess chest of Major Patrick Fergeson, the British commander who was killed there.[16]

Practical concerns were also addressed in these gatherings. At this April afternoon gathering in Asheville, Robert Vance, Zebulon's brother, joined with the Rifles' Captain McDowell and others to draw up a resolution calling on Governor Ellis to convene the legislature as promptly as possible to respond to Lincoln's call for troops. It also named a committee to visit the governor "with a view to procure arms for such volunteer companies as may now be in this section, or which may hereafter be raised." The document ended by assuring Ellis that "we are rejoiced at the entire unanimity which pervades our commu-nity in this trying emergency, and as one man, we are determined to defend the honor and dignity of our State to the last extremity."[17]

So amid the political posturing and community celebration, the Buncombe Riflemen joined the Burke Rifles as the first two companies from western North Carolina to enter the war. The fact that they arrived in Raleigh in time to become Company E of the 1st North Carolina Regiment added to their luster, as did their participation in the first battle of the war, a relatively minor skirmish at Big Bethel, near Hampton, Virginia, on June 10. News of that Confederate victory and of "the noble stand our troops made" generated much excitement in the mountains and, combined with the more substantial Confederate victory at Bull Run a month later, no doubt encouraged the momentum for new enlistments through the summer.[18]

If not quite as all-purpose as the Buncombe County gathering on April 18, similar meetings, equally enthusiastic, convened throughout western North Carolina during the rest of the month. A day earlier, a brass band toured Yancey County in order to gather troops. Both there and in neighboring Madison it was reported that "all turned out for the South."[19] In Hendersonville, a banner stretching across the main street proclaimed: "Old Rip's Awake," a reference to secessionists' feeling that North Carolina had re-earned her earlier nickname as the Rip Van Winkle State for her reluctance to secede sooner.[20]

These efforts to rally enlistees accelerated in May and June. If some local leaders like Nicholas Woodfin used such occasions for political gain, more seemed preoccupied with assuring themselves of military leadership roles, and they recognized that their own initiatives in organizing companies was the surest means of securing those positions. Thomas Clingman and David Coleman in Buncombe County, Robert Love in Haywood, Thomas Crumpler in Ashe, William C. Walker in Cherokee, William Holland Thomas in Jackson, Lawrence Allen in Madison, James Byron Gordon in Wilkes, and John McElroy in Yancey were among those who resigned from legislative or other government offices to return home, to put together companies, and to lead them off as their captains.[21]

Zebulon Vance was among the first to do so. Even as a committed Unionist, he had declared to his constituents his intentions if war did come: "Then your fate is mine . . . you shall have, if necessary, my blood upon the battle field." When he returned to Asheville to make good on that promise, he spoke for most other political leaders when he said: "If war must come, I preferred to be with my own people. . . . [I]t was better, whether right or wrong, that communities and States should go together and face the horrors of war in a body."[22]

Two weeks after the Buncombe Riflemen's departure, Vance had no trouble assembling another 113 Buncombe County volunteers and nearly 40 from surrounding counties to make up his "Rough and Ready Guards." They marched out of Asheville on May 3 to almost as much pomp and circumstance as the Riflemen had; and they received even more attention once they were en route. Given Vance's statewide prominence, various newspapers reported on his troops' march. One reported them to be "in good spirits and full of fight, singing 'I'm Bound To Go To Richmond Right Away.'" A band serenaded them as they passed through Salisbury, then called for Vance to make a speech, which the local newspaper described as one "abounding with common sense, honesty, candor and quaintness. He said many things in an excellent manner."[23]

In the southwestern corner of the state William Holland Thomas met with Cherokee Indians late in May and soon afterward organized two hundred of them into a company known as the "Junaluska Zouaves." Thomas's achievement much impressed Raleigh newspapers. One exclaimed, "This is most remarkable. Out of a nation of some 1500, they muster 200 warriors for the defence of North Carolina"; another warned that "Northern barbarians with

Zebulon B. Vance, ca. 1860 (North Carolina Division of
Archives and History)

A. Blinkun at their head" should guard their scalps when they heard the Cherokee war whoop.[24]

A Haywood County woman provided a progress report on the steady stream of enlistments from that far corner of the state. She told her sister early in June: "One company has gone from Haywood and another will start in a few days. Mr. Ls is the 3rd one gone from Franklin [Macon County], one from Jackson, 2 from Buncombe, one from Henderson."[25] Despite the fact that it was among the most sparsely populated of any mountain county, Jackson quickly raised two companies, making it one of the first counties to supply its share of Governor Ellis's quota. By the end of June, in fact, local leaders informed the gover-

William Holland Thomas (North Carolina Division of Archives and History)

nor that nearly all single males in Jackson had enlisted and a third company was being made up primarily of married men.[26]

Even residents of the northwestern counties, where Unionism had been more entrenched, responded with enthusiasm. In Lenoir, a "great regimental muster" met on April 27 and raised a one-hundred-man company by the end of the day. Calling themselves the Caldwell Rough and Ready Boys, they were caught up in what one witness called "a state of feverish excitement." Fellow residents were quick to declare themselves "in readiness at any and all times . . . to march in defense of the rights and honors of the South against the aggressions of the North."[27]

Watauga County representative George N. Folk was one of the legislators who gave up a seat in Raleigh to return home and organize military companies under their leadership. On May 11, Folk announced his intentions to a large gathering in Boone in what one recruit described as "a some-what firey speech" in which he "dwelt at large on the attempt of the North to dominate the South and abrogate her rights under the Constitution." At the conclusion of his speech, Folk called for volunteers and asked Harvey Davis, whose diary provides this account, to lead a march in which all volunteers were to join. Folk's efforts proved successful, as Davis reported: "It seemed as if the whole assembly of citizens soon were in line." But, as Davis described, the celebration hardly ended there. Over the next four weeks of drilling, company members were "invited and partook of several public banquets, set by the hospitable citizens of this county."[28]

Even in Wilkes County, western North Carolina's strongest bastion of Unionism, the situation seemed much like that elsewhere in the mountains. James Gwyn characterized a gathering in Wilkesboro on April 30 as "a large collection of people & a great deal of excitement—most everybody now for the South." Calvin Cowles commented a bit more cynically, "Liquor flowed freely and there were ½ doz. fights."[29] In a letter to a friend a day later, Gwyn probed beneath the celebratory surface to note that "not many volunteered, only 40 or so & only 6[00] or 700$ raised to pay them." He confided that "the people seemed pretty nearly united in the Cause of the South—but I think if an influential man had got up and espoused the other side, he would have had a good many to join him."[30]

Gwyn was astute in observing that "influential men" had much to do with the tone set at these rallies. But their effectiveness in recruiting efforts had as much to do with community spirit as it did with their rhetorical skills or individual clout. Peer pressure and male camaraderie no doubt played a big part of the outpouring of volunteers in those heady days of April and May. When given the option, as most were in those early months, men and boys chose to enlist with friends and acquaintances and to serve under the command and care of men they knew and trusted. Likewise, families often felt better committing their sons to the guardianship of respected local leaders.

In his study of Ashe County during the war, Martin Crawford relates a very telling example of these localized priorities. Henry King Burgwyn Jr., a brash nineteen-year-old planter's son from eastern North Carolina and all-too-recent graduate of the Virginia Military Institute, was determined to lead a company of his own into battle and came to Ashe County to recruit such a following. He was completely stymied in his efforts, committing only two recruits—both Virginians—to his company during two weeks in the area. In contrast, Thomas Crumpler, the county's twenty-six-year-old state legislator with no military training, returned home and had no trouble putting together a cavalry company, the Jeff Davis Mountain Rifles, with himself as its captain.[31]

Community support for these locally raised companies involved more than ceremonial send-offs. The collective investment in these troops was most clearly delineated in the variety of local efforts to finance and supply them. Several counties issued court-endorsed taxes levied on their residents for the purpose of purchasing uniforms and equipment for the men and boys they sent off to war. Transylvania County went further: it borrowed $1,500 from the Asheville branch of the Cape Fear Bank in order to send off each of the volunteers in its first company with $15 cash in hand.[32] Even more creative was the solicitation of Thomas George Walton in Morganton. He raised a local cavalry company, "to aid in driving the Northern vandals from our soil," by securing pledges from twenty-five Burke County citizens "to contribute for the use of said company when organized the various items annexed to our signatures." The multicolumned list that followed indicated six donors for horses, four for guns, three for uniforms, twelve for blankets, and, from various donors, $300 in cash.[33]

Two communities in Rutherford County—Rutherfordton and Burnt Chimney (present-day Forest City)—competed to see which could mount and put into service a full company first. The Burnt Chimney Vols won the contest by departing for Raleigh on June 3. But the Rutherfordton Riflemen were only a day behind them and became part of the same regiment upon reaching the state capital.[34] A second-place finish did not diminish the pride of county seat residents. Ellen Mitchell, on behalf of "the ladies of Rutherfordton," congratulated the eager, young warriors-to-be on how quickly they had responded to the call to arms and emphasized the localized context of their achievement. "The ladies feel proud of the Sunny South, proud of the Old North State, but prouder still of this glorious mountain county whose sons, at the first sound of the tocsin of war, have rushed to the standard of our insulted country; and who being among the first in the field, will bear a part of the glorious work of driving out of Virginia the vandal hordes."[35]

Ministers often spoke at the rallies, offering prayers for the troops, for the new nation, and for an early peace, and sometimes overseeing the distribution of Bibles among the departing troops. Their presence imbued these occasions with a sense of spiritual and moral authority, which carried over to Sunday services as well, at which an entire congregation could be swept up in the emotionalism and patriotic fervor of sending their men off to war. William Graves, a Presbyterian minister who served multiple congregations in Haywood and Jackson Counties, presided over several occasions. On May 2 he preached to a "crowded house" in Webster, Jackson's county seat. Seated next to the pulpit was a company of volunteers which was to head out the next day. "It was a solemn and interesting time," Graves recalled later, "which brought forth many prayers and tears." In a similar scene in a Waynesville church a month later, after his sermon "many mothers and sisters came forward and bid their sons and brothers farewell!" Finally, he held communion services for departing troops on a Saturday in June, which "were interrupted by a barbeque in the neighborhood for the purpose of calling out the people to complete yet another volunteer Company."[36]

Ministers often enlisted with men from their communities, serving as chaplains in some cases, in others as officers.[37] They were criticized in some quarters for getting too caught up in secular matters and shirking their spiritual obligations. Early in June, a Clay County Unionist complained: "The war excitement has engaged the minds of every man in this County. The Preachers have quit preaching. The Churches are lingering under a fatal disease. They are upon the stool of do-nothing. It seems that they are all gone astray, mixing and mingleing with the world."[38] On the other hand, ministers had their own complaints. William Graves, for example, acknowledging that "Haywood & Jackson have turned out about 550 volunteers," lamented that "the excitement & confusion have caried [sic] the minds of the major part of this community too much from the great subject of religion."[39]

Where they did stay in their pulpits, clergymen throughout the Carolina highlands delivered messages on Sunday mornings that assured their congregations of the righteousness of the Southern cause in God's eyes, and the ultimate victory that would come of it. In June the Presbyterian minister in Lenoir stressed the virtues of independence and drew his text from James: "Whoso looketh into the perfect law of liberty . . . shall be blessed in his deed." A month earlier and a block away, Lenoir's Methodist minister used the story of Noah and the flood to illustrate God's efforts to save his chosen people while destroying the wicked. The ark apparently represented the Confederacy, which would keep the South afloat as God washed away Northern wickedness.[40] Episcopalians throughout the region and throughout the South heard similar sermons on July 21, as their ministers coordinated their efforts and used the Hebrews' exodus from Egypt as an analogy to Southerners' separation from the Union.[41] The churches served in other ways as well. In the spring of 1862, all of the major churches in Asheville agreed to donate their church bells, which would be melted down and recast as cannon, to the Confederate cause.[42]

In these congregational settings, women were as much the recipients of these messages as men. Church services, in fact, provided the most traditional and regularized communal outlet in which these themes and issues were addressed. Yet the circumstances of these initial war months provided women with other, less traditional venues for playing active roles in local affairs. As Ellen Mitchell's rousing speech before the Rutherfordton Riflemen indicates, wives, mothers, and daughters were allowed prominent roles, both visibly and vocally, in these proceedings, roles that served to accentuate what Asheville citizens called the "entire unanimity" of the communities involved.

Women often provided picnics for local companies as they drilled, or delivered token gifts or supplies to the troops they visited. Buncombe County women routinely visited troops from all over the mountain region as they trained at the camps established in Asheville during the summer and fall. Harvey Davis of the Watauga Rangers described the entertainment such women provided during a visit three days after the Rangers arrived at Camp Woodfin. He noted in his diary that Asheville women sang "Dixie" for the troops, which was the first time he and his companions had heard the song. After they sang, he noted, "Sergt. Todd drilled quite a squad of the ladies amid much amusement of us soldiers." Two weeks later the "ladies of Asheville" presented his company with a flag.[43]

The feminine presence at these events is particularly striking in contrast to its absence from the many public meetings held only weeks and months earlier, at which political issues were debated, resolutions were composed, and delegates were named. War differed from politics, it seemed, and the ceremonial and ritualistic nature of these latter gatherings offered women legitimate roles denied them in the decisive events leading up to the war. Men acknowledged and appreciated their new roles. The Rutherfordton Riflemen responded to Miss Mitchell's speech with three cheers "for the ladies of Rutherfordton." They marched around the courthouse square several times, finally halting again in front of the hotel, "amid a shower of bouquets and the cheers of the ladies."[44]

Women also figured more prominently in male rhetoric than had been the case during the secession crisis, perhaps an indication that many people realized that, unlike the political ramifications on which the secession debates centered, war would effect all elements of society, regardless of class or gender. Sacrifice quickly became a watchword for women's role in the war. As early as April 23, Salisbury's *Carolina Watchman* acknowledged how emotionally wrenching women would find the experience ahead of them, but it laid out a theme that would be echoed throughout the mountains in the months to come: "The millions of weeping mothers, wives and sisters, and the millions of prayers going up from hearts burdened with grief, will not restrain the voluntary human offerings which are to be made in defense of our rights and honors, but rather increase them, and nerve them for the conflict."[45]

The communal nature of women's initial responses to the war no doubt buffered them from personal anguish, and the patriotic efforts that engaged them muted private reservations, at least temporarily. The most obvious form of collective activity that engaged women during these early weeks was their creation of flags or banners to be presented to departing troops, as Ellen Mitchell did with such eloquence in Rutherfordton. When Caldwell County's first company of men was prepared to leave for Raleigh in mid-May, Mary Ann Jones in Lenoir informed her aunt that "[t]he ladies in town are hard at work. . . . Miss Sallie has almost finished the flag—'tis beautiful. The ladies of Lenoir have conferred upon me the honor of presenting it to the company 'The Caldwell Rough and Readys.' "[46] Laura Norwood, a twenty-one-year-old teacher, shared that honor with twelve other young women, all dressed in white, for a later company's send-off on July 31. The fact that the youngest sister of the company's captain gave up a silk dress to provide the material for the flag was widely circulated among Lenoir residents.[47] Amid the general euphoria, such gestures were tempered on occasion by the sobering realities of just what these women were sending their men off to do. In Hendersonville, young women presented the departing Hendersonville Guards with a flag on which they had stitched the words: "Follow your banner to victory or death."[48] (One wonders if these well-intentioned women ever considered the effect a flag emblazoned with the word "death" across it had on troops rallied into battle behind it.)

These gender-based appeals were especially effective forms of community pressure for those enlisting and kept the defense of hearth and home at the forefront of the rationales for fighting. Women not only took pride in the sacrifices they made but made sure their husbands appreciated the local status their military service conferred upon those they left at home. Ella Harper of Lenoir informed her husband, George, that she felt "a high degree of satisfaction" knowing he had answered his country's call to service. She told him that she had met a woman whose still-at-home husband made them both the subject of local gossip and disapproving glances. "If it was me," she stated, "I would be ashamed."[49]

The waverings of a woman in Surry County, just east of Ashe, regarding her husband's enlistment provides a vivid illustration of the extent to which wives not only contributed to community pressures but were susceptible to them as well. Some of the young men who made up the first wave of enlistments from that foothills community had second thoughts about military service and soon began to back out. Letitia Norman, whose husband, William, was a member of their unit, apparently saw this as an opportunity to keep him at home as well. But, as William recalled later of the backsliders, "their cowardice and toryish principles, talked of in every crowd, caused Letitia to reconsider and begin to think that, if I was to get a substitute or back out, it would affect my standing as well as hers, for she knows that a great many would accuse her of providing recreant to my duty."[50]

Women quickly found even more functional ways to support troops and to interact with each other. In the same letter in which she announced her role in a flag presentation, Mary Ann Jones also revealed that women in Lenoir were already engaged in an even more traditional and long-term activity—making "bandages and lint for the volunteers."[51] By early 1862, the *Asheville News* and other newspapers published lists of items donated to specific troops from ladies aid societies in various mountain communities.[52]

The ultimate result of all of this activity was an unusually large outpouring of highlanders into Confederate service. According to state historian Samuel A'Court Ashe, whose *History of North Carolina* is the most frequently cited source on enlistment figures, thirteen mountain counties supplied 4,400 soldiers to the Southern cause by the end of October 1861. Calculating that they were drawn from a total population of 68,000, Ashe maintained that one in fifteen mountaineers volunteered for Confederate service over that eight-month period, as opposed to the one in nineteen who volunteered from the rest of the state.[53]

The rest of the state took notice of this unusually large contribution in manpower from the mountains in 1861. On May 7, a Greensboro newspaper noted: "The hardy sons of the mountains are beginning to pour down. . . . We learn from members of the legislature that 'the mountains are in a blaze.' Volunteer companies are forming every where." The author of the article revealed his perceptions of the western counties as a frontier wilderness when he commented: "These are men enured of hardships and accustomed to the use of the rifle and will be terrible in battle."[54] The *Raleigh Register* praised highlanders' dramatic response to the state's call to arms. "The mountains are pouring forth their brave sons in great numbers," it exclaimed in July, "and still they come."[55]

By mid-June the number of mountain recruits was such that the state military command established one of four new training camps in Asheville.[56] Camp Patton's establishment there acknowledged not only the sheer number of new soldiers in the vicinity, but also the fact that Asheville was already viewed as an especially strong bastion of Confederate support. According to one historian, Asheville was "one of the most bitter towns in the state in its hatred of all things Northern," and it came to serve as a significant center of Confederate activity throughout the war.[57]

Baylis M. Edney, a Buncombe County lawyer with considerable militia experience, was named the commander of Camp Patton, and he provided frequent progress reports to the new governor, Henry T. Clark. (Governor Ellis had died on July 7.) On July 11, a week after his appointment, Edney reported that four companies were training there, with five more on the way. Two weeks later, ten companies were engaged at this "School of the Soldier," at which point Edney proposed creating a 2,400-man brigade of those he trained there, with himself at its command. By August 4, he informed Clark that "four or five Regiments can be made here in one month." With considerable pride in his achievement and what it reflected of the mountain region's contribution to the cause, Edney added, "So you may judge to what extent our people will aid the South in this great war."[58]

As for the makeup of these early companies, two studies of local enlistment patterns in mountain communities confirm similar trends. In comprehensive profiles of Ashe and Buncombe County recruitment patterns, Martin Crawford and Jim Taylor suggest that in many respects the men in the mountains who first responded to the call to arms were not so different from those elsewhere in the Confederacy. Both studies indicate that the majority of volunteers in 1861 were more likely to be single than those the next year and that they were generally younger. Crawford's calculations indicate that two-thirds of Ashe County recruits were unmarried and that of those, over four-fifths still lived with their parents. Taylor's analysis of Buncombe County indicates that 1861 recruits were on average five years younger than those who enlisted in 1862 and that the vast majority came from households that included other adult males.[59] A report from Henderson County in May 1861 confirms these findings and indicates that local observers were very much aware of such trends. In describing the departure of the Hendersonville Guards, the local Presbyterian minister noted, "Of the ninety men who compose the company, only two or three are married. The remainder are hardy, vigorous young mountaineers."[60] Both Crawford and Taylor also indicate that the earlier recruits in their counties left not only larger but also more affluent domestic situations than would be the case later in the war.[61]

All of these factors—age, marital status, financial well-being, and household size and makeup—suggest that the first men and boys to commit themselves to Confederate service were more dispensable than those who would follow them in the months and years ahead. With men's absences perhaps less of a hindrance to the continued functioning of farms, businesses, and households, this first wave of departures had less of a material impact on their families and communities than would later be the case. These tangible factors were just as significant as the martial spirit that continued to pervade the western counties in keeping morale relatively high throughout the summer and early fall of 1861.

Yet, while geographical and socio-economic factors combined to shape the course of early enlistments, they also suggest the divisions still inherent in mountain society that would resurface once the euphoria of the war's opening months subsided. Even during this period in which enthusiasm and unanimity for the cause were at their height, there were a number of subtle and not so subtle reminders of the very real divisions among mountain residents in the pre-Sumter months and ominous indications of the serious disaffection that soon would plague the region. It took an observant James Gwyn to note the superficial and short-lived enthusiasm of Wilkesboro's Confederate rally at the end of April; in the contrast between the crowd's liveliness and the actual number of recruits signed on, and the amount of money raised to support them, he recognized just how transparent the community's unified front actually was.[62]

In at least two similar rallies elsewhere in the mountains, tensions were blatantly expressed. Madison County's first public gathering centered around the May 13 vote for delegates to the secession convention. Tensions ran so high that day that it became the scene of a widely publicized shoot-out over the issues at hand. As elsewhere, liquor had flowed freely in the county seat of Marshall, and the sheriff's high spirits and intoxication led him to stand in the middle of town shouting, "Hurrah for Jeff Davis and the Southern Confederacy!" When a local farmer responded with a cry for "George Washington and the Union," the sheriff drew his pistol, accusing those in the gathering crowd of being "a set of Damd Black republicans and lincolnites." Aiming his gun at another known Unionist, he opened fire and struck his antagonist's son instead. The wounded boy's father, in turn, shot and killed the sheriff. During the street fight that ensued between Unionists and secessionists, the killer fled from Marshall, hid out in the surrounding wilderness, and eventually went to Kentucky, where he enlisted in the Union army.[63]

A string of incidents almost as volatile occurred in Hendersonville. On the day before the election, Alexander Jones, one of the few mountain Unionists on the ballot for convention delegates, faced a rowdy crowd and was "invited from the stump and threatened with a ride on one of Lincoln's rails." He claimed that guards the next day announced that they would hang or shoot anyone who voted for him and that several who did were so mobbed. When North Carolina's ordinance of secession was announced a week later, one young Confederate exchanged shots with a local Unionist and then in front of a tense, but generally approving, crowd chopped down the pole bearing the American flag.[64]

The Unionists in Hendersonville may have found themselves much outnumbered, but there were more alarming signs of divisiveness elsewhere in Henderson County. Confederate recruitment officers in Edneyville, some ten miles from the county seat, reported to Governor Ellis that in that section, "they are as deadly hostile to our raiseing volunteers & the whole defence of the south as any portion of Pennsylvania." He reported that "Houses & other buildings have been burned already by them—& our neighborhood has to hire night guards." This was the only outright defiance to Confederate recruitment mounted in the region, and it alarmed the Southern sympathizers in the area, who implored the governor to provide "relief from these painful apprehensions."[65] Although these kinds of incidents were rare during the spring, they signified the very real limitations of the unanimity of spirit so apparent elsewhere in the region. Other signs of anxiety and apathy were close behind and foreshadowed even more completely the disaffection ahead.

Volunteer companies continued to organize throughout the fall and winter— steadily in some areas, more sporadically in others. But as their departures became more routine, they also generated less enthusiasm. The novelty and spontaneity of the send-offs had worn off by the end of the summer. In September, a Waynesville woman reporting on the farewell ceremonies planned for the Haywood Sharpshooters noted a shift in mood and expediency. "Well, I do say hurrah for Haywood," Robina Norwood wrote somewhat sarcastically to her cousin. In recounting the movement of the regiment from Waynesville to nearby Asheville over three weeks earlier, she commented: "Their departure has certainly been very gradual; they have been *starting* ever since they left here and have now got on the road in good earnest. A good many of the Haywoodites went to Asheville *two weeks* ago to see them off; and thus had the pleasure of paying a hotel bill, which none of them relished, without having witnessed the object of their visit."[66] A Macon County recruit, growing impatient with delays once his company had reported to Asheville, complained to his wife after three cold and frustrating months there that "[w]e are very willing to leave this Buncombe War & goe to Jeff Davises War."[67]

Uncertainty over the terms of enlistment also became a deterrent to recruitment efforts in the fall. The transfer in June of certain regiments of state troops to the Confederacy meant alterations in their terms of service, which created confusion about the status of new companies established after that point.[68] Mercer Fain of Cherokee County, in attempting to organize a cavalry company, found that "thir is a diference of opinion hear as to the Army regulations" and requested that Governor Ellis clarify the terms on which his men would be received.[69] William Walker, also of Cherokee County, learned after putting together his own company of twelve-month volunteers that no more such companies were being accepted and that they would have to serve for the shorter of three years or the duration of the war. Walker complained to the governor that he felt such a shift in terms was unfair and feared that he would have difficulty holding on to his recruits under the new terms. "I have volluenteered [*sic*] for the Defence of my Country," he concluded. "I hope to have An Opportunity of Doing So."[70] A report from Waynesville in early September that local recruiters were "again calling for volunteers and calling almost in vain" was echoed in several other counties as well.[71]

Outside of the public realm, doubts as to the wisdom of waging war were expressed with increasing frequency. Josiah Cowles and his nephew Calvin conceded—if only in private correspondence with each other—the gloom with which they watched the tide turn so dramatically. On April 19, Josiah told Calvin that war would be "a horrible state of things to contemplate and all for the insane ambition of demagogues and [designing] politicians," who he denounced, claiming that peace could be restored if only one hundred of the leading politicians of each side should be hanged as traitors. Two weeks later he confided that he remained "sick at heart" at recent developments and that "I fear for the worst, they may fight for years Kill & destroy lives & property & then they will have to negotiate. Why not do it now[?]"[72] The younger Cowles, equally distraught, invoked vivid imagery to express his own fears: "What a sad spectacle our once glorious country presents—rent in twain and the dismembered parts crying aloud for blood—the blood of brothers."[73]

Women, too, found that the excitement of which they had been so much a part in the spring rapidly deteriorated into less glorious realities. They were soon confiding to their husbands or to other women their reluctance to give up their men to Confederate service. Laura Norwood, who had presented a flag to Caldwell County's first troops with such pride, seemed to undergo a change of heart within a month. In response to news that her brother, Thomas Lenoir, was organizing his own company late in May, she took a most rational approach in arguing against it. "I am decidedly of the opinion that you can serve your country better by staying at home and making bread & meat for our soldiers to eat than by going to be a soldier yourself at this stage of the game." She reasoned that "there seems to be no lack of troops in the field at this time and there are many more that are willing to go and who cannot serve their country so well in any other capacity."[74]

In mid-June, Norwood's cousin in Waynesville expressed her own hopes about the fate of the Haywood Invincibles. Noting that they seemed disappointed that they would be training in Asheville rather than going on to Raleigh, she confided, "For my part I am very glad they were detained at Asheville, for I know many of them will come home for a short time. . . . I hope they will never get any further."[75] When her husband announced that he was reenlisting after his six-month term was up, she wrote, "We were all so disappointed to hear of his enlisting again when he might without dishonor have come home from which he had been so long absent."[76]

Foreshadowing what would be a very real concern later in the war, Robert

Vance in Asheville informed his younger brother that rumors of soldiers' wives without food were unfounded. On May 28, he told Zebulon, then stationed with the Buncombe Rough and Readies in Weldon, that in reference to one of the privates in his company, "there never was a baser falsehood than that Jos. Randall's wife has nothing to eat. She has shoes 2 or 3 dresses and plenty to eat and so with every man's wife left behind." He told his brother: "Charge the men to believe no lie, for I am here and I say that none shall suffer." But he went on to say that requests for food had, in fact, already been met: "Newton Patton's wife was here to day. I gave her Bacon & flour."[77]

Some women, who had not yet felt any real hardship as a result of their husbands' absence, simply resented the fact that not all wives had made the sacrificial offerings to the Confederacy that they had. Only two months after her husband, Alfred, raised a company in Macon County and marched off to Asheville in November, Mary Bell expressed her bitterness toward those who had not done likewise. She admitted that for herself and a neighbor, "our daily prayer is that a draft will come and take every married man that can leave home as well as our husbands can. It makes us very mad to see other women enjoying themselves with their husbands and ours gone." A month after that, she expressed in even stronger terms what was fast becoming a far more widespread source of discontent: the inequalities in local enlistments. "Whilst some are made to mourn all the days of their lives on account of some dear one who had died whilst fighting for their country," she complained to her husband, "others will be glorying in the wealth they have made by staying at home and speculating while the war was going on and other poor wretches were fighting for them."[78]

At this early stage of the war, a much more serious—and far less personal—home front issue was the vulnerability of certain mountain areas to pockets of militant disaffection within or just beyond their borders. In the flurry of troops' gathering and moving off to Raleigh and beyond, some highlanders became concerned over the lack of protection such activity meant for their own homes and communities. The unrest in Henderson County in May made residents reluctant to enlist in regular companies. In an apologetic letter to the governor in June, Frederick Blake, to whom Ellis had given a commission and charged with raising a company, had to report that "my success thus far has not been very flattering, as men are extremely averse to leaving their crops so near harvest unless obliged to do so."[79]

Governor Ellis no doubt recognized Blake's excuse as rather feeble, for he had other, far more forthright informants in Henderson, who had explained the real source of enlistment problems there—that volatile "disaffected region" around Edneyville. Given the threats from that militant Unionist community, the men who had enlisted under Baylis Edney's command or in other companies from the county and to a greater extent "the Female society at large" were greatly concerned "that as soon as we leave that bloodshed[,] house burning & death will commence." Edney urged the governor to make some provision for civilian protection before the scheduled departure of his troops. Ellis could suggest only that a committee of safety be created and that the Buncombe County militia might be called out if necessary.[80]

Later in the fall, the volatile situation in East Tennessee and the vulnerability of the North Carolinians along its border had a serious effect on continued enlistments. In some counties, the areas bordering Tennessee contributed far fewer Confederate enlistments than did other sections of the county. Ashe County's North Fork area bordered Tennessee's Johnson County, where, by October, the violence of Unionist sympathizers was causing alarm. It is no coincidence that North Fork provided fewer men per capita to Confederate service than did any other part of Ashe.[81] By the same token, the lack of response to enlistment fervor by those in the upper Toe River valley, situated along the state line, contrasted sharply with that in the lower part of the valley. Nearly all of the eighty-six Confederate volunteers that came out of the valley, one of the most sparsely populated areas of the Carolina highlands, were from its lower section.[82] Although to some extent lower enlistment rates correlated with Unionist sentiment in those areas, they also indicated the reluctance of men living near the Tennessee border to leave their homes and communities unprotected from the military threat they felt was so close at hand.

Residents in the southwestern corner of the state also had second thoughts about the strong demonstrations their young men had made in their commitment to Southern independence only a few weeks earlier. Jackson County leaders, who had taken such pride in the two companies they had put together and sent off, noticed soon thereafter the void they had created locally. Those companies had taken most of the county's single men. A third company being formed was made up primarily of married men, who petitioned Governor Ellis late in June to allow them to stay in the region to protect their own citizenry. "We think it probable that there will be need for at least one reagement in the western part of the state," the spokesmen for the company reasoned. Although they were willing to go wherever they were assigned, they "would prefur if any forces are station[ed] in the west that they have the preferance as the company will be composed of men with families."[83]

Also in June, a group of seven men from adjacent Macon County, calling themselves the Nantahala Rifles, reminded Governor Ellis that East Tennessee "is contiguous to us." Given that "the express purpose" of certain known Tennesseans living near the border "to live and die under the Stars & Stripes, together with the smothered disaffection in our very midst," they proposed that a portion of the cavalry regiment they had raised locally be allowed to train in Franklin, the county seat, rather than in Asheville. "As a result," they reasoned, "more men will be induced to volunteer. . . and much disaffection will be given an eternal quietus." But they also told Ellis that they expected Tennessee's Confederate governor, Isham G. Harris, to "throw a large body of troops into East Tennessee, which will have a tendency to drive the Union men there to our mountains until they can be reinforced by [President] Lincoln and here commit depredations." Again, having a body of cavalrymen stationed in Franklin would serve to resist "and thus perhaps terminate a civil war and prevent our *Republicans* from rising to their relief."[84]

It is unlikely that Ellis would have seriously heeded such pleas from the state's highlanders during the summer, but we will never know, given his sudden death in July. By the fall, his successor, Governor Henry T. Clark, did acknowledge the mountain communities' concern that the drainage of manpower from the west for military service elsewhere had left their own home front vulnerable. In mid-November, Clark informed Judah Benjamin, who was then acting Confederate secretary of war, that he had received numerous requests for assistance from that part of the state. "Border warfare must ensue," he wrote, "and unless our people are protected they may be somewhat affected either by the superiority of the traitors or [by] their artful promises. That portion of NC is now very weak and exposed from the large and undue proportion of volunteers furnished from this section."[85]

The priorities of western North Carolinians changed fairly quickly over the course of 1861 for a variety of reasons. The early euphoria of the spring rapidly deteriorated as many mountain residents came to realize over the course of the summer and fall that the conflict could last far longer than they had originally anticipated. With that realization came another: that the initial waves of enthusiastic enlistment had imposed new vulnerabilities on those still at home—

whether from food and labor shortages on farms, from military threats from
Tennessee, or from more localized disruptions brought on by the disaffected
elements in the area who never had embraced the Southern cause. As later
chapters will reveal, all of these concerns, both individual and communal,
would soon become much more tangible and far more intense for western
North Carolinians and would remain so for much of the war's duration.

UNIONISTS

Lincolnite Proclivities—Matters of General Notoriety

PERHAPS no assumption about the Civil War in Appalachia has been more
pervasive than that southern highlanders were predominantly Unionist.
Chroniclers of the region from the war years to the present have characterized the region as outside the mainstream of Southern sentiment in its antisecessionist, anti-Confederate, and postwar Republican tendencies. Certainly
the greatest attention paid to Appalachia during the war was to the volatile
situations in the most solidly and militant Unionist sections of the mountain
South, East Tennessee and what would become West Virginia during the
middle of the war. The loyalist majorities in those sizable highland regions led
to the widespread conclusion that Unionism was a natural sentiment in the
areas in which slavery played a minimal role and thus applied to all parts of
Southern Appalachia.

With the war barely under way, a Minnesota journalist articulated the basic components of the viewpoint that would prove so durable. "Within the immense district to which the designation of Alleghania is here applied," he wrote in November 1861, "the slaves are so few and scattered" and its residents exhibit "a complete dedication . . . to Free Labor." He singled out East Tennessee and western North Carolina as "faithful parts of the Union" ripe for a counterrevolution against the Confederacy, a movement that Abraham Lincoln should encourage and support. "Within this Switzerland of the South, Nature is at war with Slavery, and the People are ready to strike for Liberty and Union."[1] In the years after the war, such ideas were both consciously and unconsciously perpetuated by Appalachian spokesmen and outsider observers, with little if any effort made to distinguish variations in mountain sentiments from one section of the region to another. By the end of the century, Berea College president William Frost proclaimed that "when the civil war came . . . Appalachian America clave to the old flag," and few historians found any reason to challenge his simplistic assessment.[2]

Although long forgotten or ignored once such stereotypes began to emerge, there is abundant evidence from contemporary accounts and postwar chronicles that residents, participants, and outsiders were all well aware of clear distinctions between attitudes in western North Carolina and other parts of Southern Appalachia, particularly East Tennessee. The Carolina highlands never became the Unionist stronghold that existed across the state line to the west; Unionist sentiments, in fact, were less pervasive in the western part of North Carolina than they were in many parts of the state's piedmont.[3] And yet, as in other parts of the South, the surreptitious and fluctuating nature of wartime Unionism in western North Carolina resulted in ambiguities, variations, and complexities that continue to challenge scholars today.

By the time the state voted itself out of the Union in May 1861, with overwhelming support from Carolina highlanders, political Unionism dissipated in the region. Unlike in East Tennessee or northwestern Virginia, the Unionist movement in western North Carolina was more typical of that elsewhere in the Upper South in that it lost whatever momentum it had maintained up until the attack on Fort Sumter and Lincoln's subsequent call for troops. The highlanders who were initially reluctant to support the Confederate cause clearly demonstrated the conditional nature of their Unionism. Many, perhaps most, quickly capitulated to the swelling tide of secessionism and support for the war already under way. A McDowell County farmer's assessment of his own wavering loyalties typifies that of many highlanders. "At the beginning of the rebellion I sympathized with the Union cause; I first voted in favor of the Union, and the next time in favor of the States going out of the Union. The big fellows told me it was obliged to go out of the Union, and I voted accordingly."[4]

Those who continued to oppose secession and the Confederate war effort suddenly found themselves to be a beleaguered minority.[5] Ostracized, harassed, and stigmatized within their communities as "Lincolnites," "Tories," and "abolitionists," they proved unable to sustain a consistent platform or an organized, readily identifiable group of adherents, so their movement soon took on a more subversive character with little voice or visibility during the war's early months. In an observation equally applicable to western Carolina communities, an East Tennessee Unionist noted the extent to which localized pressures made this sudden enthusiasm for the Confederacy almost contagious in his own area. "Sympathy with friends and kindred," wrote Oliver Temple, "became the bond that united the South. Tens of thousands of men who had no heart for secession, did have heart for their neighbors and kindred. This almost universal fellowship and sympathy drew men together in behalf of a cause which one-half of them disapproved."[6]

Alexander H. Jones, Henderson County's most ardent Unionist, was forced to acknowledge the extent to which Unionist convictions had evaporated by late April and early May, but he, too, noted the pressures that forced many men into rather shallow commitments to the new Southern order. He tried to rationalize the sudden shift, claiming that only five days' notice of a second vote on a secession convention proved "fatal to the Union men." When the question was posed, "If North Carolina is called upon for men, are you going to fight for Lincoln or for the South?" Jones complained bitterly that "few were found now who would face the music and become a candidate in favor of the Union." That lack of moral courage on the part of former Unionist spokesmen, he claimed, was compounded by the fact that "the mouths of the Union men [were] almost completely gagged."[7]

The initial fervor for secession among North Carolina highlanders did perhaps stifle or intimidate those who opposed it. But much of their subsequent silencing must also have resulted from their recognition that their numbers within the region had dramatically decreased. As noted earlier, just after an enthusiastic Confederate rally in Wilkesboro, James Gwyn described the dramatic shift in that community's sentiments but noted the superficial nature of the change, asserting that "an influential man . . . espousing the other side" could easily have swayed many in the crowd to abandon their newly acquired allegiances.[8]

Both Jones and Gwyn recognized that the void in a local Union leadership was crucial in their failure to buck the tide of the much more dynamic and united secessionist front. Strong leadership was perhaps the most distinguishing factor in East Tennessee's Unionist movement, which enjoyed the presence of a far more politically powerful, articulate, and committed Unionist elite than ever existed in western North Carolina. Andrew Johnson, William "Parson" Brownlow, and Thomas R. R. Nelson were more effective in shaping and rallying Unionist convictions among their constituents and readership both before and during the war than those in like positions and of like mind across the state line to the east.[9]

Over the course of the war's first year, local pressures on individuals not in support of the Confederacy continued to mount. According to an Ashe County Unionist, "as the Fall and Winter of '61 to '62 passed slowly on, I began to realize that I must suppress my convictions on the issues of the war, though my faith grew stronger on the side of the North. . . . Those in sympathy with the Southern cause grew still more arrogant, and no one's life and property were safe if it was known he was in sympathy with the Union."[10]

Yet just as many Carolina highlanders' commitment to the Union proved ephemeral in the secessionist surge of the spring and summer of 1861, it became increasingly obvious in the months that followed that many of those who swore allegiance to the Confederacy did so merely "from the teeth out," as one mountain resident put it.[11] As the war progressed, Unionist sentiment in the mountains was revitalized and manifested itself primarily as war-weary disaffection and disillusionment with both the tolls taken by the conflict itself and the demands of Confederate policy. The latter half of the war also saw the political revitalization of Unionist sentiment in the form of a statewide peace party. That, along with the Union occupation of East Tennessee in the fall of 1863, led many highlanders to sense that the Union would ultimately prevail. The peace party also made residents more confident in taking a stronger pro-Union and/or anti-Confederate stance, though doing so never proved free of risk anywhere in the region.

Wartime Unionism in western North Carolina, in other words, hit its stride only during the second half of the war and reemerged primarily in response to the exigencies of the war rather than to any deeply held love of the Union or opposition to slavery or slaveholders, sentiments that many people assumed were indigenous to mountain society. It also differed from the Unionism of the antebellum or secession period in that it was not as politicized. Our perceptions of prewar Unionism are based largely on the rhetoric and writings of politicians and journalists. It was through a political forum and as a political agenda that such opinions were conveyed up until the Confederacy assumed its final form. But once the war was under way, as Unionism took on a less public and more subversive nature, it became, for most western North Carolinians at least, an experientially based concept that we know largely as a result of postwar testimony by participants, witnesses, and other contacts, both friendly and hostile.[12]

The ideological determinants of wartime (as opposed to prewar) Unionist sentiment among western Carolinians remain particularly elusive. The records of the Southern Claims Commission, a federal agency that was established in 1871 and operated for nearly a decade to compensate Southern Unionists who provided goods and services to the Northern war effort, are a rich source of firsthand testimony by thousands of those seeking to demonstrate their loyalty in answering questions posed on lengthy claim forms.[13] But nowhere among those questions is the crucial inquiry as to why such claimants believed and acted as they did. Other testimony by individual Unionists only hints at the reasons for their minority allegiance, and much of that testimony appears to have been prompted by superficial sentimentality or self-serving hindsightedness.

The vacillation exhibited by so many highland Unionists suggests not only that they took stances that were nonpoliticized in nature but also that they were more opportunistic than ideologically committed to the cause. The actual determinants of Southern Unionism were perplexing to sort out, and even more so when applied to this mountain setting where they so often proved transitory, undemonstrative, and often well disguised. While the literature on Southern Unionism continues to grow, explanations for its origins remain obscure.

Paul Nagel has demonstrated the strength of the concept of Union as it developed from the Revolution up until secession. It was, he maintains, a "verbal icon." As a symbol, an image, and an ideal, the Union came to embrace the American qualities of "Mission, Destiny, Providence, Nature, Spirit, Immortality." The potency of those associations led one commentator in 1861 to call the Union "a holy instrument around which all American hearts cluster and to which they cling with the tenacity of a semi-religious attachment." If such hyperbole is contradicted by the crisis that came to a head that year, it may well describe the sentiment that made many Southerners reluctant to embrace its antithesis, disunion, when faced with that option.[14]

There is evidence, if scanty, that such idealistic patriotism did motivate the wartime allegiances of a number of highlanders, and that such intangibles inspired and gave meaning to their wartime loyalty. Oliver Temple explained the basis of Unionism among East Tennesseans: "They were full of patriotism and had been taught from childhood to resent an insult, and especially one to the flag of their country, the emblem of liberty."[15] Mountainous Union County, Georgia, which borders southwest North Carolina, was formed and named in 1832, during the nullification crisis. According to local tradition, a representative from the region rose in the Georgia state legislature and proposed that the new county be called "Union! for none but union men reside in it!" That legacy carried considerable weight three decades later: the county proved to be one of the most concentrated Unionist strongholds in the north Georgia mountains.[16]

In his postwar memoir, Henderson County's most outspoken Unionist, Alexander H. Jones, explained his loyalty: "[I]n my youth I read the life of Washington, Marion, Putnam, and the history of the United States. In a word, I was taught to love the Union next to my God."[17] For Jones, and other Unionists, his own military service often translated into a sense of patriotism that made separation from the Union objectionable. The fact that Jones enlisted for post–Mexican War military service and served under Winfield Scott provides further explanation for his abiding attachment to the Union.[18] The strong Unionist enclave of Shelton Laurel in Madison County stemmed in part from the Revolutionary War activity of two of its early settlers, Roderick and William Shelton, who established their homes in that remote mountain locale soon after fighting for American independence. Andrew Johnson was aware that many of his East Tennessee constituents were also descendants of Revolutionary patriots, and in his antisecessionist rhetoric he played upon the linkage between their nationalism and their pride in their ancestors who contributed to that cause.[19]

The people who moved through the mountains during the war and interacted with Unionist residents there were not much more helpful in explaining the roots of their sentiments; the dependence on local Unionists' aid and protection and later the gratitude for both led fugitive chroniclers to romanticize their highland benefactors. J. Madison Drake wrote of the Caldwell County Unionists he met: "In all my wanderings, I had never seen a more intelligent or determined people. Mingling with them, as I did for weeks, I thought of the brave defenders of the Tyrol, or the hardy Waldenses, fighting and dying among the hills for dear Liberty's sake." A New York war correspondent characterized the Unionists he encountered as "natural antagonists of the Slaveholders; lovers of the Union for the Union's sake, [who] regarded as an enemy whoever would seek its destruction," while a Wisconsin colonel found them to be "men who would suffer privations, and death itself, rather than array themselves in strife against the Stars and Stripes, the emblem of the country they loved." Albert Richardson, another wartime correspondent for the New York *Tribune* who also found himself a fugitive in the Carolina highlands, wrote of the "large number of the Union mountaineers" he encountered: "Theirs was a very blind and unreasoning loyalty, much like the disloyalty of some enthusiastic Rebels. . . . They had little education; but when they began to talk about the Union their eyes lighted wonderfully, and sometimes they grew really eloquent."[20]

If patriotism to the United States remained the common denominator in these descriptions of mountain loyalists, only occasionally did these fugitive memoirs cite slavery as a reason behind mountain Unionism. Although the paucity of slaves in the southern highlands is often, and quite naturally, cited elsewhere as a basic cause of opposition to secession and the Confederacy, explicit opposition to the peculiar institution was rarely evident to observers. As Carl Degler has noted, "The history of Union sentiment in the South is quite unlike the story of Southern antislavery."[21]

One exception is found in a turn-of-the-century reminiscence titled *Adventures of a Conscript*, by W. H. Younce, an Ashe County Unionist, although he is not fully convincing in crediting his Unionism to abolitionist sentiments. "Living in the midst of slavery," Younce wrote forty years after the fact, "and daily observing the evils of the whole system, I had become thoroughly imbued with the anti-slavery doctrine." Thus, when Southern secession led to civil war, he maintained: "I was ready and willing to fight for my country under the old flag, but could never consent that my weapon should be drawn in what I believed to be an unworthy cause."[22] The most striking aspect of such an unequivocal antislavery statement was its rarity among Carolina highlanders, who had never supported even fledgling abolitionist movements, such as those that had briefly thrived in East Tennessee.[23]

Far more often, it was a fear for slavery's future outside the Union, particularly its vulnerability should civil war result, that fueled much of the Unionist sentiment during the secession crisis. Although Basil Armstrong Thomasson, a schoolteacher and farmer in Yadkin County (adjoining Wilkes to the east), was no supporter of slavery, he resented the breakup of the Union over threats to the institution, particularly when it was unlikely to survive a war. He wrote in his diary on April 20, 1861: "[Pa] told us the war had commenced in

Charleston some two weeks ago. *Where* and *when* will it end? And what will be
the result? Freedom to the slaves? I think so. The South has commenced the
war, and now I do not believe the North will ever listen to any terms of peace
which do not include 'Freedom to the slaves.'" In a letter to his brother,
Thomasson confided, "The people of the North have set in to free the negros,
and the South too it seems to me has taken the right course—the shortest way—
to arrive at the same end."[24]

Basil Thomasson expressed such thoughts privately, but other individuals
with more of a vested interest in slavery's survival made them publicly. In his
argument that "by throwing off those guarantees—the Constitution and the
Union—southern states has done the cause of slavery more injury than anything
else could have done," Alexander Jones reflected the greatest concern of many
of the highlands' most prominent Unionists, that their slave property was less
vulnerable within rather than outside the Union.[25]

Many Unionists equated the war with slave unrest and expressed their resentment at secessionists, whom they blamed for both. An Indiana soldier
making his way through Henderson County was confronted by three young
women whose father was a tenant on the Flat Rock estate of Confederate
secretary of the treasury Christopher Memminger. The Hollingsworth sisters,
who were outspoken Unionists, as were their more discreet parents, mistook
the fugitive for a Confederate deserter and berated him and his fellow Confederates for their misguided zeal that had disrupted their lives and their society.
"For a few niggers," the oldest sister charged the soldier, "you've driven this
country to war, and forced men into the army to fight for you who don't want to
go, and you've got the whole county in such a plight that there's nothing going
on but huntin' and killin' . . . all the time." Their father's position on a
slaveholding estate gave these women a vested interest in the stability of slavery,
but they made it clear that they resented the institution that had brought on the
hardship and uncertainty of the war.[26]

A number of large slaveholders in the region remained committed Unionists
throughout the war. John Horton and Lewis Banner were among the largest
land- and slaveowners in Watauga County; they were both actively engaged
in Unionist subversion throughout the war, "secreting, hiding, and feeding"
Union prisoners who had escaped from the Salisbury prison.[27] David Worth,
his father-in-law, and his brother-in-law took a more neutral stance in Ashe
County's North Fork, where they owned nearly two-thirds of the community's
slave populace.[28] Wilkes County's most active entrepreneur and second largest

slaveholder, Calvin Cowles, was also its most outspoken antisecessionist before the war, and he remained a committed, if somewhat muted, Unionist
during the conflict.[29]

There are enough such examples of Unionist leanings among western North
Carolina's established elite to dismiss antislavery sentiments as a source of the
region's anti-Confederate stance. Yet evidence also supports the more general
assumption that Southern Unionism was a function of lower-class resentment of
slaveholders, particularly as the war continued, exacting more and more hardships on those least able to make the sacrifices demanded of them. Echoing the
antislavocracy rhetoric so common among Tennessee Unionist leaders, Alexander Jones called North Carolina's Confederate leaders "bombastic, high
falutin, aristocratic fools [who] have been in the habit of driving negroes and
poor helpless white people until they think they can control the world of
mankind."[30]

Yet what is most striking about Jones's bombast is how rarely such opinions
were expressed by other Carolina highlanders during the war. Tempered perhaps by the fact that the secession debate in the region was itself never framed in
class terms, since Unionists and secessionists alike made slavery's protection a
priority, the wartime dialogue over slavery as a source of class tensions was
equally vague, leaving the exigencies of the war itself as the prime source of
tensions between the region's elite and nonelite populace. New York journalist
Sidney Andrews made the point quite explicitly during his tour of the postwar
South. "I was somewhat curious to see the Unionism of Western North Carolina of which we heard so much during the war," he wrote in 1866. He concluded that it "was less a love for the Union than a personal hatred of those who
went into the Rebellion. It was not so much an uprising for the [federal]
government as against a certain ruling class." Andrews acknowledged the existence of a more principled Unionist leadership within the region, characterizing
the leaders he had encountered as "many intelligent men, whose Unionism is of
the judgement and affection, and whose speech on almost every phase of the
question at issue would do no discredit even to the radicalism of Massachusetts." But he was correct when he dismissed their influence after Fort Sumter
as negligible and their following as minimal.[31]

Only as the oppression of Confederate policy and local efforts to enforce that
policy began to stir resentment did Unionist ranks begin to swell. According to
Andrews, it was "a rebellion against the little tyranny of local politicians" that
was "unquestionably at the foundation of much of the opposition to the Davis

government."[32] That "little tyranny" no doubt referred to the implementation of Confederate policy by county officials or home guard units that proved more and more unpopular over the latter war years. The basis of mountain Unionism, then, lay in that significant segment of the populace that had neither deep-rooted loyalties to either cause, Union or Confederate, but for whom the actions and policies of the latter proved more offensive than those of the former.

But how does one measure the extent and characterize the nature of Unionism in western North Carolina? Part of the problem in doing either lies in the scattershot nature of Unionist sentiment in the region. There was almost no area of the mountains in which Unionist households could not be found. Fugitive narratives reveal that there were networks of Unionists that provided aid, shelter, and protection in virtually every county in the region. On the other hand, there was no part of the region in which Unionists ever felt safe or secure enough to do so openly.

Because so many escaped prisoners from Confederate prisons at Salisbury and Columbia moved into the highlands to their west in an attempt to reach East Tennessee, the Union-occupied territory most accessible to them, their narratives provide particularly rich, if impressionistic, contemporary accounts of the region's political leanings. Like so many other treatments of the subject, many of their descriptions exaggerated, at least initially, the extent of Unionist sentiment in North Carolina's mountains or tended to see all highland populaces as committed to the Union. A New York officer who moved into the Blue Ridge foothills after escaping from Salisbury commented that western North Carolina "was to the full as loyal as West Virginia."[33]

Some escapees actually entered highland areas with a false—and dangerous—sense of security based on such assumptions, and were quickly disillusioned. Another fugitive from Salisbury noted that once he and his fellow prisoners moved into the Carolina highlands, "we experienced little trouble finding 'friends,' for they were everywhere." Yet they were soon thereafter startled to find themselves face to face with a local Confederate officer who charged them with being "d—n Yankees." The prisoners panicked, but the officer quickly alleviated their fear by informing them that as the father of three sons killed in battle and another dying of fever in a Delaware prison, he had lost all interest in the war. He allowed the Union men to proceed unharmed, but once out of his sight, they raced away, still unsure of his intentions or truthfulness. They agreed that "hereafter we must be more careful, and not act on the hypothesis that every person we meet is devoted to the Union, even though he is a *North* Carolinian."[34]

William H. Parkins's initial assessment of the region is perhaps more accurate. Parkins recalled that as he moved through the southwest corner of the state en route from Georgia to Tennessee, "I knew that we were now approaching rapidly the border country where some were Secessionists and others Union people, and that with each step we took our danger from bushwhackers and scouts increased." He noted the kind of evidence that confirmed the volatility of the region—a burned cabin, destroyed corncribs, the furtiveness of men he encountered along the road. "All showed me," Parkins concluded, "that we were gradually getting into the bloody ground of western North Carolina and East Tennessee, where neighbor fought with neighbor and brother slew brother."[35]

In general, these Union soldiers' narratives suggest that allies were to be found in every part of western North Carolina but that nowhere could one ever assume they made up a majority of the populace. Yet despite the seemingly disparate nature of Unionist configurations in the Carolina highlands, there were several concentrated pockets of Unionist strength as well. Wilkes was unquestionably the most Unionist of North Carolina's mountain counties. As indicated earlier, an overwhelming number of its voters (97 percent) had opposed a convention to consider North Carolina's February 1861 secession referendum. While their reversal of opinion in the May 20 balloting and their initial enthusiasm for the Confederacy and the war effort suggest that their commitment to the Union had been only superficial, it reemerged to the extent that Wilkes gained a reputation among deserters and other Union fugitives as being a particularly sought after refuge. One escapee referred to it as "a county so strong in its Union sentiments that the Rebels call it 'the Old United States.'"[36] Certain communities within the county, such as Trap Hill and Mulberry, were particularly assertive in their loyalty to the Union. Confederates in Wilkesboro noted with dismay the activities of Trap Hill residents who raised their own local Union militia company and, along with others in the county, marched into the county seat in August 1863, raised a large Union flag, and held a rally in the town square. One local woman reported that Union sentiment was as prevalent among the women as among the men and noted with alarm that "[s]ome of the people about here have actually rejoiced at the death of Genl. [Stonewall] Jackson."[37]

Most other mountain counties had far greater pro-Confederate majorities than Wilkes, and yet there were a number of intensely Unionist communities scattered throughout the region. The Edneyville area of Henderson County (discussed in Chapter 3) was obviously firm enough in its loyalties and had the manpower to strike fear into many of the Confederate men and women living elsewhere in the county.[38] Pro-Union residents of Crab Creek in newly formed Transylvania County outnumbered Confederate sympathizers by six to one, according to a local observer, and the remote community sent over a hundred men to the Union army. Joseph Hamilton, a leading citizen and colonel of the local militia before the war, was elected captain of a Federal company he organized locally, which served with the 2nd North Carolina Mounted Infantry, one of the state's two Union regiments.[39]

In many instances, proximity to the Tennessee border shaped a community's proclivities toward Federal loyalism. Studies of both Ashe and Yancey Counties reveal far stronger Unionist sentiment in the more remote northern sections of each county, which in both cases also happened to border Tennessee. Martin Crawford, in the most extensive study of mountain Unionism at the local level, characterized such commitments in Ashe County as essentially an extension of East Tennessee Unionism. He discovered that two-thirds of the Ashe County men who enlisted in Union regiments were from the North Fork district, and that most of them joined a Tennessee cavalry unit. As early as August 1861, Jennie Lillard, a North Fork resident, explained her community's Unionist majority, noting that the town was only six miles from the state line and "consequently close to the Tory hot bed."[40]

A Unionist fugitive moving through Watauga County late in the war commented on how deserted he found Boone, its county seat, only a dozen miles from the state line. "I was told," he said, "that the village had once been inhabited by Union-loving people, who, not liking the Jeff. Davis rule, had stampeded for Tennessee."[41] A local Confederate official described the Laurel Mountains of Madison County, also near the Tennessee border, as an area "where lawlessness reigned supreme and all claimed to be Union men."[42] Residents of Marshall, Madison's county seat, were among the few western North Carolina applicants to the Southern Claims Commission who acknowledged that they lived among other Unionists. A witness for one claimant stated that "the locale in which he lived was strongly Union and a great number of his neighbors went through and joined the Union army." Another testified that all of his near neighbors were Union men and that he had "lived on the route that was travelled mostly by parties moving through the lines—some were also aided by my relatives."[43]

Yet western North Carolina's proximity to the far more prevalent Unionism across the state line did not necessarily make loyalists out of Carolina residents. An analysis of divided allegiances in the Toe River valley before and during the war concludes that despite its remoteness and location in Yancey and Mitchell Counties, adjacent to Tennessee, approximately three-fourths of the valley's inhabitants were firmly committed to the Confederate cause once the war was under way, despite an almost evenly divided voting record on the secession issue two months earlier. The community closest to Tennessee, in southwest Mitchell County, was, in fact, the valley's most neutral, displaying neither the ardent Unionism of the minority nor the pro-Southern sentiment of the major-ity of Toe River valley inhabitants.[44] (Cross-state influences worked two ways as well. Historian Durwood Dunn has noted that in the predominantly Unionist community of Cades Cove in the Tennessee Smokies, the Confederate sympa-thies of a few younger men were due to strong kinship ties with pro-Southern Yancey County residents, whom they often visited.)[45]

Despite the presence of Unionist communities within easy access to Ten-nessee, the impression that emerges from the narratives of Union fugitives fleeing through the Carolina highlands, and from much of the Southern Claims Commission testimony from the region, is that Unionists there were more likely to be situated in more remote valleys or along ridges that physically isolated them from other residents of like sentiments and were more likely to have only Confederate neighbors. When two slave women gave directions to a Camp Sorghum escapee in Transylvania County to the home of a white Unionist who would be a valuable guide through the mountains, they instructed him to approach the sixth house after crossing a particular bridge along his route, warning him to count carefully, for approaching any other house before or after could prove to be a costly blunder.[46] A Southern Claims Commission agent's summation of the claim of Nehemiah North of McDowell County described a situation that many, if not most, mountain Unionists faced: "It appears from his testimony that the region where he lived was violently rebel—that for 12 miles around there were only five or six Union men—who were known to each other, but who were obliged to keep silent as to their opinions except when they talked to each other."[47]

Much of the difficulty in detecting patterns or pinpointing reliable indicators of Unionism is what appears to be the sheer randomness of such allegiances, within not only communities and neighborhoods but also households. In some instances, it was the stamina or depth of conviction toward a cause—either Union or Confederate—that determined its home front adherents, and thus degrees of allegiance could vary greatly.

Divided loyalties within families took a variety of forms, in terms of generation and gender. Southern Claims Commission files contain testimony from several western Carolina fathers who maintained that their love of the Union outweighed parental bonds. In at least three such cases, Unionist landholders disowned their sons when they volunteered for Confederate service.[48] Other highlanders who served in the Union army noted that they had brothers, fathers, or sons in Confederate service. Sidney McLean of Madison County joined Federal troops in Tennessee despite the fact that he had five brothers at the time in the Confederate army.[49]

Husbands and wives sometimes found themselves on either side of the issue as well. Union fugitive Madison Drake wrote of a pro-Confederate "vixen" he and his party encountered in attempting to move through Caldwell County. She gave them a vehement tongue-lashing once she learned of their identities and took special pleasure in telling them of a Yankee who had escaped from Salisbury only to be captured and hanged in nearby Lenoir. Once she confirmed "that we were Yankees" she added that "she would gladly assist in hanging us on the same tree." But all hope of aid from this household was not lost, for the crippled husband of this outspoken rebel witnessed the scene. "While his spouse was declaiming against us so virulently," Drake wrote, "he remained a passive listener; and when she concluded her tirade, he winked at us significantly, and hobbling off the stoop, bade us follow him." Once safely out of earshot of the cabin, this "happy or unhappy husband," married only six weeks, informed his visitors that he had served in the Confederate army until he was wounded and discharged. Two of his brothers had been captured in battle, had "taken the oath," and were doing good business in the North. He was determined to do likewise, and with the threat of conscription looming, he saw Drake and his companions as a means of his own escape. He "resolved to befriend" the Union fugitives and help them get through to Union lines. In return, he asked that they return with other forces and take him prisoner so that he could join his brothers in the North, thus escaping not only Confederate oppression but that of his shrewish bride as well.[50]

Confederate husbands and Unionist wives seem to have been the more common configuration of divided households. Pennsylvania officer David Stafford encountered such a situation after his prison escape. Moving north across the Blue Ridge toward Virginia, Stafford misunderstood the instructions of earlier contacts and stopped at the wrong house along his route. He found himself at the door of a Confederate captain's home. Fortunately, the captain's wife answered the door and she quietly informed the fugitive of his mistake, telling him he should have gone one house farther, where her parents, "good Union people," would take him in.[51]

A Macon County incident involved yet another variation of divisions in families and among neighbors and the subterfuge in which they engaged—that between a Confederate son, his Unionist mother, and their neighbors. As Michael Egan, a Pennsylvania captain, and his fugitive band moved into Macon County, they encountered Henry Grant, a "fire-tried Unionist, brave, prudent, determined, and inflexible." Grant offered to provide the group with shelter but noted "a slight obstacle in the way—there is an armed rebel soldier in the house." This young Confederate was visiting his widowed mother who lived in an adjoining house. To their surprise, they found that she "had no real sympathy with the Southern cause," despite the fact that her only child was fighting for it, and she agreed to help conceal the identities of the fugitives for the duration of her son's visit.[52]

The fact that spouses were forced to hide their loyalties from one another, that parents and children were sometimes unaware of each other's true allegiances, and that neighbors concealed from other neighbors their sentiments regarding the war demonstrates how surreptitious Unionism remained in the North Carolina mountains. Michael Fellman's observation of civilians in guerrilla-torn Civil War Missouri applies to western North Carolina Unionists as well. "Loyalty was not the safest and most common presentation of self during this guerrilla war," he writes. "Prevarication was. Frankness and directness led to destruction more often than did reticence and withdrawal."[53]

The experience of Alexander Jones in Hendersonville provided an early lesson to other Unionists. He was, by his own admission, unflinching in his anti-Confederate stance, and as a newspaper editor he had a ready outlet for making his views public. "I endeavored to give the people the benefit of the great arguments in favor of the Union," he wrote. "My editorials were determined and uncompromising. I was dubbed by the disorganizers an abolitionist, a Tory, a Lincolnite, etc." His unveering efforts to rally wavering local Unionists well after the war was under way and his increasingly conspiratorial contacts with East Tennesseans led to "daily threats" on his life and "much uneasiness" on the part of his family. Perhaps inevitably, he was arrested and imprisoned by Confederate forces in Asheville. He was eventually transferred to prison camps in Raleigh and then Richmond, where in the fall of 1863, he was conscripted into a Virginia infantry company, despite his advanced age. He eventually deserted that enforced service and escaped to Cincinnati, where he spent most of the rest of the war.[54]

Even in areas of relatively heavy Union concentrations, Unionist merchants, such as David Worth in Ashe County's North Fork and Calvin Cowles in Wilkesboro, were restrained enough by social pressures and business concerns to claim only "neutrality" as far as the war was concerned. Cowles, as one of Wilkes County's most prominent and probably wealthiest residents, found he had to be particularly heedful that his anti-Confederacy stance not offend customers or clients on either side. In September 1863, Calvin's brother urged him not to express his true sentiments publicly, even in Wilkes County, one of the most vital Union strongholds. "There is great trouble in store for all of us," Josiah Cowles warned Calvin, "and it is best for every one to preserve silence on the political affairs of the day. . . . I beseech you to be very careful of what you say."[55]

Although Southern Claims Commission files offer few clues as to the initial determinants of wartime allegiance to the Union, they provide numerous examples of the ingenuity displayed by mountain Unionists in concealing their true leanings from those in whose midst they lived. The affidavits of over two hundred western Carolinians indicate both the variety of role-playing to which many Unionists resorted over the course of the war, and the questionable nature of such roles, which belied the sincerity of their commitments to either side. In their concerted efforts to portray their loyalty as consistent and deep-rooted, the duplicity of many applicants is all too apparent.

Joseph Green, for example, a middle-aged farmer in Rutherford County, admitted that he took a job making twenty pairs of shoes a month for the Confederate army. But he dismissed these business dealings with those he claimed to have opposed on the grounds that it kept him from having to join that army himself. He gave up this contract when he was elected justice of the peace, in itself an unlikely achievement for a committed Unionist in a Confederate county. Practically the only basis for his claim of loyalty was that on April 23, 1865, almost two weeks after Lee's surrender at Appomattox, Green very willingly allowed a small Yankee occupying force to use his house as its headquarters.[56]

Few other claims were as weak or unconvincing as Green's, but many document the extent to which self-professed Unionists attempted to support either
side when it worked to their advantage, thus rendering their true loyalties
somewhat questionable, or at least compromising their identities as Union
supporters. Like Green, Elisha Blackwell, a Cherokee County farmer, profited
from working for the Confederacy before he eventually cast his lot against it.
Blackwell worked at a Confederate saltworks in Virginia for several months
(which a neighbor claimed he did to escape conscription at home) and at a local
ironworks, from which he transported iron just across the state line to Cleveland, Tennessee, for the Confederate war effort. But he insisted that even as he
was paid by Confederate authorities for this service, he was also escorting "into
Federal lines" the families of Unionist refugees to visit their husbands and/or
fathers hiding out in Tennessee. Blackwell claimed that he gave money on
occasion to fugitives moving through the area to join the Union army in Knoxville. He insisted that he had "hated to see this thing [secession] come on—
I wanted the Old Government to stand," but he waited until March 1865 to
join a Union company in Athens, Tennessee, and served with it uneventfully
until July.[57]

Clark Rogers, a farmer of modest means in Macon County, provided an
unusually detailed account of his wartime activity. His story suggests the degree
to which some Unionists managed to keep their proclivities hidden. Rogers left
his farm, three miles from Franklin, and moved to adjacent Haywood County
early in 1862 to avoid pressures to enlist in the Confederate army. He left a wife
and teenage son behind. Over the course of the next two years, he managed to
serve as coroner, deputy sheriff, and justice of the peace, all positions he
claimed to have sought in order to avoid conscription, along with "many other
devices too tedious to mention." Although forced to serve in the home guard in
Waynesville, he insisted that he did so only briefly and had only pretended
to do so willingly. He even admitted that he was once asked by Confederate
authorities and offered funds to accompany a group of new recruits to join
rebel forces near Kinston in eastern North Carolina, which he did without
compensation.

During this apparently successful deception, Rogers actively engaged in a
variety of pro-Union pursuits. He aided both Confederate deserters and Union
soldiers who had escaped from Confederate prisons by feeding them, hiding
them in his home, visiting them in their remote mountain hideouts, carrying
messages from them to their families and other contacts, and warning them of

home guard or other enemy troop movement in the area. Some family members were among the recipients of his help. He also admitted that some of his relatives had served in the Confederate army, but he insisted that "on some, I did exert an influence against their entering and serving in the rebel army." He stated that "I induced two of my brothers to leave said service, concealed them at my house, and afterward aided them in crossing the line into the Northern States. Two or three of my cousins and others accompanied them at the same time."

Rogers's true feelings were common knowledge among his acquaintances in Macon County. His lawyer, William L. Love, testified that he had frequently heard Franklin residents refer to him as "a tory, a traitor to his home and to the South . . . his Lincolnite proclivities were matters of general notoriety." Another of Franklin's more prominent citizens, James M. Lyle, stated that he had heard Rogers say that if forced to serve with the home guard that he would shoot the other way—he was not going to shoot toward the Yankees.

Yet despite his reputation at home, Rogers managed to conceal his Unionism and subversive activity from Haywood County authorities until the spring of 1864, when a careless slip of the tongue led him to express some "anti-rebel sentiments" that a number of Waynesville citizens happened to hear. This led to his arrest by Confederate authorities and a very brief stint in the local jail. While his ability to manage dual identities served him well for much of the war, it compromised his credibility to the Southern Claims Commission board, which denied his claim on the grounds that "his official career is inconsistent with adherence to the cause of the Union" and noted that it was very unlikely that his Confederate neighbors would have elected him to responsible office or that Confederate authorities would have selected him as a trustworthy agent had he been a Union man.[58]

Other Unionists engaged in such deceits as well, which allowed them, like Clark Rogers, to avoid Confederate military service or to operate in positions of power and authority otherwise unavailable to them. Even involvement in some of form of Confederate military service became the means by which some Unionists concealed their true feelings from a community demanding proof of their loyalty to the Southern cause.

In moving through Wilkes County in 1864, Union prison escapee William Burson was struck by how many of the Confederate home guard in the county were actually Unionist in sentiment. He asked one guard why he served in this capacity when it was against his principles; he replied that "it was merely to keep out of the army."[59] Home guard duty was sometimes forced upon men suspected of Unionist sentiments, and they later claimed to have taken advantage of that militia service by engaging in subversive activity or supporting fellow Unionists in their communities. William Donaldson of Cherokee County testified to the Southern Claims Commission that in the summer of 1863 he had been arrested, "held under Rebel guard for several days," and then released on the condition, and the threat of death, that he serve in the county's home guard. One of his duties was to distribute provisions to the widows and children of Confederate soldiers. But, Donaldson said, "these orders were not strictly obeyed as I divided the provisions with the widows and children of loyal men."[60] Drury Weeks, another Cherokee County Unionist, was ordered to assist with the distribution of salt to destitute families "loyal to the Rebel Government." Weeks not only persuaded the official in charge "to allow all, irrespective of party or politics, to have salt," he also sometimes weighed out the salt for Union families himself.[61]

The jailer in Morganton was an ardent Unionist who "as a jailor and a poor man . . . had to be very quiet and prudent." Two Union officers placed in the Burke County jail testified to his great kindnesses toward them.[62] In Transylvania County, escaped Union prisoners were surprised to find that the sheriff proved himself to be among their most effective allies. One described Sheriff Hamilton as "a very earnest Union man, who was willing to assist the Union cause in every way that he could." He, too, was compelled to serve in the home guard, whose primary duty was to search out and arrest deserters. He reported that when he participated in such raids "he always tried to manage to send word ahead that they were coming" and, on at least one occasion, chose not to divulge to his fellow raiders a Unionist neighbor he discovered hiding under his bed during such a raid on his house. Hamilton and his wife secretly operated a way station for fugitives moving from South Carolina toward East Tennessee. Known as the "Pennsylvania House," it proved a convenient hideout and rendezvous point for numerous escapees, and from it, Sheriff Hamilton organized groups to move together toward Knoxville and furnished guides to get them across the Smokies.[63]

Other Unionists were forced to act out rebel roles in order to alleviate suspicions or to avoid harassment within their communities. When faced with conscription, some joined Confederate companies and marched off to battle, with full intentions of deserting as soon as possible. To avoid imprisonment for his Unionist activity, W. H. Younce, a twenty-year-old native of Ashe County, was allowed the option of taking an oath of allegiance to the Southern cause, and then "volunteering" to join a company of the 58th North Carolina Regiment then forming in Jefferson. Younce described his departure in the midst of a gathering of well-wishers. Although he was merely one of fifty young men enlisting, he recalled that "I was the hero of the occasion, and the crowd became so enthusiastic that I was carried on the shoulders of some of the younger men to a platform and force to make a short talk." Apparently Younce's treasonous past was well known, and the community took heart that he had seen the error of his ways. "There was more rejoicing over one sinner that repented than over ninety and nine that went not astray," he wrote. Yet, he concluded, "they could not read my thoughts. My purposes were the same, and I believed that I would find refuge under the flag of my country some day."[64]

Other reluctant Confederate soldiers, equally unsold on the cause for which they were forced to fight, even carried their role-playing into battle. The Wilkes County deserters hiding out with William Burson told him of just how active their military service in Virginia had been. "They declared that they could not fight against their principles—though forced into several hard battles in the vicinity of Richmond, said they always shot so high that no one was ever hurt by their bullets, as they expected to be killed themselves, and wanted to die with a clear conscience."[65]

A Wisconsin fugitive fleeing across western North Carolina was impressed by the number of self-proclaimed local Unionists aiding his efforts who had earlier fought for the Confederacy. He noted the irony in their role reversals. "Here we were," he wrote of his band of fugitive prisoners, "four Yankee officers, in the heart of the enemy's country, in a mountain fastness, surrounded by some of the men who we had encountered in battle's stern array at Bull Run, Roanoke, Newbern, Fredericksburg, and on other ensanguined fields, who now were keeping watch and ward over our lives, which they regard as precious in their sight—willing to shed their blood in our defense."[66]

In other cases, ambivalent family loyalties were less duplicitous but proved just as advantageous. Napoleon Banner and G. W. Dugger of Banner Elk in Watauga (later Avery) County sent five sons between them into Union regiments in Tennessee but were themselves "detailed" by Confederate authorities to employment at the ironworks in nearby Cranberry. These entanglements secured their safety, as Dugger's son Shepherd explained: "The Yankees passed over Napoleon for working for the South because he had three sons . . . in the Federal army, and the Homeguard let him off for being a Union man because he was hammering iron for the Confederacy." The elder Dugger was spared for the same reasons. "Thus," Shepherd Dugger summarized, "father and Napoleon sat on the top of a four-point barbed wire fence that divided the two armies, and so well did they balance themselves that they sat there four years and never got the hide split."[67]

Certainly the most unequivocal commitment western Carolinians could make to the Union was enlistment in the Federal army. The increasing number of such enlistments during the latter half of the war is one of the clearest demonstrations that such loyalties were escalating. To join the Union army, a Southerner, of course, must have had access to it, and because of Carolina highlanders' proximity to East Tennessee and even access to Kentucky, joining the Union army was an option available to them throughout the war. A few western Carolinians did so at the beginning of the war, thus making a commitment to the Union cause as firm and as full as one could, but one not without risks. Union volunteers often acted in groups. One such band of at least eight young men, all but one related to the others and including two sets of brothers, gathered in a cabin in Banner Elk in August 1861 and after dark, moved quietly and cautiously across the state line only a few miles away to enlist in Union service.[68] In Madison County, also bordering Tennessee, a group of teenage boys attempted to "go through the lines" in the summer of 1861. They encountered a home guard border patrol that prevented them from crossing into Tennessee and, in the words of one of those involved, "deterred them from carrying their proposal into effect at that time."[69]

It was not until in late 1863 that such sporadic and relatively isolated efforts became more systematic and widespread. Ever growing disaffection with Confederate policy and home front hardships combined with the Federal occupation of East Tennessee generated wholesale defection by Carolina highlanders across the state line into Union army units. Within weeks of General Ambrose Burnside's occupation of Knoxville in September 1863, men and boys from Cherokee, Jackson, and other southwestern counties moved across the state line. On October 6, there were enough of them to form four companies in Knoxville and two more in Walker's Ford, which together would form the core of the 2nd North Carolina Mounted Infantry.[70]

By 1864, one could often merely wait at home for the opportunity of Union service to come knocking. In February, Ambrose's replacement, General John Schofield, authorized George W. Kirk, a Greenville, Tennessee, native who belonged to the 2nd North Carolina, to organize another new regiment. Kirk formed the 3rd North Carolina Mounted infantry with men and boys from East Tennessee and western North Carolina by sending recruiters and raiders across the state line into adjacent Carolina communities, such as Madison County, where he was particularly successful. His example was followed by later expeditions that moved from Knoxville across the Smokies into the southwestern counties of North Carolina.[71]

Alexander Jones claimed that at least 5,790 white males from North Carolina's twenty-one westernmost counties "crossed the lines." Three-quarters of that number, he said, enlisted in the Union army, while 183 lost their lives in attempting to get through.[72] Jones may have padded his numbers, given his tendency to exaggerate the extent of Unionist sentiment in region, but no historian since has provide any other figures to either confirm or challenge that 1866 estimate.

Yet even if these figures are accurate, they provide only one indication of Unionist sentiment in western North Carolina. By the same token, an allegiance to the Union, either long held or newly established, was not the only incentive that sent North Carolina men and boys into Union companies in Tennessee. Chapter 5 deals with the variety of factors that pulled or pushed western Carolinians "across the line." For civilians, the threat of conscription or for deserters, the constant efforts of the Confederate army or home guard to find them were enough to send them into the other army. Thus, even joining the Federal army—once the supreme demonstration of one's commitment to the Union cause—had become by the war's midpoint an action inspired by other feelings as well, ranging from anger or revenge to disaffection or sheer desperation. Thus, not even enlistment could be viewed as a strict measure of loyalty to the Union, and the motivations behind anti-Confederate thought and action remain as elusive and complex as ever. Consequently, what being a Unionist meant in western North Carolina varied considerably over time and according to circumstance.

Guerrilla Warfare

Rule by Bushwhackers, Tories, and Yankees

In November 1864 Rufus Lenoir described what had become an all too familiar source of anxiety throughout the Carolina highlands. "The robbers & bushwhackers in Wilkes and Caldwell are becoming more insolent & aggressive," he wrote to his brother Walter. "We never go to bed without thinking they may come before morning. I fear western N. Carolina will be ruled by Bushwhackers, Tories, and Yankees."[1] These fears were by no means new. Although the intensity of violence and disruption had certainly increased during the war's final year, many mountain residents had suffered the effects of a military presence, however minor, from the beginning of the war and would experience even more indignities as the conflict in the Carolina highlands increasingly came to be characterized by terrorist tactics and guerrilla warfare.

The remoteness of North Carolina's mountains served to insulate residents from some of the full-scale military activity that plagued much of the South during the war. The mountains' rugged terrain discouraged large armies from fighting and foraging in the region. The sheer presence of soldiers, whether friends or foes, could be devastating to an area in terms of their requirements for food, forage, horses, and other supplies, which often became a major drain on local resources. The additional impact of a major battle or campaign often left an area devastated for months afterward, until the balance of human, natural, and social resources could be restored.

While western Carolinians escaped that level of upheaval, they were never completely free of military intrusion. From the war's beginning, a primary concern was their vulnerability to the Union presence just across the state line in East Tennessee. Tennessee had been the last state to secede from the Union and did so by a closer vote than any other Confederate state. Much of the reluctance to join the new Southern nation was concentrated in the eastern third of the state, a highland area not unlike western North Carolina in terms of terrain, socio-economic makeup, and slaveholding status. Yet whereas Carolina highlanders quickly capitulated to their state's secessionist majority after Fort Sumter and Lincoln's call for troops, East Tennesseans maintained a far more determined and effective Unionist leadership in Andrew Johnson, William "Parson" Brownlow, T. R. R. Nelson, and others, who not only kept Unionist sentiment very much alive within that region but also stalled a state vote on secession until June 8, 1861. No other state left the Union with greater internal opposition or with more pronounced regional differences of opinion: fully two-thirds of East Tennesseans still opposed joining the Confederacy when their state did at last join.[2]

Southern officials were worried enough about these newest Confederate citizens that they acted quickly to move military forces into Tennessee's high-lands. Residents viewed the military presence as a hostile occupation, and the army's repressive measures inspired widespread resistance by Unionists, who still made up a healthy majority of the region's populace. Their resistance culminated in a carefully planned series of railroad bridge burnings on November 8, which backfired. The Richmond government viewed the upheaval in East Tennessee as treasonous, declared martial law, and expanded the military presence there to enforce it.[3]

The vigorous suppression of Unionist activity, including the executions of bridge burners and the shutting down of "Parson" Brownlow's *Knoxville Whig* and other pro-Union newspapers in the region, led many residents to flee east across the North Carolina border in search of a safe haven in the remote Laurel

Mountains of Madison County. Among them was Captain David Fry, the notorious ringleader of the "bridge burners," who used his base there to lead raids back into Tennessee, where he and his followers engaged in "taking money, powder, threatening death, and on occasion beating Southern men." The presence of these renegades served as a catalyst for Carolina "tories" in the area to undertake a more aggressive stance themselves. Local sympathizers found Fry's band and others a convenient means of casting their own lots with the Federal forces, with Watauga County, as much as Madison, supplying what were rumored to be substantial numbers of Unionist recruits. Such activity alarmed other western Carolinians, who were quick to demand military protection from state leaders. As early as mid-November, Governor Henry T. Clark ordered Colonel Robert B. Vance's regiment back from Knoxville to the state border in order to prevent further Unionist infiltration across the state line.[4]

A Federal invasion from Kentucky wrested temporary control of the Cumberland Gap from its Southern occupiers in early 1862, which further frightened Confederate sympathizers in the North Carolina mountains. Some of them suggested taking the offensive and sending their own troops westward to put down Union forces well before they had a chance to move into North Carolina. Marcus Erwin in his *Asheville News* suggested on January 30 that several of the companies still stationed in Buncombe County be mobilized for this purpose. "They are tired of listless inaction and would hail with joy the order to march." Noting that "the tide of battle is rolling to the immediate borders of our State on the northwest" and that "East Tennessee may soon become the next theatre of war," Erwin warned that "Western North Carolina's turn would come next. We would suggest that the best way to keep the war from our own borders is to go over and help our Tennessee friends drive the vandals beyond the limits of that State." The same editorial also urged that local militia companies be fully prepared not only to defend their own communities but to mobilize "to strike when the hour shall come." Building to a hearty exhortation, Erwin concluded: "The riflemen of the mountains have never been conquered. Freemen they have lived and freemen they will die. Men of the Mountains! Be ready at the tap of the drum!"[5]

A more widely held sentiment throughout the region was that a strong defense should take precedence over an aggressive offense. Too many mountain men had already been called away for service elsewhere, leaving their own lands and families far more vulnerable to attack than should have been allowed. Less than a month after the *News*'s call for sending more North Carolinians into

Tennessee, Confederate lieutenant W. F. Parker, a Buncombe County native then stationed near Knoxville, wrote his hometown newspaper, urging that the best engineers be enlisted to design and place "inpenetrable fortifications" at Paint Rock, on the well-traveled turnpike along the French Broad River from Greenville, Tennessee, into North Carolina, and at all other passes along the state border, "to keep the invaders out of our mountain country." Parker added what must have been a chilling warning to those in his hometown: "I cannot, in good faith to my beloved Buncombe hills, close this paper without . . . one more hint. It is this: I have it from the lips of some of the Union leaders, that the Federal forces intend to sack Asheville, as soon as they can possibly get there. They actually hate Asheville with a perfect hatred," which was due, no doubt, to the armory already operating there and the city's role as the region's center of Confederate mobilization efforts.[6]

In some parts of the mountains, local citizens had already taken matters into their own hands with a strategy of an offensive defense. Unwilling to wait for outside protection, Confederate sympathizers in particularly vulnerable areas declared themselves unwilling to enlist for regular military service and instead organized guerrilla units to combat the Union threats at home. As one high-lander informed the governor, "We have many Union men in disguise among us, and we think that it would be bad policy for us to strip ourselves entirely of our true grit." As early as July 1861, a group of Jackson County men, calling themselves the "Horse Cave Wolf Hunters," expressed their willingness to cross the state line to attack Union forces without any official military sanction or compensation. In addition to defusing any threat to their own homes and families, they boldly declared that they would "pay themselves out of what they may be able to get from our Enemyes by conquest not calling on the government for any thing."[7]

Caldwell County citizens went so far as to hire their own intelligence service so as not to be caught off guard by the threat from the west. Edmund Jones wrote a cousin in April 1862 that "we recently sent an agent, a sort of spy, to East Tennessee, to ascertain the state of affairs there and to make some arrangement with two southern men by which they could act in concert and keep each other posted." Jones told his cousin that the agent had already informed his clients that "it was, or is undoubtedly, the intention of the Lincoln forces to penetrate into this section," and Jones insisted that they would meet a strong defense if they did. "Well, maybe they will get here . . . but they may be sure of one thing—many of their bones will be left to bleach on the hills and in the valleys which line the way. They will encounter more than one 'Thermopylae,'" he confidently proclaimed.[8]

Union forces never got as far east as Caldwell County, but infiltration from Tennessee intensified in the spring of 1862 as both Federal and Confederate forces pushed into other parts of the region. Early in April, Gen. E. Kirby Smith, who commanded the Confederate occupation force in East Tennessee, sent three companies under the command of Lt. Col. David M. Key to clean out the Union bands still wreaking havoc from their Madison County base, despite the fact that ringleader David Fry had been captured during a reckless raid into Kentucky a month earlier. The rugged terrain and thick underbrush of the Laurel Valley worked to the disadvantage of the regular troops and to the advantage of their targets, who were able to shoot at the columns in gray and then disappear into the woods. Key's men made no captures, though the commander claimed that they killed fifteen of the "outlaws" and suffered two fatalities before abandoning their three-day mission and returning to Tennessee.[9]

Somewhat more successful was a more localized attempt later the same month to round up Unionists in Laurel Valley, that "general resort and hideout for outlaws." Editor Marcus Erwin, practicing what he preached in his newspaper, led a large contingent of Buncombe County militia northward, had them block escape routes from the Laurel Valley, and flushed out eighty anti-Confederates. All were taken prisoner and about half were forced to enlist in the Confederate army. This proved a Pyrrhic victory in that those forced into Confederate service soon deserted and that it only inflamed tensions in that area, leading to perhaps the most infamous incident in the Carolina highlands' war nine months later.[10]

In May, a raid into Haywood County by a small Federal force from Tennessee led to the forced release of a Unionist man condemned to death in Waynesville. Although a minor incident, it alarmed citizens there and throughout southwestern North Carolina, who realized how vulnerable they were to such attacks.[11] The most prominent resident of that part of the state, William Holland Thomas of Jackson County, had already expended considerable energies establishing a strong home defense. Earlier in 1862, during the last days of his final term in the state senate, before he returned home to form his own legion, he drew up a proposal for an extensive defense system that involved fortifying all of the passes through the Blue Ridge and Smoky Mountains, most of which were formed by rivers flowing into Tennessee from North Carolina—the French Broad, Big Pigeon, Little Tennessee, New, and Hiwassee. Thomas himself would take charge of defenses on the Oconaluftee River, Jackson County's most accessible artery from Tennessee.[12]

To enact his plan, Thomas began the recruitment of what would become the famous Thomas's Legion, consisting first of two companies of Cherokee Indians and ultimately fifteen more of white recruits from Haywood, Cherokee, Jackson, and Macon Counties. Although he was able to resist Jefferson Davis's proposal for using the Indian companies in the swamps of eastern North Carolina, Thomas was unable to keep them in western North Carolina but acquiesced to their assignment to East Tennessee in April 1862. Yet, even as he led his legion to Kirby Smith, to whom they would report, Thomas continued to push for protection for southwestern North Carolina. He informed Governor Clark: "I have determined to raise a guerrilla force to be used with my Indians for the local defence of the Carolinas, Virginia, and East Tennessee."[13]

Although Thomas's plans never materialized, he continued to stress the importance of local defenses and their relevance to larger strategies. In a letter to Governor Zebulon Vance, his longtime political acquaintance, in November, Thomas proposed that all men between the ages of thirty-five and forty who lived west of the Blue Ridge be provided arms and ammunition and be required to guard their own communities and homes. At the same time, regular Confederate forces should be placed "at every pass in the Smoky Mountains from Ashe to Cherokee [Counties]." As he had done before, Thomas stressed the geographical significance of the southern highlands in justifying this military attention: "As long as we can hold the Country encircled by the Blue Ridge and Cumberland mountains . . . we have the heart of the South. The loss of this country larger than England and France is the loss of the Southern Confederacy and we sink under a despotism."[14]

Of particular note in Thomas's letters is what had changed between April and November 1862 besides the occupant of the Governor's Mansion. Through the spring, it was the incursion of Federal troops from Tennessee that most worried Thomas and other western North Carolina residents. But in November, he expressed a new concern. His asking for further defenses for his region indicated that more than the borders alone needed guarding. He wrote, "[T]he Western Counties are in danger of being over run by deserters and renegades who by the hundred are taking shelter in the smoky mountains."[15] What earlier in the year had been a localized problem in the Laurel Mountains, coming largely from Tennessee, had become a problem that was to plague the entire mountain region for the duration of the war. Certainly the single most important impetus for this shift was conscription.

On April 16, 1862, the Confederate Congress passed the first conscription law in American history. This legislation required all able-bodied white males from eighteen to thirty-five years old to be available for up to three years of service in the Confederate army or, if the war lasted longer, for its duration. Equally crucial, those already in service as twelve-month volunteers were required to serve an additional two years. Five days after this law was passed, the legislators in Richmond passed a supplementary act to exempt state employees, industrial workers, ministers, teachers, and other professionals. These exemptions led to some abuses of the system, but most Southerners, including mountaineers, especially resented those who could afford to pay substitutes to serve in their stead.[16]

Few legislators had anticipated just how unpopular the new policy would be or what political or military backlash it would provoke. For no part of the Confederacy was this more true than the mountain South. The only two North Carolinians to vote against the act in Richmond were both from mountain counties.[17] Given how few residents in the region would ever benefit from the exemptions, and given their awareness of the regional, as well as the class, bias of such exemptions, resentment ran high from the beginning. The war, more than ever, came to be perceived as what so many had already called it: "a rich man's war and a poor man's fight." One small farmer spoke for many western Carolinians when he informed Governor Clark, "I have no negroes to defend and will not take up arms for the South."[18]

Other reactions from the mountains were equally strong and often far more bitter in tone. W. W. Stringfield, a Confederate captain in East Tennessee who was recruiting soldiers for Colonel Thomas in the North Carolina Smokies when the Conscription Act was passed, later characterized the hostility with which highlanders viewed it: "It was the desperate act of unwise if not desperate men, whose minds were not moulded after the manner or matter of our great Declaration of Independence but rather of the crafty politician and thoughtless slave-holder."[19]

The sacrifices highlanders had already made to the war effort contributed to their resentment of the new act. Given that the vast majority of eligible men from the mountain counties were already in service and that there were far fewer slaves to keep farms productive than was the case elsewhere in the state, they felt that the policy was prejudicial to their region. A citizen of Stokes County, just east of Surry and Ashe, expressed the frustrations of many when he pointed out that 1,300 men from his county were already enrolled and 1,100 of them were in active service. The wives and children left behind were already suffering from crop shortages and other deprivations; to take the few men left would prove disastrous. "If all the conscripts from my county are taken off," he noted, "it will be impossible for those left behind to make support for another year."[20] Another westerner made the point far more contemptuously to a Raleigh newspaper editor: "Will you be so kind, Mr. Editor, as to inform Jeff Davis and his Destructives, that after they take the next draw of men from this mountain region, if they please, as an act of *great* and *special* mercy be so gracious as to call out a *few*, just a few of their exempted pets . . . to knock the women and children of the mountains in the head, to put them out of their misery?"[21]

Such contempt was not only aimed at Davis "and his Destructives" but at local officials as well, particularly in personal attacks made on those charged with raising troops under the new law. An anonymous letter to Governor Vance from Columbus in Polk County in September 1862 targeted Johnson Ward, the colonel of the county's militia. "The people will not submit much longer to such rule as Ward [Militia] & Co.," the writer warned, calling him "one of the most obnoxious men in the County to a very large majority." Ward claimed that he had orders from the governor "to take all men liabel [*sic*] to Conscript & tie them and bring them to Jail an carry them off in chains if necessary," but the writer and others in the county were skeptical of Ward's orders. They even questioned the legitimacy of the election that put him in so authoritative a position. "Ward is one of the most miserobel corrupt men in power in any way in N.C. or any whare els," his critic seethed. "He is of the worst Stock ever raised in our State his father was whipe at the whiping post and Stood in the Pillery at Rutherfordton."[22] Although it is unlikely that such character assassination proved an effective means of convincing Vance of the injustices of conscription, the letter does convey the personal animosities and localized divisions the policy imposed on many mountain communities.

Far more powerful an argument against conscription, and perhaps the most eloquent plea to the governor from the mountains, came from a longtime friend and political colleague, David Siler of Macon County. As older men were being organized into a company in Franklin in November 1862, Siler urged that the company be allowed to serve locally, or that for every able-bodied man taken from the county, another be retained. "We have no hesitation in believing that it is our duty to stay here and provide for the helpless while it is in our power to do so," he wrote. Siler explained that family councils had already met and decided who should stay and who should go and noted that "those on whom the lot fell to stay in many instances made the greater sacrifice of feeling." If such concessions were not made, Siler warned, the consequences would be grave both for those left at home and to the ultimate resolve of those in military service. "You know all about men and their powers of endurance and of their wives and children," he told his friend. "They can turn away from the graves of comrades and brothers firm in their resolve to die . . . for the sake of objects coming to their recollections with thoughts of home. But what consolation or encouragement can come to a man's heart in an hour of trial from a home where the helpless are perishing for want of his hand to provide?"[23]

Most concerns focused on the new manpower that would be drained from home and hearth, but there were equally vehement objections to the provision of the act that required soldiers already serving to remain enrolled. The timing of new legislation proved especially poor, given that it was passed just as many soldiers' initial twelve-month enlistments were about to run out. Randolph Shotwell of Rutherford County called the act "a piece of injustice," noting that men in Southern service suddenly found "all their fond anticipations blasted and years of service before them with very little prospect of one in a dozen of them ever seeing home again unless as a cripple, or diseased wreck of his former self," a prospect that stirred "a strong feeling and not a little indignation."[24]

Matthew Love of Henderson County was a lieutenant in the 25th North Carolina Regiment, made up almost entirely of recruits from the state's southwestern corner. Four days after passage of the Conscription Act, he informed his father that "there is a good deal of dissatisfaction in camp concerning the press law[.] some say they are going home when their time is out regardless of consequences."[25] Norm Harrold, an Ashe County soldier, wrote a scathing indictment of the new law to Jefferson Davis from a camp in eastern North Carolina. His letter concluded with a not so fond farewell: "And now bastard President of a political abortion, farewell. 'Scalp-hunter,' relic, pole, and chivalrous Confederates in crime, good-bye. Except it be in the army of the Union, you will not again see this conscript."[26]

Both Love and Harrold confirmed what David Siler had foreseen from a home front perspective—that an even more significant effect of conscription than popular disaffection was that it dramatically escalated desertion rates. The mountains were hit particularly hard by desertions, which compounded the manpower shortage that rendered highland families so vulnerable. Women were quick to recognize the connection between conscription and desertion. In November 1862 Ella Harper of Lenoir confided to a brother-in-law that "if there is not something done for the support of the soldier's families, they *will not* stay away when their wives write to them they are suffering for the necessarys of life, and many of them are doing that now."[27]

Governor Vance recognized the dual threat that conscription posed for the residents of his native region. Not only did it increase the desertion rate and force into hiding many seeking to escape such service altogether, it also drew away men who would otherwise have been at home to deal with the disruptions caused by these "disaffected." In January 1863, Vance wrote to Confederate secretary of war James A. Seddon about "the increase in desertion" across the state. Although he felt confident that home militia could be entrusted with controlling the problem in the piedmont and coastal plain, the governor informed Seddon that "in the mountains of the West the case is different." He explained: "The enforcement of the Conscript law in East Tennessee has filled the mountains with disaffected desperadoes of the worst character, who joining with the deserters from our Army form very formidable bands of outlaws, who hide in the fastnesses, waylay the passes, rob, steal, and destroy as pleased. The evil has become so great that travel has almost been suspended through the mountains." The extent of their activity was such that local militias had proven "too feeble to resist them," in part because so many eligible men were in service elsewhere. Vance thus proposed creating a new company of regular troops to put down the lawlessness, to arrest deserters and conscripts, and to restore order to the region.[28]

The literature on desertion in North Carolina is vast; for no other state has historical analysis of the problem been as extensive. This is no doubt due to the fact that while North Carolina sent more troops into Confederate service than any other state, it also had the highest desertion rate. Some estimates place the number of Tar Heels who abandoned the army over the course of the war at nearly 24,000.[29] By far, the greatest number of desertions were by Carolina highlanders. According to historical sociologist Peter Bearman, who has provided the most numerically sophisticated analysis of desertions by region within the state, the rate of desertion in the mountains was just over 24 percent of all men who enlisted from the region, as compared with a mere 12 percent for the state as a whole.[30] In the most extensive quantitative study of desertion

within a single regiment, historian Jim Taylor found that the 60th North Carolina, made up largely of Buncombe and Madison County enlistees recruited by
Col. Joseph McDowell of Warm Springs in the spring of 1862, suffered from an
inordinately high rate of desertion, which began almost from the time the
regiment was established. Between July 1862 and December 1864, 351 men
deserted, a third of its total force of 1,051 men. In 1864, desertions averaged four
men per week.[31]

An extraordinarily large number of deserters ended up in western North
Carolina not only because highlanders were leaving the army at over twice the
rate of North Carolina troops as a whole, but also because many soldiers from
other areas took refuge in the remote reaches of the Blue Ridge and Smoky
Mountains. At the beginning of 1863, Governor Vance estimated that there were
as many as 1,200 deserters hiding in the mountains. On January 26, he issued a
proclamation exhorting all North Carolina soldiers "illegally absent" from their
units to return to duty and stated that the full powers of the state would be
brought to bear in their capture and punishment if they refused to do so.
"There shall be no rest for the deserter in the borders of North Carolina,"
Vance asserted. Well aware that many men abandoned their military commitments in order to meet the needs of their families, he insisted that "they will add
nothing to the comforts of their families by hiding like guilty men in the wood
by day and by plundering their neighbors by night, they only bring shame and
suffering upon the innocent." He closed with the assurance that the state, along
with its counties, was working to provide food for the families of enlisted men
and promised "that the wife & child of the soldiers who are in the Army doing
his duty, shall share the last bushel of meal & pound of meat in the State."[32]

That message may indeed have served as a deterrent for at least some North
Carolina soldiers. John W. Reese, a poor Buncombe County farmer who was
not among those who abandoned the 60th Regiment, for example, told his wife,
who was urging him to come home, "If you say for mee to cum I shal cum. But I
have studied it all over long ago . . . I want to do the Best I can for my family and
myself. To stay hear at aleven dollars a month—you cant live on that while stuf is
so hy. well to run away and go home and have to lay out—I cant help you to
anythiung to liv on. that seem to me lik that will not doo. I wood Bee a drawback
instid of a help to you and the children . . . I think I will cum home any-
how if you think we can make out By my doging about to keep out of the
ways."[33] Reese continued to weigh the needs of his family against the practi-

"Union Bushwhackers Attacking Rebel Cavalry"
(From Browne, Four Years in Secessia*)*

cal burdens of desertion on them all—both financial and logistical, given the punishment that the government and local authorities were threatening to inflict on deserters.[34]

Another western Carolina regiment, the 64th North Carolina, was particularly plagued by desertions, and the way in which authorities ultimately dealt with the problem led to one of the most infamous episodes in the mountains' guerrilla war. This regiment had been formed in Madison County in the summer of 1862 and was commanded by first cousins Lawrence Allen and James Keith, both of whom were members of the ambitious county seat elite of Marshall. This band of soldiers, made up of primarily Madison men, along with recruits from Henderson and Polk Counties and East Tennessee, was not a particularly willing or eager group of soldiers, having only enlisted under duress and the threat of conscription. In addition, class tensions were more pronounced in this regiment than in most, given the conspicuous contrast between the affluent commanders Keith and Allen and the relatively poor farmers who fell under their command. The troops' disdain for their leaders and the reluctance with which many joined the 64th were compounded by the distasteful activity in which they were forced to engage, activity that soon encouraged desertion on a large scale.[35]

From bases in Greenville and Knoxville, the members of the 64th were to patrol areas in the North Carolina and Kentucky mountains troubled by bushwhacking activity. The assignments proved unsettling. As its regimental historian, Captain B. T. Morris, later described its adversaries, they were "of such fierce audacity and viciousness that only severe and caustic measures would suppress them." In an attempt to explain the drastic actions that would later make the 64th and its leaders so infamous, Morris noted, "When an officer finds himself and men bushwhacked from behind every shrub, tree or projection on all sides of the road, only severe measures will stop it." Only those who know the region "can have an idea of the hardships endured," Morris claimed, referring to the frustrations faced by conventional troops confronting a most unconventional opposition. "Our enemies were at home—knew all the roads, by-ways and trails, and were much in heart of the success of their arms elsewhere. . . . They never gave us a fair fight, square-up, face-to-face, man-to-man, horse-to-horse."[36]

Such vulnerabilities and frustrations contributed to what were already personnel problems within this regiment of "rough mountain boys," problems Morris characterized as "friction, jealousy, dictation, and some tyranny." Not surprisingly, given the proximity of the 64th to its members' homes and families, desertions from the regiment were rampant. At one point, three hundred men abandoned the regiment together, most of whom returned to Madison County to hide out in the rugged wilderness close to home.[37] Julius Gash of Henderson County, the commander of a cavalry company of the 64th, complained bitterly: "My company has about 'gone up' too. All deserted or at home without leave." He expressed his bewilderment as to why they left: "I have learned during this war that there is no Confidence to be placed in white men. I'll swear men have deserted my Company who I had the most implicit confidence in and men too who had been for near twelve months good Soldiers as I thought was in the Confederate Army." "A man who is void enough of principal to desert his County in so perilous a time as now" should be shot, he insisted. "There is a day when I'll get revenge from deserters. Mark it! When I think of a deserter, I get so mad it bother me to keep from saying Cuss words!"[38]

Gash and no doubt other officers of the 64th especially resented the fact that many of the men who deserted their ranks joined the Unionists, refugees, and bushwhackers who continued to wreak havoc in that still troublesome Laurel Valley. It was there in January 1863, as both state officials and western Carolinians came to recognize the extent of these upheavals as a serious regionwide crisis, that the highland war's most extreme showdown between Unionists and Confederate forces took place. The "massacre" at Shelton Laurel (as the community in the Laurel Valley was known locally) came to define the new terms under which the war would be waged in the mountains while drawing new attention to the Carolina highlands from both Confederate and Federal officials. Although the incident is perhaps the best documented aspect of the war in the region, thanks to Phillip Paludan's excellent book-length account, *Victims*, the basic outline of the story demands retelling here.[39]

In the winter of 1862–63, the deserters from the 64th and other disaffected fugitives were joined by John Kirk, a brash young Union guerrilla raider, who, according to differing accounts, had moved into the Laurel either seeking refuge from Confederate forces (most likely the 64th North Carolina) or on a recruitment campaign where, according to Lawrence Allen's memoir, "lawlessness reigned supreme and all claimed to be Union men."[40] Confederate authorities in Marshall responded by shutting off those men and their families from county distributions of the much needed and ever more scarce salt, which was a necessity in the fall and winter, especially for curing and preserving meats and hides. At Kirk's instigation, a band of fifty-some Unionists plus the deserters from the 64th and other fugitives formed a raiding party and headed across the county from Shelton Laurel to Marshall to take for themselves the salt they so desperately needed to survive the winter. On January 8, 1863, they attacked the town, taking salt and other merchandise and foodstuffs from the village's few stores. Before leaving, they ransacked Colonel Allen's home on Main Street, one of the town's largest and an obvious sign of his affluence, and harassed his wife and three sick children.

When Keith and Allen, the commanders of the 64th, heard of the attack on their hometown, they moved quickly. Although they were in different places when the news reached them, the two men, with the authority of Henry Heth, then the Confederate commander of the Department of East Tennessee, mobilized 200 and 300 troops, respectively, and moved by different routes toward that "insurrectionary country" to put down once and for all those who had made it so.

As Allen's men moved across Madison County toward Marshall, hampered by bushwhacking snipers all along the route, Keith's men headed directly into the Laurel Valley, where they launched an intensive search for those who had participated in the salt raid on Marshall. Armed with ambiguous orders from General Heth, they harassed—and even tortured—the women of Shelton Laurel in a vain attempt to force them to reveal the whereabouts of their husbands and sons. Although many of those participants in the raid had anticipated Confederate reprisals and fled the area, Keith found and arrested fifteen men and boys (only five of whom, by some accounts, were among the Marshall raiders).

By this time Colonel Allen had joined Keith in the area, bringing with him the news that his son had died of fever and one of his two daughters was likely to succumb shortly, thus adding to his troops' indignation over the raiders, who had actually stolen the blankets off the children's sick beds. The rage this turn of events elicited, along with the general tensions imposed by the invisible enemy the 64th found itself confronting once again in this increasingly frustrating assignment, did not speak well for the fate of Keith's fifteen prisoners. Two of them escaped, but the others, under the assumption that they were being escorted to Knoxville for trial, found themselves forced off the road into woods not far from their homes. Keith's soldiers ordered them to kneel in a row in groups of three to five and executed them. Nearly all of the thirteen victims were related to each other. Seven shared the Shelton name; both the oldest, sixty-five years old, and the youngest, twelve, were named David Shelton. The latter watched his father and older brother shot in the first group and put up the most impassioned plea for mercy before he was killed with the second group.[41] After a quick and only partial burial of their victims, the troops returned to Tennessee, leaving family members to discover the grisly site the following day.

Confederate officials were aghast at the enormity of the crime committed by their troops. Governor Vance had known earlier of the 64th's expedition into Madison County and its purpose but had warned Henry Heth: "I hope you will not relax until the tories are crushed, but do not let our excited people deal too harshly with these misguided men."[42] As detailed reports of the atrocity reached Vance over the next few weeks, particularly those of Augustus S. Merrimon, the district attorney for the mountain region, he became increasingly incensed. He agreed with Merrimon, who had insisted that "the parties guilty of so dark a crime should be punished. Humanity revolts at so savage a crime." In communications to both Heth and Secretary of War Seddon, Vance demanded that they authorize a full investigation into what he characterized as "a scene of horror disgraceful to civilization" and that James Keith, in particular, be punished as the officer who ordered the killings. Keith was court-martialed. He resigned his commission in May but was not held by army officials, who allowed him to return home to Madison County, where he managed to evade further efforts at arrest and prosecution until the war's end. Lawrence Allen, who was viewed far more sympathetically by authorities given the raid on his house and family and the subsequent deaths of his children, received a much less harsh punishment for his role in the massacre, a mere six-month suspension from active duty.[43]

The Shelton Laurel massacre was not an isolated incident, nor can the severity of the atrocity committed be blamed solely on policy decisions or misjudgments on the part of commanders Heth, Allen, or Keith; rather it represented the most extreme manifestation of escalating tensions between lower-ranking troops and civilians, as guerrilla warfare blurred the lines between combatants and noncombatants and obscured the rules of war that defined both. It demonstrated the frustrations of soldiers confronting an elusive enemy, who Captain Morris, the 64th's commander, claimed "never gave us a fair fight, square up, face-to-face." Morris's troops abandoned any sense of a "fair fight" themselves, using instead the very terrorist tactics that they claimed to have so abhorred. Thus they confirmed that Confederates had the same "desire to fight like bushwhackers rather than play by the rules" that historian Kenneth Noe noted of "angry, frustrated Federal soldiers" in southwest Virginia who faced a similar "invisible and dangerous foe."[44] Those frustrations were compounded in Madison County because so many of the combatants on both sides lived in the area. The localized and even personal contexts were vital to the tensions that resulted in the raid on Marshall and its repercussions at Shelton Laurel, as they would be in so many other instances in the Carolina highlands.[45]

If this crime signaled to both Confederate and Federal authorities the new terms by which guerrilla war would be waged throughout the Carolina highlands, its message to western Carolinians was that the Confederate army was no longer a desirable presence in their midst. In the spring of 1863, other Confederate incursions served to further alienate residents of the region. In March, a cavalry squad from Atlanta, led by the volatile George W. Lee, who had made it his personal mission to put down Unionist resistance in the north Georgia mountains, crossed the state line into Cherokee County, North Carolina, where he and his men abducted eight suspected Unionists (all over conscription age, and one at least sixty years old) and brought them back to Georgia. The abductees were soon released and allowed to return home, but Governor Vance protested vehemently against such treatment of North Carolina civilians by troops outside the state and insisted that he would authorize county officials "to call out the Militia and shoot the first man who attempts to perpetrate a Similar outrage." Within a week, a similar cavalry raid from Tennessee, led by Gen. Gideon Johnson Pillow, to "enroll and arrest conscripts without the shadow of law and in defiance of the proper authorities" prompted Vance to threaten "resistance and bloodshed" if such raids across state lines were not stopped.[46]

Yet a military presence of some sort was very much needed in the mountains, and another "startling occurrence" two weeks after the Shelton Laurel massacre made it clear that local authorities alone could not control the upheavals in their own counties. Early in February 1863, militia units in Yadkin County found themselves facing disruptions by nearly a hundred men who had "taken to the woods" to escape conscription. In a report to Governor Vance, local resident R. F. Armfield explained that "although the militia officers exerted themselves with great zeal, . . . these skulkers have always had many more active friends than they had and could always get timely information of every movement to arrest them and so avoid it. . . . [E]mboldened by their numbers and the bad success of the militia officers in arresting them, they have armed themselves, procured ammunition, and openly defied the law." They even sent "menacing messages" in the form of death threats to certain officers.[47]

The standoff came to a head when twelve soldiers happened upon sixteen bushwhackers who had taken shelter in a schoolhouse just outside of Yadkin-ville. A brief shoot-out resulted in the deaths of two men on each side before the "desperadoes" in the schoolhouse made their escape and retreated into the hills, where Armfield felt it unlikely that they could be taken. "The section of the country in which they lurk is so disloyal," he maintained, "and the people so readily conceal the murderers and convey intelligence to them, that it will be exceedingly difficult to find them, even if they do not draw together a larger force than they have yet had and again give battle to the sheriff and his posse."[48]

Following so closely behind the Shelton Laurel massacre, this incident alarmed western North Carolinians and set off "wild rumors of organizations of armed tories throughout the mountains, bent on sacking towns and the plunder of loyal men."[49] In response to the rumors, Vance endorsed the proposal of Baylis M. Edney of Buncombe County and other mountain residents that "local organizations of the Militia or State Forces be formed to operate against these Marauding Bands" and that conscription be temporarily suspended in "the Counties west of the Blue Ridge" so that men could stay home and serve in these newly formed groups. But Confederate officials in Richmond were reluc-tant to put conscripts to such use within their own communities simply because of the local animosities they could aggravate. Perhaps with the lessons of Shelton Laurel and the Yadkinville schoolhouse skirmish in mind, Secretary of War Seddon argued in March that "the use of these men exclusively or mainly against the marauding and disaffected classes of their vicinity might engender the worst sort of civil strife and lead to inextinguishable feuds and mutual reprisals to the grievous affliction and waste of the whole region."[50] Within a few short months, the scenario he described proved tragically accurate.

These disruptions proved to be too great for either type of military force to put down, and by mid-1863, western Carolinians, who were even more concerned with their vulnerable position, sought relief from the same sources. Late in July, the new editor of the *Asheville News*, Thomas W. Atkins, and other "citizens of western North Carolina" informed Seddon that "the safety and security of . . . our homes and property are seriously menaced and openly assaulted by herds of disloyal citizens and gangs of deserters from the Confederate army." As Vance did earlier, they urged the secretary to waive conscription requirements for highland men, noting that if the men remaining were forced into service, "we shall doubtless fall an easy prey to the malicious hands of marauders, which now openly parade themselves in the different counties, west of the Blue Ridge."[51] A group of Watauga County citizens made the same plea in a petition to Jefferson Davis, reasoning that "we are in close proximity with the most disaffected portion of East Tennessee and our people are liable to be plundered and murdered." They asked their president to detail for local defense at least a hundred men eligible for conscription "so that they may afford protection and make a support for those who would otherwise suffer."[52]

The reversal of military fortune that took place in East Tennessee late that summer posed even more of a threat to North Carolina's mountain residents. From June through September of 1863, Federal forces under William Rosecrans and Ambrose Burnside moved eastward into the region and occupied Knoxville and much of the rest of East Tennessee. Suddenly, the Union army was within easy reach of western North Carolina, and the earlier Confederate raids from across state lines paled in comparison to the prospect of Federal attacks from the same direction. Panic seized highlanders, who called for ever more troops to defend them. Forced to preserve precious resources in manpower for more important theaters of war, Richmond authorities created the Western Military District of North Carolina and in September placed the governor's brother, Brig. Gen. Robert B. Vance, in charge of all local defense units and the scattering of regular troops.[53]

The necessity for this new military presence was quickly demonstrated by a series of minor raids by small Union forces from Tennessee on Carolina communities. In mid-September, a party of between 200 and 300 Federal troops attacked and held Waynesville. That unexpected incursion so alarmed neighboring Buncombe County officials that they ordered home guardsmen to dismantle bridges leading to Asheville in order to protect the Confederate armory there. Although the Federals soon abandoned Waynesville and made no further move toward Asheville, Confederate authorities decided that the region was no longer safe and moved the armory to South Carolina.[54]

Further Union incursions that fall met much stiffer resistance. Goldman Bryson, a Cherokee County native who had defected to East Tennessee and Federal service, was one of the most aggressive of the raiders crossing into western North Carolina. As captain of the 1st Tennessee National Guard of about 150 men, who Braxton Bragg labeled "mounted robbers," Bryson organized a group of raiders from Cherokee County and from north Georgia, a stronghold of loyalism just across Cherokee County's southern border. According to an admiring Union veteran, the group rampaged along the border area of the three states, "protecting loyal citizens from being impressed by the conscript law . . . and giving aid to loyal men moving through the federal lines when they could no longer withstand the hardships of the rebels." The group was more elusive then other raiding parties in that its members did not operate as an official Federal army unit but "stayed at their homes, and got together when the occasion required."[55]

Bryson's activity proved enough of a nuisance to Confederate residents that Bragg ordered a Confederate force into the mountains to destroy his party. While on a recruiting mission to his home county in October, Bryson and his men were ambushed about fifteen miles east of Murphy. A brief skirmish led to the deaths of two of Bryson's men, the capture of fifteen, and a quick retreat by the rest back to Knoxville. Bryson sought refuge in his own neighborhood. Persistent soldiers, led by twenty-five Cherokee Indian trackers from Thomas's Legion, tracked him to his home and shot him as he tried to flee. The next day, one Confederate observer reported with amusement that the Indians made quite an impression wearing Bryson's bloody uniform on the streets of Murphy.[56] News of his death was heartily hailed from Asheville to Athens, Georgia. The latter town's newspaper proclaimed: "Thus ended the inglorious career of this tory chieftain, who has made a name and fame by the side of which that of Benedict Arnold stands in enviable contrast."[57]

Despite this setback for local Unionists, the Federal occupation of East Tennessee provided a ready escape for many previously secret Unionist Carolinians who found themselves under intense scrutiny and increasingly harassed within their own communities. More and more of them were willing to make the long and often dangerous trek across the Smokies and Blue Ridge to enlist in Federal service in Tennessee. One observer reported to Governor Vance that several groups of from forty to sixty men each were traveling westward to join Burnside's army. At the same time, increasing numbers of fugitives—either Unionists avoiding conscription or other forms of persecution elsewhere in the state, or Union soldiers escaping from Confederate prisons in Salisbury, North Carolina, or Columbia, South Carolina—found escape routes through western North Carolina that would lead them to sanctuary in the nearest Union-occupied territory accessible to Southerners. The rugged, sparsely settled terrain offered them good hiding places, remote roads, and enough of a sympathetic populace to lend support and assistance along the way. A network developed among western Carolina's pro-Union minority that one "passenger," a New York cavalry captain, described as "an underground railway, as systematic and as well arranged as that which existed in Ohio before the war."[58]

But not all fugitives moved all the way through the Carolina highlands into Tennessee. Compounding the new Union threats from the west were other forms of disruption to the east that meant an equally troubling new presence in the mountains. The volatile situation that had developed in the Laurel Valley in 1862, in which fugitives joined forces with local dissidents, was by early 1863 replicated throughout the Southern Appalachians. Deserters from Virginia and eastern North Carolina armies often moved westward, either retreating back to their highland homes or seeking the refuge of the remote mountains for the first time. In either case, they added to the swelling numbers of other fugitives or outliers who were largely local men forced into hiding to evade conscription. Often they acted individually in their subterfuges, concealing themselves in woods or caves near their homes, from which family members cared for them and often served as guards and protectors against sometimes intense and even brutal efforts by local authorities to take them.

Some of the best descriptions of these men are those provided by Union soldiers who themselves became fugitives moving through the area. According to one, "Outliers . . . camped in the mountain fastnesses, receiving their food from some member of the family. Some of these men had their copper stills in the rock houses [as locals referred to caves], while others more wary of the recruiting sergeant, wandered from point to point, their only furniture a rifle and a bedquilt."[59] J. Madison Drake of Wisconsin wrote of meeting "hundreds of this class" as he moved through the Wilson Creek area of Caldwell County in 1864. Some, he noted, "had resisted the conscriptions of the rebel authorities through two years and more of vicissitudes and suffering." He bemoaned the sacrifices they had been forced to make: "Many of these 'lyers-out' before the war were in comfortable circumstances, possessing pleasant and profitable farms, but the rebellion and its dreadful consequences had reduced them to their present wretched condition, many of them being utterly penniless . . . because of their devotion to the Government."[60] An Ashe County deserter described those with whom he hid out as practically hermits. He noted that although they managed to avoid conscription for as much as three years by lying low in the woods, "they had to lie in the mountains like wild animals, their beards and hair grew down over their shoulders, and they were really like wild men."[61]

But if some men bore their fugitive status alone and passively, many others banded together to become the common and much feared combination that Rufus Lenoir referred to as "Bushwhackers, Tories, and Yankees." In effect, deserters became bushwhackers from the point at which they abandoned the army and headed home. As one Confederate officer noted of the situation among North Carolinians:

> Desertion has assumed . . . a very different and more formidable shape
> and development than could have been anticipated. Deserters now leave
> the Army with arms and ammunition in hand. They act in concert to force
> by superior numbers a passage against bridge or ferry guards, if such
> are encountered. Arriving at their selected localities of refuge, they
> organize in bands, variously estimated at from fifty up to hundreds at
> various points. . . . These men are not only determined to kill in avoiding
> apprehension . . . but their esprit de corps extends to killing in revenge
> as well as in prevention of the capture of each other.

He also noted the intimidation they inspired: "[W]hile the disaffected feed them from sympathy, the loyal do so from fear. The latter class (and the militia) are afraid to aid the conscript service least they draw revenge upon themselves and their property."[62]

Traditional strongholds of Unionist sentiment in Wilkes, Caldwell, and Yadkin Counties, in particular, reemerged as centers of resistance, and they quickly attracted more and increasingly militant disaffected to their ranks. In June 1863, a Confederate observer said of deserters and outliers: "[I]n the disloyal counties formerly Unionist—as Yadkin and Wilkes—they number hundreds and are committing depredations on persons and property."[63] By then, their numbers in Rufus Lenoir's own county, Caldwell, had swelled to between 200 and 300, and in both Wilkes and Yadkin, to as many as 500.[64] Such bands added greatly to the insecurity of many mountain residents as their rampages through farms, neighborhoods, and towns became more frequent and more daring. Disaffected bands in Yadkin were secure enough in their number to openly taunt Confederate sympathizers. A local woman complained to her husband that "the tories term every southerner Secessionist, and call in addressing them 'you secessionist' etc. I do wish that something could be done to stop this miserable increase in tory feeling."[65] Some residents blamed their neighbors for creating an environment conducive to such activity. A young Julia Gwyn informed her uncle that women in Wilkes exhibited loyalist sentiments at least as strong as their husbands and sons. She blamed wives in particular for the vast number of deserters in her area, recognizing that it was their pleas that had brought so many men back home. Their swelling numbers were such, Miss Gwyn reported, that "they have a regular union company up at Trap Hill" and "march under an old dirty United States rag!"[66]

Trap Hill had already earned notoriety throughout northwestern North Carolina as an especially dangerous enclave of disaffection. A small rural community in the northern part of Wilkes County, it was home to John Quincy Adams Bryan, one of the most fervent Unionists in what had always been the most Unionist of mountain counties. As his anti-Confederate sentiments grew more militant during the war's early months, his reputation spread and Trap Hill began to attract deserters, conscript-evaders, and other Unionists, who Bryan managed to mold into a quasi-military company. They soon took the offensive, roaming the county harassing residents and easily spurning the feeble efforts by the home guard to stop them.[67]

Several piedmont counties just to the east of Wilkes had also emerged as hotbeds of dissidence and disruption, and the situation was desperate enough by August that Governor Vance asked Secretary of War Seddon for "a good strong regiment" from Lee's army to restore order. "The vast numbers of deserters in the western counties of this State," Vance wrote, "have so accumulated lately to set the local militia at defiance and exert a very injurious effect upon the community." Home guard units were not capable of dealing with this scale of insurrection and, in some cases, according to Vance, were "rendered timid by fear of secret vengeance from the deserters." Robert E. Lee responded by sending Vance two of his North Carolina regiments, the 21st and 56th, and a cavalry squadron under the command of Gen. Robert F. Hoke. The governor directed the general to "proceed to Wilkes and adjoining counties of this State and use every effort to capture the deserters and conscripts, and break up & disperse any organized bands of lawless men to be found there, resisting the authority of the Government."[68] The troops moved quickly into the area, and after facing enough resistance in the piedmont counties of Forsyth and Randolph Counties, regrouped, with Hoke leaving half of his force in Yadkin County and accompanying the rest to Wilkes County. There, over the course of the next six weeks, they aggressively searched for and captured numerous deserters and conscripts, though they never faced J. Q. A. Bryan's elusive Trap Hill band directly.[69]

Unionist brothers Calvin and Josiah Cowles worried about the impact of Hoke's efforts. Josiah, in Yadkin County, warned his brother in Wilkesboro: "There is great trouble in store for all of us and it is best for every one to preserve silence on the political affairs of the day. . . . [T]he guard [are] in heavy force and are determined to go to Trap Hill & arrest every rebel to the southern cause [and] take every sympathizer that they can get hold of. Should they succeed in getting hold of any of the leaders they will be hung like dogs."[70]

Josiah Cowles's fears proved well founded. Despite the failure of Hoke's forces to take Bryan or his Trap Hill band, Calvin reported that "arrests of citizens as well as conscripts and deserters is a daily occurrence." He was especially bitter about the treatment accorded the families of these deserters. He confided to his father-in-law, William W. Holden in Raleigh, "[Y]ou would be perfectly shocked if you could know half the atrocities they have committed on our people." He told of the father of a deserter who was forced to give up his brandy supply at bayonet point, after soldiers had already stolen all of his grain. He was equally outraged by their treatment of "one old helpless bed-ridden mother, with 3 sons in the army (C.S.A.) and 3 in the bushes" who was "despoiled of her property." In short, Cowles wrote, "many deserters families have been deprived of all means of subsistence & left to starve this winter." "Is this not making war on women & children?" he asked. Although he expressed such sentiments privately to a politically sympathetic correspondent, Calvin

Cowles's views were widely known in the county. Eventually he was arrested but not imprisoned for his active support of Unionist political efforts and for his refusal to take on home guard duties.[71]

While the high number of arrests by Hoke's troops—reportedly 500 in Wilkes by late October and over 3,000 throughout the area a month later— allowed them to claim some success in their mission, whatever gains they made in restoring order and stifling dissent proved all too temporary. By December Wilkes residents were again complaining of a conspicuous "tory" presence, noting that there was little evidence that the two-month purge had had much effect on either their activity level or their continued defiance of local authority. They were all too aware that this meant that they faced 1864 with little prospect of any return to peace or stability.[72]

Similar disruption in Henderson County attracted official attention because of the affluence of the victims and thus the apparent class tensions involved. But as in Wilkes, the movement of regular troops into the area to restore order offered only a temporary reprieve at best. Just as the Unionist enclaves in Henderson had been among the most violently disruptive during the secession crisis, they continued to serve as what one resident termed "a hiding place of tories & deserters . . . who live by pilfering & marauding." Bushwhackers there targeted Flat Rock, in particular, since it still attracted a number of South Carolina planters and their families during the late spring and summer months. More than a year after its infamous encounter at Shelton Laurel, the 64th North Carolina was assigned to the area in mid-1864 in order to break up these "bands of robbers." The assignment proved particularly troublesome. So audacious were these marauders that they sometimes attacked residents in their own homes, looting as they went. With the new regimental protection of the 64th, headquartered at the Farmer Hotel, many families brought their furniture and other valuables to the hotel for safekeeping.[73]

A particularly shocking incident in June 1864 intensified fears in this affluent resort community. According to a report written by "a friend" three days after the events it described, a squad of six men stopped at Beaumont, an imposing stone estate built in 1840 and occupied by Andrew Johnstone, a rice planter from Georgetown, South Carolina. The intruders asked to be fed, and the Johnstone family graciously offered its hospitality to the men, with the daughters entertaining them with piano music and German "musical lore." The guests became "rather free in their manners," which led Johnstone to suspect they were about to rob his family. He hinted "to his girls to retire & be on the watch against pilfering," and the dinner proceeded smoothly. As the men rose to leave after the meal their leader pulled a firelock from his knapsack, shouted, "Boys are you ready?" to his comrades, and announced that they were taking Johnstone prisoner. When Johnstone reached for his own pistol, the marauder shot and killed him in his front hall. Johnstone's young son Elliott hurried to his father's body, took his pistol, and fired wildly at the intruders, killing two and injuring a third. "Heroic boy!" proclaimed the friend in the narrative of the tragedy. "Worthy of the fiery ardor of his Elliott ancestry & the intrepid nerve of his fallen sire."[74] But the message for other friends and neighbors was that no one was exempt from the wholesale violence that had come to characterize the war in many parts of the North Carolina highlands.

Confederate control seemed to have given way to similar levels of upheaval and lawlessness in the southwestern corner of the state. The failed attempt by Confederate captain J. N. Bryson to bring back deserters from that area to their post at Loudon, Tennessee, in June 1863 emphasized just how serious the disruption there had become. Bryson explained the failure of his mission to his commander: "[T]he outlaws are a terror to the citizens, and especially the soldiers' wives who are alone. They are killing cattle, sheep, and hogs; also stealing bee-gums, breaking into smoke-houses, milk-houses, &c." He said that they had threatened his life and told him that neither he nor the officers accompanying him "should ever return to the command to report how affairs were going on there." As for who "was doing the mischief," Bryson supposed them to be "deserters from different commands and some conscripts who have never been in camps." In short, he reported, it was unsafe to send troops back into that area, given the numbers and the vindictiveness of those they had encountered.[75]

Given regular troops' reluctance to confront this kind of opposition and their ineffectiveness when they did so, putting down guerrilla activity often fell to home guard units. In June 1863, Governor Vance had authorized the establishment of such units in response to pleas from mountain residents for military protection. In all counties west of the Blue Ridge, men not subject to conscription were instructed to form companies that would serve only within their own counties. They would serve without pay but would be provided arms and ammunition by the state. Their purpose, according to Vance, would be "to repel invasion, break up and arrest gangs of deserters, preserve order and enforce the laws."[76] All western counties quickly established home guard companies under these terms, but they remained relatively ineffective in achieving

"Rebel Mode of Capturing Escaped Prisoners"
(From Glazier, The Capture, the Prison Pen, and the Escape*)*

the aims Vance laid out. Much of their ineptness was due to a lack of will in their pursuit of their targets. By this point in the war, those available to fill home guard ranks were men who had to be forced into this localized military duty; thus, many found they had little stomach for waging war on their kinsmen or neighbors.

Elkanah Turbyfill of Haywood County, for example, had been appointed to the home guard at the beginning of the war, his primary duty having been to arrest deserters and send them back into Confederate ranks. According to his postwar testimony, when his closest friend and neighbor deserted the army and returned home after a year of such service, Turbyfill "went into [his] house, took down [his] gun, & said: 'Pluma [his wife], I am going to war. I would rather fight the enemy than my neighbors.'"[77] The former sheriff of Transylvania County was a closet Unionist who, like so many others, was forced into home guard duty. He confided to a fugitive that he once sheltered that although he always responded to the call for a hunting expedition to round up deserters, he always tried to send word ahead to them or their families that they were coming.[78] At least one man met his death while engaged in such dubious duty. An Asheville woman wrote of a friend's husband, Dick, who, as a home guardsman, had been in pursuit of a renegade band when the group captured him. So enraged were these "torys" at the home guard of which Dick was a part for "steeling their plunder" that they killed him. She quoted his wife as saying, "Poor Dick she knowes it was mighty against his will to ingage in steeling . . . but they are commanded they have to obey."[79]

Some observers made little distinction between the pursued and the pursuers in these situations. W. H. Shelton, a Union fugitive from Pennsylvania, accurately described the home guard members as he saw them: "These mountain soldiers were mostly of two classes, both opposed to the war, but doing home-guard duty in lieu of sterner service in the field. Numbers were of the outlier class, who wearied of continual hiding in the laurel brakes, had embraced this service as a compromise."[80]

The waning morale of the Confederate troops stationed in the mountains, as well as their dwindling numbers, compounded the insecurities of highlanders. By one count in early 1864, the Western Military District of North Carolina found itself with only about half of the men assigned for duty within the region (591 out of 1,122 men listed). By another count, the three Indian companies of Thomas's Legion and two regiments, the 62nd and 64th, totaled only 475 regular infantry and 250 cavalry on duty.[81] So dismal a showing no doubt reflected the fact that the duties assigned to soldiers in their own areas became more onerous as resistance became more intense. Both home guard units and regular troops found it increasingly difficult to wage war on neighbors and other local acquaintances. An officer in Thomas's Legion who was charged with putting down Unionist activity along the Tennessee border complained: "It was painful and humiliating to have to arrest anyone, but after living and associating with people for weeks and months it was very disagreeable duty to arrest them impress or confiscate anything of theirs."[82]

A series of military encounters in early 1864 pointed up just how ineffective both regular troops and home guard units were in defending North Carolina's mountains from Union attack. Gen. James Longstreet provided western Carolinians with a brief respite from Union raids when he and a small Confederate army advanced on Knoxville in November. Although the general was ultimately unsuccessful in retaking the city from Federal control, his presence in the area did eliminate most movement by Federal troops across the state border through year's end. But by January, that lull was broken when Longstreet ordered Gen. Robert B. Vance, the commander of the Western Military District of North Carolina, to move west "with all available forces" and reinforce Confederate efforts in Tennessee. The governor's brother led a force of five hundred troops from Asheville in an arduous midwinter trek across the Smokies to Gatlinburg, where, on January 12, he split his forces and led about a third of them in the attack and capture of twenty-eight Federal supply wagons.[83] But miscommunication and poor judgment made that achievement short-lived. On the assumption that William Holland Thomas, as ordered, was about to join him with reinforcements, General Vance failed to post pickets as he moved to join the rest of his troops. A detachment of Pennsylvania cavalry caught him and his (by then) substantial entourage by surprise and captured the chagrined general and fifty of his men.

This was not only a major setback for what was one of the largest military missions ever initiated from western North Carolina; it also had major political implications. Robert Vance would spend the rest of the war as a prisoner, and his brother blamed Thomas and another cavalry leader, Col. James L. Henry, for failing to provide reinforcements as ordered. The governor attempted to have both officers court-martialed, but Thomas's connections with the Richmond government helped them narrowly avert that indignity.[84]

The aborted expedition invited retaliation, and by February, Union troops in Tennessee were again making raids into southwestern North Carolina. Major Francis M. Davidson led a force of six hundred Illinois cavalrymen across the state line with orders to search out and destroy Thomas's Legion, three companies of which had returned home with the colonel to Cherokee County. Davidson's men encountered their targets only a few miles over the state line, about ten miles west of Thomas's home at Quallatown. Although caught by surprise, Thomas's men, particularly the Cherokees, rallied their forces quickly enough to sustain an hour-long skirmish. There were major discrepancies in the results reported by the two sides of the so-called Battle of Deep Creek. The Illinois troops declared their expedition a "complete success," claiming to have killed 137 men, and taken over 50 captives, including 22 Cherokees, in what one participant called "one of the most daring raids of the war." Thomas minimized his losses but could hardly claim victory.[85]

Other attacks by both Union troops and local "tories" quickly followed. Wisconsin troops numbering at least 250 followed in Davidson's path, moving unmolested through Cherokee County and into Jackson County, where a brief engagement with local home guardsmen left eight men dead and where Union troops destroyed or confiscated much food and property.[86] C. D. Smith, of Franklin, Macon County's seat, expressed the fears of many in that part of the state when he wrote: "We are in a truly deplorable condition. There is no reliable forces in the country or between us and the enemy. Col. Thomas had been pretending to picket the passes at the Smokey mountains, but to no purpose as recent facts go to prove."[87]

In April 1864 a different sort of raid put other western Carolinians into just as much of a panic. A band of seventy-five bushwhackers, led by Montrevail Ray, a local tory leader, descended upon Burnsville in Yancey County. Faced with little home guard resistance, these "tories" broke open the county magazine and took all of its arms and ammunition, raided a store for its provisions, including 500 pounds of bacon, and attacked the home of confederate Captain Lyons, the local enrollment officer, wounding him slightly before he escaped. Gen. John W. McElroy, the home guard commander for the region, reported the raid to Governor Vance, declaring that "the county is gone up." Not only the home guard but all the citizens "ran on the first approach of the tories." McElroy used the incident to put the larger crisis into perspective for the governor. "It seems to me," he wrote, "that there is a determination of the people of the country generally to do no more service to the cause. Swarms of men liable to conscription are gone to the tories or to the Yankees . . . while many others are fleeing east of the Blue Ridge for refuge." He concluded: "If something is not done immediately for this country, we will all be ruined, for the home guards now will not do to depend on."[88]

The governor hardly needed to be convinced. The day before McElroy wrote him, Vance had made another, more desperate plea to Secretary of War Seddon to suspend conscription in his home region. He reiterated that "the mountain counties of North Carolina . . . are filled with tories and deserters, burning, robbing, and murdering," but he added that the region was more vulnerable than ever because Longstreet's troops had left East Tennessee. With no Confederate resistance present there, the condition of western Carolinians "will be altogether wretched, and hundreds will go to the enemy for protection and bread."[89]

It is telling that in this plea Vance only asked for a suspension of conscription and not for additional troops to be assigned to the region. The reason: many of the Confederate soldiers who moved into the area proved nearly as great a menace to local residents as those they came to combat. Caldwell and Burke County residents complained about Longstreet's artillerymen and their horses, who were "impressing corn, and eating out the country." The 56th North Carolina Regiment was sent to arrest deserters and conscripts in neighboring Wilkes and Ashe Counties, but, according to residents who complained to

Governor Vance during his visit there, the troops harassed and terrorized disaffected civilians. Even more offensive to most, however, they seized both horses and cattle from "loyal citizens" and sold them in neighboring counties, dividing the profits among themselves.[90] Again, Calvin Cowles was among the most outspoken about the abuses imposed on Wilkes County residents. Describing the actions of the 56th to the governor, he wrote, "There is too much Brandy in the county for them and not enough corn." He urged Vance to call them out of the area, noting that "famine is sure and speedy unless they are removed or made to get their subsistence from other sections," such as eastern North Carolina or South Carolina. "These troops," he concluded, "might find more useful employment elsewhere—they are good fighting stock but there is nobody to fight here and inaction will tend to enervate and paralyze them."[91]

A report to Vance on Col. John C. Vaughn's command in April 1864 vividly reinforced the point that demoralized and undisciplined troops had become more a part of the problem than the solution in the mountains. Confederate officer Lt. J. C. Wills of the 32nd North Carolina reported that he encountered Vaughn's men in Watauga County. He wrote from Boone: "Half a mile behind him I met some half doz. of his soldiers, and I continued to meet them in squads, of from two to twenty, all the way to this place (Boone)—straggling along without the shadow of organization or discipline. . . . The whole command (some seventeen or eighteen hundred men) just disbanded, and turned loose, to pillage the inhabitants, and thoroughly did they perform their work."[92] (Ironically, Lieutenant Wills's major source of irritation seems to have been that Vaughn's men had left his own troops very little to "pillage" for themselves.)

Not unexpectedly, these demoralized forces did not react effectively when, two months later, Federal forces again turned their attention to western North Carolina In the spring of 1864 Gen. John Schofield, the new commander of the District of East Tennessee, charged Maj. George W. Kirk to raise a regiment in East Tennessee and western North Carolina. Kirk's mission was to capture Camp Vance, a Confederate training camp in Burke County, then to proceed eastward to inflict what damage he could on the Western North Carolina Railroad running to Salisbury, specifically to destroy its bridge across the Yadkin River, and then to move on to Salisbury to liberate Union soldiers held at the Confederate prison camp there.[93]

Kirk, a carpenter and a politically active antisecessionist from Greene County, Tennessee, who had piloted fugitive Unionists and escaped prisoners across the mountains into Federally occupied territory, was only twenty-six years old and had already earned a reputation as an effective scout and cavalry leader. He headed two regiments of cavalry, the 2nd and 3rd North Carolina Mounted Volunteers, made up of highlanders he had actively recruited during numerous ventures into Unionist communities on both sides of the state line.[94]

The raid on Camp Vance was a particularly daring one, given that its location, two miles east of Morganton, was nearly seventy miles from the Tennessee line. Yet Kirk, with 130 men, made the two-week trip across the mountains undetected, catching the camp commanders completely off guard early in the morning on June 28. The Confederate forces surrendered the camp after a minor skirmish, and Kirk's men soon found themselves with 277 prisoners. By this point in the war many of the camps newest prisoners had been less than willing conscripts, so Kirk felt secure enough to turn some of them from prisoners into recruits and actually arm them, as he did several deserters who had been imprisoned in the camp's guardhouse. From there, Kirk moved directly to the terminus of the Western North Carolina Railroad nearby, where his men destroyed the depot, an engine and several cars, and a large store of grain.

The quick reaction of a local telegrapher prevented the raiders from carrying out the rest of their assignment. He alerted Confederate officials in Salisbury of the attack and urged that troops be sent to stop the Yankees. Without the element of surprise and burdened with an unwieldy number of prisoners, Kirk abandoned his plans for moving farther east and turned back toward Tennessee, bypassing Morganton and moving quickly toward the steep mountain passes in western Burke County. Home guards from both Morganton and Lenoir had by then been alerted to the raid and were in hot pursuit. The Morganton contingent, along with reinforcements made up of guards from the Salisbury prison, caught up with Kirk at Winding Stairs near Brown Mountain, about fourteen miles west of Morganton, just before he and his entourage moved on into Watauga County. With the advantage of the higher ground in a narrow pass, Kirk easily repelled his pursuers. In the skirmish that ensued, William Waightstill Avery, Burke County's largest planter and one of the state's most effective secessionist leaders, was the first to fall. Avery was at least as much in command of the group as its titular leader, fellow planter and lawyer Thomas G. Walton, and his death, with another five or six casualties quickly following, panicked the rest of the home guard, who retreated down the mountain. Kirk then moved back to Tennessee, with almost no resistance, detouring once to set fire to the house of the new commander of the Western Military

District of North Carolina, Col. John B. Palmer, in Mitchell County. He arrived triumphantly in Knoxville, virtually unscathed, where he turned over to Federal authorities 132 prisoners, 32 slaves, and 48 horses and mules. But perhaps most impressive, he added to his own ranks 40 new recruits.[95]

The significance of Kirk's success was not the physical damage done—which was quickly repaired—or even the closure of Camp Vance but rather what it revealed so painfully about the weakness of Confederate defenses in western North Carolina. The rampant lawlessness and upheaval throughout the region had already indicated as much, but this failure of the home guard to provide any effective military resistance to so small a band moving through three counties illustrated the point more graphically—and more embarrassingly—than any defeat preceding it. Colonel Palmer immediately attempted to absolve himself of blame. In a report to Richmond written on July 4, he insisted that "if the citizens of Morganton had notified me of Kirk's presence in their vicinity, I could have captured their entire band." "I fear this is but the prelude to something more serious," he warned, and he made a strong case for the inade-quacy of the manpower assigned him: "It is 250 miles from Virginia to the Georgia State line. I am forced to keep most of my troops posted from Yancey to Cherokee Counties, in order to guard as far as possible against raids into the country opposite the enemy's lines. I have not the force to resist successfully any serious demonstrations on the part of the enemy."[96]

For the many western Carolinians who had found themselves harassed far more by Confederate troops than by Kirk's raiders, there were other sides to the issue of a regional defense. Calvin Cowles, for example, acknowledged the inadequacy of local resistance to the invasion: "The pursuit is said to have been very feeble & the manner of the pursued quite defiant." But he also expressed a far more cynical view of local reaction to the raid: he was afraid that the pressure for a more substantial defense would be bring Confederate troops back into the area. If "the pretense that troops are needed to repel the 'Kirk raiders,'" proved successful, he opined, the "scenes of Aug. and Nov. 1863 [when the 56th North Carolina had so plagued Wilkes County citizens] will be reenacted in our midst." He noted wryly the dilemma faced by those in need of such protection: "There are some men here who want to be guarded all the while but they are mighty stingy of their 'tators' not being willing to give one to a Soldier even though he stands guard over them."[97]

The inadequacy of Confederate defenses became even more evident through the rest of 1864, as violent clashes erupted between bands of pro-Southern and pro-Union forces and the lines between regular and guerrilla military efforts blurred further. Disaffected elements—Unionists, Confederate deserters, and men evading conscription—became even more openly defiant and their resistance was more effectively organized. Evidence indicates that the Heroes of America, a subversive Unionist organization based largely in western piedmont counties, had spread into the mountains as well, thus providing structure and leadership for those who rallied to its cause. In a letter to Gen. John C. Breckinridge in August, Governor Vance described the situation. "The warfare between scattering bodies of irregular troops is conducted on both sides without any regard whatever to the rules of civilized war or the dictates of humanity," he wrote. "The murder of prisoners and non-combatants in cold blood has, I learn, become quite common, and, in fact, almost every other horror incident to brutal and unrestrained soldiery."[98]

That Vance, a zealous defender of the Confederacy, did not distinguish between the activities of Southern units and their opponents is revealing. Fully apprised of Confederate abuses in Wilkes and other mountain counties the previous fall and winter, the governor acknowledged that there was enough reprehensible behavior on both sides to merit condemnation. Yet nothing came of his suggestion that General Breckinridge bring all local groups under regular army control, and the situation continued to degenerate through the fall. All commitment by regular troops to maintain order seemed to have been abandoned, as their efforts to maintain their own supplies meant looting the very populace they were supposedly protecting.

By year's end, even as prominent a force as Thomas's Legion had become problematic in that regard. Ill equipped and poorly clothed, its companies were scattered widely across several southwestern counties, some of them in disarray and all but dysfunctional. In response to numerous complaints from the area, Governor Vance (still resentful of Thomas's failure to support his brother Robert in their bungled mission into Tennessee the year before) reported to Richmond in December that Thomas was "worse than useless; he is a positive injury to that country. His command is a favorite resort for deserters; numbers of them, I learn, are on his rolls, who do no service."[99] Colonel Palmer confirmed Vance's judgment, noting, "Thomas's Legion, as at present organized, is of but little, if any use, either for local defense or for aggressive movements."[100]

Only days later, in response to General John C. Vaughn's complaint that civilians in Watauga County had lynched two of his cavalryman, the beleaguered governor showed him little sympathy. In a scorching letter, he reprimanded Vaughn and his men: "No one can more deplore the *quasi* warfare between the troops and the citizens than myself. But sir, the conduct of many of your men . . . in parts of our mountain country has been sufficient to drive our people to desperation. The stories of robbery and outrage by them would fill a volume and would fully justify the immediate & indiscriminate slaughter of all men caught with the proofs of their villainy. From looking upon them as their gallant protectors, thousands in their bitterness of heart have come to regard them as their deadliest enemies."[101] By the latter part of 1864, Vance's characterization of the breakdown of military activity and civilian unrest in the North Carolina mountains as "quasi war" was entirely accurate and obviously a reflection of the numerous reports and complaints he had received from western Carolinians for at least the last year. The situation had spun completely out of control, and both the governor and military officials in the mountains realized how helpless they were to stop it.

POLITICAL DISSENT

We Are Tired of This Desolating, Ruinous War

D ESPITE the surface enthusiasm for the war in western North Carolina
through the spring and summer of 1861, significant opposition to the Confederate war effort soon developed.[1] While many factors contributed to this
growing disillusionment with the rebellion against the Federal government, two
were of decisive importance in North Carolina's mountain counties. The first,
and without doubt the most critical, was the imposition of military conscription
in the spring of 1862, which forced men who felt no enthusiasm for the new
government to defend it with their lives or to become outlaws in their own
communities. An increasing number chose the latter course, while others deserted from the army and returned to the mountains. As Chapter 5 made
apparent, the influx of deserters and draft dodgers contributed greatly to the
instability and tensions generated along the highland home front and created a

cycle of escalating local violence that poisoned relationships in many mountain communities.

Seeking redress from the cruel dilemma in which conscription placed them, many dissatisfied mountaineers turned to politics for solutions. Unfortunately, the antebellum political system had fostered profound cleavages of its own in the western counties, which were only exacerbated by the distressing wartime pressures.[2] Although the rhetoric of Southern nationalism decreed that the old parties be abandoned, old political allegiances were not forgotten. Informal structures lacking the cohesion of the older parties existed below the surface until the spring of 1862, when the gubernatorial election prompted the re-creation of formal organizations. In some cases, former adversaries found it necessary to put aside accumulated grievances and to work together against lifelong allies. As the war lengthened and conscription threatened virtually all voters, an active peace party challenged newly created parties for local, state, and national offices. Some of the supporters of the peace movement were active opponents of the Confederacy. Leaders of traditional political parties, frightened by what they perceived to be treason by their opponents, sometimes resorted to extralegal measures to insure that they retained power. The result was that by the spring of 1865, the combination of resistance to conscription and political upheaval had shattered the civil society that had sustained the economic and social structures that supported the traditional lifestyle in western North Carolina.

Carolina highlanders reacted violently against conscription in part because they had been persuaded by the antebellum rhetoric of Thomas Clingman and other Southern rights leaders that the imposition of national government controls on their lives was unacceptable. Clingman had called himself a "States' Rights Whig" and articulated a program based on "the rights of the States, strictly defining the powers of the Federal government."[3] He continued his warnings against "aggression," which would be the inevitable result of Republican control of the national government. In February 1861, Clingman stated in a Senate speech that the people of North Carolina would be called on to fight against the secessionists in other Southern states if they remained in the Union. The publication of Abraham Lincoln's proclamation of April 15, 1861, and his letter to North Carolina governor John Ellis calling for troops confirmed Clingman's prediction. The Federal government's demand that the people of western North Carolina comply with this "coercion" was unacceptable to a majority of the highland population, including many former Unionists.[4] As noted earlier, mountain men demonstrated their commitment to the new nation by volunteering for military duty at an even higher rate than men elsewhere in the state.

Bowing to this tradition of government noninterference, the Confederacy began the war with an all-volunteer army, following the pattern of all previous American military organizations. By the late fall of 1861, nearly half of the new nation's armed forces consisted of men who had agreed to serve for twelve months and no more. In a vain effort to persuade these increasingly disgruntled veterans to remain in the service, the Confederate Congress passed a bill to entice volunteers to reenlist. The terms offered a $50 bounty and a sixty-day furlough. Even the usually reticent Robert E. Lee termed this enactment "highly disastrous" and, equally important, ineffective. Virtually none of the twelve-month men rejoined the army. Facing the depletion of the Confederate army just as the Federal offensive began in the spring of 1862, Jefferson Davis pushed passage of the Conscription Act that so quickly redefined the relationship between his government and its constituents.[5]

This new law was a radical departure from Confederate Southern rights rhetoric. All men between eighteen and thirty-five were obligated to serve three years in the military unless they could persuade some person not covered by the legislation to accept payment and act as a substitute for them. Those already in the army—the main targets of this legislation—were required to remain in the service. They were given a sixty-day furlough and the opportunity to elect their company officers to assuage their outrage. On April 21, a week after that act's passage, the Confederate Congress compounded the resentments of its citizenry by implementing a "class exemption" system that allowed state employees and certain skilled workers exemption from the military.[6] While the conscription policy was absolutely essential to the survival of the Confederacy, it appeared to many in western North Carolina to be a repudiation of the justification for the new nation.

Ironically, men in western North Carolina were subjected to a form of the draft even before the passage of the Confederate legislation. In February 1862, Governor Henry T. Clark, seeking to counter the presence of the Union army in the coastal part of the state, "ordered that one-third of the state militia be drafted and organized into state regiments." This action was fiercely resisted in some piedmont counties and generated considerable dissatisfaction in the mountains.[7] Only the later passage of similar national legislation defused the protest against this state law. Many Unionists and others who sought to avoid active service dated their open opposition to the Confederacy to this particular development.

As objectionable as the legislation was, its actual implementation added greatly to the disruption of mountain society. Even before the enforcement of the conscription legislation, western North Carolina soldiers were asking to be relieved of their military obligations, and the new laws only increased such requests. The discretion accorded to local authorities in responding to those pleas led to the serious abuse of the coercive power of governmental authority at all levels. The combined militia of Madison and Buncombe Counties, for example, marched into the remote Unionist areas of Madison County and rounded up eighty men, half of whom they impressed into Confederate service.[8] In Polk County, a former county sheriff arranged to have many conscripts arrested by incumbent law enforcement officers and released only when they agreed to serve in a company he had organized.[9] For the wealthy, substitutes provided a legal avenue of escape. Millington Lytle, for instance, placed an advertisement in the *Asheville News* saying: "I want a substitute to go in Capt. West's Company, Col. McDowell's Battalion, and will pay a liberal price." Lytle probably had little difficulty finding men to take his place since the *News* had run a notice a month earlier that three or four "Able bodied" men were willing to be substitutes "for a satisfactory compensation."[10] The combination of overly zealous local officials and the obvious inequities of the substitute system added to the already substantial disapproval of the conscription system.

This outrage manifested itself in a series of challenges to Confederate authority. The number of requests for hardship exemptions increased rapidly, but fewer seemed to be granted.[11] Potential Macon County conscripts adopted an ingenious device for meeting home front needs: men of draft age made a private agreement that designated who would join the army and who would stay home and provide for the families. Those who remained behind were devastated when the Confederate government refused to honor their private pact and forced them into the army.[12] Other men secured jobs that would exempt them from service under the Confederate legislation. Mail deliverymen were exempt from the draft, so in Rutherford and Polk Counties, a number of possible conscripts divided mail routes amongst themselves in order to avoid military service.[13]

Such exemptions or other legal remedies did not apply to the vast majority of the men subject to the draft. Hundreds of men in like circumstances and an even greater number of deserters moved into the hills to hide out, thus creating the military crisis discussed in Chapter 5 as well as a political crisis as state and national leaders sought unsuccessfully to enforce the new laws. The situation became so serious that by August 1862, Governor Clark had decided that only by offering amnesty to the deserters who would return to their units could this problem be solved.[14] Neither Clark's appeal nor later ones by Governor Zebulon Vance persuaded many of the deserters or conscripts to defend the Confederacy. By June 1863, 232 men from Madison, Henderson, and Polk Counties had deserted the 64th North Carolina Regiment alone. Repeated calls by the Confederate government for more men between the ages of seventeen and eighteen and thirty-five and forty-five only drove more desperate men into the hills for refuge. In December 1862 Gen. John W. McElroy observed, "I am sorry to state that our mountains are full of Deserters and Tories and I fear their numbers will be augmented by the last enrollment of Conscripts." Two years later, the problem was just as acute, as a Buncombe County man noted: "And as to conscription here it will increase Abes Army as much now as before or more."[15]

The issue became more than a state or local concern when troops from neighboring states forced men from western North Carolina into Confederate service. Governor Vance protested to Governor John Letcher of Virginia that troops from that state were forcing men from Ashe and Alleghany Counties into a Virginia cavalry regiment. An Alleghany resident reported to Vance in January 1863, "In our family they arrested a Youth not 15 years old with the intention of taking him into Va, I learn, without right or authority to do so." This and other incidents led Letcher to acknowledge the legitimacy of Vance's complaint and put a stop to Virginia troops' incursions across the state line.[16] In 1863 Georgia cavalrymen under George W. Lee raided Cherokee County and Gideon Pillow raided Yancey and Madison Counties, abducted local residents, and forced them into Confederate service.[17] Vance again strongly protested to officials in both states, but this time it took several months before Confederate authorities made any attempt to return the citizens to their highland communities. He warned that there would "be resistance and bloodshed" by his mountain constituents unless such unauthorized raids ceased.[18] But it was not the threat of such violence alone that worried the governor; he recognized that these abuses of conscription policies further undermined public acceptance of the system and of the government that had set it in place.

Vance and other state and local officials sought to end conscription in the western counties, but they met only resistance from the Richmond government. As early as November 1862, the governor requested that President Davis dissolve the draft in the mountains. The governor's unsuccessful plea was followed by another doomed petition from the region's state legislators, as was a petition of Henderson County citizens to Secretary of War James A. Seddon requesting an end to conscription so that enough men could be retained to defend their homes against the deserters. This appeal was rejected because reliance on solely local conscripts was thought to lead to local "feuds and mutual reprisals."[19] Only in the late spring of 1864, after Vance's continued pleas to suspend conscription, did Seddon offer a slight concession by allowing local enrolling officials more discretion in enforcement.[20] That minor relaxation of national policy proved too little too late and had very little effect on morale in the mountains.

Further confusing the issue were two decisions made by Richmond Pearson, chief justice of the state supreme court. In his role as a district appellate judge (and thus without the backing of the other two members of the court), Pearson issued rulings that aided those seeking to avoid Confederate service. One opinion forbade state officials from enforcing conscription on the grounds that the act was national legislation and therefore could be enforced only by national powers. Since the Confederate government could not spare extra men to hunt down draft evaders in North Carolina, Vance ignored this ruling until the entire state supreme court overturned Pearson's decision.[21] In a much more controversial decision—which was eventually overturned late in the war by the full court—Pearson also ruled that the men who had provided a substitute to do their service could not be coerced into the Confederate army when new conscription guidelines with expanded ages of eligibility went into effect. Pearson issued writs of habeas corpus freeing the men who had been arrested after their substitutes had been drafted.[22] These decisions affected less than 1 percent of all western North Carolina men exempted from conscription, but they seemed to offer protection for all those who sought to avoid Confederate service. Although Vance protested Pearson's ruling, he refused to ignore it, despite demands from Confederate authorities that he do so.[23]

Another exemption to the draft on which Congress voted in September 1862 was equally damaging to Confederate efforts to recruit disgruntled mountain men. Responding to the fact that the number of white males was reaching a very low level in many black belt districts, which threatened racial control, Congress allowed the exemption of one white male for every twenty slaves on a plantation.[24] Even with Lincoln's Emancipation Proclamation signaling that slave control laws were losing their force, many western North Carolinians deeply resented "the twenty nigger law." They felt that the wealthy were being offered a way out of the military that was unavailable to the poor. All the exemptions that the elite could more easily claim increasingly led those opposed to the war to cite class favoritism as a justification for their resistance.[25] Resentment became so great in western North Carolina that some men were reluctant to take advantage of opportunities for exemption offered them. The owner of the largest hotel in Asheville, for example, refused to hire a substitute because "some very harsh things already having been said about him in reference to the war he is very adverse to a step of that kind."[26]

The coercive power of the Confederate and state governments remained strong throughout the war, however. No combination of deserters, draft evaders, and Unionists was strong enough to assume military control of any significant segment of the North Carolina mountain counties. Even after Ambrose Burnside's army occupied Knoxville in July 1863, opposition to the war in western North Carolina remained poorly organized and subject to repression by state and national authorities. The only legitimate form of protest and vehicle for reform available to western North Carolina dissenters was North Carolina's competitive political system (which was rather ironic since that very system had been a major source of many of the divisions and animosities during the sectional crisis and continued to be during the war).

As noted in Chapter 3, the brief respite in the fragile coalition of Whigs and moderate Democrats in resisting secession prior to April was shattered by the attack on Fort Sumter and replaced by a spontaneous and seemingly bipartisan burst of enthusiasm for secession and the Confederate war effort. Many former Unionist leaders felt betrayed by the Lincoln administration's failure to withdraw Federal troops from the fort and quickly embraced secession and the Confederacy. Old partisan differences seemed to disappear as both Clingman and Vance resigned from Congress and returned to lead North Carolina regiments in the Confederate army.[27] Yet, beneath this surface unanimity were signs that political differences would continue to play an important role in wartime western North Carolina.[28]

The political battles began before the state had formally severed its ties with the Union. Although the opening contests took place in Raleigh, mountain politicians quickly became involved. Despite the near unanimity for secession among North Carolinians by the time the secession convention met in May, some suspected the former Unionists as only "lukewarm" adherents of the Confederate cause. Their suspicions proved correct, since those late converts, while voting unanimously to take the state out of the Union, organized a separate caucus at the state convention with William W. Holden, the editor of the *North Carolina Standard*, its most prominent spokesman.[29] They remained a minority, however, and the secessionist majority and Governor John B. Ellis began to organize the state government in a largely partisan manner. Vance reported: "I am . . . in rather low spirits at the way things are managed at Raleigh. I see a pretty determined purpose to carry on affairs under a strict party regimen; none but Locos and Secessionists will be appointed to the Offices."[30]

In this increasingly acrimonious atmosphere, the fall election campaign of 1861 took place. The extent of partisan bitterness was revealed when the former Unionists ran a separate presidential electoral ticket in the fall canvass. Since both Unionists and Confederates supported Jefferson Davis for president, there was no reason for the ticket headed by former Whig governor William Alexander Graham to appear on the ballot except to attack the early secessionists and to protest their administration of the state.[31] The antisecessionists could use against them recent Confederate setbacks, including the disaster at Fort Hatteras, which gained them strong public appeal. In addition, there were increasing indications that small but significant pockets of resistance to the Confederacy existed in several mountain counties.

Against this background of greater organization among former Unionists statewide, the 1861 congressional campaign in the mountain counties drew a crowded field of candidates. In the absence of formally structured parties, a number of self-nominated candidates sought the support of the voters. By the time the campaign entered its final month, the desire for victory over the opposition led to a party consensus that reduced the field to two primary candidates. The former Whigs concentrated their support on Allen Davidson of Cherokee County, who had been nominated previously by the former Unionist caucus at the state convention. The opposition charged that Davidson "considered it his duty to advocate submission to Lincoln and when in convention openly declared that it was a *bitter* pill to vote for the ordinance of secession."[32]

The Democratic-secessionist candidate was state senator and secession convention delegate William Holland Thomas of Jackson County. His stature as merchant, large landowner, and slaveowner had made him a dominant presence in the region, but it was his position as legal chief of the eastern group of the

Cherokee Indians that proved to be a major campaign issue. Resentment of Thomas's protection of one racial minority led to suspicions of this attitude toward the other—and specifically toward his commitment to slavery. In response to the charge "that he had as leve be catched a voting in the ballot box with a free negro as an Indian," Thomas responded that he was the victim of "low vulgar prejudice." He also charged that the convention had gerrymandered his district to weaken Democratic-secessionist strength and that several state employees were canvassing actively for his opponent. The combination of these factors placed Thomas in a difficult position.[33]

The election results from the mountain district confirmed Thomas's fears. Davidson won a decisive victory similar to those achieved by Vance in the two previous elections. Despite all of the traumatic events that appeared to destroy party lines, the 1861 contest confirmed that old allegiances survived the transition into the war. Davidson was convinced that these alignments were permanent and that he would defeat any Democratic-secessionist who ran against him in 1863.[34] The Whig-Unionist alliance received confirmation that their reluctance to join the Confederacy was still endorsed by much of its highland constituency. Speaking for a revitalized political faction, William Holden proclaimed: "Proscribed, crowded out, and crowded down, suspected, maligned, and almost crushed, the old Union men are determined *now* to make a stand, and to appeal to the people. *This course has been forced upon them*."[35]

Holden's call for partisan resistance would find expression in the 1862 gubernatorial campaign. The continued absence of formal party structures led to a drawn-out and confusing nomination process. The Charlotte *Democrat* nominated Charlottean William Johnston to be the secessionist—now named Confederate Party—candidate. Johnston was presented as a compromise candidate, a Whig who supported John Bell in the 1860 presidential election but who also advocated secession well before the firing on Ft. Sumter. The Confederates hoped his candidacy might bring an end to partisanship and suggested that representatives from all counties meet at a gubernatorial nominating convention, agree on a candidate—presumably Johnston—and then hold an uncontested election.[36] Holden, who was denied the opportunity to run for governor in 1858 by a bitterly contested Democratic gubernatorial convention, scornfully rejected the Confederate offer. With the Confederate Party's electoral strategy in disarray, party newspapers across the state, including the *Asheville News*, dutifully endorsed Johnston.[37]

The opposition—now called the Conservative Party—led by Holden sought

William Woods Holden (North Carolina Division of Archives and History)

to find a suitable candidate to oppose Johnston. When early favorite William A. Graham refused to run, Conservative leaders, including Holden and Graham, turned to Colonel Zebulon Vance to be their nominee.[38] Enthusiastic meetings in the mountain counties of Rutherford, Polk, and Wilkes ratified the decision of the party leadership. The popular former congressman from the mountain district agreed to run but announced that he would remain in the army and would not campaign for the office.[39]

The election that followed was particularly bitter, with few substantive issues discussed. Instead, the personalities and weaknesses of the candidates became the focus of the newspaper stories that dominated the debate. Since neither Johnston nor Vance made any public appearances, editors grasped at straws. The Conservative Party papers noted that Johnston's business interests were located in South Carolina, and they attacked him as an outsider. In addition, the Conservatives blamed Johnston's allies for starting the war and running the state military effort ineffectively.[40] In turn, the Confederates attacked Vance and his supporters for conducting a "party canvas" in the midst of a national crisis. In addition, Vance was accused of fabricating and inflating his war record and using it for political purposes. Finally, the thirty-two-year-old Vance was attacked for simply a lack of substance or seriousness. The *Raleigh Register* asked: "With a heavy debt to manage and provide for, what knowledge, experience or ability would 'Zeb Vance,' the young stump-speaking, joke-telling, huzza-boying party politician bring to the talk?"[41]

The bitter campaign in the state as a whole was duplicated in the mountain counties as well. Henderson and Polk County officials who supported Johnston and the Confederate Party were replaced in a partisan purge. Only in the governor's race did highland voters rise above petty partisanship. As a native of the region and someone familiar to most western Carolinians, Vance drew support from both antebellum parties. Ironically, his status as a Conservative attracted the support of voters who were most dissatisfied with the war, while his presence in the army encouraged the voters who were committed to Southern independence at all costs to vote for him. The result was that Vance overwhelmed Johnston in both the mountains and the state in the July and August elections.[42]

When the state legislature met in the fall, the Conservatives seized control of the state and local governments. Vance's chief supporters received their rewards. William A. Graham was elected to the Confederate Senate and William Holden was restored to his former position as state printer.[43] Confederates were particularly incensed by the election of Jonathan Worth as state treasurer, since as a member of the state legislature, he had opposed calling a secession convention even *after* the firing on Fort Sumter. But it was in the appointments made to local offices that Vance and the legislature had the greatest impact. In all parts of the state, former Whigs were named justices of the peace, district solicitors, and election officials, and local positions created by the wartime emergency suddenly became Whig strongholds. Since the Democrats had been in charge of the state government for more than a decade, this abrupt change of personnel and the new Whig strongholds they created amounted to a political revolution at the local level, and the so-called Confederates became increasingly alienated from traditional political activities.[44]

The political changes continued in the winter and spring of 1863. Confederate Party frustrations in the mountains prompted the party's leaders to resort to military force to try to regain their ascendancy. The Shelton Laurel massacre in January put Conservatives on the defensive, since its perpetrators, most of whom were Madison County natives, counted themselves as party sympathizers.[45] In an attempt to distance themselves from such Confederate excesses, Conservative officials like district solicitor Augustus Merrimon and Governor Vance badgered Confederate government civilian and military officials to bring those who authorized the killings to justice.[46]

A second significant incident was more directly partisan. Frustrated Cherokee County Confederate Party members contacted Confederate troops in Georgia and encouraged them to enter their county, which resulted in the incident described earlier. The eight men were arrested for disloyalty to the Confederacy and taken back to Georgia for trial and then forced into "voluntary" service in the Confederate army. Congressman Allen Davidson was particularly incensed by the affront in his home county, noting: "I am sure that this is all persecution because that community were not original secessionists." He identified the chief perpetrator as a political opponent, whom he was determined to destroy. He wrote to Vance: "If nothing else is done, I am determined to write home to shoot Ramseur down in the road, or anywhere else and get rid of him."[47] Eventually Davidson and Vance brought enough pressure on the Atlanta military authorities that the Cherokee County men were released from their Georgia units and returned home. Nevertheless, Davidson was particularly concerned that the incident might be used to intimidate his political allies.

Davidson had good reasons to be concerned about his chances for reelection. Chosen as an opponent of the original secessionists, he had become part of the Conservative Party in 1862. Like many Conservatives, he supported the goal of Southern independence but thought it legitimate that his political allies share in the patronage opportunities. Increasingly satisfied that this was the case at the local and state level, Davidson sought positions for his associates at the national level. His most successful effort at that level was a brigadier general appointment for Robert B. Vance, the governor's older brother. But Davidson's success at obtaining patronage for the party followers could not shield him from widespread criticism of his support for unpopular legislation. For example, Davidson had voted in favor of a series of taxes, including the hated tax-in-kind, in order to provide a sound financial basis for the war effort. In a confidential letter, Davidson admitted that it was a "rip snorter" of a bill. The tax-in-kind impost required families to give 10 percent of their harvest to the Confederate government, a levy Jackson County residents used force to prevent Confederate soldiers from collecting.[48] This outrage undermined Davidson's position and made him vulnerable to challenges from several sources.

Ironically, the initial challenge to the incumbent came from one of his political allies, John D. Hyman. Hyman, Vance's partner in the *Asheville Spectator* since 1855, asked Davidson, Vance's cousin, to voluntarily relinquish his seat. This split in the Conservative ranks confused local party leaders and threatened to end the party's brief period of success. Both candidates and other party officials appealed to Vance to choose between the two claimants. Vance sought to persuade Hyman to withdraw from the contest but failed to do so.[49] Thus, the Conservative Party was irreparably divided before the active campaign actually began. Although both men agreed that the war must continue and that blame for all Confederate failures rested with the Davis administration and the original secessionists, neither man would withdraw and leave the field open to the other.

Hyman's challenge to Davidson prompted other ambitious mountain political figures to contemplate offering themselves as potential candidates. This large number of self-selected aspirants was a clear indication that the traditional party discipline was falling apart in the face of mounting pressure brought by the war. Davidson and Hyman were joined by fellow Conservative William L. Love and Confederate Party members Baylis M. Edney and Marcus Erwin. The tactics adopted by Love and Edney, in particular, illustrate the expediency to which candidates resorted even during this period of national crisis. Edney circulated a petition calling for an end to conscription in the western counties and took the document to Richmond. In mid-April 1863 he returned to the mountain region claiming, inaccurately, that his trip had been successful. Love used his position as a member of the Conscript Examining Board to give unwarranted deferment to healthy men for physical disabilities. To further confuse the situation, the governor's brother, Robert B. Vance, hinted that he could be persuaded to run for Congress as a Conservative.[50]

The unity of the Conservative Party was further ruptured by the appearance of a powerful peace wing in the party. As early as June 1, 1863, Henderson County Conservative Party leader Leander Gash wrote to Vance urging an end to the war. In protesting the governor's renewed efforts to prosecute deserters, Gash defended them and their motives for abandoning the war effort:

> The true course in my opinion in most of the cases is they are tired of a war that they can see no hopes of ever being ended by fighting and not a few of them believe they nor the South would be benefitted by it if the North was conquered. Thousands believe in their hearts that there was no use in breaking up the old government and that Secession was wrong in the beginning and can hardly be made right by fighting. And further they believe that the longer the fight is continued and kept up the more and harder the difficulties to settle; that the South could have got a better settlement at the end of the first year of the war than can be had now. . . . The longer we continue the war the worse for us as well as the North.[51]

After the crushing Confederate defeats at Vicksburg and Gettysburg, an increasing number of mountain people began to appreciate Gash's perspective. They were particularly distraught about the large number of western North Carolinian casualties in Pennsylvania. Raleigh *Daily Progress* editor J. L. Pennington was disturbed by the same developments. He had already stated on April 3 "that the parties who commenced this war must eventually settle it by compromise and conciliation, we think it better done now than at the end of one or two years or more." In a July 15 editorial he issued a more insistent call for an end to the fighting on any basis that would preserve slavery and Southern independence.[52]

Two days later, William Holden's *North Carolina Standard* endorsed the call for a peaceful solution to the conflict and an end to the senseless slaughter of young men. Calling on the people to take control of government policy on this issue, Holden urged them to speak out: "If they want peace, let them say so, and let them state the terms on which they would have it." Holden even suggested a plan of action that he hoped would bring peace: "Let our next Congressional elections turn on the proposition that Congress shall appoint commissioners to meet others on the part of Lincoln, to make an honest effort to stay the effusion of blood by an honorable adjustment." Holden's crusade suddenly raised the stakes of the mountain congressional race to be held that fall.[53]

Pennington and Holden struck a responsive chord in terms of public feeling

about the war. Almost immediately, public meetings began to be held throughout the state, and the results of these gatherings were published in the two
men's newspapers, beginning with the July 21 issue of the *Daily Progress*,
in which Pennington called upon "the people of North Carolina to hold meetings in their respective counties and declare whether they shall be freemen or
slaves."[54] The impact of these peace rallies in the mountains was dramatic.
Robert Vance reported to his brother that there was a "clamor" for peace and
that not even a militant speech he had made as the region's newly commis-
sioned brigadier general could stem the tide.[55]

Full reports exist for nine of the peace meetings held in the mountains in July
and August 1863. Gatherings were held in small communities in Buncombe,
Henderson, Rutherford, and Watauga Counties. Despite their often rather remote locations, the meetings reflected a mature understanding of the issues
confronting the mountain people at the time. Most of the groups, as dedicated
Conservative Party followers and patriotic North Carolinians, protested the
appointment of a Virginian as the chief collector of the tax-in-kind for their
state, a minor issue that served as a symbolic means of protesting Davis's
administration of the war effort.[56] The unpopularity of the Richmond government was clearly one of the most important motivating forces behind these
meetings. The tax law itself was also the target of earnest protest, and several
groups pledged not to support any candidate for Congress who did not agree to
repeal the despised tax-in-kind altogether. Two of the gatherings added to these
demands the cessation of conscription in the mountain counties.[57]

Party leaders may have expected this sort of political debate, but they were
not prepared for the resolutions that challenged the broader aims of Confederate
policy. In particular, Confederate Party members and moderate Conservatives
led by Governor Vance were appalled by calls for a convention to negotiate
a peace. The attendees of one meeting held in Reems Creek in Buncombe
County, Vance's birthplace, even seemed willing to sacrifice Confederate independence to achieve peace. One of their resolutions read: "That we are tired of
this desolating, ruinous war, and will vote for no man to represent us in any form
who will not publicly pledge himself to make use of . . . all the means in his power
to bring about a reconciliation between the contending parties." The momentum for the peace movement resulting from these meetings was considerable,
and those in attendance often agreed to send delegates to nominate a "true"
Conservative for Congress at a September 4 meeting in Hendersonville.[58]

Political leaders at the state level pushed the peace initiative as well. William

Holden became the recognized leader of the peace wing of the Conservative Party. In an effort to retain the unity of the party and as a means to prevent the growing peace sentiment from becoming overtly anti-Confederate, Governor Vance met with the powerful editor to attempt to dissuade him from carrying the peace campaign any further. Holden refused to back down, arguing that he was simply following and reporting on popular discontent rather than creating it.[59] When the two men parted without reaching an agreement, the peace movement in the mountains had an identified spokesman and came to recognize itself as being part of a broader effort. The rift within the Conservative Party was formally acknowledged in the July 28 issue of the *Standard*, in which Holden made clear his differences with the governor. He noted that Vance wanted peace also, "but he regards peace movements among ourselves with no overtures of the kind from the North as premature and injudicious." Holden went on to declare that he, like other peace proponents, opposed "reunion" with or "submission" to the Lincoln administration.[60]

Holden's disclaimer notwithstanding, some highland peace advocates began to move beyond the carefully worded phrases of the Reems Creek meeting to more open hostility toward the Confederate government. The peace meeting in Henderson County in July was the first to elicit radical statements. Alexander H. Jones, the region's most outspoken Unionist, addressed the large assembly and delivered a scorching anti-Davis and antiwar speech. Some of the spectators interpreted his remarks, probably accurately, as a call for reunion and reconstruction.[61] A similar spirit was evident at a peace meeting in Rutherford County, where local delegates were being chosen for the September 4 congressional nominating convention. After the convention delegates intentionally avoided making any specific statements, moderate Conservative state legislator Rufus Bryan offered this resolution: "[W]e are unwilling to accept any terms of peace not based upon the separate & entire independence of the southern Confederacy as we do not consider any other as honorable." By more than a two-thirds majority, the motion was defeated, and local newspaper editor George W. Logan was nominated as the candidate for the peace forces.[62] Equally troubling to Confederate Party loyalists and moderate Conservatives was the number of local officials, including law enforcement officers, who endorsed the peace movement.

The growing outspokenness and radicalism of the Conservatives' peace wing led to a strong reaction by the Southern nationalists in the mountains. One wrote to Vance on August 29 warning that the Tenth Congressional District contained many *"dirty cowardly submissionists."* He named Logan and *Hendersonville Times* editor William Dedman as two such leaders to be on guard against.[63] The antipeace faction did not limit itself to private complaints. When the peace convention met in Hendersonville on September 4, some two dozen Confederate soldiers interrupted the proceedings and dispersed the participants before they had named a nominee. When Dedman attempted to print a story about the disruption of the meeting three days later, the same soldiers forced him to close his press.[64] Governor Vance's growing awareness of the civil strife brewing over the congressional elections induced him to issue a proclamation the same day the soldiers shut down Dedman's paper saying, in part, "I, therefore, implore you my countrymen, of all shades of political opinion, to abstain from assembling together for the purpose of denouncing each other."[65] On September 9 the violence against peace advocates shifted to Raleigh, where two days of tumult involving Confederate soldiers and Holden's supporters left the offices of the *Standard* and a rival paper in shambles.[66] Holden's account of those harrowing days soon reached the members of the highland peace movement, who realized that their adversaries would go well beyond traditional political discourse to oppose them.

The mountain peace leadership began to move more cautiously than before. No new public peace meetings were held, and private letters to Vance and other officials became much more circumspect. William Dedman agreed to limit his criticism of state and national leadership and was allowed to resume publication of his paper. Then at a little-advertised meeting in Hendersonville on September 28, the peace Conservatives completed the process that had been disrupted earlier in the month and nominated George Logan for Congress.[67] Taking a cautious approach to the contest ahead, they requested that Logan carry on no formal campaign. In addition, the platform was very brief. Its main plank read, in part: "[W]e desire to hold ourselves guiltless of the shedding of one drop of blood beyond that which is necessary to the securing of an honorable peace with our enemies." In an apparent effort to assure mountain voters that they were sincere Southern patriots, the convention participants then resolved: "That we deprecate the spirit of desertion . . . and would advise all absentees to return to their proper commands till a permanent peace can be secured."[68] Since it was assumed that the men who had deserted from the army would attempt to vote for Logan, the peace Conservatives were denying any connection with more subversive elements of the peace movement.

Logan followed the advice of the convention and refused to take part in the debates that traditionally marked a mountain congressional contest. Instead, he depended upon open letters to his constituents printed in the *Hendersonville Times* and the *North Carolina Standard*. In his letter of acceptance, he ignored the question of the deserters and concentrated on the peace issue. He argued that it was "the *only practical issue now before the people*, and upon which the election *must turn*." Logan continued with an analysis of the means by which peace could be brought to the western North Carolina mountains. Like most North Carolina peace advocates, he sought to ally himself with the "*fair minded men of the North*."[69] He did not name individuals but indicated that they were members of the Democratic Party of New Jersey and the lower Midwest, whose opposition to the war was well known, if ultimately ineffective in forcing Lincoln's hand at negotiating with the Confederacy.

The candidates opposing Logan attacked this issue of collusion with Northerners but found themselves frustrated by his unwillingness to take part in the dialogue of the campaign or to canvass for votes. When Confederate Party candidate Marcus Erwin challenged Logan to a debate in Hendersonville, Logan replied with a letter to Dedman's *Times*, in which he stated simply: "My friends know my principles."[70] Implying that his opponents did as well, Logan went on to write that nothing he could say would win any additional votes. The peace Conservatives did not give up on the public campaign, however. William Holden provided considerable publicity in the *Standard*; he even printed Logan's voting tickets and sent them to peace supporters wrapped inside of their weekly issues of the newspaper. Other prominent local spokesmen, including Leander Gash, Alexander Jones, and William Dedman, spoke to groups in many parts of the district. The meetings were held without incident since they were usually held in communities in which local officials were sympathetic to the movement.[71]

The peace movement's greatest advantage, however, was the disarray in the ranks of the opposition. The moderate Conservatives who were loyal supporters of Governor Vance remained disastrously divided over incumbent congressman Allen Davidson and John Hyman. Davidson was haunted by his support of unpopular tax laws and by charges that he had voted against a pay increase for soldiers. Hyman was himself a controversial figure who had alienated many potential supporters with his harsh rhetoric as editor of the *Asheville Spectator*. The opportunistic tactics of William Love and Baylis Edney were exposed sufficiently to force them to withdraw from the canvass, and Robert Vance decided not to run, so *Asheville News* editor Marcus Erwin was the sole Confederate candidate to run against Hyman, Davidson, and Logan.[72]

The canvassing took place in the middle of a significant drop in the morale of western North Carolinians. The summer's crushing Confederate defeats convinced many mountaineers, as it had Holden and Pennington, that the chance for Confederate military success was limited. The gloom was so deep that even the Confederate success at Chickamaugua in September 1863 could not offset the Union occupation of nearby Knoxville. Hundreds of men from every mountain county were killed or injured in these major battles, and grief became a part of life for many highland families. The Confederate Party candidates throughout the state sensed this mood and were forced to acknowledge voter anger. In an attempt to salvage support, they once again sought to persuade President Davis to end conscription in the mountain counties.[73] His refusal to consider the request left the Confederate candidates with little to offer the voters who wanted a change.

In mid-September, the ineffectiveness of the Confederate military was brought home to residents of western North Carolina. A small Union force dashed through the Smokies and seized the Haywood County seat of Waynesville. After destroying some property, they returned to East Tennessee without being seriously challenged.[74] In itself of little consequence, this raid added greatly to the impression that the war was indeed being lost and that further fighting was futile. The inability of the Confederate army to defend mountain residents or maintain order in the highlands further undermined civilian morale in the region.

The beleaguered mountain voters went to the polls in early November and provided no firm verdict on the war and future policy. Unfortunately, complete election returns have not survived, but enough data are available to trace the broad outlines of the results. Logan was elected to Congress, but he received substantially less than a majority of the votes. Only that he was able to carry his own county of Rutherford with 851 votes out of a total of 1,160 insured his election. Apparently, he carried only five more of the fourteen remaining counties in the district, and these only by pluralities. Erwin won pluralities in three traditionally Democratic counties and came out slightly ahead among the soldiers, winning 585 out of 1,187 military votes. These successes allowed Erwin to finish second with approximately 30 percent of the votes. The remainder of the ballots was split between Hyman, who carried his home county of Henderson and won pluralities in several small counties, and Davidson, who finished a dismal last.[75] The regular Conservatives were stunned by their loss and may have sought to nullify the returns. As a result it was not until four weeks after the voting that the returns were made official.

As a Confederate congressman, Logan addressed the concerns voiced by the peace movement. The biographers of the Confederate Congress identified Logan as one of the four most consistent opponents of the Davis administration in that body. At the opening of the 1864 congressional session, Logan introduced legislation "to protect citizens . . . from unjust and illegal impressments." A short time later he proposed a bill to end the tax-in-kind. When the congress rejected that initiative, he offered a substitute that would have exempted families of living or dead soldiers from the tax. These measures were supported by virtually all western Carolinians as a means to bring relief to a starving people. Another widely popular economic measure was Logan's effort to retain some semblance of a community economic structure. He offered a bill "to exempt a tanner, a blacksmith, a shoemaker, and a miller for each square mile of land." This proposal would have provided not only the manpower required to sustain the local economies of the mountains but also a means for many more mountain men to legally avoid military service. Reflecting the economic interests of the elite and the need to retain every available source of manpower, Logan also sought to limit the power of the central government to impress slaves. Ironically, the one piece of legislation that Logan did not introduce was the one that would have facilitated the peace process. Instead, he followed the lead of fellow North Carolina peace advocate James T. Leach, supporting his resolutions calling for peace meetings between North and South.[76]

Buoyed by the election of at least five peace candidates from North Carolina to the Confederate Congress, William Holden pushed for an active peace policy at the state level in December 1863. Holden announced that the leading issue of the 1864 gubernatorial campaign would be whether the candidates would agree to call a special state convention or to send state delegates to a national convention to seek a peaceful end to the war. Since several mountain peace meetings the previous summer had called for precisely such a move, Holden's call was well received in the western counties.[77] An alarmed Governor Vance, who recognized that the peace issue had already defeated his allies in several districts, acknowledged the potency of the issue. On December 30, 1863, Vance attempted to neutralize the impact of the peace movement with a preemptive policy maneuver. He wrote to Jefferson Davis: "After a careful consideration of all the sources of discontent in North Carolina, I have concluded that it will be perhaps impossible to remove it except by making some efforts at negotiation with the enemy."[78] Vance expected little to come of this effort, but he did hope that the failure of a public attempt at peace would force the peace advocates to recognize that their alternatives were Confederate independence, to be achieved only by continued war, or peace and Federal reconstruction.

The Logan wing of the Conservative Party in the western counties immediately seized upon Holden's call for a state convention. Its advocates quickly scheduled a second series of public meetings seeking to pressure Vance and the state government to support them. W. E. Blanton of Rutherford County spoke for many when he informed the governor, "[W]e the people of North carolina wants a convention called soon to meet at some point to see if this miserable war cannot be stopt. We Elected Gen. Logan for that purpose."[79] Hyman warned his former partner that a petition had been signed by Henderson County men who "openly avow that the object of the movement is to take North Carolina back to Lincoln."[80] Other meetings taking place and petitions circulating in the mountains made the same points and demanded that Vance call a special session of the legislature to authorize a peace convention. By mid-January 1864, Holden had intimated that he would challenge Vance for the gubernatorial office if the governor did not support the peace effort.

Vance moved quickly to blunt the impact of the peace movement on the Confederate government's war effort and his reelection campaign. Ironically, Holden's challenge brought Confederate Party leaders in the mountains to Vance's defense. Confederate congressional candidate Marcus Erwin warned Vance that the peace movement threatened to split mountain society even further. He prophesied that the movement "will divide our people into two parties each eager to bathe their weapons in the other's blood" and urged Vance to speak out against Holden and his followers.[81] Former senator Thomas Clingman wrote to Vance assuring him that he would publicly support his bid for reelection and that he would discourage any Confederate Party nomination to oppose the governor.[82] Erwin's and Clingman's sentiments were apparently shared by most mountain Confederate Party members, and they offered no public opposition to Vance's candidacy. Thus Vance turned his attention to winning as many Conservative Party votes as possible.

Sensing that the crisis in the mountains would grow worse if it was not immediately addressed, Vance decided to meet the peace movement directly. On February 22, 1864, he opened his gubernatorial campaign before more than

2,000 mountain voters in the community of Wilkesboro. Vance opened the meeting with the question, "Now what is it you desire above all other present earthly good?" The audience responded, "Peace, Peace, We all want peace." Vance gracefully acknowledged this response and the benefits of peace with quotations from the Bible. He admitted that the crux of the campaign was whose plan would most rapidly and successfully bring about this highly desirable state. Mixing humor with commonsense arguments, the governor addressed his fellow mountaineers for nearly three hours in an effort to convince them that Holden's convention plan would only lead to greater problems. He maintained that a convention could do only one thing that the state legislature could not do—remove the state from the Confederacy. And if the state left the Confederacy, even worse events would transpire. North Carolinians would find themselves at war with both the Union and the Confederacy; or if the state allied itself with the Union, mountain men would be drafted into the Federal forces and be required to kill their fellow Southerners. Vance reminded his audience that Kentucky "undertook to be neutral. She declared that she would take no part in the quarrel. But Mr. Lincoln soon thrashed neutrality out of Kentucky, made her furnish her quota of men, and subjected her to her share of all of the burden of the government."[83] While Vance's arguments may have converted some mountain voters, many were still fearful that he supported Jefferson Davis's recent suspension of the writ of habeas corpus.

That suspension, which was specifically aimed at Holden and the North Carolina peace movement, changed the nature of the canvass in the mountains. Holden officially announced his candidacy in early March and declared that he would not campaign directly before the people—using the 1862 election as a precedent and an excuse for not debating his highly skilled opponent. Citing the suspension of the writ, Holden also announced that he would cease publication of the *Standard* for fear of government intervention.[84] While this tactic of avoiding debate had worked effectively in 1863, it was much less successful in 1864. Unlike in 1863, the peace Conservatives faced a united opposition. Moderate Conservatives, opponents of Holden, and Confederate Party members lined up behind Vance. In addition, Vance quickly sensed that the emergence of the question of civil liberties as a major issue would allow him to appeal to many advocates of an early peace.

Vance also recognized that Holden's failure to canvass actively presented the governor with a significant opportunity to reach voters, and he began an active personal tour of the state and North Carolina military units. Vance also traveled to Virginia and over a ten-day period in March spoke to the substantial number of North Carolina voters who were in the Army of Northern Virginia. Using the coarser language of the veterans he was addressing, he praised the troops for their successes against the massive forces of the Federal army. At one point he asserted, "Boys, you must fight till you fill hell so full of Yankees that their feet will stick out the windows."[85] Vance also hoped to stem the growing tide of deserters from North Carolina regiments by assuring the soldiers that their state and local governments were providing food and other necessities to their families back home. The officers of the units were very encouraged by Vance's message, but Holden maintained that the privates were not persuaded. One mountain soldier, Jesse M. Frank of Watauga County, wrote home: "I will say to you that Gov-Vance has been threw the army making stump speaches. That is a thing near all the soldiers in regular service dispise to here."[86] These speeches established Vance as the candidate committed to fighting until independence was achieved.

Returning to North Carolina, Vance tried to reach out to mountain voters using the issue of civil liberties. Between June 14 and June 23, he spoke at Rutherfordton, Hendersonville, Asheville, Marion, Morganton, and Lenoir. In these appearances, Vance attacked the Davis administration for suspending the writ and defended the North Carolina Supreme Court's right to protect men from Confederate conscription. His strategy of making the increasingly unpopular Davis the scapegoat for the failures of the Confederacy was a brilliant success. His campaign platform captured his anti-Davis, pro-independence stand:

> The supremacy of the civil over military law.
>
> A speedy repeal of the act of suspending the writ of habeas corpus.
>
> A quiet submission to all laws, whether good or bad, while they remain on the statute books.
>
> No reconstruction or submission, but perpetual independence.
>
> An unbroken front to the common enemy; but timely and repeated negotiations for peace by the proper authorities.
>
> No separate State action through a convention; no counter revolution; no combined resistance to the government.
>
> Opposition to despotism in every form, and the preservation of our Republican institutions in all their purity.[87]

This series of appeals attracted both Confederate Party members who would vote against any avowed peace candidates as well as the Conservative Party members who were more concerned about abuses of civil liberties than peace.

Vance's skillful campaign before the public weakened Holden and put him on the defensive. Holden was forced to try to tie Vance to Davis. He correctly noted that the Confederate Party leadership supported Vance, and he contrasted Vance's leadership with that of Governor Joseph E. Brown of Georgia, who, Holden maintained, had taken early and advanced positions on the peace question. Vance countered by having the Raleigh *Daily Conservative* reprint his official letters challenging President Davis's authority.[88] In addition, Vance's numerous speeches pointing out the limitations of the state convention as a vehicle to bring peace forced Holden to abandon the convention as an electioneering device. In late May, Holden's claim to the leadership of the Conservative Party in the state was seriously undermined when only five state legislators voted against resolutions endorsing Vance's administration.[89] At this point, state treasurer Jonathan Worth, a strong advocate for peace, attempted to persuade Holden to withdraw from the race. Holden refused but soon found his campaign in even deeper trouble.

Vance's supporters revealed the existence of the Heroes of America in June 1864 and attempted to tie Holden to this avowedly Unionist organization. The Red Strings, as they were often known, sought nothing less than the destruction of the Confederacy. Although centered in Raleigh and based primarily in the state's piedmont, they were active in the mountain counties as well. They provided safe havens for Federal prisoners of war who escaped from the prison at Salisbury. They organized themselves at the local level, and local law enforcement officials may well have been members in several highland locations. They may even have provided some of the structure for the Logan campaign in 1863.[90] Holden denied Vance's charges that he was a Red String member and once again affirmed that he would accept no peace that did not come with Confederate independence.[91] Thus, the peace movement found that it could offer few options that Vance was not already claiming as his own.

Ironically, a series of outside forces served to weaken the peace effort without any assistance from the Vance campaign. For the duration of the campaign— from February through August—the Confederate currency crisis abated. During those months, a reformed currency actually produced a slight deflationary trend. While prices still remained much too high for the average mountaineer, the inflationary spiral stopped.[92] At the same time, the Federal war effort was apparently stymied by the effective defensive tactics of Joseph E. Johnston before Atlanta and Robert E. Lee before Richmond. Union soldiers were being killed in large numbers without gaining their major objectives. Lincoln's prospects for reelection in November looked dim, and his cabinet had signed a blind memorandum outlining the administration's policies in the face of that lost election. The drop in Northern civilian morale was matched by a temporary rise in Southern spirits. Some mountain voters who had given up hope for Confederate independence earlier now saw one last chance for success. Then in late June Colonel George Kirk conducted his raid on Camp Vance in Burke County.[93] While this raid, like earlier ones, pointed up the continuing weakness of the Confederacy, it also prompted many mountaineers to view the Federal army as the enemy and served to identify the peace advocates as traitors to the South.

By the time the balloting took place in August, the peace forces were in complete disarray and the Vance campaign was growing stronger every day. Holden's support in the region was particularly weakened when Hendersonville *Times* editor William Dedman sold his paper when local Vance supporters threatened to conscript him unless he did so.[94] In addition, Vance's supporters printed their ballots yellow instead of the traditional white in an attempt to identify and thereby intimidate Holden supporters.[95] Mountain men in the military (who voted early) found it virtually impossible to cast a vote for Holden, and Holden's overwhelming defeat in late July among the military discouraged many of his mountain followers. When some of Vance's supporters continued to try to identify Holden's backers as they did at Marion in McDowell County, there is little surprise that Vance won by margins as big as 113 to 3 in many western precincts.[96] Holden, in fact, won only Wilkes County in the mountains, and even here his margin of victory was very slight. The peace movement in western North Carolina had been outcampaigned and crushed in the climactic election of the war.

In less than two months, however, the movement reemerged with growing strength. The Confederate defeats at Mobile, Atlanta, and in the Shenandoah Valley revealed the true weakness of the Southern military position. In the late fall, a number of mountain legislators supported the resolution introduced into the state senate by John Pool that read in part: "Resolved, that five commissioners be elected by this General Assembly, to act from other States of the Confederacy, as a medium for negotiating a peace with the United States." The ambiguity of the peace movement in North Carolina remained. The Pool resolution, which lost in the Senate by a 24 to 20 vote, still did not clarify the conditions or the terms under which such negotiations would have taken place.[97] Also, as had been true throughout the period, the North Carolina peace activists were still dependent on some sort of positive response from the North, which at that point seemed forthcoming.

Three North Carolina congressmen, including George Logan, did clarify their position in a resolution proposed by Congressman James T. Leach that offered, "That whenever the Government of the United States shall signify its willingness to recognize the reserved rights of the States and guarantee to the citizens of the States their rights of property, as provided in the Constitution of the United States and by the laws of Congress . . . we will agree to treat for peace." In effect, the Confederacy agreed to a reunion with the United States if the Federal government would retain the institution of slavery. This explicit platform might have been the basis for further negotiations, but the Confederate Congress overwhelmingly defeated it. Thus, the North Carolina peace advocates found themselves unable to offer a practical escape from their state's difficulties. Holden adopted the Leach resolutions, stating: "We would negotiate with the government of the United States, and we would obtain the best terms we could for North Carolina."[98] The success of Sherman's march through the Carolinas and the capture of Fort Fisher outside Wilmington threatened to bring the full horrors of the war to North Carolina. In a secret session, the legislature elected four commissioners to meet with Jefferson Davis to seek ways to achieve an end to the conflict. This, the North Carolina peace activists' final effort, failed.[99]

The situation in the mountain counties deteriorated even more rapidly. Despondent civilians wrote increasingly demoralizing letters to mountain soldiers, which led to a catastrophic rate of desertion of western North Carolina troops. By February 1865, the *Asheville News*, the Confederate Party's organ in the mountains, reported that the party was willing to accept peace under any conditions. Within a month, however, the paper had ceased publication, indicating the complete bankruptcy of the Confederate cause in the mountains.[100] Unionists and peace advocates became bolder in their demand for an immediate cessation of hostilities. The region's military commander, General James G. Martin, reported in early March: "I am confidently informed there have been secret meetings held in nearly all the counties west of the Blue Ridge, to send delegates to a secret convention, which was to meet, and did meet, at Marshall in Madison County . . . to take steps to organize a new State of the eastern portion of Tennessee and Western North Carolina."[101] This meeting was quickly followed by the devastating Stoneman's Raid through the mountain counties, which coincided with the surrenders of Lee's and Johnston's armies and the war's end.[102]

The Confederate government's decision in the spring of 1862 to force western North Carolina men to join or to remain in the army was a fateful one. While conscription was critical for the immediate survival of the new nation, it had undermined the legitimacy of the Confederacy for many mountain residents and had as much to do with the disruption of their lives and was as much the source of their disillusionment with the war effort as any other single policy imposed by that government. Not powerful enough to challenge the Richmond government directly, the individuals who opposed conscription and other Davis administration programs turned to politics to seek redress for their grievances. They tended to support Vance in 1862, Logan in 1863, and Holden in 1864, with increasingly radical solutions to the problems that faced them. Politics proved to be an imperfect vehicle to oppose Confederate policies, however. In part this was because the antebellum political system on which wartime partisanship had been established was too divisive and thus poorly suited to provide community-saving solutions under the pressure of modern war. In addition, election results provided no clear-cut guidelines for elected officials to follow. The only development accurately reflected in this turbulent political landscape was the progressive disintegration of the society and the institutions from which that society had been derived.

ECONOMIC STRAIN

Laboring under Grate Disadvantage

AT the end of October 1861, Elizabeth Watson in Jackson County wrote to her husband, James, then stationed in the Confederate army in East Tennessee, about conditions at home. Like many letters from wives at home to husbands in the service, the economics of the household, the community, and the region were a regular, and often substantive, part of the report given. In this case, Elizabeth told James: "Times in our county is hard for the poor class of people for every thing is giting so deer that they cant by hardly a noughf to live on[.] Salt is from nine to ten dollars a sack her and evry other thing in proportion. Thier is good crops made in our county I think corn can be bought at 50 cts. all through the winter and now the people is . . . halling off thier meet. I dont now how we will git our nessaryes for money is scarce here."[1]

Only six months into the war, the economic stresses of the war that Elizabeth

Watson described—the scarcity of cash, the high price and limited supplies of staples, especially salt, the drainage of vital foodstuffs to troops or larger markets, and the concerns of surviving through the winter—served as a grim preview of the hardships so many others would experience in the months and years ahead. The Civil War would test the strength and durability of the economy and community in western North Carolina throughout its duration. Its particular stresses for many rural highlanders were caused by the removal of the margin of safety that tenants and yeoman farmers sought to build into their lives. That strategy, so basic to an agricultural economy, called for preserving some surplus production in case of adverse weather or other unforeseen setbacks. With so many of the most productive farm workers absent, families and communities found it more and more difficult to produce even that small a surplus, and when outside forces intervened, real hardship resulted. Thus, late spring and early fall frosts that might have been a minor irritant in the past became a matter of grave concern.

The problems that so concerned Mrs. Watson and other poor families did not become widespread until nearly a year later. The summer and fall of 1862 appeared to be a time of particular crisis. Farmers in Rutherford, Polk, Caldwell, and Wilkes Counties were among those who lamented the terrible drought of that year that reduced crop yields by at least one-third. In addition, an epidemic of hog cholera threatened the other staple of the mountain diet during that same period.[2] Such setbacks proved especially ominous because they forced the consumption of most of the surplus resources during the winter of 1862-63, which meant there would be little to fall back on during the ensuing years of the conflict.

In this atmosphere of growing scarcity, it became more apparent than ever that the nuclear family was the most basic unit of production and consumption. The dislocations caused by the war illustrated the importance of each productive member of the family. As David W. Siler of Cherokee County explained to Governor Vance: "Our people . . . have learned to subsist mainly on the immediate productions of their own labor. Deprive us of that labor and the innocent & helpless must perish." He went on to ask: "What consolation or encouragement can come to a mans [sic] heart in an hour of trial from a home where the helpless are perishing for want of his hand to provide?"[3] Husbands were not the only crucial members of the household. A crippled father in McDowell County asked that his two sons be returned from the army to help him with his work. A blind Polk County woman asked Governor Henry Clark that her fourth son be denied permission to join his three brothers in the army; she needed him to work the farm.[4]

The death of a wife could be as devastating to a family as the loss of a husband or son, as a group of Wilkes County petitioners indicated in their appeal for an exemption for a soldier who had just become a widower: "Mr. Burgess has within the last few days lost his wife leaving him six little children, the youngest only a few days old & the largest not able to do anything in the shape of work and without any assistance in the world Save the father. . . . [W]e most humbly pray your excellency to do whats [sic] in your power to get a discharge for Mr. Burgess that he may save his little children from starvation."[5] There is no record of what action, if any, was taken on this appeal, but it is likely that if Burgess was not given legal sanction to return home, he may well have chosen the option such suffering inspired among so many other Confederate troops from western North Carolina—desertion.

A combination of early frost, wheat rust, and drought continued to greatly reduce food production in many parts of the mountains from 1862 on. Both governors Clark and Vance, along with other Confederate authorities, were constantly reminded by highland residents that they in particular suffered by the shortage of manpower, since, unlike families elsewhere in the state, they had few slaves to fill the labor needs left vacant by those in military service. The absence of adult males also left no one to break the sod during spring planting or to haul heavy rocks and timbers from newly cleared fields. While women and adolescents could and did plow the fields that had been used in previous years, the absence of fathers, husbands, and older sons meant that many other fields lay fallow.

Serious setbacks in agricultural production resulted. As early as February 1862, James Gwyn of Wilkes County expressed his concern over "the great scarcity of grain in this Country" and that much of what was being produced was being distilled. Such scarcities meant higher prices, leading Gwyn to ponder, "What will the poor who have no money to buy grain do?"[6] Women often bore the brunt of these and other economic woes, which were often among the more unexpected consequences of the war. A Waynesville woman expressed the frustrations of many others when she wrote in December 1862: "When the war broke out all I thought about was our friends going off & getting killed. I did not think about the small pox and evry kind of disease getting all over the country, and people starving to death and all that. . . . As I heard an old woman say the other day, 'seems like this country is might nigh tore up!' "[7]

Out of such desperation, both poor men and women did what few, if any, ever would have considered before the war: they wrote their governor. Henry T. Clark, governor until September 1862, and then Zebulon B. Vance, received hundreds of letters from male and female constituents, some of which were barely literate and crudely written, not unlike those that wives—often the same women—had been sending to their husbands, fathers, and sons. They reported on a variety of hardships they faced and begged for relief of various sorts. Many expressed the sentiments of Maryann Arrowood of Henderson County, who in November 1863 made a simple but powerful plea to Governor Vance: "There will have to be something don for us or we will all perish to deth." A Jackson County woman informed him that the wives and children of Cherokee Indians were "living on weeds and the bark of trees."[8] As the situation became more critical, civilians and soldiers joined their wives to put increased pressure on state and Confederate officials, who were forced to alter established policies. As described in Chapter 6, Vance's attempt at the most obvious solution—to put an end to conscription so that enough men could be retained in the area to feed the population—fell on deaf ears in the Richmond government.[9]

Another option for alleviating distress was government assistance, which North Carolina attempted to implement. In an unprecedented series of actions by both state and local governments, Raleigh officials provided money, food, and other necessities to county committees to distribute to the needy, while local elites rallied in official and unofficial ways their own resources to meet the needs of families. In the fall of 1862, Caldwell County appropriated $1,000 to buy corn for soldiers' wives.[10] By the following spring, several of the westernmost counties, like those throughout the state, had appointed commissioners and several subcommissioners to oversee the distribution of tax funds for the relief of the poor. Yancey County officials devised a formula for such distribution in which widows and children of deceased soldiers received two shares each, while wives and children of soldiers still alive and in service received a single share.[11]

In implementing such relief, lists of indigent wives of soldiers were compiled and circulated; some that have survived provide revealing details as to the circumstances and extent of various local efforts. The records of Wallins Laurel District in Madison County include the names of sixteen women, followed by columns of figures indicating the number in their families and the allotments of corn, bacon, and salt provided them.[12] A similar document for a Wilkes County district records not the foodstuffs to be distributed to the sixteen households it lists but rather the makeup of each family—all mothers with anywhere from two to eight children—and the "amount of providsions" each currently had on hand. Typical among them was Emmaline Barnett, who had three children under the age of six and only one hog and three bushels of corn with which to feed them; and Roda Dowell, a widow with five children under the age of fourteen (and two sons in Confederate service) who was only slightly better off with "4 bushels of corn, 10 to 12 lbs of bacon, 1 Milch cow & calf & a head of Hogs."[13]

Local elites often exhibited a sense of noblesse oblige in their recognition of the plight of the needy in their midst and often divided up among themselves, by neighborhood within their counties, responsibilities for donations. In Cherokee County, commissioner N—N. Davidson instructed William Walker: "I understand you have twelve sacks of corn now at your place. You will please distribute eight sacks of corn among the people of your beat. This is more than their proportional part of what is brought, though I understand your people are suffering and you had better divide it among them as equanomically [*sic*] as you can." Davidson then asked Walker to send the other four sacks by the first available wagon moving toward his part of the county for distribution there. He concluded his letter with a discouraging word: "Say to the people not to depend entirely on the county corn for support as I cannot get it hauled as fast as they can consume it."[14]

Other individuals used their role as landlords to help alleviate the suffering of their destitute neighbors. Joseph C. Norwood of Caldwell County indicated in the fall of 1863 that he had allowed "wives and widows of soldiers" to cultivate "patches" on his farm, as did other landowners in that area. He noted of the tenants: "[T]he women begged to retain their rent, expecting to get it at a low rate. I thought it was best to give it to them, as a low price in Confedte money woult amt. to nothing—& we find it necessary here to be very liberal with the soldier's families."[15]

Unionist wives were, for the most part, denied a share in either government-sanctioned efforts or the personal extensions of charity. Their particular plight evoked concern only among those who had similar sympathies, such as Calvin Cowles, who pondered their fate in a letter to his brother Josiah in November

1863. "What is to become of the poor families who they have despoiled?" he asked. "[F]amilies of Deserters and out-lyers—God only knows—there is no eye to pity, no hand to save. Some have not a bushel of corn nor a pound of meat yet neighbor's would think it an indictable offence to furnish them with a days ration or even to aid some of these poor mothers to bury a dead child." A month later, Cowles described the situation even more pointedly to his father-in-law, William W. Holden, in Raleigh. Confederate soldiers had deprived Unionist sympathizers of their grain and livestock. "Milch cows have been driven away from crying children & weeping mothers because the Fathers have been recusant—one old helpless bedridden mother with 3 sons in the army (C.S.A.) and 3 in the bushes has been despoiled of her property." She was not unlike many other deserters' families, Cowles reported, who "have been deprived of all means of subsistence and left to starve. . . . Is not this making war on women and children?"[16]

The economic difficulties families faced during the war were also a result of the disruption of the market economy on which the broader mountain community was so dependent. Although most western North Carolina farm families were subsistence farmers—that is, they worked to provide for their own needs—they were constantly involved in an exchange of goods and services. For example, they required a miller to grind their grain and corn into flour and meal. They also needed salt, which had to be purchased from local merchants, to preserve the meat they raised and slaughtered. Although the 1860 census reveals that mountain families were more likely to meet their own manufacturing needs at home than the families in other parts of North Carolina, the specialized skills of the tanner, wheelwright, miller, and blacksmith were essential to every family, regardless of how self-sufficient or isolated they might be.[17]

While this system of trade has often been portrayed as a simple exchange of goods, it was, in fact, based on a monetary value being assigned to most parts of the transaction. Even under the pressure of war, barter was sometimes handled on an approximate cash basis. Typical was the proposal of Wilkes County farmers to Calvin Cowles: "We received a note from you stating that you was anxious to swap beef hides for leather. We will swap at the old prices if that will suit."[18] Cash not only remained the basis of commodity exchange, it also was the measure of value for the most basic of economic goods—land. Unlike real property in other parts of the South, where it was treated as a disposable resource, landholdings in Appalachia were usually the measure of a highlander's wealth and a source of speculative investment.[19] (Slaves were traded through regionally determined monetary values as well, as Chapter 9 will demonstrate in detail.)

The most critical services required by mountain families were those of the blacksmith and miller. Surviving letters and petitions from many parts of western North Carolina to Governor Vance testify to the impossibility of producing goods without the help of a smith. A Haywood County farmer noted that his area was "disorganized" without a blacksmith, while Caldwell County petitioners asserted "we are laboring under grate disadvantage in our neighborhood for want of a Blacksmith."[20] A petition from McDowell County asked that the Broad River District be provided with a miller since the farm families had to transport their grain to be ground over five miles of poor roads. Robert Love of Haywood County informed the governor that miller Elisha P. Hyatt had been unexpectedly conscripted. "He is absolutely necessary in this neighborhood as a miller," Love wrote. "We cannot get along well without him." Leander Gash of Henderson County complained that with the influx of deserters into the area, even their duties as home guardsmen interfered with the services they could provide. "Millers, Blacksmiths & all other exempts are dragged into this deserter catching," a futile effort, he claimed, that "will hardly render much valuable service to any body."[21]

While smiths and millers were vital to the survival of mountain farmers, many other craftsmen were also essential for sustaining the highland economy. Tanners and shoemakers proved to be nearly as important to civilians as to soldiers. Particularly when preparing for the cold winter months, farm families were aggressive in expressing their concern about securing adequate footwear.[22] In addition, millwrights who could repair mill machinery and keep the mills running were considered as essential as the millers whom they kept in business. Probably the most valuable single individual was the jack-of-all-trades. Burke County citizens, including a number of women, described one such man in their petition to win an exemption for him from Governor Vance: "We feel that his services are indispensable in the neighborhood where he resides—He is the only mechanic in the neighborhood—he makes looms, bed steads, trays, chairs[,] tables, chests, stocks[,] scythes, plows &c &c."[23] Clearly the loss of an individual like this could cripple the productivity of any locality.

Other hardships and deprivations served to indicate the extent to which western North Carolina farmers were integrated into a market economy. First and foremost was the emphasis farmers placed on the lack of adequate transportation and transportation routes. This concern was made manifest by mountain voters long before the Civil War, with the widespread political popularity of internal improvement efforts in the region, from turnpikes to railroads. Despite their strong advocacy, mountain leaders had only begun to implement their coveted rail system when the war began. Thus they had to make do with a road network that could not withstand the demands placed on it by the war. By the spring of 1863 Macon County farmers expressed their concern that many of the bridges on the turnpike between their area and Asheville were "entirely gone" and travel was quite hazardous. Citizens of newly established Mitchell County demanded that their wheelwright be returned to them and that a wagon-making factory be built in their county to insure that they could travel. Citizens reasoned that the solution to the problem of hauling heavy loads in Transylvania County would be the return of a teamster from the army.[24] Even government officials were forced to admit that the normal pattern of transport to western North Carolina had been destroyed. Nicholas W. Woodfin of Asheville, who served as North Carolina's salt commissioner at Saltville, Virginia, expressed his frustration in the fall of 1863 that he could not ship his precious cargo to many mountain counties because so many roads were impassable.[25]

Another indication of mountaineer dependence on commercial transactions was the unexpected demand for cloth-making equipment and yard goods. The Appalachian woman weaver has long symbolized the basis and the continuity of the southern highland handicraft tradition. Every mountain home was reputed to contain a spinning wheel and a loom to turn wool from the farm's sheep into thread and yarn, which was then woven into cloth. Yet during the war, many western North Carolina families had stopped producing their own clothing. In many cases, households lacked even the basic cotton and wool cards needed to prepare the fibers for the process of making thread and yarn.[26] Other weavers simply refused to consider starting from that basic level and insisted on obtaining commercially produced thread and yarn. Still others disdained any use of the loom at all and demanded access to the finished product.[27]

Western North Carolina merchants sought yard goods from outside of the region, and on occasion, wives urged their husbands in service to send them yarn, thread, and cards if they knew them to be stationed in the vicinity of cities where they might have access to such goods. Under pressure from local women, Joseph Cathey, a Haywood County merchant, sought to secure yarn from a South Carolina source and offered to pay "500 dollars in S.C. money and the balance in Confederate money." The demand for cloth became so great that in the spring of 1864 a group of businessmen in Buncombe County sought government assistance to construct a textile factory near Asheville, though nothing came of their efforts.[28]

Some farm families depended on the market even for food. Although this dependency undoubtedly was the result of wartime conditions, those involved did not find the practice of directly purchasing food supplies unusual or unacceptable. Martin Crawford points out in an economic study of Ashe County in the 1850s that even tenant farmers in that county began to devote more of their land to grow grain for the market and thus had less acreage to provide all of their own food needs.[29] There is ample evidence that the war accelerated this trend. In fact, many families resented more the prices they had to pay than the fact that they had to purchase the goods. A Cherokee County woman, for example, complained to Governor Vance of how exploited she felt by such price gouging: "My husband has been taken away from myself & family as a disloyalist whitch I think has been caused by desyning men that wont go into the army themselves but prefer to stay at home & speculate by selling the wives of soldiers good[s] at 500 per cent." Other families did not bother to request an allotment of food but rather asked for cash stipends with which to purchase their own food supplies.[30]

In other cases, local citizens were disturbed by the farmers or merchants who were draining the food supply in their area by seeking higher prices elsewhere. A Macon County report to the governor indicated that a merchant was moving "some 2 or 3 hundred bushels of dried fruit across state lines into Ga. to be distilled into brandy."[31] Alexander England, a poor farmer in Transylvania County, received a request from his two sons in Confederate service that he send them ten to fifteen gallons of brandy, which they proposed selling to their fellow soldiers for a greater profit than he could make selling it locally.[32] Both actions violated a new state law that prohibited for the duration of the war the distillation of fruit into liquid form.

One final factor tied these rural families and communities to the broader market economy. Economic historian Winifred B. Rothenberg has argued that the uniformity of prices on products sold in a market center and on the same goods in a rural community indicates that these two localities are part of the same market system.[33] Throughout the war, people in the western North Carolina counties faced the same problems of high commodity prices, speculation, and inflation suffered by urban Confederates. According to one study of the tremendous impact inflation had on this region during the war, "The price of eggs increased 1666%, . . . bacon 2272%, flour 2777%, . . . and corn and potatoes shot up 3000%."[34] Despite Governor Vance's desperate attempts to regulate supplies and prices, the extraordinary cost of these items as well as salt, shoes, and other grains left highlanders as defenseless as residents of any other part of the Confederacy, thus negating any claim that the citizens of western North Carolina were isolated from market forces.[35]

The broader economic forces that affected western North Carolinians in general was significant, but the complex mix of landed and commercial elite, yeoman farmers, tenants, and slaves that lived in the region insured that the market's impact would not fall equally on all residents. For slaveowners and merchants, the local economy was tied directly to commercial transactions originating outside of the mountains, and they used mountain products supplied by the poorer elements of their communities to trade with suppliers and businesses regionally and nationally. The war had made yeomen and, in turn, tenant families even more dependent upon both that trade with the outside world and the local merchants who conducted it for part of the goods they required to sustain themselves. At the same time, these groups lived in an interdependent local economy in which local exchanges of goods and services provided much of their basic necessities. It was this interdependency that even Elizabeth Lawson, whose letter opens this chapter, recognized.

This inequality of economic opportunity and the fact that some of the more affluent had the means not only to profit by wartime circumstances but to do so by taking advantage of the very consumers most at their mercy provoked the strongest resentment. Alfred W. Bell expressed the anger many of his fellow citizens of Franklin felt at a particularly egregious example of such profiteering at their expense. He reported to Governor Vance on the activities of a H. W. Nolen, a Massachusetts native who had settled in the area just before the war, who was "carrying on the shoe and boot business" and charging customers "twice the pr ct. allowed by law" for this most basic of necessities.

> The citizens have been very much enraged at his course, having completely monopolized the shoe business, he bought up all the leather he could, made it into shoes & sold it to the citizens and soldiers at high figures—they being compelled to buy. He has been speculating in Brandy, and in fact in everything he has been engaged in, extortioning upon the poor wives of soldiers by selling them shoes at astonishing rates. . . . It does not look right that this Yankee pet should be permitted to extortion and amass a fortune

off of those who are defending our rights, when the County is demanding and entitled to his services it should have them.

Bell went on to inquire about what he heard was a policy put in place by Vance by which anyone overcharging more than 75 percent for goods or services would be subject to conscription. Apparently, Nolen had made himself exempt by petitioning for the postmaster's position in Franklin.[36]

In complete contrast to the concerns of the rural agricultural community that characterized most of the North Carolina mountain society during the war was an attempt made by local businessmen and the Confederate government to introduce a major industrial enterprise into the region. The primary impetus for this business came from local entrepreneurs in the region's largest town. As early as July 1861, William L. Henry of Asheville was corresponding with Governor Henry T. Clark proposing to manufacture "Rifle guns" for the Confederacy.[37] Nothing came of that particular venture, but the idea of constructing an arms factory was not forgotten. It was resuscitated when Col. Robert W. Pulliam became the agent for the Confederate Ordnance Bureau in his home region of western North Carolina in August 1861. Pulliam contracted with a company in which he had a financial interest to assist him with the task of obtaining and repairing small arms. His fellow entrepreneurs were Col. Ephiram Clayton and Dr. George Whitson of Asheville. Clayton, who specialized in producing finished timber and directing small construction projects was put in charge of adapting his large wood planing building to function as a gun factory.[38]

Like most businessmen in the mountains at this time, Pulliam, Clayton, and Whitson ran their organization with a minimum of structure. Pulliam, for example, did not submit his contract to Richmond for approval, and he purchased all of his supplies locally and without authorization. In addition, he ran the fiscal side of the business out of his store and often issued store script instead of currency for wages.[39] According to a list Pulliam submitted to Confederate authorities in November 1862, 107 workers were employed at the factory. Not surprisingly, 87 of the workers were eligible for the Confederate draft and 8 others were subject to service in the state militia.[40] Although these figures do not demonstrate that his primary motive for starting the business was to provide a safe haven for men evading the draft, there is little doubt that workers were attracted to the business by the draft exemption extended to them. In January 1862, this concern was functioning well enough to start producing rifles. All of this was revealed to an astonished Josiah Gorgas, chief of Confederate Ord-nance, in November 1862 when A. A. King, master armorer of the Asheville factory, wrote to inquire where he should ship 200 rifles recently completed at the works. The meticulous Gorgas was stunned to discover in the center of the Confederacy this arms producing factory, whose existence was previously un-known to him.[41]

Gorgas immediately dispatched W. S. Downer, superintendent of armories, to inspect the plant and to report back to him. Downer's report was devastating. He stated: "Mr. Pulliam has a great deal of private business to attend to, which from what I can learn, keeps him absent from the Armory the greater portion of the time." Downer's assessment of Whitson was equally unnerving: "He is a gentleman of general genius but no practical knowledge of mechanics," but he had nevertheless directed part of the operations of the rifle making until re-cently. The workers were no better at their work. The dismayed Downer relayed to Gorgas that "the tools and machines . . . were mere makeshifts and the work carried on almost at the discretion of the men employed." The result was that "the guns were made worthless and the labor performed . . . worse than thrown away."[42] It is probable that Pulliam and his associates were not deliberately defrauding the Confederate government. They were simply doing business in the casual manner that had been acceptable to their regular moun-tain customers. It was most unusual for managers and workers in highland commercial establishments to be highly skilled specialists. Instead, alike the farming population they served, highlanders found that talented generalists—jack-of-all-trades—were more useful to the local economy than were highly skilled specialists in a single trade.

Clearly, the Confederacy could not afford to allow resources to be used in this manner. Within a month, Capt. Benjamin Sloan was appointed to assume command of the newly discovered works. Sloan, a former Confederate Ord-nance inspector at the large Tredegar Works outside of Richmond, understood how a modern factory should be organized.[43] Unlike the small businesses started in Haywood, Jackson, and Macon Counties before the war, which were characterized as "small, poorly capitalized, [and] short-lived," the armory was well capitalized and attracted a large labor force.[44] Sloan estimated that in the first three months of operation he would require $32,000 to run the armory. Among the larger items in the budget were $18,000 for "Labor & Stock fab-ricating new rifles," $6,500 for "Pur. & fabrication for new machy. & Tools," and $1,000 for "Completing New Smithery." Sloan's total request for funds,

which included start-up costs, for April through June 1863 rose to nearly
$46,000.[45] The commander's first task was to complete the building of two
brick structures to house parts of the manufacturing process and to secure the
machine tools necessary to fabricate the weapons. Sloan reported to Gorgas on
April 15, 1863, that all of the tools and machines needed to begin production
had been assembled at the armory.[46] Now all that was needed was an adequate
workforce and the raw and finished materials necessary to produce rifles.

Having a skilled workforce was essential for the manufacture of rifles in the
Confederacy. Because each factory had its own set of specially created tools (as
was obviously the case at Asheville), "Confederate guns were all practically
hand-made, with very little interchangeability of parts."[47] To help secure an
adequate workforce, Sloan reappointed Clayton to a key managerial position
overseeing "all Carpenters work and control of the teams and teamsters, wood
choppers, Coal Burners and saw mill hands." Sloan defended his choice of
Clayton to Gorgas by noting his "knowledge of the people and his influence
with them." Further considerations were that the main building of the armory
was Clayton's reconditioned planing factory and the armory was located on his
land.[48]

Clayton's role was absolutely crucial because many of the local men had
never worked in a carefully structured environment with rules governing many
of the work practices. For example, Sloan found it necessary to decree that
workmen would no longer receive their pay at Pulliam's store. A couple of
months later, an obviously irritated Sloan announced that workers who left their
work area without permission of their foreman and the master armorer were to
forfeit double their pay for the time missed.[49] Many workers were unable to
accept the demands placed upon them by the new workplace. Of the approximately 123 workers employed by the armory in January 1863, Sloan fired 20.[50]
This 16 percent enforced turnover in one month was most likely an indication of
the resistance on the part of many local men to the new discipline required by
factory work.

Since most of the workers at the armory were subject to conscription and
would be liable for military duty if they lost their positions, a semblance of
discipline was maintained among the factory workers. The men worked a ten-
hour day during the winter and an eleven-hour day during the summer, when
there was more daylight. They apparently were expected to work on Saturday
but were granted time and a half when they worked longer hours and double
time for any Sunday work. They were paid on a sliding scale of daily wages that

varied from $5.15 for a foreman to as little as $1.00 for an unskilled laborer. A teamster with his own wagon and four horses could earn as much as $8.00 a day.[51] Even considering the high rate of inflation that plagued the Confederacy, these wages were very substantial, especially considering the fact that a private in the Confederate army was paid $11 a month. The major problem that these workers faced was finding adequate housing. Asheville was a small town of fewer than 1,000 persons in 1860. The result was that "[t]here are no houses rented by the Govt. which can be used by the operatives." Instead, many of them were forced to stay at the only hotel, which charged a monthly rent of $12 a room. These high housing costs and the rapid increase in inflation led to periodic increases in compensation for armory workers and price increases for suppliers.[52]

Despite the ample wages and the threat of conscription, Sloan found it difficult to retain an adequate workforce. Part of the reason was that Sloan proved to be inefficient in sending workers who had lost their jobs into the army, as he was expected to do. To secure a more compliant workforce, Sloan, as many elite Southerners had done for more than two centuries, turned to hiring African Americans. He placed an advertisement in the *Asheville News* to hire "Ten negro men" in March 1863.[53] Black workers were resented, however, by the local community that suddenly found itself overwhelmed by the number of slaves who had escaped into the mountains or who were moved in from low-lying areas by their masters.[54] Allen, a slave hired out to the armory by his owner, W. F. M. Galbraith of Yorkville, South Carolina, was severely whipped by a mob on the evening of January 13, 1863, when the local ruffians caught him walking the streets of Asheville without a "pass" from his employer. Allen had run away from the armory for one day, but as Captain Sloan reassured Galbraith, he soon returned and proved to be a reliable worker.[55]

Even with a more reliable workforce, Sloan's problems did not abate. Many of the mountain workers at the factory were forced to master a skill. They were divided into four departments—"Locks, Stocks and Machine, Smith shop, and Barrel."[56] Each of these specializations was directly related to the production of rifles, the chief function of the armory. In addition, the armory required substantial numbers of employees to purchase supplies, cut wood, haul materials, and perform other nonmanufacturing tasks that allowed the factory to function. These other jobs included completing construction work on the three buildings that made up the factory complex. Correspondence found in the armory's letterbook indicates that skilled personnel were scarce and difficult to retain.

Even when all personnel were in place, Captain Sloan could not guarantee that they would be able to work. As defense of the operation became a priority, Sloan and his workers were forced to take time from their intense production schedule to insure that their facility was safe from hostile raiders. Just a few weeks after he took over, Sloan requested weapons for his workers from the government in Richmond. The Unionist raid on nearby Marshall in early January 1863 to secure salt and other supplies denied them by their Confederate neighbors alarmed Asheville's residents, who assumed that further raids would be directed at them.[57] In response, Sloan reported: "The operatives have been organized into a company to resist any attempt to destroy Government Property at this place, by disloyal persons." Five months later, Sloan was appealing to Richmond for some artillery, which he felt would be most useful to "intimidate the disloyal."[58]

Although the loss of production was a major concern for the worried commander, it was not the only one. Sloan reported to his superiors that "many of these men indeed will embrace the first opportunity of joining the enemy."[59] Sloan's suspicions of his workers' loyalties were exacerbated by three peace meetings held in the Asheville area in July and August 1863.[60] While these gatherings were technically protests against Confederate policies, they were generally viewed as welcoming the end of the war, even if it meant the loss of Southern independence. Thus, even under the best of circumstances, the workforce at the Asheville Armory must be judged as poorly prepared both in skills and motivation to perform their tasks efficiently.

Even if the dubious loyalty and lack of industrial discipline could be overcome, there was no guarantee that the rifles would be produced in great numbers. Sloan's successor, Captain C. C. McPhail, was asked to evaluate the workers in December 1863, and he concluded: "There are, I find, very few first class workmen among the employees here, they are mostly novices & learning the various branches of the profession." Earlier, Sloan himself had fired an engineer at the plant for "repeated and dangerous neglect of duty."[61] There is no reason to doubt McPhail's assessment, and the general absence of industrial skills among mountain workers was a formidable barrier to the construction of other manufacturing entities requiring trained workers. This incompetence was not limited to workers at the immediate site. The most glaring example was the poor performance of the company that produced pig iron, the most critical material used at the armory. McKinna and Orr (which eventually became McKinna and Patton) operated a small mill owned by Leonard Cagle in the Davidson's

River community of Henderson County. Sloan was displeased with both their labor and their product and at one point dismissed all of their employees and ordered them into the army. Apparently he did not follow through on this threat because they were still contractors when McPhail took over. In his usually frank manner, McPhail assessed their performance: "The quality of your iron is, I must say, miserable, arising from palpable neglect & want of exercise of proper attention & skill in forging it. The quantity also falls below what might be reasonably expected."[62]

A second and equally vexing conundrum the embattled commanders of the Asheville Armory faced was the transportation system that served the arms factory. Since western North Carolina did not provide many of the raw materials and finished products needed to manufacture rifles, these supplies had to be brought in from outside the region. The most efficient way was to transport the goods by rail to the edge of the mountains in eastern Tennessee, upper South Carolina, or Burke or Rutherford Counties in North Carolina. From there they would have to travel by "stage line" to Asheville. At best this was a cumbersome system, and under the pressures of the war, transportation in the mountains became even more problematic. Sloan and McPhail were forced to approach local suppliers whenever possible, and they often proved to be unreliable and recalcitrant. Pulliam's tanning company, Gains and Deaver, was one example. The owner of this concern refused to do business with the armory after he was replaced as one of the armory's directors. As a result, most of the armory's employees were forced to go without shoes during the harsh mountain winter of 1862–63.[63]

Even when local suppliers did agree to furnish needed items, Sloan and his successor could not count on the contract being carried out. This was particularly true in regard to foodstuffs. Volunteering and conscription removed many of the farm workers from the population, and production of food supplies began to decline significantly. By 1863, the threat of starvation was quite substantial in many sections of North Carolina. Under these circumstances it is not surprising that both Sloan and McPhail resorted to threats to obtain the food for which they had previously contracted.[64] Sloan even resorted to the strategy of prepaying for part of a farmer's crop as an inducement for him to sign contracts with the armory. Even this expedient was not sufficient to insure a steady supply of food and fodder for the armory. Sloan was forced to contract with out-of-state farmers to supply the goods he was unable to obtain in western North Carolina. This strategy was only partially successful because of the wretched transportation system. When the factory was able to purchase corn from a South Carolina farmer, Sloan was forced to pay the man to store the grain until the commander could obtain a sufficient number of wagons to transport the foodstuffs.[65]

No sooner had the armory reached a relatively acceptable rate of production in the summer of 1863 than the exigencies of war intervened and halted production. With the Union occupation of Knoxville under Ambrose Burnside in early September, the civilian population of Asheville panicked. Assuming that Burnside's next objective would be the factory complex in their own city, they deluged Governor Vance with demands that the armory be better defended or closed.[66] Captain Sloan apparently was similarly anxious and wrote to Gorgas suggesting "the propriety of removing the Government Machinery from Asheville to some safer place." He followed that letter with one directed to the director of Confederate conscription in North Carolina in which he released nearly his entire workforce to the army.[67]

When it became apparent that Burnside had neither the means nor the intent to move on Asheville right away, Sloan attempted to resume a lower level of production while preparing for a quick exit if necessary. Josiah Gorgas had become increasingly dissatisfied with Sloan's management of the operation, so he replaced him with C. C. McPhail. McPhail had no time to restore the factory to full production because late in October a raid by Union army forces from Tennessee on nearby Warm Springs convinced the new supervisor that the armory continued to be a magnet for the enemy. On October 24, he ordered the "master armorer" to dismantle the machinery and prepare it for transport to another site, which Gorgas would soon decide to make Columbia, South Carolina. With the release of the few workers remaining by the end of the month, the Asheville Armory was closed.[68]

Since the enterprise was ended by military rather than economic considerations, one must speculate as to the financial viability of this first attempt to introduce a large manufacturing concern west of the Blue Ridge in North Carolina. It is quite clear that this manufacturing complex was well capitalized for its time period. In 1863 alone, the Confederacy invested approximately $192,000 in equipment, supplies, and labor.[69] Despite this substantial infusion of capital, the armory ran a deficit each month for which an accounting was recorded. For nine months in 1863, the deficit beyond what the Confederacy had already invested was $167,000.[70] Despite this unprecedented investment of resources, the factory did not achieve high production rates at any time in its existence. The maximum output of the 150 to 200 workers at the armory complex was 200 rifles a month (which it appears was rarely achieved, since only 900 rifles were produced by the armory).[71]

Although the pressures and inefficiencies of war explain some of the problems faced by this manufacturing unit, it would appear that if the armory had been a private business it would have failed financially. Since no entity in the South except the Confederate government would have made this large an investment in manufacturing in western North Carolina before the appearance of the railroads, this episode appears to confirm that the region was simply not capable of supporting such an enterprise. Although this experiment was a failure in many respects, it did inspire others to attempt to invest in the region. Other enterprising souls were willing to build a powder mill in Asheville to complement the armory. And a man writing from Madison County called on Governor Vance to support the creation of textile mills in the region only six months after the armory closed.[72]

The 220 pages of records kept by the commanding officers at the armory do confirm many of the observations made by other inhabitants of the region. First and foremost, they show that supplies of many necessities were very scarce in western North Carolina. Foodstuffs, leather, horses, and iron all had to be imported from elsewhere. When supplies were purchased, the transaction was on a strict cash basis, which seems to confirm that the region was well attuned to the workings of the market economy. The willingness of many men to forsake their farms and accept factory wages further confirms the basically commercial outlook of the mountain dwellers. At the same time, the employees' sloppy work habits and unwillingness to accept the discipline of the shop floor, as well as the management's lack of quality control, indicate that highlanders had not yet absorbed the mentality of an industrial workforce. While those who worked in the armory benefited financially and were able to provide for their families, their presence in the region may have harmed many other residents. Because these factory hands had a relatively large amount of cash on hand, they undoubtedly contributed to the rapid inflation that took place.

If these factory workers were able to avoid, for a few months midway through the war at least, the economic devastation that took its toll on the vast majority of Carolina highlanders, they were not the only ones in the region to do so. Much of the landholding and commercial elite of western North Carolina weathered the war with far less hardship or suffering than did many of their neighbors. Those who had access to slaves or other forms of purchased labor often profited from their use, and some of them did so in unscrupulous ways. In addition, the families in which a member had a marketable skill that was highly valued or had accumulated substantial holdings before the war found it much easier to obtain basic necessities, and even luxuries on occasion.

One couple, whose wartime experience can be re-created in considerable detail, serves to illustrate how some families could manage to hold their place among the elite without problem. Mary and Alfred Bell of Macon County actually improved their economic and social status over the course of the war. Married in 1856, the Bells moved from northeast Georgia to Alfred's former home in Franklin, Macon County's seat, just before the war began. Alfred was a dentist, and he opened a lucrative practice in Franklin, as well as joining his father's jewelry and clock-making business. Mary and Alfred bought a house in the village and a farm outside of town. Alfred turned over most of his farmland to two tenants, whose activities he closely supervised.[73] Although Alfred joined the Confederate army with his own company of local men in November 1861 and remained in service for most of the war, Mary was able to retain the two tenants on their farm and even purchased slaves for the first time. Apparently, Alfred had accumulated sufficient cash reserves, the Bells had access to scarce labor, and Mary proved to be an able enough manager that they never suffered the severe deprivations that many yeoman families did.

Mary proved particularly adept at handling cash transactions, all of which she regularly reported to Alfred. She agreed to pay a local man to cut wood for her for $0.75 a month in early 1862, repaired a soldier's watch for the princely sum of $20 in mid-1862, and credited an account for $1.64 for the sale of two hams at the end of that year.[74] But she also grew more and more self-assured in conducting other types of business as well. She was especially proud of her skill at bartering, which, as the war went on, became an increasing—but never exclusive—means of doing business locally. She became more proficient and confident in handling often complex transactions that sometimes involved a variety of currencies as well as produce. Her April 1864 report provides a typical example of the descriptions of negotiations she sent to her husband. The report also confirms the community dependency and intricate local trade network and credit system that had been instigated at least in part by the exigencies of the war in the Carolina highlands. "John McConnel has paid me five bushel [of corn] and says that I will have to wait until he goes south after corn before he can pay me anymore," Mary wrote. "Mr. Lores Ell owes me 4 bushels for Apples which he promised to bring this week but has not done yet. Alfred and Simeon still owes me the 4 bushels they have not brought any corn yet. Alfred sent me two hames which I credited on the old account which leaves him $1.64 in debt. Albert has only paid 1 ¼ bushels which leaves him in debt 3 ¾ bushels, Joe 2 ½ bushels, Arthur 1 bushels, Adie McConnel 1 ½ bushels." In the same letter, Mary also describes her attempts to get payment for corn sold on credit to a neighboring woman, payment of which was to include dried fruit; her unsuccessful attempts to obtain straw from some of the people who still owed her for corn; and a neighbor's payment of a past debt in wheat, freshly milled into what she reported was good flour.[75] By December she was swapping cows with Amanda Cunningham and had made a deal in which she took particular pride: she traded a calf to Benny Dobsom for his sow that should have young piglets within the next two months. "I want to raise my own meat," she wrote to Alf, and two men told her "they would have give two such calves for such a hog." One of them, Mary boasted, "says I can Cheat!"[76]

In addition, prominent lowland families, many of whom had long enjoyed summer homes in the Carolina highlands, moved into the area for the war's duration and brought substantial resources with them. These included the family of Confederate secretary of the treasury Christopher G. Memminger, who retreated to his estate in Flat Rock,[77] and that of Confederate general Leonidas Polk, who recognized early that Louisiana would be an inhospitable area for a wealthy pro-Confederate family. Polk selected Asheville as a safe haven for his wife and adolescent children. His daughter Katherine described their stay in Asheville in almost idyllic terms: "My Father always thoughtful & provident had some twenty excellent negro men & their families brought that sommer [sic] from the plantation in Miss. I think Mack brought them on—these my Brother hired to neighboring farmers, their wages to be paid in supplies of Bacon, wheat, flour, potatoes, etc.; in that way provisions for the family were secured so long as hostilities lasted."[78]

Since many of these pampered elite settled in a few villages in the mountain region, rural highlanders came to see these resort communities as centers of prosperity compared to their own, bleak surroundings. The salt raid by men from Shelton Laurel on the town of Marshall was just one manifestation of individuals acting on this perception. Local newspaper advertisements often reflected the affluence of the residents in certain towns. In the *Asheville News* in November 1864, for example, just as the Confederate nation and economy came crashing down, merchant J. M. Blair announced that he had for sale French flannel, English calico, Irish linen, and "Gent[lemen's] Lamb's Wool Drawers."[79]

Although there appeared to be few visible changes in the region's economy when the conflict ended, several important developments had occurred. Many households and communities had suffered the permanent loss—through death or injury—of crucial members of their economic teams. The difficulties created by this situation were compounded by the animosities between individuals, families, and communities created by the events of the war. Deflation and currency shortages caused by the freeing of the slaves and the repudiation of Confederate money added to difficulties facing those who sought to return to the enterprises that had sustained their families before the fighting. In addition, the war reinforced the growing tendency for trade patterns to follow along rail lines. Thus as the South sought to industrialize after the war, western North Carolina farmers and businessmen were increasingly cut off from the growing trade that took place. Western North Carolina towns remained small and underdeveloped, while Atlanta, Knoxville, and Charlotte expanded rapidly. Although the mountain counties were generally able to avoid the growing dependency of many parts of the South on cotton production, there is little question that the region was economically weakened by the war. In addition, much of the social cohesion that characterized mountain economic communities before the war had been destroyed.

WOMEN AT WAR

Assuming All the Duties of the Sterner Sex

L ATE in the summer of 1863, an anonymous "Voice from Cherokee County" wrote a letter to the *North Carolina Standard* in Raleigh, bemoaning the oppressive impact of Confederate policy on the state's mountain region. He paid tribute to the highlanders he maintained were most victimized by those hardships—the women, that "class of beings entitled to the deepest sympathy of the Confederate government . . . the wives, children, mothers, sisters and widows" left behind by the troops fighting for the Southern cause. This voice from the state's westernmost county went on to extol "the thousand instances of women's patriotism, in resigning without a murmur the being in whom her affections centered, to all the horrors of war, who after her husband's departure, uncomplainingly assume all the duties of the sterner sex; accompanied by her little brood, labor from morn to night in the corn-field, or wield the axe to fell the sturdy oak."[1] The glorification of Confederate womanhood was obviously well under way by the war's midpoint and was pervasive enough to have reached one of the most remote parts of the Confederacy. Yet even there, the hyperbole of heroism obscured the actual plight of mountain women. While women did indeed spend much of the war laboring in cornfields, chopping wood, and caring for growing "little broods," they did not always do so "uncomplainingly" or "without a murmur."

As was demonstrated in Chapter 3, highland women were caught up in the same patriotic fervor that swept the state and the region in those heady opening days and weeks of the war. Many of them played vocal and visible roles in the first mobilization efforts of western North Carolina's men as they marched off to Confederate service. But the enthusiasm and unity of purpose that held sway in the spring and summer of 1861 proved ephemeral as the harsh realities of the war's demands soon set in. The strains of war tried mountain women in different ways and to different degrees, and their varied responses provide important insights into the complexities of the region's wartime experience.

Increasingly, scholars of the Confederacy have turned to the plight of women and its impact on the war effort and have discovered a complex set of circumstances that led Southern women to react to the crisis in a variety of ways. To some historians, they were active and crucial agents in bringing about Southern defeat. According to Drew Gilpin Faust, "Southern women undermined both objective and ideological foundations for the Confederate effort; they directly subverted the South's military and economic effectiveness as well as civilian morale."[2] Faust and other historians have described in detail how Southern women were brutalized by events of the war and have carefully documented their growing disenchantment with and erosion of support for the war effort.[3] Others have stressed the resiliency of women and their growing empowerment as a result of the new responsibilities and independence thrust upon them in the absence of husbands and other manpower.[4]

The full spectrum of mountain women's experiences in and responses to the war confirms the complexities of both the society of which they were a part and the varied ways in which the war effected that society. Women's socio-economic status and geographic location within the region had much to do with determining the extent of their vulnerabilities as they faced the variety of problems that so plagued the region: attack by enemy forces; harassment by deserters and other bushwhackers; social, political, and economic tensions; and most universal of all, varying degrees of material deprivation and scarcity. As demonstrated in Chapter 7, members of the elite slaveholding families in areas relatively insulated from military or paramilitary disruption were often able to maintain their basic lifestyle, and even prosper. The vast majority of mountain families, however, had fewer resources on which to draw and faced starvation and economic ruin. Only in areas subjected to full-scale guerrilla warfare or, by the end of the war, to more traditional military invasion did the upheaval cut across class lines and expose households of all sizes and means alike to the full destructive force of the war.

The beginning of hostilities in 1861 forced women in western North Carolina to confront direct challenges to their normal patterns of life. As their familiar circumstances, routines, and relationships disintegrated, or threatened to disintegrate, they worked hard to preserve the aspects of their lives they most valued. For some women, partnerships with their husbands remained their highest priorities, and early in the war, some wives took extraordinary initiatives to remain with their enlisted spouses. Malinda Blalock, who lived in the Grandfather Mountain area of Watauga County, was sixteen years old when she disguised herself as a soldier, adopted the name Sam, and joined North Carolina's 26th Regiment with her new husband, Keith. Described by a fellow soldier as "a good looking boy . . . weight about 130 pounds, height five feet, four inches," she was apparently successful in disguising her identity for the month or so that the couple served in eastern North Carolina. While she was never under fire, she did share all of the other physical dangers of army life. Only when Keith contracted a rash in their swampy surroundings and acquired a medical discharge did Malinda reveal herself and demand a discharge as well. The muster records for the 26th Regiment include a brief entry: "Mrs. L. M. Blalock, discharged for being a woman."[5]

A Macon County wife simply joined her husband in the field, although the couple's domestic squabbles in camp made the arrangement a short-lived one. According to the account of a fellow enlistee in July 1862, "a certain Mr. McLane, having tried the sweets of married life at home was not willing to surrender his domestic joys on coming into the army and so brought Mrs. McLane along with him" when his company was assigned to duty in East Tennessee. A dispute between the couple over laundry duties led to a public row, "a regular dog and cat fight in which the wife came off as conqueror having placed her antagonist hors du combat by mashing his nose with a bottle." A subsequent trial by his fellow enlistees led to "the loving pair" being confined to the guardhouse until arrangements were made to send Mrs. McLane back home to Macon County.[6]

Malinda Blalock, alias "Sam" Blalock
(Southern Historical Collection, University of North Carolina)

More often, women found themselves taking initiatives in more localized military activity, either offensive or defensive. The very nature of guerrilla warfare often forced women into such unconventional roles. In his study of guerrilla warfare in Civil War Missouri, Michael Fellman wrote: "Disintegration, demoralization, and perverse adaptation engulfed women's behavior and self-conceptions as it assaulted the family and undermined male-female and female-

female . . . relationships." Women "were compelled to participate, which they did with varying degrees of enthusiasm, fear, and rage."[7]

That range of experiences is evident among western North Carolina's women as well. Some sources, such as postwar Southern Claims Commission applications (of which 20 percent of the sixty successful claims by western Carolinians were filed by women) tended to stress the victimization of Unionist women by the Confederate majority in whose midst they lived. The report of Louisa Stiles from Cherokee County was one of the hardest hitting and obviously impressed claims officials, who summed up her case: "The claimant is a widow, and exhibits in her testimony very bitter hostility to the Rebels and for very sufficient reasons. Her husband, two sons, and two brothers were killed by Rebels while in the service of the Union Army, and she was threatened, attacked and robbed by them because of her Union sentiments and associations."[8]

While such traumas forced some women into the depths of despair and desperation, other women, both Unionist and Confederate, rose to the challenge with heroic exploits that earned them prominent places in the local lore that emerged after the war's end. A Haywood County woman risked her life by purposely leading a small militia group into an ambush created by anti-Confederates in the area. The death of one of the men engaged in the ensuing skirmish made a widow out of another local woman and left her eight children fatherless.[9] Cynthia Parker, the wife of Confederate colonel James H. Parker of Sparta, earned widespread acclaim in Alleghany County for a daring intervention in a local skirmish. Alerted by firing guns and riderless horses running in panic through town, she mounted her own horse and rode immediately to the site of the gunfire, where she helped nurse wounded home guardsmen. Later the same day, she retrieved and delivered the town's mail, which had been abandoned by a cowardly courier who had not been willing to put himself within firing range.[10] In mid-1864 some women in Wilkes County were reported to have formed a group that joined with deserters and Unionists and participated in raids on Confederate families in the county.[11]

Many mountain women with Unionist sympathies either acted as lookouts and guides for escaped Federal soldiers or actively abetted their efforts to cross the mountains undetected. They provided food and shelter, gave directions, and even escorted hundreds of fugitives to the safety of Union lines in East Tennessee. The accounts of those on the run, either Confederate deserters or Union escapees from Confederate prison camps, reflect how impressed they were by the strength, resourcefulness, and courage of the women they encoun-

"Meeting with Deserters" (From Drake, Fast and Loose in Dixie*)*

tered. Quite naturally, it was Unionist women who emerged as the most celebrated figures in Federal soldiers' escape narratives. Numerous descriptions of
their actions demonstrate the extent to which women were integral participants
in the subversive activity that undermined Confederate strength in the region.
They were often surprisingly militant, as revealed through a variety of physically or verbally aggressive responses to enemy incursions.[12]

A Federal captain from Wisconsin, J. Madison Drake, recounted an incident
in which a "noble woman," known to him only as Mrs. Estes, discovered him
and his companions as they hid in a ravine near her remotely situated cabin.
"She was a typical woman of the North Carolina mountains," Drake wrote. "No
shadow of fear manifested itself in her somewhat masculine features, as she
boldly advanced toward us." She demanded that the men identify themselves,
warning them that "you must not use deceit or you will be shot down where
you stand. A dozen true rifles are now levelled on you, and if I raise my hand
you will fall dead at my feet." Drake concluded, "We had never met such a
woman . . . certainly the bravest of her sex." Once he and his companions
confirmed their identities as Northerners and assured her that they posed no
threat to her deserter husband, she became a warm and generous ally, taking
them into her cabin, feeding them, and eventually instructing them on the safest
and shortest route to Tennessee.[13]

Women like Mrs. Estes often proved to be among the most outspoken partisans in the region, and fugitive narrators never resisted the temptation to describe their tough-talking devotion to the cause. A "voluble, hatchet-faced, tireless woman" in Cashiers hosted a group of refugees who "listened in amused wonder to the tongue of this seemingly untamed virago, who . . . cursed, in her high-pitched tones, for a pack of fools the men who had brought on the war."[14] According to a Maine native moving through that region, an elderly woman in Henderson County, Aunt Becky, told him: "I ain't afraid of those rebels. I tell them 'you may hang old Aunt Becky if you want to, but with the last breath I draw I will shout, Hurrah for the Union!' "[15]

Local Unionists were aware of the suffering endured by these women and the fortitude with which they faced it, as a would-be poet from Taylorsville acknowledged in a verse sent to Governor Vance:

> Then Chiear up you union ladies bold
> For of your courige must be told
> How youv withstood abuses
> When your property theyd take
> The witty ancers you would make
> That would vanish thir rude forces.[16]

Although such militant women—either Confederate or Unionist—were no doubt a distinct minority, the strains of localized conflict encouraged them to defend themselves and their families in increasingly assertive ways. In a recent study of guerrilla warfare in the Sandy Basin community of western Virginia, Ralph Mann noted that the very nature of such conflict often meant that men and women faced their enemies together and provided mutually supportive roles in which they protected each other and their property.[17] An elderly Unionist who lived in the remote Nolichucky Valley in southwestern North Carolina told a fugitive guest of how well his daughters, "three comely, bright-eyed, lithe but buxom mountain maidens," protected him from conscription. "Old Yank," as he was known, had been harassed by Confederate neighbors, for both his nickname and his well-known sympathies for the Union. During one attempt to force him into Southern service, Old Yank recounted, "I just reached 'round the door and pulled out my Henry rifle, an' my gals understood it an' got their double-barreled shotgouns, an' I just told them boys I had lived too long in the mountains to be scared that way, an' if they . . . laid hand on an ole man like me they'd never do it agin, fur my gals had the bead on 'em."[18]

Reports by state and Confederate officials confirmed that growing numbers of mountain women encouraged their more vulnerable husbands, fathers, and sons to hide out in nearby wilderness areas while they remained at home to protect them from hostile Confederate conscription officers or Union raiders. In a curious reversal of gender roles, women stood on the front lines of the home front as guardians of their homes and of the men who could not risk doing so themselves.

The letters of Cornelia Henry provide a rare example of the communication between husband and wife that captures the essence of women's roles as informants, advisers, and co-conspirators. William Lewis Henry was forced to hide in the woods near his Haywood County farm when a raid by George Kirk and his men moved into their area in January 1865. Although only a few hundred yards separated the couple, Cornelia wrote William a lengthy letter alerting him to the danger he was in and urging him to escape. "Oh papa, for my sake and our children's sake leave tonight if you can possibly get through," she urged him. A neighbor had reported that "there was 15 Yankees at the Murry place this morning" and that they "are on the watch for you." Apparently, William Henry had driven away hogs confiscated by Kirk's men, and Cornelia informed him that "they intend to kill you." She gave him very specific advice on how to make his escape: "Trust no one but keep away from the house. . . . Stay where you are for fear they will catch you. Go lie in some thicket till you leave and try to leave tonight. . . . I will not be easy till I know you are gone. May God protect you and watch over you in this trying hour. Stay away from the road. Go way off. . . . Disguise yourself and pass under a fictitious name. Oh yes, leave and try to get out." Cornelia assured William that she was safe and that "if the enemy occupy the country long I will try to come out to you some way as soon as I am able." As to the great length of her missive, she told her husband, "I can't quit writing, you are so dear to me."[19]

Cornelia Henry escaped physical harm by her husband's pursuers, but other wives and mothers faced with the same responsibilities for protecting their men were not as fortunate. In the 1930s, a Madison County man told of his grandmother's experience. Her husband had gone to join Union forces in Tennessee, but home guards, "the hatefullest, most thievin' bunch there ever was," were convinced that he "was home layin' out." In an attempt to force his wife to reveal his hiding place, they dragged her out of her house, placed her fingers between two fence rails, and walked along the top one. When that torture failed to evoke any information, they turned on her five-year-old son, threatening to hack his dog to death with an axe if he didn't tell where his father was. When he refused, they made good on their threat.[20]

Likewise, there was little gender distinction in the torture Confederate troops inflicted on Unionists in the Shelton Laurel community of Madison County. As noted in Chapter 5, soldiers seeking information as to the whereabouts and activity of local "Tories" in Shelton Laurel subjected their wives and even elderly mothers to extreme measures of brutality. Both an eighty-five-year-old and a seventy-year-old woman were among several women whipped, beaten, and bound to trees (in some cases suspended by nooses around their necks) in efforts to make them disclose the whereabouts of their sons.[21] In defending such actions later, Col. James Keith admitted only to the whippings, which he justified both on the grounds of their effectiveness in extorting information from unwilling witnesses and of the women's identities. "These women," Keith wrote, "as well as a large majority of the females in that section are base prostitutes and devoid of moral worth."[22] (Yet this kind of behavior was hardly one-sided. Shelton Laurel Unionists had ransacked Confederate commander Lawrence Allen's home as part of their raid on Marshall. They terrorized his wife, who was home alone with their three sick children, two of whom died shortly thereafter.)[23]

The "temporary hangings" suffered by Shelton Laurel women were inflicted upon women in other areas of western North Carolina as well. In Wilkes County "the Home Guard and a kind of independent company, professing to put down robbery," according to a witness's later report, "have hung women till nearly dead (some of them pregnant), to make them tell on deserters in the County."[24] In Macon County, residents expressed genuine shock that "bushers cutting up back in this country . . . killed Bryon's wife and wounded two of his daughters." "Such men," an acquaintance of the family declared, "ought to be hung by the heels."[25] Cherokee County lore includes the story of Ann Tatham, whose husband was rumored to have gold hidden on their remote farm near Valleytown. An unruly band of men found her home alone and tried to force her to reveal where the gold was hidden. They hanged her from a beam in her kitchen to make her talk. After raising and lowering her four times, she still refused to divulge any information. The accounts of what took place next differ. According to one, her intended executioners departed, leaving her slumped on her floor, presumably dead. Another version made Mrs. Tatham more assertive: after the four hangings, she managed to struggle free of the rope and make her escape to an orchard after shooting one of her torturers.[26]

Confederate cavalry squads who were seeking to confiscate new horses
became much feared for their treatment of women and their random destruction of property. Raiders in Cherokee County terrorized the wife of Unionist
Thomas Runnion with threats that "if she didn't leave they would burn the
house & her in it."[27] According to a complainant in adjacent Jackson County,
both their threats and their "conduct in impressing, lying, & stealing would
make a man conclude that Lincoln's Devils Incarnate was amongst us."[28] These
tactics by soldiers outraged the residents of Alleghany County in the spring of
1864 when "some 5 or 6 of them undertook to rape a very decent white woman
& some of the neighbors heard her screams & immediately went to her assistance and relieved her from their foul hands." The neighbors pursued the
soldiers and engaged them in a brief skirmish in which one person on each side
was killed. Local civilians were upset by the behavior of these cavalrymen, but
infantrymen stationed in the area were enraged and disheartened as well. "The
men who compose this regiment were very nearly all from the western part of
the state," they told Governor Vance, "and it makes them very low spirited to
[know] that they are here defending the cause while our country and own
soldiers are destroying their homes."[29]

Highland women on the westernmost edges of North Carolina were especially vulnerable to attack by Union raiding parties once Federal forces took
control of East Tennessee. Between September 1863 and April 1865, at least six
Union raids across the state line thoroughly disrupted life in a number of
mountain communities and farms. Margaret Walker of the remote settlement of
Valleytown in Cherokee County, only a few miles from the Tennessee border,
recounted a particularly harrowing incident. On October 6, 1864, a party of
twenty-seven Unionists and bushwhackers stormed the Walker home, having
targeted her husband William Walker as the head of the local "home guards"
and in turn assuming he had guns and ammunition stored on the premises.
After ransacking their house and outbuildings, they forced William to accompany them, announcing to Margaret that they were going to execute him. The
following morning, she set out with her sister to follow their trail, hoping more
realistically to recover her husband's body than to save his life. She was unable
to do either and never after learned his fate.[30]

Some women felt they were secure enough in their circumstances to take a
more cavalier, even callous, attitude toward these kind of attacks. Unlike many
of her fellow residents in Macon County, Mary Bell in Franklin claimed to have
had no qualms about one of the most serious enemy incursions into her area. In

February 1864, 250 men of the 1st Wisconsin Cavalry launched a raid from Tennessee into southwestern North Carolina. Although the troops never got closer than twenty miles from Franklin before turning back, its residents panicked at this closest call yet to a military attack by Union forces. By the time Bell reported the incident to her husband, then stationed in Alabama, the excitement had waned and fears had subsided. But she mocked her neighbors—men and women alike—for what she considered vast overreactions. "I guess you have heard," she wrote, "of the great yankee and tory raid we had or at least expected to have. . . . It was the most ridiculous thing I ever heard of. I think evry man in Macon Co., except those that were too old to get away, skidaddled—home guards, preachers, doctors, and all." Mrs. Bell was no more sympathetic toward the frightened women left behind by Franklin's male population in her description of the two or three days in which they had to endure "fine times during yankee holadays." She described a variety of mishaps other women encountered in their efforts to hide their valuables and livestock and safeguard their homes as little more than slapstick. Alfred Bell took just as jocular a tone in his response, noting that "we are glad to hear that the people at home had all escaped the yankees so well by flying to the mountains and staying there untill the women and children ran the yankees back." He later commented: "The home guards of Macon should have a flag presented to them by the ladies for their gallantry."[31]

Of course, only those who had the luxury of viewing enemy attacks from a distance could be so smug. As discussed in Chapter 7, women and children left alone at home were most vulnerable to the economic devastation the war inflicted on so much of the mountain region. Far more wives and mothers struggled to survive starvation than the abuses of hostile troops. In waging their often desperate war against poverty, however, they had ready support of the noblesse oblige of county officials and more affluent neighbors, whose relief efforts to "indigent wives of soldiers" kept many families alive through the bleak winters of the midwar years. But foodstuffs for distribution were sometimes in short supply, and not all families were granted equal access to it. The loyalties of household heads were often the criteria by which his family was deemed worthy of relief.

By late in the war, some of the women who either were denied county aid or found it woefully inadequate mobilized to take more drastic measures to feed themselves and their children. Replicating the bread riots in Richmond and other Confederate cities in the spring of 1863, about fifty Yancey County women broke into a Confederate warehouse in Burnsville in April 1864 and carried off sixty bushels of "Government wheat." The women's success inspired a male raid on Burnsville the following day. A "band of tories" consisting of seventy-five men attacked both a magazine and a commissary, taking arms and ammunition and some 500 pounds of bacon. "The county is gone up!" bemoaned the commander of the home guard brigade in that region.[32]

In January 1865, women raided graineries in Hamptonville and Jamesville in Yadkin County. In a report of the latter incident to her aunt, Lizzie Lenoir in neighboring Wilkes County provided a vivid description of the Jamesville raid and why it failed: "[A] band of *women*, armed with axes, came down in the place to press the tithe corn, &tc., brought wagons to carry it off. There was only one man in the place, and he (Leonidas like) stood in the door of the house and bid defiance to the crowd. You know women generally want to carry their point, and it was with great difficulty that our hero could withstand them. They were happily thrown into confusion by an old drunk man coming up with a huge *brush* in his hand, striking their horses with it, causing them to run away with their wagons and some of *them* in it." She concluded smugly, "They didn't get any of the corn."[33]

Lizzie's amusement reflects her lack of empathy for the desperate plight of the wives and mothers driven to such drastic measures. Her commentary on the earlier, more successful Hamptonville raid reflects the partisanship behind her lack of sympathy. In this incident the women "took as much as they wanted without meeting any resistance. They were doubtless instigated to this unbecoming behavior by *men*, who were afraid to undertake the scheme themselves. Deserters perhaps or distillers." "The degeneracy of the times," she concluded, "is truly alarming."[34]

Much of that degeneracy was due to the breakdown of local institutional sources of support. Often still in formative stages when the war began and further weakened by war-related turmoil, these traditional outlets proved woefully inadequate in meeting the increasingly critical needs of women and their families. Religious organizations played a diminished role in mountain life during the war, despite a spiritual revival that swept through the Confederacy. Some churches simply closed their doors as more and more clergy were called into service. In September 1862, a Wilkes County petition to Governor Vance informed him that the "Churches in the county is left allmost without ministers so many of them has gone to volunteer in the service." A year later, conscription efforts meant that even fewer clergymen remained at home. A report in November 1863 indicated that only twenty-one ministers in the region had been exempted from Confederate service, leaving more than four hundred congregations in the state's twenty westernmost counties in need of their services.[35] Despite the increased efforts of these few men to divide their time among as many congregations as they could, they held fewer and fewer services.

In the early months of the war, ministers had been instrumental in providing support for and sustaining morale among the women in their congregations. The many women who were, as the war continued, eventually deprived of such reassurances, or even of the regular interaction with other women at Sunday services, therefore, found the loss significant.[36] The absence of both ministers and laymen potentially could have afforded an opportunity for women to play a greater role in congregational affairs, but the necessities of the moment could not overcome ingrained traditions of gender restrictions within church organizations. The Silver Creek District of the Primitive Baptists, for example, opened its quarterly meetings to all male members in order to avoid gender-integrated sessions.[37]

The church was not the only institution that provided decreased levels of support to women and their children during the war years. A shortage of instructors forced a number of highland communities to abandon their schools. And although the state government urged that women be hired to replace departed male teachers, the little evidence available about mountain education during the war indicates that there was no dramatic change in teacher employment patterns.[38] Even though a number of women had taught in mountain schools before the war, there were so few of them in the three hundred district schools in the region that they alone were unable to keep the schools open once the war was under way.[39] The Holston Conference Female College (actually a Methodist academy) in Asheville faced great pressure to close during the war.[40]

Like churches and schools, local governments also lacked the resources to remedy the growing problems that their constituents experienced. As early as the spring of 1862, Henderson County officials found it difficult to purchase food for the poor. Speculation in grains and other foodstuffs had driven prices so high that county officials did not have the resources to provide for every needy family. Two years later, the problem was even more pervasive. A Jackson County woman reported to Governor Vance circumstances typical of many mountain communities: "Our county agent the Rev Wm Hicks told the people at church last Sunday that he could not provide food for the wants of suffering familys . . . and they must look out for themselves."[41] Thus many women dis-

covered that the communities that had supported them economically and provided them with some measure of physical security could no longer do either.

That breakdown contributed to the variety of stresses that forced some
mountain women, both Confederate and Union, to actually flee their homes.
Although few in number compared to the massive displacement that took place
in other parts of the Confederacy, some women and their families became
refugees, often moving to live with kin or neighbors elsewhere in the region or
beyond. Such upheaval proved demoralizing and even debilitating for many,
even when such a move was short term and of little distance.

Several Haywood County women retreated to the homes of family or friends
in Asheville after a series of raids in their area late in 1864. Just after Christmas,
Cornelia Henry wrote to her young son that his Aunt Jane and her baby "had
been driven from her home by the mean old yankees and tories." She went on
the describe the Christmas treats his siblings, still at home, had enjoyed and
assured him that "the yankees have not got Santa Clause yet!" Much more frank
in an accompanying letter to her sister-in-law Dora in South Carolina, Cornelia
confided of "Sister Jane" that "the yanks have treated her badly. She looks old
and care worn." Cornelia then went on to reveal her own emotional fragility.
"Oh, Dora!" she wrote, "if this war last one year longer I shall be prematurely
old . . . it really seems to me sometimes I can't stand it. I am afraid I shall be a
lunatic when this war is over." Referring to the continued absence of her
husband and the uncertainty of his return, she concluded, "Oh! Tis perfect
agony. My life is no pleasure to me at all."[42]

The wives and families of known Unionists suffered far harsher displacement
experiences; they were often forced from their homes and communities by the
threats and harassment of their own neighbors. Mary Orr of Transylvania
County suffered a particularly harrowing experience. When her husband abandoned Confederate service early in 1863 and, along with her father, joined a
Union company that formed locally and headed for East Tennessee, Mary and
her newborn baby took to the road with other family members, an ordeal she
endured until August 1864. She later recalled the experience: Mary and her
sister-in-law were milking cows when they saw a distant crowd moving toward
them. Her initial fright at the approach of such a mob subsided as it came close
enough for her to recognize the group as her own mother and her nine children.
Poverty and local harassment at home in nearby Henderson County drove her
mother to attempt a move to Knoxville with her children to "join the Yankees,"
which her husband, Mary's father, had done. Mary joined the expedition,

reasoning that "my husband is there and my mother is going, and the 'Rebs' will starve us to death and what do I want to stay here for?" Faced with rough terrain, raging rivers, and roaming Confederate troops and home guards, the band of twelve women and children proceeded slowly across the mountains. Seeking food and shelter from a variety of hosts, rich and poor, friendly and hostile, Orr and her family eventually crossed into Tennessee and reunited with her husband and father. She wrote later, "There is no one knows the trials and hardships of the Southern men and women, except those who endured it."[43]

Mary was far less bitter than many highland women forced from their homes. In an 1887 memoir, a Union private who served at a refugee camp for Unionist civilians in Alabama wrote of the Appalachian women who had sought safe haven there and their determination that the Confederate neighbors from whom they had fled would pay dearly for their intolerance. "I heard them repeat over and over to their children the names of men which they were never to forget, and whom they were to kill when had sufficient strength to hold a rifle," he recalled. "These women, who have been driven from their homes by the most savage warfare our country has been cursed with . . . impressed me as living wholly to revenge their wrongs."[44]

Class distinctions often colored women's refugee experiences. The resources one could bring to such a move determined how bearable it proved to be, and the advantages of privilege often offset the traumas of displacement. Asheville, Hendersonville, and Flat Rock continued to be a haven for planter women and their families from lowland South Carolina and other parts of the South who were seeking a comfortable retreat from which to ride out the conflict. Mary Chesnut was one of several women who moved back into the area for extended stays. Katherine Polk's sojourn with her family to Asheville from their Mississippi plantation in the fall of 1862 offers a striking contrast to the experiences of Mary Orr or Cornelia Henry. In the carefree life it describes Polk's account of their stay in the region's largest and most affluent community appears to be unique among wartime journals. She referred to the community as "a beautiful little village among the mountains of western N. Carolina," where "by degrees, the family gathered," and she noted that they settled into a very large house that her father had rented in advance, which "proved extremely comfortable & restful after all the weary wanderings." Her brother hired two local farmers to provide all of the provisions for their family "so long as hostilities lasted," their efforts no doubt aided by the twenty slaves and their families they brought along. Katherine extolled the beautiful scenery, delightful climate, and the lively social life in which she had settled: "We met some extremely agreeable people in Asheville, great hospitality was shown us by people in the town & in the surrounding country, many charming friendships were formed."[45] Although she described the shattering of that idyllic existence when Union troops moved into Asheville in the war's final days, few other women in the region were enjoying life as much at the war's midpoint.

In other respects as well, elite women throughout the region were spared many of the hardships and traumas of their less fortunate highland compatriots. With some significant exceptions already noted in earlier chapters, few of the region's wealthier households were ever subjected to the same levels of physical violence or even threats that so many of those of more modest means were forced to suffer. The mistresses of such households did not suffer the same degree of economic deprivation and desperation that other women did, nor were they daunted by the new responsibilities thrust upon them. In a recent study of women in antebellum Yancey County, anthropologist Mary Anglin reminds us that many women were capable of running farms unaided. The 1860 census lists thirty households headed by women; from more detailed statistics for eleven of those households, Anglin discovered that these women adopted a variety of strategies to survive. Two of them had access to male slave labor and were able to run relatively large agricultural operations that produced above average amounts of fruits and grains. Another woman farmer who proved more successful than her male counterparts in her agricultural output of livestock and grain was sixty-five years old and operated her concern with no male assistance.[46] Such examples indicate that resourceful women in the mountains were capable of surviving wartime challenges as long as circumstances allowed them to adopt peacetime strategies.

Mary Bell of Macon County provides the best documented example of a highland woman who adapted successfully to the exigencies of war. Her skills at financial management of her husband's accounts have already been cited in Chapter 6; but those duties represent only a part of her wartime success story. When her husband, Alfred, raised a company of volunteers and marched off to war in November 1861, Mary was thrust into a position of considerable responsibility. Far more than many women in her situation, she not only rose to the challenges she faced, she was also completely aware of her achievements and took real satisfaction in the growing empowerment that accompanied them.

In addition to the care of her growing family (she bore two children and lost another during the war, which means she was pregnant for over a third of the war), Mary's new responsibilities were as manager of the farm she and her husband, Alf, owned and as fiscal agent for Alf's business interests. Unlike many mountain women thrust into such circumstances, Mary never lacked for male workers on her farm, which was located a mile or so from town, or on her substantial garden plot in town; nor for that matter did she ever lack for male advice. Two tenants—one white, one black—continued to work different sections of the Bell farm under her close supervision. Alf's father and brother, both Franklin residents, were also regular sources of support, advice, and, on occasion, manpower. In November 1861, Mary wrote to Alf in the first of many letters that would be for her a typical combination of reporting and inquiry: "Your father is shucking corn tonight. Tom is done sewing your wheat, he did not sew any rye for you, did you want him to sew some?"[47]

Nevertheless, it is clear from both Mary's and Alf's letters that the bulk of responsibility for both business and farm lay with her. His early letters to her included detailed instructions about how she should deal with a variety of financial concerns, from negotiating with hired hands or, in the case of slaves, with their owners in collecting debts owed him, paying his own debts, and authorizing new loans, most often to men in his company or their wives. During the same period, her letters to him were full of questions that reflected her unfamiliarity and uncertainty in fulfilling these new responsibilities. Mary reported in April 1862 that Alf's brother had proposed a swap of some property but that she declined what was most likely an advantageous bargain, because, she wrote, "I was afraid to do it for fear it might not prove good and you would not like it."[48]

Although Mary was firmly in control of her garden plot, her early reports on the farm operations indicate her detachment and uncertainty. She indicated dutiful adherence to Alf's instructions and demonstrated little initiative or judgment on her part. It was obvious that she took little pleasure in these duties. Yet her self-confidence was quickly bolstered by her success and by the respect she found herself commanding from other Franklin residents, male and female. By the summer of 1862, she had begun to exercise her own discretion in making loans to Captain Bell's men, all of which she reported to him so that he might collect from them when they returned to camp and were paid. She wrote in August that "as usual I had to loan some of your men some money." After describing five-dollar loans to three men and the mother of another, she rationalized her generosity: "I seem to have their good will as well as their Capt. And I thought perhaps I had better keep it by being good to them."[49]

Mary conveyed new self-assurance and self-satisfaction in her reports of her activities and decision making in both agricultural and financial matters. At times Alf had to remind her merely to keep him abreast of the farm's progress, with his letters far more full of questions than were hers. Particularly revealing is the extent to which she had come to describe their farm operations in first-person singular: "I think I will have a clover patch by next year"; or "*My* horses are fatter than any my neighbors work horses"; or "I like *my* darkies better than I did at first."[50] While she still complained about the burden she bore, she did so with far less rancor than had been the case two years earlier. She took pride in how hard she worked and on occasion openly acknowledged her achievement. "I do not want to boast any," she wrote Alf in April 1864, "but I think you can say now that you have a wife that does not eat any idle bread although she can eat a good deal when she can get it."[51]

With the growth in her self-confidence, her dependence on Alf had diminished dramatically. She opened a letter in June with a revealing exclamation: "O! Would that you were here today." But the reason behind her urgent desire for her husband's presence at that point was not for his help, as it had been in the past, but rather, to show him her achievements: "I would take you over the farm and show you our prospect for a crop." A month later, she could barely contain her exuberance as she wrote, "I felt so good that evrything [*sic*] went right with me. I do not think any person could have made me mad for two or three days if they had spit in my face."[52]

As that statement alone indicates, neither Mary Bell's circumstances nor her state of mind typified by mid-1864 those of most mountain women, very few of whom would claim that "evrything" was going right, or that they "felt so good."[53] The vast majority of Carolina highland women were far less privileged than Mary Bell or Katherine Polk and did not enjoy either the financial or human resources on which those women had to draw. Bell's and Polk's situations as well-connected residents or welcome visitors in a close-knit community gave them options and opportunities not available to the many poor or more remotely situated (and thus far more vulnerable) women who struggled to survive both the economic and agricultural burdens that had become increasingly dire as the war wore on.

At the same time, there is evidence that these more privileged women formed stronger bonds with each other than did poorer women and drew heavily on the resources, both psychological and material, that such kinship or friendship provided them. In a recent study of Caldwell County's elite women during the war, David McGee has observed that these women formed intimate bonds with each other, with constant visits and correspondence providing a strong network of emotional support and material comfort, but such support did not easily cross class lines. McGee notes that their voluminous correspondence rarely makes mention of women outside of their own circle, and that their few efforts at charity seem to have been more through institutionalized outlets, such as the Soldier's Aid Society or their churches, than through personal contacts with local women in need.[54] Even a call by Governor Ellis in the spring of 1862 to raise money for a gun boat for the protection of the North Carolina coast generated more interest and activity among western North Carolina's more affluent women than did the welfare of the indigent wives and widows in their midst.[55]

Curiously, gender distinctions were evident in the sense of obligation community members felt toward their less fortunate neighbors. While landlords and county officials used their economic resources and political authority to provide some relief to that ever growing segment of the population, their wives rarely demonstrated the same charitable impulses. As already noted, Lizzie Lenoir expressed only contempt for the women engaged in bread riots in her area. There was never any indication that Mary Bell ever felt any obligation or compassion for the many Franklin women forced to cope without the many resources upon which she could draw. Though she occasionally, if begrudgingly, provided aid to the wives of men under Captain Bell's command, she became cynical of the fact that this generosity failed to win their loyalty to her husband. Both Bells expressed contempt for the wives of men in Alf's company, in which power struggles over rank were reflected in tensions among the women left at home. He complained, for example, that Salina Reid had failed to take his side in regimental politics, telling Mary, "[S]he ought to remember my father halled wood for her when her own father would not do it and my wife loned her money when she needed it. Such ungrateful women I have no use for."[56]

David McGee relates a particular incident revealing the callousness of Lenoir's more privileged women. Elizabeth Morrow, a poor widow whose husband had served as a private in the company commanded by George Harper, approached the commander's wife, Ella, to ask if she could assist in assuring the return of her late husband's belongings from Harper. Such items were usually sold, with the cash sent to the family, but Mrs. Morrow explained that they would prove more valuable than Confederate money at present. Ella Harper passed the message on to her husband, but with only in a perfunctory tone, which suggests she had little interest in the outcome of the matter or in her neighbor's fate and indicates she had no sympathy for Mrs. Morrow. On the other hand, a female refugee from Virginia who gave birth and became ill while she was in Lenoir evoked much concern and compassion from Ella Harper and her friends, even though she was a complete stranger to them all. That she was of their class seemed to determine the level of empathy they bestowed upon her.[57]

Privileged women's neglect merely added to the hardships that the collapse of more conventional networks of support created for the vast majority of highland women. As the lifestyles and economic bases of all western North Carolina women disintegrated under the weight of the war, they sought to defend the only way of life that they knew. Drew Gilpin Faust has noted the number of Southern women who yearned to be men so that they might make themselves useful to the Confederacy. North Carolina's highland women were among those expressing their desire for what Faust calls "a magical personal deliverance from gender restraints." Mary Bell said as much. "I wish I could be both man and woman until this war ends," she wrote in desperation in the spring of 1862.[58]

But Bell had nothing so magnanimous in mind as contributing to the war effort of the Southern nation; she simply yearned for the strength to keep her farm, family, and finances afloat. That commitment to such limited or localized goals was one shared by most highland women, regardless of class. Sheer survival—their own and that of their households—remained the prime motivation of women throughout the region who rose to the many challenges thrust upon them. When the home guard of Rutherford County failed to respond to a Federal raid late in the war, several local women requested guns to defend themselves. "Please order out the Militia of Rutherford," they petitioned Governor Vance in January 1864, "or send ammunition and arms enough to supply the Ladies and we, for the *name* of the Old North State, will defend their homes for them."[59]

In other efforts as well, women "assumed the duties of the sterner sex" to keep their communities functional and their households intact. They signed petitions in large numbers seeking to retain the blacksmiths, millers, tanners, and other craftsmen on whom their local economies so depended. They were even more assertive in the defense of their families: they hid their husbands who deserted from the army; they endured harassment and injury to protect family members from violent gangs; and they worked against impossible odds to provide adequate food for themselves and their children. In some cases, they even rioted and stole food.

The geographical isolation of western North Carolina could not prevent the institutional collapse of its communities nor shield its women from the consequences of such intrusions of a modern, war-torn world upon their lives. Mountain women bore the innumerable tragedies that marked their lives during the war with a grim determination to preserve a familiar world. Their efforts to retain their traditional lives and community structures forced these women to challenge Confederate policies—both actively and passively; and in so doing they contributed to the failure of the South to establish its independence.

SLAVERY

Many Negro Buyers in This Part of the Country

O N October 7, 1861, Colonel George Bower, the largest slaveholder in Ashe County, drowned during a trip to Raleigh from his home in Jefferson when his two-horse carriage overturned as he attempted to ford the swollen Yadkin River near Wilkesboro. Two days later, Calvin Cowles, his friend and a fellow slaveholder from Wilkesboro, reported the tragic incident in a letter to William W. Holden in Raleigh. Cowles stated that Bower had been accompanied by a slave, who had urged him not to attempt the crossing given the force of the current. "The Carriage capsized and all went downstream," Cowles wrote, "except the Negro who fortunately escapd to tell the story. The alarm being given, 20 or 30 people went immediately through a drenching rain," where they searched in vain for the elderly colonel's body.[1] In his account of the incident in the *North Carolina Standard* a week later, editor Holden shifted words just enough to imply a somewhat different scenario: The "negro boy who was driving him" used the occasion to make his escape.[2] Soon thereafter and ever since, the standard version of the incident has been that, as Ashe County's sole history states, Bower drowned "while pursuing a runaway slave."[3]

It is tempting to speculate both on Holden's reasons for altering the story behind the slave's escape and on how the slave became the cause of Bower's death rather than his attempted savior. Perhaps the ominous implications of that latter version proved too useful to resist: that less than six months into the war, a powerful slaveholder had already fallen victim to his human property. Bower's death may have been an extreme portent of the fate of his counterparts throughout the South. It also had significant implications for western Carolinians, for he was part of a rather striking statistic: he was the first of four of the region's forty largest slaveholders to die violent deaths at or near their homes over the course of the war. Those losses, which were compounded by numerous battlefield casualties among the sons of the highland elite, prompted Governor Zebulon Vance to observe just after the war that in western North Carolina, "many old families are almost extinct in the male line."[4]

Yet if the war took an unusually heavy toll on the mountains' slaveholders, the institution of slavery suffered remarkably little. It continued to thrive economically and proved so resilient that few highlanders took seriously the possibility of its demise until the waning weeks of the conflict, when military invaders finally subjected the Carolina highlands to the full thrust of its destructive might. Only at this point did the system show any real signs of collapse, and even then, it died a lingering and relatively uneventful death in much of the mountain region not in the path of Union troops. Despite a vast literature documenting the broad range of emancipation experiences of bondsmen and -women throughout the Confederacy and the border state South, little attention seems to have been paid to the impact of the war on the economics of slavery, or on the continued utilization of slaves as commodities, except as they were engaged in the Confederate war effort.[5]

Because of their insulation from any major military incursion until the war's final weeks, elite highlanders in North Carolina enjoyed the continued stability and profitability of slavery throughout the war years. Despite the turbulence, tensions, and hardships the war imposed on so many other aspects of mountain life, an active slave trade continued unabated throughout the region. The increased demands for and value of slaves blinded many of the beneficiaries of slavery to the possibility of Confederate defeat and the end to slavery as an inevitable function of that defeat.

It is rather curious that mountain masters and mistresses exhibited so little concern for the security of their black property holdings during the war, especially given the uncertainties of the immediate prewar years. The sectional crisis had spawned new fears across the state of insurrectionary or subversive activity among its slave population. A major thrust of the rhetoric during the secession crisis had been warnings of the effect of war on slavery's stability and, indeed, survival.[6] A Raleigh newspaper editor expressed the concerns of many mountain residents when he noted in February 1861 that if armed conflict was to come, "the negroes will know, too, that the war is waged on their account," and they will "become restless and difficult to manage."[7]

Western Carolinians on both sides of the secession debate utilized fear tactics to make their case, outlining scenarios of upheaval aimed at slaveholding and nonslaveholding highlanders alike. Democratic spokesmen W. W. Avery and Marcus Erwin printed a circular warning of the "terrible calamity of having three hundred thousand idle, vagabond free negroes turned loose with all the privileges of white men" if Republican coercion went unchallenged. Asheville resident William Vance Brown, taking the opposing view, pointed out that if war did break out, slaves would suddenly become detrimental to Southerners. The North, he wrote, "can do awful damage & destruction by & through our slaves. Once arouse them to insurrection & they will carry murder, Rape & arson into the midst of our firesides."[8] Western Carolinians were aware of the specific implications of such consequences for their own highland region, many having heard or read Georgia governor Joseph E. Brown's much-quoted warning to his north Georgia constituents that emancipation would mean slaves would swarm into the hills and "we should have them plundering and stealing, robbing, and killing in all the lovely vallies of the mountains."[9]

Yet, once the war was under way, there were few signs that mountain whites took seriously or even remembered such predictions. From late 1861 on, the Asheville Mutual Insurance Company ran with more frequency its newspaper advertisements for "policies of insurance on white and slave lives . . . giving the insured perfect security against loss." Yet these ads played on owners' heightened anxiety about the security of individual slaves, not on fears of either massive insurrection or the system's collapse, losses which the company would not likely have covered.[10]

One reason mountain residents were not worried was that the value of slave property continued to soar—or appeared to soar—for most of the war's duration. Although slavery had never been as demographically significant or economically vital to southern highland society as elsewhere in the South, the latter antebellum years had proved very healthy ones for the slave trade in western North Carolina.[11] There are few indications that the vitality of the local slave trade diminished as a result of secession and the war. Highland slaveholders were quick to finesse the wartime labor shortages by hiring out their own slaves and serving as agents in renting or selling the slaves of others. The widespread practice of hiring slaves for long and short terms had long been integral to the institution's viability in the southern highlands, and that flexibility allowed the region to adapt more effectively than other parts of the Confederacy to new labor demands.[12]

The Carolina highlands were deluged with slaveholders and their slaves from vulnerable coastal regions stretching from tidewater Virginia through low country Georgia. Refugees, both black and white, poured into various North Carolina communities to avoid the disruptions and threats posed by the movement of armies elsewhere. Governor Zebulon Vance viewed this shift with some alarm, complaining to Jefferson Davis in October 1862, "Thousands are flying from our Eastern Counties with their slaves to the centre & West to devour the very short crops and increase the prospect of starvation."[13]

Highlanders themselves seemed to view this influx in a more positive light than Vance did, however, perhaps because of the caliber of the refugees seeking asylum in their midst. Charlestonians and other South Carolina planters with summer homes in Flat Rock and Hendersonville often retreated there with much of their slave force. Among them were Christopher Memminger, Senator Thomas J. Semmes of New Orleans, Mary Chesnut, and assorted Middletons, Rhetts, and Lowndes.[14] As already noted, General Leonidas Polk moved his family to Asheville for the duration of the war, after the fall of Nashville and then New Orleans, both of which his wife had called home, and the destruction of his daughter's Mississippi plantation. "Always thoughtful and provident," according to his daughter Katherine's account, Polk arranged for "some twenty excellent negro men & their families" to be brought up to join the family, while Mrs. Polk had other slaves of her own brought to Asheville from New Orleans.[15]

More often, slaveholders opted to send their human property out of the reach of Confederate impressment officials or Union liberators. On the one hand, the demands for slave labor in constructing coastal fortifications made slaves ready targets of the Confederates. On the other, state officials were convinced that Federal forces occupying the eastern part of the state were actively encouraging slaves to escape, which prompted Governor Vance to issue a policy statement informing easterners that "it is the duty of all slaveowners immediately to remove their slaves able to bear arms." Vance's order was a response to more general instructions issued from the Confederate administration in Richmond in March 1863 that planters in coastal South Carolina, Georgia, and Florida withdraw their slaves into the interior, "since they were liable to be lost at any moment." For slaveowners in South Carolina, in particular, western North Carolina was a viable site for such interior transfers.[16]

Even before such moves became official policy, highland opportunists had reached out to eastern owners with tempting leasing or purchase offers. Nicholas W. Woodfin was the most aggressive in making this pitch. Along with other Asheville businessmen, he had actively advertised for hired slave labor to construct the long-anticipated Western North Carolina Railroad long before war seemed a possibility. With no intention of letting its progress lag once the conflict was under way, Woodfin continued to run advertisements in newspapers across the state well into 1862. In December 1861, one such notice called for "100 able-bodied negroes," while another in March 1862 sought fifty more. Woodfin used a personal approach in offering his services as broker to his slaveholding friends who wanted safe havens for their slave property during the war. In May 1862, he wrote former governor and Asheville native David L. Swain, who was then living in Chapel Hill as president of the University of North Carolina, with the following proposition: "Now upon the subject of your negroes. If you will send them up to this country I can yet hire them to advantage for the rest of the year. The men especially will command high prices, particularly before harvest commences. There is great demand for labor indeed. . . . It won't be as easy to place women & children, but it can be done."[17]

William Holland Thomas went so far as to suggest that such arrangements be made official policy. While encamped at Knoxville, Colonel Thomas wrote to Governor Vance in November 1862 suggesting that "able bodied negro men" in eastern North Carolina be "employed by the State and transferred from their present positions to work on the extension of the Railroad." The advantages of such a policy, Thomas maintained, were twofold: It would protect the human property of the eastern owners; and the troops that would otherwise be protecting slaves could be used in the defense of the state's western borders, which he felt was the greater priority. But Thomas also shared Nicholas Woodfin's inter-

est in seeing the much-delayed railroad, in which they both were heavy inves-
tors, finally reach across the Blue Ridge.[18]

Calvin Cowles, the most energetic of Wilkes County's entrepreneurs, was
equally aggressive in attempting to bring new slave labor into the area, particularly through hiring contracts that allowed him to sublet the slaves he had
hired to his neighbors and relatives. His correspondence over the first two years
of the war is replete with pleas to slaveholders in which he confirms the rich
opportunities his area could offer. He informed a Mississippi business contact
of the high demand for adult males, who were then commanding annual rates of
$125 or $150.[19]

By June 1862 Cowles complained that "hirelings cannot be had for money
nor love" and asked his brother, then in eastern North Carolina, "Can't you
catch me a Negro or two and send them up?" He intensified his search, asking
particularly for blacksmiths or carpenters but willing to consider any women
and children that might be for hire. In 1863 he offered to rent at least one of the
several farms among his vast landholdings to any refugees seeking to move from
war-torn areas who could bring slaves with them. During one of his regular
mercantile purchasing trips to Charleston and Savannah in April 1863, he
bought a slave as well. He reported to his wife that he had bought "Nancy," a
forty-year-old "cook, washer, and house servant," for $805 at the slave mart in
Charleston but that he had had no luck thus far in finding a "boy" of comparable worth.[20]

Cowles's attempts to make outright purchases may have proved futile, but his
efforts in the long-distance hiring of slaves seems to have paid off. Throughout
the latter half of the war he corresponded with a variety of eastern North
Carolina owners regarding the maintenance and welfare of their slaves, who
were under either his own care or that of the individuals to whom he had rented
their labor. When his sister in Lenoir expressed concern over her financial
situation in November 1862, Cowles urged her to hire out her slave, Wash,
noting that "prices rule high here, . . . [and] he ought to fetch you some money
as his work is in demand."[21]

Woodfin and Cowles were by no means alone in these pursuits. Some highland residents viewed the care and supervision of others' slaves as a service as
well as a financial opportunity. Allen Davidson, for example, wrote in February
1863 from Cherokee County that he and other family members were willing to
oblige relatives in middle Tennessee who wanted to send their slaves "up here
this summer." "I would be glad if they'd do so," Davidson wrote. "Uncle

Harvy's folks would take some and us two or three for a fair price board and clothe them."[22] But for most such opportunists, buying, selling, and trading slaves were strictly business transactions and these kinds of arrangements were made through past business connections. Mountain merchants found that their many antebellum contacts with South Carolina and Georgia markets were effective conduits for moving slaves into the Carolina highlands for both short- and long-term usage, thus creating a vigorous regional slave market up until the final three or four months of the war.

The effect of this activity was a considerable expansion of the mountain slave population. A Haywood County resident noted in May 1863 that the number of slaves in that county "has increased very rapidly since the war commenced." At least one Asheville resident was alarmed enough about the number of slaves being brought into Buncombe County from the coast that he informed fellow Buncombe native Governor Vance in March 1863 that citizens there wanted more protection "from Negro Ravages."[23]

Yet despite the influx of new blacks into the region, the demand for them increased, and therefore the hiring rates they commanded rose dramatically. A Rutherford County owner hired out six slaves for an annual fee of $618, almost twice the fee he had asked for two years earlier. Joseph Corpening in Caldwell County hired out four of his slaves, two men and two women, on annual contracts, and his accounts show that these transactions remained steady throughout the war years, despite the dramatic rate increases. William, an adult male, earned Corpening a $28 annual fee in 1861. That rate doubled over each of the next two years to $47 in 1862 and $104 in 1863. By 1864, Corpening charged $510 for William's services, and in January 1865, $525. The fees Corpening charged for the other male and one of the two women were comparable to those he charged for William, so that a total of $113 collected in January 1861 for the four had grown by January 1864 to $1,165.[24] These figures say as much or more about the dramatic depreciation of Confederate currency as they do about the increased value of slaves. But the perception was as important as the reality, and mountain residents interpreted these rising values to mean slaves were an increasingly profitable investment; that perception in itself had much to do with the vitality of the slave market in the region.

More often than not, the purchases and sales of black bondsmen and -women were negotiated locally, but they were never confined to one region. Like Woodfin, who went to purchase slaves in Charleston and Savannah, many highlanders were very much aware of current prices in these major markets and the options for sale or purchase they continued to offer. In May 1863, Calvin Cowles advised his sister in the aftermath of the capture of her two unruly runaways: "Robert could have been sold in Charleston for $2500, but I presume you allowed your philanthropy to influence you in marketing him—he is with old friends. In Wash's case, I advise you that you put him on the block in Richmond . . . he has forfeited all claims on your sympathy—get the most you can for him."[25]

The contrasting experiences of two highland families in the wartime slave trade illustrate the variety of scenarios in which these business ventures could play themselves out. The extensive correspondence of the Lenoirs, who were one of the most established families and largest slaveholders in western North Carolina, reveals the family's very different approach to its black property compared to the approach reflected in the letters of Alfred and Mary Bell, who broke into the ranks of slaveholders for the first time during the war. Yet behind the actions of both Bells and Lenoirs lay some shared assumptions about the future security and profitability of slavery in their region.

Colonel Thomas Lenoir, the eighty-year-old patriarch of the venerable Fort Defiance plantation in Caldwell County, died in March 1861 and left his three sons and several sons-in-law to face the early months of the war with the additional burden of settling his substantial estate, including the distribution of his sixty-one slaves. Two of the Lenoir sons chose to stay at home and concentrate on their new responsibilities as managers of their father's wealth. Thomas, the colonel's eldest son and namesake, who was forty-four years old when the war began, toyed with the idea of raising a company but seemed to submit to his sister's argument against it. She wrote, "There are many more who are willing to go who cannot serve their county so well in any other capacity. . . . [T]he corn & bacon & beef you can raise will be quite a consideration and I fear that your constitution would not hold up long under a long campaign."[26] Thomas opted to become the productive citizen his sister described but chose to do so not at Fort Defiance but at "the Den," a crude but vast farm that was part of the family's extensive holdings in Haywood County. Rufus, thirty-six years old and the youngest of the three brothers, stayed at home to manage the Caldwell County plantation. Walter, the middle son, served the Confederate cause militarily.[27]

The burdens of the war, compounded by the responsibility of their father's estate, particularly his slave property, weighed heavily on the Lenoir brothers. The lion's share of that burden fell upon Rufus, the sole adult male remaining at Fort Defiance. But he never lacked for long-distance advice from Walter, wherever he was stationed. While at Kinston, North Carolina, in April 1862, Walter lectured his younger brother on investment opportunities for the more liquid part of his inheritance. He advised Rufus not to acquire more real estate because of their already extensive holdings and pointed out that most forms of personal property were unreasonably high priced at the time, though he knew they "must fall when public affairs again become settled by peace; and unless with a view to an early profit, [I] would not deem it prudent to invest largely in such property." But, Walter continued, "there are two kinds of personal property which form exceptions in this respect, negroes and cotton, both of which are depreciated in value, the first from political considerations & the peculiar character of the war waged by our powerful and unprincipled foe, & the other on account of the blockade." While there were risks in investing in either commodity, Walter reasoned from his eastern North Carolina vantage point that "for long investment and in a mere pecuniary point of view, I would prefer buying negroes or cotton near the point where they are in the greatest present danger & removing them to the mountains to any other investment in personal property."[28]

But Walter Lenoir acknowledged his brother's doubts about slaveownership. "I know that for reasons not pecuniary, you be altogether averse to owning any more slaves than you are already responsible for," he wrote Rufus, and urged him to buy up as much cotton as he could instead.[29] Walter, too, was ambivalent about the human portion of their inheritance. Well before the war, in fact, he had expressed serious misgivings about slavery on moral grounds. After a slave of his was caught breaking into a store in 1858, Walter confided to Thomas: "I feel determined at present never to own another slave. Both Nealy [his wife] and I have concluded after our limited experience with slaves that the evil of being a master and mistress of slaves is greater than we are willing to bear unless imposed upon us by some sterner necessity belonging to our lot."[30]

Thus, neither he nor his brothers embraced their new, vastly expanded slaveholdings with enthusiasm. But with the war under way, and their support of the Confederate cause nominal at least, they no longer invoked any ideological underpinnings for their distaste for their black property. They insisted instead—mainly to each other and to other family members—that it was the burdensome and often frustrating responsibilities incurred to which they objected. This sense of burden in itself may have been a part of their legacy from their father, who had long felt that the number of slaves he had inherited from

his own father was far in excess of the labor needs of the Fort Defiance operation. Although he complained on more than one occasion that they were
"eating up all the profits" of their plantation production, he was bound by a
strong sense of noblesse oblige to retain "his people."[31]

While the colonel had instilled in his sons a paternalistic respect for slave
family ties, they were far quicker than he had been to sell much of their excess
personnel. The pressure to do so was constant, a reflection of the wartime surge
in market activity in the area. James Gwyn, an heir by virtue of his marriage to
the colonel's daughter, recognized the potential and pressed his in-laws to make
slaves as large a share of his portion of the estate as possible. He specifically
asked for young slaves, a reflection not only of his faith in the institution's
future but also of his awareness of the prices they commanded in an optimistic
local market.[32]

When in early 1863 their father's estate was settled and the slaves had been
divided, the Lenoir brothers moved quickly to convert sizable portions of that
property into cash. Rather than carrying through with a public auction as they
had advertised, they opted for private sales and seemed quite pleased with the
prices they garnered. But Gwyn by then was a little more cautious than he had
been a year and half earlier, more because of doubts about fluctuations in the
value of Confederate currency than about the demand for slaves. "I have had
several persons to see me to buy George and his family," he wrote in January,
"but I have not sold them yet and I hardly think I will for a while at least, altho' I
do not think I will keep them, but maybe they are as safe as the money I would
get for them." Yet he was also adding to his holdings. He purchased several
slaves from the estate of an elderly widow with no heirs and seemed to take great
satisfaction in the fact that he acquired them "at two-thirds of traders' prices as
the will directed."[33]

In May 1863 Walter (who had returned home from the war as an amputee
several months earlier and had moved to Thomas's Haywood County farm)
noted that the value of his slaves had doubled since their assessment at the time
of his father's death. Gwyn wrote his brother-in-law Rufus from Wilkes County
two months earlier that "there are many negro buyers in this part of the country.
I dare say it is the same way with you & that you obtained large prices." Gwyn
went on to complain about his failure to anticipate how rapidly prices were
climbing and that he had succumbed too soon to market demands: "I had to
sell one of Byram's and Betsey's children (Polly) which I disliked very much but

she got too far along in the sleight of hand to keep; I only got $1250 for her—could now get $1800. I also sold Lark a few weeks ago, for $2000 which I then thought an exorbitant price but it seems there is no telling what property will go for."[34]

Despite their preoccupation with the profitability of their black property they intended to sell, the Lenoirs were equally involved in the care and supervision of the slaves they retained. Except for the mention of minor problems encountered in the adjustments of slaves moved between Fort Defiance and "the Den," the brothers' reports to each other of slave activity varied remarkably little from those of antebellum years, as daily life at both sites continued to be dictated by the seasonal demands of agriculture. Perhaps the biggest social event of the war years was a double wedding of two slave couples at the Den. Walter provided his mother at Fort Defiance this tongue-in-cheek description: "Uriah and Delia, and Pervis and Lizzie was married here last night by Lewis Welsh, Esq. (of African descent) Who is duly authorized by the law (Ethiopian) to celebrate the vows of matrimony and also to hear and determine actions of debt and pleas of assault and battery and other breaches of the peace among the descendants of Ham. . . . The Squire very prudently united the couples as husband and wife as long as there was no deficiency over which they had no controll."[35]

While Walter's tone suggests full approval of the ceremony, which was perhaps a reflection of the Lenoir's longstanding sensitivity to the family life of their slaves, it is also probable that he and his brothers viewed the affair in the optimistic terms of prospective property expansion, and even potential profits, that such unions could generate. For both the Lenoirs and Gwyn continued to make periodic sales—usually but not always in family groupings—throughout 1863 and into 1864. They never seemed to have had trouble selling slaves to residents of Caldwell or neighboring counties, and while they became more and more hesitant to accept payment in Confederate currency, they seem to have been pleased with the profits accrued from such transactions.[36]

A very different story, but one equally indicative of the dynamic wartime slave trade in the Carolina mountains is that of Alfred and Mary Bell in Macon County. Macon was far removed and in many respects very different from Caldwell and Wilkes Counties. It was more deeply entrenched in the mountains and thus more remote and more sparsely settled than the fertile river valleys of the Blue Ridge's eastern foothills. Macon County had only half as many slaves and a third as many slaveholders as Caldwell in 1860, yet the system there showed as much vigor and vitality as it did in the more affluent community of which the Lenoirs were a part.[37]

When the Bells moved to Franklin in 1860, there were eleven slaveholders in the village. But like many of their nonslaveholding neighbors, the Bells took advantage of the sources of both white and black manpower available in the community. From the time of their arrival until at least the end of 1862, they entrusted their farm to a white tenant and two slaves, Tom and Liza, both of whom were hired on an annual basis from the county's largest supplier, Dillard Love, whose ninety-five slaves made him western North Carolina's fifth largest slaveholder in 1860.[38]

After Alfred Bell's enlistment in November 1861, Mary continued to rely on the labor of their tenant and hired slaves. She appeared to be responsible for the supervision of the slaves and was often frustrated by the discipline problems due to their proximity to their owner's farm and thus to the slave community from which they had been removed. Her difficulties in controlling their movements or their work rates were such that by the fall of 1862, she was ready to dispense with hired slave labor altogether. While both Mary and Alf weighed the option of employing other white workers, they were even more inclined to the option of purchasing slaves of their own.

As a result of certain profitable investments, in addition to Mary's collection of back payments for her husband's dental services and their share in Alf's family's jewelry business, the Bells were in the unusual position of having accumulated considerable capital early in the war, and like many young Southern couples, they saw slaves as a natural, indeed sound, investment. By December 1862, Alf was eager to make some sort of investment because he was nervous about the stability of the Confederate currency they were accumulating. "I don't think it good policy to keep money on hand," he wrote Mary. "I want you to invest what you have in something, either for a negro or land." He trusted her judgment in choosing which and thanked God he had a wife "who is not extravagant and is always trying to lay something up for the future."[39]

Slave trading was brisk in Macon County during the second year of the war, and the Bells were very much interested in purchasing Martha, a cook, and her child from Dillard Love, a pair in whom there was considerable interest by other local residents as well. Despite their interest in Martha and her interest in belonging to the Bells (she told Mary that she would "beg Mr. Love to sell her" to them), John Ingram, who had himself recently entered slaveholding status with the purchase of four other bondsmen, beat the Bells in acquiring these two additional hands. The couple did not acquire any slaves that fall, but at some point in 1863, they received a female slave named Eve as payment for accumulated debts owed Alf.

Their new bondswoman soon proved to be a nuisance to Mary Bell, and Alf assured her that there was no shortage of buyers in Franklin. With landholding becoming more of a priority for him, he suggested she trade Eve for one of several tracts of land he would like to have owned. In March 1864 he instructed her to try the Silers first and to "give any price for it that you think we can pay and live afterward." "I want the land bad" was his final word on the subject. At the time, Alf was stationed in Alabama, his greatest distance yet from home, and his advice reached Mary too late. It crossed in the mail a letter from Mary Bell in which she announced: "Well, I believe I told you that you need not be surprised if [I] made a nigger trade. Well I have done it." What she had done, in fact, was to negotiate, with the help of Alf's brothers, the purchase of a slave family from Charleston. "I have swaped [sic] Eve for a man, woman, and child . . . and gave $1800 to boot," she explained.[40]

A Mr. Kilpatrick had purchased the couple and their daughter through a Charleston agent. Worried about his own mounting debts and recognizing that he had overextended himself with his new slave property, he agreed to let Mary Bell purchase them. In Alf's brother's explanation of the transaction, he assured Alf that Mary had pulled off a real bargain and had purchased these slaves at far less than their current value in the mountain market. Mary described the slaves in rich detail: Trim, a thirty-five-year-old cooper who had built paint buckets in Charleston, his wife, Patsy, forty years old and pregnant, and Rosa, their three-year-old daughter. Mary suggested that these were not the first low country slaves who had been moved into her area when she wrote of Patsy, "She is like all the other south niggers—don't know much about the work as we do . . . but she is willing to try to learn to do anything." Mary seemed to pride herself on the firm stance she took with her new charges: "I have told both [Trim and Patsy] that if they do not make my crib full of corn that I will sell them both in the fall for enough to fill it."[41]

Alf was obviously taken aback by the news of Mary's purchase. But comforted by his brother's insistence that the deal had indeed been a bargain, he stifled criticism of his wife, limiting his initial comments to: "I supose [sic] you will have negroes enough to make corn and rye this year. . . . Well, if they will suit you I am glad for the trade. I will try and pay the money." A week later he seemed even more resigned to his new status. "I hope we now can get along without having any thing to do with Loves negroes," he wrote. "I do crave to be independent and unbeholding to any body."[42]

Mary seemed to revel in her new situation. At the end of her glowing descriptions of her new workforce, she declared to Alf, "[I]f this war would just end and you could be at home, I would be satisfied." In July she wrote, "I like my darkies better I believe than I did at first. . . . I feel so good that everything went right with me." By the fall of 1864, however, Mary's euphoria was deflated by the fact that Patsy was not only not pregnant but had also suffered a series of fainting spells that rendered her more of a burden than a help. Trim's skill and energy had not lived up to Mary's high expectations either. "These low country negroes," she wrote in November, "are not like ours in their work nor anything else. . . . I have almost lost confidence in anybody."[43]

Yet Mary did not appear to be disillusioned with the burdens of slaveownership. From early fall on, she proposed to her husband further slave purchases either to supplement or to replace the family she owned. In particular, she had her eye on a slave couple, Betts and Alfred, that she felt "would suit us as well as any we could get." She also learned that Mr. Kilpatrick, from whom she had purchased Trim, Patsy, and Rosa, was willing to buy back at least the father and daughter, although she grudgingly admitted he would probably have to accept the sickly Patsy as well.[44]

Despite her urgency to take advantage of these opportunities, there is no indication that any such trade or purchase ever took place, since Alf's return home in February 1865 ended Mary's vivid record of the couple's slaveholding experience. Yet the mere fact that within three months of the war's end such transactions were still taking place in the Franklin area suggests that slavery's death in the Carolina highlands came both suddenly and unexpectedly. It is tempting to judge Mary Bell as shortsighted in having made such risky investments in 1864, or to suggest that Alfred's preference for land over slaves indicates his foresight as to the latter's precarious future. Yet there is no evidence that he had any doubts as to either the Confederacy's ultimate victory or slavery's continued, and even safer, existence under that new regime. Had he had any qualms about the risks involved, he certainly would not have been so quick to encourage Mary in her pursuit of more slaves.

The Bells were not alone in their assumptions. That the vitality of the highland slave trade hinged on the ever growing threats to black property elsewhere in the Confederacy seems never to have worried the highlanders taking advantage of the bargain rates on slaves. Even those selling slaves, like

Kilpatrick, cannot be credited with any more prescience than those they sold to. It was, after all, at the end 1864, with Lee's surrender less than four months away, that he indicated his willingness to buy back all three of the slaves he had earlier sold to the Bells.

Thus the Bells, more so than the Lenoirs, but probably not unlike the majority of mountain slaveholders, were caught very much by surprise when all of their plans, maneuvers, and even skill in playing the slave market came to naught. That Mary Bell moved as readily and as enthusiastically into the ranks of slaveholders at the very point at which the institution was crumbling elsewhere suggests not only how healthy the market continued to be in the mountains during the war's final year but also how few doubts either she or her community seemed to harbor about its continued viability and profitability.

Even Lincoln's Emancipation Proclamation, the development that turned the war specifically into a struggle over slave liberation, caused less of a stir among highlanders than residents elsewhere in the state or in the South. No doubt many highlanders were alarmed by the possible scenarios its enactment could generate. Mary Taylor Brown, the wife of one of Buncombe County's substantial slaveholders, wrote that upon hearing of Lincoln's proclamation she "was roused to a feeling of indignation inexpressible!" Under the assumption that Lincoln had coupled the arming of slaves with their liberation, she declared it "to be the work of the Devil or of some arch-fiend in his employ."[45]

Yet there is little evidence that such fears were strong enough to have any negative effects on the marketability of slaves or on the commitment of mountaineers to the cause for which they were fighting. For many Southerners, Lincoln's revolutionary edict signaled new challenges in maintaining white solidarity across class lines in support of the Confederate cause. They feared that, just as Lincoln intended, his proclamation would drive a wedge between the slaveholding elite and the nonslaveholders willing to fight for state rights or their new Southern nation but not willing to risk their lives to protect the property of their social superiors.

This was a legitimate concern in western North Carolina, where some highlanders detected in the new terms of the war the impetus for rising numbers of deserters from the Confederate army, particularly among those who felt "they had nothing to fight for . . . but the negroes."[46] In reflecting on the impact of the Emancipation Proclamation many years after the war, Zebulon Vance stated: "[I]t did more than anything else to alienate the affections of the common people. . . . [I]t opened a wide door to demagogues to appeal to the nonslaveholding class, and make them believe that the only issue was the protection of slavery, in which they were sacrifices for the sole benefit of the masters."[47]

Yet while there is some evidence of such sentiments among nonslaveholding mountain residents, the Emancipation Proclamation seems to have exacerbated class divisiveness far less in that region than elsewhere. There was, on the contrary, the belief among many highlanders that Lincoln's action could have the opposite effect—that of uniting whites as never before behind the Confederate cause. A Henderson County resident serving in the Confederate army near Knoxville recognized its benefits to western North Carolina's protection from Union invasion. He wrote home in October 1862 that "Lincoln's proclimation has had the happy tendency I hear of uniting the people of East Tennessee together and causing them to stem the tide of Yankee invasion that may yet set toward our own fair Southern shore."[48]

The same sort of defiance exhibited by East Tennesseans was evident among Carolina highlanders as well and may have stemmed from the fact that from the secession crisis on, their leaders had made slavery's preservation central to their reasoning as to why North Carolina either should or should not join the new Southern nation. In so doing, they had appealed successfully to their vast nonslaveholding constituency in terms of the threats slavery's end posed for them, as blacks were freed not only from their shackles but from a wide variety of other restrictions as well. David W. Siler, a large slaveholder in Macon County, wrote Vance with confidence that the prospect of slavery's demise would intensify highlanders' commitment to the Confederate war effort. "We are opposed to negro equality," he informed the governor in November 1863. "To prevent this we are willing to spare the last man down to the point where women and children begin to suffer for food and clothing. . . . Rather than see them equalized with an inferior race, [we] will die with them."[49] This was wishful thinking, perhaps, on the part of so large a slaveholder among so few, but the fears were real, and they continued to be effectively tapped by Siler's fellow mountain masters.

Privately, however, some slaveholders were more realistic, and even introspective, about the future implications of Lincoln's edict. In a letter to Governor Vance on June 1, 1863, Leander S. Gash in Henderson County worried more openly than most about the effects of the war's duration on slavery's future. Acknowledging that "the North and the balance of the civilized world" viewed slavery as the primary cause of the war and that "its abolition and destruction is regarded by many sensible men as certain and sure," Gash noted that its demise was only a matter of time. Concluding with the central tenet of the nascent peace movement, he asserted, "[T]he sooner Peace is made consentably the longer slavery may be enjoyed by a gradual extinction. But prolong the war indefinitely and all must go together and end at the same time."[50]

The news of Lee's defeat at Gettysburg forced other mountain residents to face such hard truths. Walter Lenoir, who for so long had wrestled with his doubts about slavery, grew progressively disturbed by the prospect of its demise. From the isolation of his Haywood County farm, his reflections wavered between uncertainty, agitation, and resignation at the prospects that Confederate defeat would present to the South. "I have never thought that the Yankees would succeed in liberating our slaves," he wrote his brother Rufus in July 1863, for "God will not suffer the Yankees to perpetrate so great a crime as that against us and our species." If, however, that "righteous will" was not what Southerners assumed, the abolition of slavery must remain a possibility. Walter admitted that his earlier assumptions about its consequences were those shared by most Southerners, "that such a forcible emancipation would lead to scenes of horrid massacre and butchery; that the negroes finding freedom in their grasp, and having their passions inflamed by the fierce teaching of abolitionists, would attempt to slay their masters, and that they in turn would be compelled to destroy the negroes."[51]

Yet Walter went on to confide to his younger brother that he had revised his views in light of the interaction of Union occupation forces and slaves elsewhere in the South: "I now believe that if the Yankees succeed in subjugating the white people of the South and freeing the negroes it will be without any massacre. . . . There will be no rising upon the non-combatant men, women, or children. Those of us who live to see it will see their Yankee masters set the negroes free and then govern them and their fellow citizens, their late masters and mistresses, as well as subjugated peoples are governed by other enlightened nations." He worried about but then minimized the consequences of Union attempts to arm slaves, with the curious rationale that "it is possible that even the negro disciplined and led by white men may stand fire better than we of the South have supposed" but that "amalgamation in the ranks with them . . . is so very unnatural that even Yankee fanaticism will fail in the attempt."[52]

A month later, Walter's tone had changed and he lashed out in response to Rufus's observation that in the aftermath of Gettysburg, "many in Caldwell County say we are whipped and the sooner we come to terms with our enemies the better." One of the most important reasons to resist, he insisted, was that "every reconstructionist is an abolitionist at heart, and likes Lincoln's emancipation proclamation." He went on to label them amalgamationists as well, all with "some notion of taking a negro wife," a prospect he found revolting and the prevention of which was well worth continued fighting. Yet he made even more clear that his present defense of the institution did not stem from self-interest. He confided to his sister-in-law, "You know that I had made up my mind before the war that I would not be again a slave owner, not from doubt that it was right for the people of the South in this age to continue to own their slaves. The tie that binds me to it is so slight that my slaves *cant* [*sic*] habitually trouble me much."[53]

In December 1864, Rufus wrote Walter about the problems of troublesome slaves and noted that "unless I could feel more interest in the institution as a permanent one, I do not care to be troubled with dishonest ones." Yet in the same letter he acknowledged the high prices slaves still commanded as he contemplated the sale of his "young Venus."[54] Only in February 1865 did the Lenoirs acknowledge the possibility that slavery would soon meet its end. In a family estate settlement involving the dispersal of slave property, a new conditional phrase accompanied the list of the slaves bequeathed to Walter: "provided that the events of the war do not result in the abolition of slavery or their removal from his controll as owner."[55]

Witnessing the flurry of sales activity by early 1865, one might conclude that other highlanders sensed the system's doom as well, as they, like the Lenoirs and the Bells, continued to dispose of troublesome property. Only a week after the Lenoir document was drawn up, Mary Cowles in Caldwell County reported that her uncle had sold Mike, "a scamp" and "a miserable drunkard" who she was glad to be rid of at any price. Mike's reputation was too well known for him to command the asking price of $850 in Confederate currency at an auction, though a private sale was negotiated soon afterward. Also in February Cowles's mother was forced to sell a "mean negro" of her own, and although she too could not do so locally because of his reputation for thievery, she was able to sell him to a man near Charlotte.[56] Two months earlier in the same county, Rufus Patterson recommended that his parents sell two of their particularly bothersome slaves. They were such troublemakers, Rufus wrote, that he felt sure his mother "would be decidedly happier if George & Rob are away."[57]

Yet in most cases, such sales did not reflect owners' attempts to bail out of a doomed or even declining investment option; rather it was increasing discipline problems that seem to have instigated these sales, a trend that suggests a growing restlessness and even defiance among mountain slaves. Some owners sensed this shift in mood. "A general spirit of devilment is thro' the country," Rufus Patterson observed in December 1864. "I deem it best to be constantly on the lookout. Our negros need watching."[58] In hindsight, it seems odd that their masters and mistresses did not recognize the increasing unrest on the part of so much of their black property as symptomatic of the institution's eminent collapse. And yet there is little evidence that highlanders drew any linkage between their personal problems with individual slaves and broader patterns of disruption or that they acknowledged the all too ominous reasons for this shift in behavior.

Yet slaves themselves were quick to sense the loosening of control over their behavior and attitudes, and many engaged in subversive activity of which their owners were oblivious. The majority of the many memoirs and narratives by escaped prisoners of war, deserters, bushwhackers, and other fugitives who moved through the Carolina highlands for refuge or en route to East Tennessee during the war's latter half relate countless incidents in which black residents aided their efforts. Slaves often guided fugitives through the rugged and some-times treacherous mountain terrain as they headed for Knoxville. Many opened their cabins to these men, sometimes hiding them and feeding them generously for days at a time. Others provided clothing, foodstuffs, or other supplies (more often than not their masters' property) to passersby or offered medical care.

To a number of refugees, simply the information slaves provided on the political persuasion of residents of their area was one of the most valuable services they provided. Slaves were usually well aware of which white residents in their neighborhood were Unionist, and therefore useful to fugitives, and which were to be avoided.[59] A Rhode Island fugitive recalled his exasperation with the "most ignorant man I had ever met," a lone white Unionist to whose mountain cabin he had been directed by helpful slaves. Although the hermit expressed his willingness to help him, the soldier complained that he was too ill informed to do so and that "we could do better with the negroes" in terms of information and advice.[60]

The prevalence of interracial contacts in the mountains is most noteworthy. Almost all of the fugitives who later wrote accounts of traveling through that region included references to contacts with and usually aid from slaves in an area with a relatively small black populace. But of course it was by no means only slaves in the mountains who provided assistance. Indeed their efforts

"The Escaped Correspondents Enjoying the Negro's Hospitality"
(From Browne, Four Years in Secessia*)*

typified the sort of subversive activity in which slaves throughout the South
engaged whenever the opportunity presented itself. Many of the fugitives who
made their way into the Carolina highlands had benefited from slave contacts
long before they reached the mountains and had learned to rely on black
inhabitants wherever they encountered them. A Massachusetts soldier in flight
from the Camp Sorghum prison in Columbia, South Carolina, recalled that well
before he and his party had moved into the mountains they had learned to
search out "negroes" along the way.

The uncertainty of white loyalties among highlanders made blacks even
more valuable resources. Union escapees from the Danville, Virginia, prison
warned a fellow fugitive as he moved into the Blue Ridge mountains that, given
the uncertainty of loyalties among white highlanders, he "must have nothing to
do with any body but a negro, or he's a goner." In his account of moving into
Wilkes County after escaping from the Confederate prison at Salisbury, Albert
Richardson, a New York *Tribune* correspondent, stated: "By this time we had
learned that every black face was a friendly face. So far as fidelity was con-

cerned, we felt just as safe among the negroes as if in our Northern homes. Male or female, old or young, intelligent or simple, we were fully assured they would never betray us."[61]

It was not simply kindness toward strangers that motivated the hospitality and aid bestowed by highland blacks, both slave and free. A number of the beneficiaries of those kindnesses were convinced that it was the cause for which they had fought that determined the extent of blacks' help. To Richardson, "they were always ready to help anybody opposed to the Rebels. Union refugees, Confederate deserters, escaped prisoners—all received from them the same prompt and invariable kindness. But let a Rebel soldier . . . apply to them, and he would find but cold kindness."[62] Junius Browne, a fugitive traveling with Richardson, was more eloquent in describing black partisanship as he witnessed it. "The magic word 'Yankee' opened all their hearts, and elicited the loftiest virtues. They were ignorant, oppressed, enslaved; but they always cherished a simple and beautiful faith in the cause of the Union and its ultimate triumph."[63] Others recognized the risks slaves took in offering such aid. Michael Egan, who traveled through the South Carolina upcountry on his way into Macon County, North Carolina, noted that "by betraying us to their masters they would have been duly rewarded and appreciated, while if found giving aid or comfort to escaping Yankee soldiers it would insure to them punishment, the nature of which I leave the reader to infer."[64]

A local slave who shared a prison cell in Asheville with fugitive Union soldiers who had been recaptured nearby paid a heavy price for his attempt to aid them. According to a preconceived plan of escape from the flimsy jail, this "large, powerful negro" seized the guard and held him while his white cell mates took his keys and made their exit. Intimidated by the threats of another guard they encountered, the "cowards" retreated back to their cell. On the assumption that the slave alone had instigated the attack and subsequent escape, the guard he had held ordered him to be disciplined by a hundred lashes. The New York cavalryman who related this story was particularly incensed by the unfairness of the punishment, noting that the "poor fellow was not to blame half as much as the white men" who had "basely deserted him." He told his companions that "the poor ignorant black man's only fault had been his confidence in the courage of his white associates."[65]

Self-interest was also often a motivating factor in the collaboration of mountain slaves with fugitives they encountered. Slaves sometimes took advantage of the opportunities such contacts offered to make their own escapes. When

William Parkins, for example, anticipating rugged terrain and hostile country ahead as he moved through Mitchell County, urged the South Carolina slave who had accompanied him to return home, the slave replied: "No, sah! Dis chile neber goes back to Carolina. Dar's freedom ahead of him, and he's gwine to git dar, sure, dis time. Can't turn me back now, Massa Parkins, not eban with a six-shooter. I goes wid you." "And so he did," stated Parkins, "for nearly two months without a word of complaint."[66]

William Burson, an Ohio soldier in flight from Andersonville prison to East Tennessee, met five slave men in Wilkes County who asked if they could accompany him across Union lines. Hiding out for several days under the care and protection of these slaves in the Trap Hill area of the county, Burson was joined by local Confederate deserters as well. He asked their advice about taking the black men with him. One assured him that "they were all good fellows and belonged to rebel masters whom they would be glad to see robbed of their slaves" but went on to warn him about the added risks to his own escape if he was accompanied by slaves. Their presence would probably assure that all would be hanged if captured. This notion frightened Burson's other white companions, who urged him to abandon the idea, but Burson reiterated his own resolve to contribute in this small way to the emancipation process. He maintained that "to anybody who had treated me as well as the negroes had, I would do all in my power to assist them out of bondage." His commitment remained firm, but after being warned of his impending arrest by the home guards, which required him to make a more sudden retreat from the county than anticipated, Burson "informed the darkies of our danger. 'Well, well,' they said, 'nebber mind us, massa, we'll come arter awhile.'" They never appear again in Burson's narrative.[67]

Of course, the sentiments and behavior of highland blacks were not nearly as united behind the Union cause as these accounts imply. Naturally, such accounts only rarely acknowledged instances of slaves' loyalty to or defense of their owners or their owners' property, just as later memoirs of the owners of those slaves rarely allude to slaves' behavior except to relate instances of loyalty, affection, or heroism. When enemy troops finally invaded the area late in the war, highland bondsmen and -women, like their counterparts throughout the South, reacted in very different ways, and one must rely on sources of both biases to sense the full range of their responses.

A strong black oral tradition in Burke County recounts the defiant actions of Lawson, the slave son of Hamilton Avery, during George W. Kirk's raid on

Camp Vance in 1863. According to this account, Lawson burned his master's barn during the raid and, with other slaves, joined Kirk's men as they headed back to Tennessee.[68] White Avery descendants, on the other hand, were more likely to recall the behavior of Rodman, one of Isaac Avery's slaves. After Isaac's own death and that of his son, William Waightstill, who was killed in attempting to chase Kirk's raiders out of the county, Rodman took charge of the Avery family's business affairs and farm operation, even providing funds of his own to maintain the home for Avery's widow and her daughters.[69]

In her account of her parents' war experiences in Cherokee County, Margaret Walker Freel detailed the heroics of slaves owned by fellow resident Abraham Suddereth, whose seventy-two slaves made him by far the largest slaveholder in the state's southwestern corner. During a Union raid on the county from Tennessee in the summer of 1863, the Suddereth slaves took refuge in the hills as soldiers ransacked their owner's home. The troops forced a deaf slave called "Deef Bob" to saddle an unruly stallion and to accompany on another horse the Federal captain, who claimed new ownership of the prize animal. The Suddereths assumed they had lost both slave and horse until Bob returned several days later riding the stallion. He had somehow manipulated the horse into dumping his abductor, and the horse followed Bob back home through the mountain wilderness.

During a later raid on the farm, other slaves saved the Suddereths' valuables. One removed their buried strong box and hid it in nearby woods when he heard the raiders approaching. When yet another slave stumbled upon the box while seeking refuge from the troops, he moved it to an even safer distance from the house and buried it there. The two slaves received the adulations of both white and black Suddereths, and, according to Freel, "dutifully accepted the praise and thanks of the family and modestly disclaimed any right to a reward."[70]

While the accuracy of such heroic tales told by later generations of whites may be questionable, such actions on the part of slaves were by no means unusual and are fully understandable. But so, too, are the acts of defiance and subversion that, often unbeknownst to their owners or other whites, served to destabilize, if only indirectly, the institution that defined their servitude. In short, slaves in western North Carolina seem to have responded to the war's various disruptive forces in much the same manner as slaves throughout the war-torn South. It was only that such situations came later and with less frequency than was the case in other parts of the Confederacy.

Unionist Alexander H. Jones of Hendersonville had sneered at efforts to make slavery central to North Carolinians' arguments for leaving the Union. News of Lincoln's election, he wrote, were met with the howl of "'*nigger, nigger, nigger,*' as though the salvation of the whole world depended upon the negro and slavery."[71] Highlanders, like Southerners elsewhere, did indeed make slavery's security a basic part of their rhetoric for or against secession, and with the war's end, the system's abolishment would prove one of the war's most revolutionary and long-lasting effects. Yet, ironically, once the war was under way and for much of its duration, slavery was one of the aspects of the mountain economy and social structure that suffered least.

The disruptions and discipline problems slaveowners faced remained, from their own perspectives, mere inconveniences, and few of them saw in such developments anything ominous about the future of the institution. The relative stability of the system, the increased demand for and market value of slave property, and its ever more crucial role in meeting the region's labor demands and sustaining agricultural productivity all combined to create a false sense of optimism and complacency on the part of mountain masters. Thus slavery's collapse came more suddenly to the North Carolina mountains than it did in many parts of the South, and as will be seen, the reaction of mountain masters and mistresses varied greatly to what, for most of them, was an unexpected turn of events in the spring of 1865.

MILITARY INCURSION AND COLLAPSE

Oh! This Is a Cruel World and Cruel People in It

O N September 22, 1864, Governor Vance expressed the disillusionment and discouragement that many western North Carolinians were beginning to face regarding the prospects of the war's ultimate outcome. In a long letter to former governor and fellow Buncombe County native, David L. Swain, then president of the University of North Carolina, Vance assessed the military prospects for the Confederacy and disclosed the depth of his despondency: "I have never before been so gloomy about the condition of affairs. Early's defeat in the Valley I regard as the Turning point of the campaign & confidentially, I fear seals the fate of Richmond though not immediately. It will require our utmost exertions to retain our footing in Va. until 1865 comes in. McLellans [*sic*] defeat is placed among the facts & abolitionism is rampant for four years more. The army in Georgia is getting demoralized."[1]

There is no information in this passage that was not available to any resident of the state's mountain counties. The victories of Union armies under William T. Sherman in Atlanta and Philip Sheridan in the Shenandoah Valley had convinced even the most sanguine of them, as it had their governor, that the struggle for Southern independence was doomed. And many would have agreed with Vance when he assigned blame for the predicament that they had been unwillingly forced into by the events surrounding the bombardment of Fort Sumter three and a half years earlier. He asserted: "It shows what I have always believed that the great *popular heart* is not now & never has been in this war. It was a revolution of the *politicians* not *the people*."[2]

It was not only news from other fronts that created this despondency. As already indicated, the war had seriously weakened the mountain society and economy to the breaking point by its final year. Faced with increasingly active Federal forces in East Tennessee, local leaders in the North Carolina mountains sought ways to limit the damage that the end of the conflict would produce. For those who had suffered persecution for their unwillingness to support the Confederacy or for their active support for the Union, these months were a time for increased vigilance as disappointed Southern patriots blamed them for the impending destruction of their dream. Adding to all highlanders' uncertainties about the future were the destruction of much of their transportation system and the impending end of slavery. Almost certain freedom for slaves and the diminished status of many of the region's elite threatened the very structure of the social order and power base. In the midst of all of this change and uncertainty, most western North Carolinians waited apprehensively for the end of the conflict.

Sermons preached from mountain pulpits came to reflect this mood of apprehension and gloom over the course of the fall of 1864 and winter of 1865. In Lenoir, Rev. Jesse Rankin preached from Ecclesiastes, telling his congregation that it was "better to go to the house of mourning than to go to the house of feasting . . . sorrow is better than laughter," in that it strengthened character. In December, another Caldwell County minister drew on the story of Ruth for a message that seemed particularly aimed at the women among his listeners. They should take comfort, he preached, from this woman who endured famine and despair by trusting in God and caring for her family.[3] In Asheville, a February 1865 sermon focused on the Hebrews' Babylonian exile, with the message that even in defeat God did not abandon his chosen people.[4]

Perhaps the clearest indication of the apprehension about the vulnerability of mountain society was the drastic action taken by two prominent leaders of the region to protect their families. Where the Carolina highlands had long been viewed as a safe refuge from the turmoil wrought in other parts of the South, by mid-1864 some residents had come to see it as an area from which to escape. At summer's end, Governor Vance sent his wife and four children away from their relatively exposed position in Asheville to Morganton. The seriousness of the Vances' intention to abandon the area west of the Blue Ridge is attested to by the fact that the possessions their wagon carried included their "cooking stove, . . . brass kettle and ice cream freezer."[5] The Vance family eventually decided that even Morganton was not safe enough, and Harriett E. Vance and the children moved another forty miles east to Statesville. By early 1865, even as refugees driven from their homes by Sherman's army were moving into Caldwell County, Rufus Lenoir Patterson decided that his own family's safety could not be guaranteed there, and he moved his wife, Mary, and their children fifty miles east to Salem to stay with her parents.[6] Given the prominence of both families, their departures must have proved unsettling to others in the area.[7]

Despite such displays of panic and uncertainty, most highlanders followed the example of their governor, who made a concerted effort to carry on despite the impending doom of the Confederacy. Seeing no alternative other than to try to preserve as many of their traditional social and economic relationships as possible, western Carolinians persevered. Despite all of the pressure placed on local governments by undisciplined Confederate troops, Federal raids, and the depredations of gangs of deserters and draft evaders, officials continued to do their duties. Clay County elected a new sheriff; Jacob Siler continued to collect revenue to repair the state road and contracted to have three bridges rebuilt in Macon County; Augustus Merrimon endeavored to bring murderers in Henderson and Jackson Counties to trial; Madison County officials sought to have John Ponder named collector of Confederate taxes.[8] Undoubtedly, most residents welcomed these activities as evidence that mountain society still retained its basic structure and discipline.

In private life as well, highlanders sought to give the appearance of normalcy to their lives. The Silver Creek Primitive Baptist Association held their regular district meeting in Burke County in September 1864 and planned its next regularly scheduled meeting.[9] Concerned relatives and neighbors in the Hominy Creek community of Buncombe County continued to make clothing and to preserve food to be sent to local units in the Confederate army.[10] Traditional economic activities continued despite the problems caused by inflation and shortages. The selling and leasing of land continued as the 1865 spring planting season beckoned.[11] The sale and hiring of slaves, as well as renegotiated contracts with tenants and overseers, continued with little reference to the extraordinary circumstances that might well render such transactions void.[12] The few remaining merchants continued to sell items brought in from more worldly markets, including "English Calico," "Irish Linen," and "French Flannel." (The reality of the war, however, intruded even here; the same merchant also advertised "Water Proof Gun Caps" and "Mourning Calico.")[13] No one in the western counties was likely deceived by these appearances of normality, yet such actions may well have provided some small comfort in the face of daunting challenges.

Perhaps not surprisingly, some business leaders in the mountains appeared to be more concerned with the health of their own enterprises than with the fate of the Confederacy. There was renewed interest in the two railroads that served the eastern edge of the mountain region. In December, the leaders of the Western North Carolina Railroad strongly urged Governor Vance to assume "control of the manufactures of the State at least to a great extent."[14] This proposal was designed to protect the railroad that extended into Burke County (and that was a target of Kirk's raid the previous summer) from being taken over by Confederate authorities. At the same time, the board of directors of the Wilmington, Charlotte, and Rutherford Railroad passed resolutions of gratitude for the governor's efforts to preserve the rails and rolling stock of the line from redistribution to other railroads.[15] In both instances, local business interests—and the state government as well—sought to preserve the infrastructure of the region, even though it conflicted with the more immediate needs of the Confederate government. Clearly, the mountain elite as well as other residents were trying to insure their own well-being rather than that of the Southern nation, whose days they increasingly viewed as numbered.

Unfortunately for the civilian population in the mountains, such stability was unlikely as the Confederacy died. Among the most immediate concerns was the shortage of salt. Keeping mountain residents supplied with salt, which was essential in preserving much of their food stores, had been a challenge through much of the war, but after the Federal army seized Fort Fisher early in 1865 and closed the state saltworks there, county salt agents found it even more difficult to obtain the precious preservative. Equally frustrating was the fact that a fairly ample supply at nearby Saltville, Virginia, had become nearly inaccessible since poor roads and the failing railroad system limited what could be shipped to the mountain counties. Even when salt did reach some counties, it did not always get distributed to the residents most in need. O. L. Erwin of Transylvania County reported that his supply was "dripping and waisting" because he and his agents were constantly being called out for home guard duty.[16] The result was that the region's food supply was drastically reduced by the spring of 1865.

Like the salt agent in Transylvania County, most civilians in the mountains were convinced that many of their economic difficulties would be solved if they could just retain the human resources needed to sustain their community economies. As was true earlier in the conflict, letters and petitions to Governor Vance from all parts of western North Carolina attested to the hardships caused by the absence of blacksmiths, tanners, shoemakers, and teachers.[17] These pleas changed little from the three previous years, and residents' needs seemed only slightly more acute by the winter of 1864–65 than they had been previously. The sheer increase in such communications to Vance might have meant simply that highlanders were more consciously attempting to retain as many of the traditional economic relationships as possible as the war approached its end.

A second group of letters asking for the release of men from military duty tells a much different story. As the Transylvania salt agent indicated, the men who were required to serve in the home guard were often essential parts of the wartime economy. Even though they were allowed to remain at home except during emergencies, their neighbors increasingly felt that they could no longer depend upon their skills and services. At this point, only men forty-six years old or older served in home guard units, and they were often not particularly energetic or effective defenders of the public safety in any case. Thus, petitioners to the governor and other officials urged that certain men be exempted from local defense duties because they would be much more "useful" as full-time civilians. A number of prominent residents of Henderson County, for example, protested that tanner William Patton had accumulated approximately $100,000 worth of hides that could be turned into footwear only under his direction. Since Patton apparently employed slaves to actually make the shoes and boots, some Henderson County citizens worried about problems of race control as well.[18] Other residents sent letters and petitions asking that individual shoemakers, teachers, and physicians be excused.[19]

As important as these particular cases were, some observers perceived an even broader and more acute problem. Augustus Merrimon, Vance's confidante in Asheville who was well acquainted with conditions in the more remote counties north of the town, informed the governor that farmers' output there also suffered from the constant calls on them as home guardsmen. When these demands came during the harvest and planting seasons, such defensive duties proved very real threats to communities' food supply.[20] As elsewhere in the Confederacy, resources in the Carolina highlands were being stretched far too thin by the overwhelming demands of modern warfare.

Even when sufficient people were available to process food supplies, these resources were not always used in the best interests of the community. Early in the war, the state government had forbidden the manufacture of whiskey from corn in an attempt to retain as much food for people and animals as possible. Despite a long tradition of resistance to restrictive government policies in this particular activity, the ban seems to have been generally observed. In fact, a shortage of alcohol for medicinal purposes was the unexpected result, prompting Confederate authorities to allow certain distillers in Burke County to make grain and corn into alcohol. Local residents protested. "Grain is very scarce in this community," one resident complained, "and the families of soldiers and the poor & needy will require all of the surplus which can be spared from the army, for their maintenance and support."[21]

But in the counties surrounding Burke—Rutherford, McDowell, Yancey, Watauga, and Wilkes—local residents late in the war had resumed their prewar practices and were manufacturing moonshine in tremendous volume. One stunned official reported that a local farmer "offered a certain number of gallons of 'Nick Williams' *new* whiskey in trade for a negro."[22] Although authorities found it difficult to eradicate this subversive entrepreneurship, William W. Springfield, an officer in Thomas's Legion, ordered his troops to destroy stills in Cherokee and Jackson Counties.[23] While this kind of government intervention into the economic lives of mountain residents was generally supported as long as food remained in short supply, the attempt to reallocate resources was marginally successful at best. Surviving evidence indicates that as civilian morale declined, the market for alcohol grew. At the same time, disillusionment with the Confederacy created an atmosphere in which community-sanctioned lawlessness flourished.

Sensing that the social fabric of western North Carolina was beginning to unravel, local leaders continued their efforts to ameliorate the suffering of the indigent. By 1864 and 1865, national, state, and county governments engaged in an unprecedented welfare effort. The particular targets of this relief were the suffering families of Confederate soldiers, who rarely received pay, and when they were paid, the value of the money when it was issued depreciated rapidly in the face of the raging inflation of Confederate currency. The extraordinary efforts that were made, however, became increasingly ineffective. First, the tax system was regressive since all citizens had to pay a flat 10 percent of their produce in taxes, which was a greater hardship on the poor. Moreover, as historian Paul Escott has maintained, "the government simply did not obtain enough food for the poor. The destruction and dislocations of the war were too great, and the needs of the army took too high a priority relative to civilian needs."[24] He noted too that this new form of economic dependency threatened the financial and social independence of the yeoman farmers. Mountain society was facing stresses from unexpected quarters as the Confederacy collapsed.

The most obvious cause of these social dislocations was the growing internal warfare between organized Union, Confederate, and outlaw bands throughout the highlands. The violence that had taken place in the mountains earlier in the war had been more contained, and thus more predictable and somehow more explicable. Although Confederate army units, Union raiders, and militia groups had greatly disrupted the lives of increasingly bitter civilians, they left the basic social structure untouched, except in extreme cases like the Shelton Laurel massacre. Even the individual confrontations created by personal feuds seemed to fit into the existing social frameworks.[25] By 1864, however, far more western North Carolina civilians found themselves victimized by increased abuse and terrorism from roving bands of bushwhackers or deserters, which were subject to no obvious control or authority. Even more unsettling to many was the randomness and the unpredictability of their attacks. This uncertainty and the growing meanness of spirit of the participants in this mayhem threatened to destroy the fragile economic, social, and political fabric of mountain communities.

One of the worst incidents of this new warfare took place near the Laurel region of Madison County. Three local bushwhackers, who had terrorized the county by killing and then scalping a woman in the summer of 1864, later murdered a home guard officer. The officer's companions hunted down the small gang and killed all three outlaws. When it became apparent that the fugitives were brothers, the local defense forces proceeded to the family's house and burned it down.[26]

The events in Madison County were part of an escalating cycle of violence that had begun at least two years before, but terrorist attacks were becoming ever more localized, were often in response to very particular provocations, and were usually retaliatory in nature. The brutal murder of William C. Walker, the

Cherokee County political leader and colonel in Thomas's Legion, was retaliation for three Unionists killed earlier in October 1864. Walker had been singled out as the most prominent Confederate target of five who were identified by friends of the Unionist victims.[27] It was not simply Walker's murder but the attitudes of his executioners that captured the new mean spiritedness of internal warfare. The vigilantes first physically abused Walker, who was already in ill health, kicking him and striking him in the head. When it became obvious that they were going to kill Walker, his wife, Margaret, requested that they do so on the premises, so that they could give him a proper burial. But they denied her even that, carrying him off into the wilderness to execute him. His body was never recovered. It was only through the kindness of Walker's fellow Masonic brothers that his widow and family were provided with enough food and forage to allow them to survive the war's remaining months.[28] The malice exhibited in this confrontation was typical of the growing nastiness of the internal war. Death and destruction were no longer sufficient; the infliction of pain and suffering seem to have been required as well.

Increasingly, the violence appeared to bear no relation to the issues of the war. In Wilkes County, the Harrison Church band combined larceny with self-defense. Although Church claimed to have a commission from the Federal army to perform some unspecified tasks, he spent most of his time raiding his Confederate neighbors. In November 1864, Church and his compatriots liberated three slaves in one raid and in another stole $35,000 from the home of a fellow resident.[29] On another occasion, they burned property worth $4,000 and plundered other houses. One of the victims was so enraged that he demanded that Church's "underaged" brother be killed by the authorities in retaliation.[30]

All sense of civility seemed to disappear in the county. Edward Cranor described to Governor Vance his violent encounter with Calvin Cowles, one of Wilkes's leading Unionists. Cowles, upon receiving a newspaper in which a letter from Cranor was published, apparently with derogatory comments about him, "brought it down & asked me who wrote it. I told him I wrote it; he said he did not care who wrote it but that whoever did, wrote a lie whereupon I struck him in the mouth with my fist & a general row ensued."[31] The violence directed by and at men like Harrison Church eroded civility and community ties. In February 1865 frustrated local citizens formed an independent posse, outside of the authority of the home guards, that attempted to end the violence by unleashing a reign of terror upon the families of members of the outlaw bands.[32]

Similar atrocities took place with increasing frequency in many mountain counties. In Rutherford County, Alexander Grant's family was attacked by an outlaw gang. The bushwhackers stole his money and valuables, beat him and left him for dead, and shot and killed his daughter as she lay in her bed. In a similar attack in the same county, William Fortune lost the contents of his tannery and two slaves but the outlaws retreated before inflicting any harm to Fortune or his family. As a correspondent to Governor Vance wryly commented later, "I suppose his having a double barrel shot gun well charged was the reason of their not forcing open the house."[33]

The psychological impact of such depredations could be as damaging as the physical abuse, particularly on the women at home, who felt particularly vulnerable and often defenseless. One husband in the army counseled an obviously worried wife: "Our fears often alarm us when the real danger is light. No Yankees or bushwackers [sic] are likely to do you any personal violence and being alarmed does not profit."[34] Cornelia Henry expressed her distress more privately. She recorded in her diary three different reports of murders committed in her Buncombe County neighborhood in September and October 1864 alone. At the end of the third such report—"The tories killed Mrs. Joe Bryson & wounded two of her daughters"—Mrs. Henry exclaimed: "Oh! This is a cruel world & cruel people in it."[35] She would have even more reason to express such sentiments over the next four months, as these sorts of atrocities continued.

A similar outbreak of larceny and vandalism occurred in Polk, Henderson, and Transylvania Counties, which led to reports that farmers in the French Broad River valley were refusing to plant in the spring of 1865. The fear that they would be killed while working their fields overshadowed the desperate need for their produce.[36] An Asheville man suggested to Governor Vance that the state obtain bloodhounds from South Carolina to track the band of deserters rumored to be perpetrating these outrages. He urged that "every man that shelters or protects or aids them in any way" be prosecuted, and that every deserter captured be court-martialed and shot, for "to send them to the army is only to allow them to return again or go to the enemy."[37] When some of the gang members were arrested in Polk County, a local notable lamented, "It is greatly to be regretted that any of them were taken alive & it is sincerely to be hoped for the good of our sacred cause and the benefit of example that speedy justice will be meted out to Weaver and Hamilton. They have great influence among the lower & meaner classes."[38]

As western North Carolina society appeared on the verge of collapse, larger events in the war conspired to bring the conflict to an end. The capture of Fort Fisher near Wilmington in mid-January 1865 signaled that the war was entering its final phase. Now completely cut off from the outside world, the Confederacy was clearly doomed. Shortly thereafter, Sherman's army started north from Savannah bringing its massive firepower and vindictive destructiveness into South Carolina, the seat of secessionism and rebellion. Unwilling to face the obvious consequences of these developments, both the national administration under Jefferson Davis and the state government under Zebulon Vance sought to rally public support. The failed peace conference in early February between a Confederate delegation and President Lincoln and William H. Seward simply insured that the final result would be dictated by the military.

Yet signs of the Confederacy's disintegration were apparent even in the discipline problems among Confederate troops in the mountains. An incident in Asheville in January underscored these newly emerging tensions. James L. Henry reported to Governor Vance that the cavalry company he had earlier commanded were resisting orders to dismount and serve as infantry. Henry was subsequently dismissed from that command, and news of his dismissal led the same group, as part of the 69th North Carolina Regiment, to refuse orders to leave Asheville and proceed to Tennessee. In a final address to his men after his dismissal, Henry complained of being mistreated by the Confederate leadership; at one point, according to a witness, he broke down and "cried like a child."[39] His men were shortly thereafter introduced to their new commanding officer, George Tait, who Vance apparently had sent to bring some order to this volatile situation. But Tait's presence only exacerbated the hard feelings of the troops, who attacked him. As Tait reported to a stunned governor: "Just at dark a mutiny broke out among the men, which culminated about 9 o'clock in my being severely wounded and rendered insensible by a rock which struck me on the forehead. I was unarmed and could get no assistance whatever, the insubordination extending to the entire command."[40] Not unreasonably, Tait concluded that he could not be an effective leader to this unit and resigned the appointment.

Such actions were symptomatic of the profound disillusionment and discouragement that gripped soldiers in the mountain area as much as it did civilians, now that the Confederacy was visibly on its last legs. Recognizing that their action was the most serious crime in the military law code, the men in this company of the 69th immediately dispersed. Both the officers and the private soldiers retreated into the woods to avoid their military superiors. (Interestingly, one observer noted that local residents sympathized with Tait and refused to support the mutinous actions of the cavalrymen, although many of them were neighbors and acquaintances.)[41] Other troops in the mountains demonstrated their frustrations simply by wholesale desertions. In Yancey County, Captain John Henry Ray led much of his company, some 250 men by one count, to walk away from their posts and give themselves over to Federal authorities just across the state line in Tennessee.[42]

It was into this vacuum of Confederate military power that George W. Kirk launched yet another raid into western North Carolina, apparently with the understanding that many residents there would now welcome Union soldiers' presence. But he soon found out that, as William W. Stringfield later noted, it was a welcome "with bloody hands to hospitable graves."[43] In early February 1865, Kirk led 600 men from Newport, Tennessee, into Haywood County. After brushing aside only a feeble effort by home guardsmen to hold them off, the Union troops struck several farms and households, and then moved on to Waynesville, where they spent most of a day pillaging stores and homes. They attacked the jail, liberating a number of local Unionists and deserters held there, and then burned it. This was a symbolic gesture in part, given that many Unionists from the region had been detained there throughout the war. On Kirk's orders, his troops also burned the home of Confederate leader James R. Love, which also had been the home of Revolutionary War hero Robert Love, his ancestor. They were stopped from burning the home of another of the county's prominent families, the Welches, only because friends of the Welches were among Kirk's forces.[44]

As these attacks took place, local forces mustered some resistance. While camped that night before a planned raid west into Jackson County, Kirk's troops were surprised by an attack by a group of about a hundred Haywood County men, made up of some regular troops and some home guardsmen, who opened fire upon them from the darkness. Though his men easily repelled their attackers, Kirk altered his plans for moving farther into the region and the next morning headed toward the Smokies to cross back into Tennessee. But even those efforts were thwarted as a sizable contingent of Confederates from the southwest counties gathered to ambush the Union retreat at Soco Gap, thirteen miles northwest of Waynesville. Kirk was forced to alter his route once again. This time he moved due west along the Soco Creek, where he encountered Colonel Stringfield and a battalion of Thomas's Legion, including a substantial number of the Cherokee Indians under his command. Although the Union forces again escaped after an hour-long skirmish, known locally as the battle of Soco Creek, Kirk returned to Tennessee far more exhausted and relieved than he had expected, having met the strongest defenses and hardest fighting yet in his ventures into the North Carolina mountains. The encounter was rather heartening for Stringfield, who wrote that "this raid had a good effect upon the people, drawing them more closely together and intensified Southern senti-ment." But he seemed to have been under no illusions (or so he later claimed) as to how little any of this meant by this point. "Soon after this," he reported, "the enemy everywhere became more active and aggressive. The end was now rapidly approaching, as slow as our people were to believe it."[45]

By late March and early April, Sherman's troops were moving northward into North Carolina, Grant was pursuing Lee from Richmond westward toward Appomattox Court House, and Davis's government was fleeing southward through the Carolinas and into Georgia. All of this activity coincided with an eastward movement of Union troops, led by General George Stoneman, that would cause many other western Carolinians to finally feel the full thrust of a substantial enemy force. With this month-long cavalry raid, many mountain residents, particularly town dwellers who had been insulated from much of the bushwhacking activity and short-term raids that so plagued much of the coun-tryside, suddenly came to experience the war just as many Southern civilians in Virginia, in Tennessee, in Georgia, and in other major theaters of war had done.

General Stoneman, a New Yorker, had conducted a number of raids with mixed results prior to this last major assignment—one into middle Georgia early in Sherman's May 1864 campaign (during which he had been captured and later released), and a second, far more successful venture into southwestern Virginia in December, where he destroyed railroads that may have served Lee's army later in the spring and where he leveled the Confederacy's major saltworks at Saltville. As a reward for this latter mission, Stoneman was named commander of the District of East Tennessee in February 1865 and ordered by General Grant to lead a cavalry raid into the interior of South Carolina, "visiting a portion of the State which will not be reached by Sherman's forces," including Columbia. His orders were "to destroy but not to fight battles," a strategy obviously modeled on the "total war" tactics employed so effectively by Sherman in Georgia the previous fall. A series of delays meant that Sherman had already taken Columbia and had moved on into North Carolina by the time Stoneman was ready to move. His mission was thus scaled back to the more limited mission of moving through the western and piedmont sections of North Carolina, destroying property, particularly railroads and other military resources, and liberating Union prisoners still held in Salisbury, who numbered as many as 10,000 by some estimates.[46] This strategy was designed not only to deny any logistical support from this part of the state to either Lee or Johnston but also to eliminate the region as an avenue of retreat for either of their armies.

Not until March 28 did Stoneman cross the state line into North Carolina, leading a group of around 6,000 cavalrymen, consisting primarily of units from Pennsylvania, Michigan, Kentucky, and Ohio. At the beginning and the end of his march, Stoneman would be reinforced by George W. Kirk, three weeks after Kirk's Haywood County raid. A significant number of men, including Kirk's, under Stoneman's command were "home yankees." They served for the most part in the 2nd and 3rd North Carolina Mounted Volunteer Infantries and consisted of recruits taken during Kirk's earlier raids into Madison, Yancey, and Wilkes Counties, residents of which were particularly well represented in both regiments.[47]

Stoneman's men moved quickly and quietly enough to take the town of Boone late on the March 28, with no advance warning having reached its citizens. A unit of home guardsmen was assembling just as the Union advanced guard approached, which led to an exchange of fire in which three of the guardsmen and at least two civilians were killed. The haphazard nature of the skirmish was such that a fifteen-year-old boy mounted the most effective defense. Chased by several Union soldiers, he was able to hold them at bay by shooting from behind fences and trees as they approached. He killed two of his attackers before racing off into hiding in nearby woods.[48] Union troops, at the command of General Alvan C. Gillem, Stoneman's second-in-command, burned the jail and with it most county records. They took between fifty and sixty prisoners, most of whom were elderly men, who eventually were transported to prison camps in the north, even with the war's end fast approaching.[49]

The Union forces set a pattern of disruption and destruction in Boone that they continued in Lenoir, Wilkesboro, Elkin, Salem, Salisbury, Statesville, Morganton, and Marion—though with significant variations. The resistance mounted by local residents in the raiders' path had much to do with the treatment accorded them. Caldwell and Wilkes County citizens seemed relieved that they were spared the violence inflicted on Watauga County residents. Joseph C. Norwood in Lenoir informed Walter Lenoir of Stoneman's visit, which came two days later. "We are just through with a scene of alarm and

General George Stoneman (Library of Congress)

very great danger," he began, but he went on to say, almost admiringly, that the troops "were equipped in the very best manner, and under the severest discipline and were not allowed to plunder to any great extent or commit any acts of violence."[50] Rufus Patterson's cotton factory near his Palmyra plantation was burned, again on orders from General Gillem. This was the only major damage inflicted on Caldwell County property, but even that action led to Stoneman's

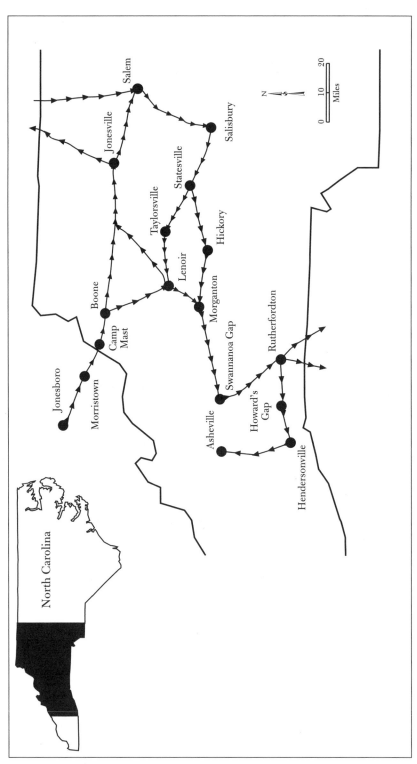

Route of Stoneman's raid through western North Carolina, March–April 1865 (University of Georgia Cartographic Services)

objection. He rebuked his second-in-command because Patterson had always maintained a "neutral" stance and had traded with Union officials in East Tennessee throughout most of the war, supplying cloth to Federal troops stationed there.[51]

Farther up the Happy Valley in Wilkes County, James Gwyn described in his diary his relief as the Union forces passed by. "We were all very agreeably disappointed; those who passed the place of Mr. Hickerson acted very well indeed, only took cattle and horses, & mules & and did not even enter our houses or do violence to our families." Gwyn confided that he himself had lain low, fearing that he would be taken prisoner. "But I need not have gone off, they would not have molested me. Those on the other side of the [Yadkin] river acted somewhat worse, but they behaved well in the main."[52]

Interestingly, class issues may have played a part in the leniency shown toward Gwyn and his neighbors. Col. William J. Palmer, who was commanding one of Stoneman's three brigades, later wrote that he respected Gwyn and Hickerson as leaders in their communities who were looked up to by their neighbors. He had earlier divulged similar empathies toward the local elite when he described another resident as "one of the finest specimens of a country-gentleman I have ever met," and "although he was a rebel, [he] belonged to the Free-Masonry of Gentlemen," and "before I knew it I found myself regretting every bushel of corn that we fed, and sympathizing with every one of his fence rails that we were compelled to burn." He continued: "We frequently meet such gentlemen in our marches, and always make it a point to leave them as far as possible unmolested so that they may remain to teach nobility by example to the communities in which they live."[53]

Such appreciation for Southern noblesse oblige was hardly typical of the Union troops' attitudes as they moved through the area. More often it was residents' compliance and cooperation that accounted for the leniency with which Stoneman's troops treated them. As the raiders reached their eastern-most point at Salem on April 10, for example, a contingent led by the town's mayor waving white handkerchiefs met them as they approached the historic Moravian community and the adjoining village of Winston. (Among the twenty-odd members of that peacekeeping group was Rufus Patterson, who had recently moved his family from Caldwell County to what he thought would be a safer area. He had only just learned that the men he was about to face had destroyed his cotton factory nearly two weeks earlier.) Their communal surrender, along with what one of Stoneman's men called "a cordial reception, very different from the greetings we usually receive," spared both Salem and Winston from any destruction.[54]

As one group of Union cavalrymen then moved north into Virginia to continue the destruction of railroads that Stoneman's December raid had begun, the largest part of his force moved toward Salisbury, the only substantial military target in the region and their ultimate goal. As the site of what remained one of the Confederacy's largest military prisons and as a collection point for Confederate armaments and state governmental records and other property, the town had no hope of receiving the same benign treatment accorded to Salem. Although they were fully expected, the Union forces met only token resistance as they moved quickly into Salisbury on April 12. They destroyed public buildings, cotton mills, and tanneries, raided the supply depots and distributed its holdings to local poor whites and blacks before burning the rest, and leveled the prison. While Salisbury certainly suffered more extensive damage than any mountain community in Stoneman's path, the general strictly enforced orders forbidding the pillage of private property or the harassment of local residents.[55]

On April 13, Stoneman's raiders turned west again and headed back toward the mountain counties. His men encountered Mrs. Zebulon Vance as they moved through Statesville. They confiscated some of her possessions, including money, until a Federal officer learned of her identity and ordered the stolen goods returned.[56] As Union cavalrymen moved back into Caldwell County on April 15, residents in Lenoir demonstrated the lessons learned earlier and again mounted no resistance. This time Stoneman left them an added burden: he deposited nearly nine hundred prisoners there, many of whom were either elderly men or disabled veterans. Lenoir women took up the charge of caring for them as they huddled in a pen next to the St. James Episcopal Church. Seeing that her community again escaped any severe repercussions from the invading Yankees, Laura Norwood declared, "I was proud of the way Lenoir acted—all stuck together and the Yankees said they liked us better than any people they had met," though she was quick to add with equal pride that they claimed "it was the d—est little rebel town they ever saw."[57]

Stoneman's troops found Morgantonians in neighboring Burke County much more defiant—as they had been during Kirk's raid on Camp Vance ten months earlier. Led by Col. Thomas Walton, with able assistance from Maj. Gen. John P. McCown, who happened to be on leave visiting relatives in Morganton, and Col. Samuel McDowell Tate, who was at home recuperating from a wound he had received in Virginia, about eighty home guardsmen

Confederate prison in Salisbury (North Carolina Division of Archives and History)

mounted as well planned a defense as Stoneman's raiders had yet faced. They destroyed the only bridge across the Catawba River east of town, forcing General Gillem and his two brigades to attempt a crossing at the closest accessible spot, Rocky Ford. Walton's men, concealed there by hastily constructed earthworks and in thick woods along the riverbank, opened fire on Gillem's men. The attack forced the Union troops to move farther downstream, where they exchanged fire with another group of Burke County guardsmen, made up mainly of seventeen-year-old boys, who, according to one observer, "fought with the coolness of veterans." The two local groups together inflicted from twenty to twenty-five casualties on the invaders and killed at least eight men, the highest losses yet experienced by Stoneman's raiders. Only when Walton's men learned that the mass of Union forces had made the crossing undetected at another ford did they retreat.[58]

Morgantonians paid a high price for their hearty defense. Stoneman had returned to Tennessee with his many prisoners, leaving his troops under command of the far less restrained Gillem, who allowed his men to engage in their most wholesale plundering yet. They moved through the town's empty streets, vandalizing almost every house and barn, terrorizing the women and children hiding within (no men remained in town), and taking firearms, foodstuffs, livestock, and any household furnishing portable enough to make off with.[59]

Despite Colonel Palmer's partiality toward "country-gentlemen," the area's elite in Morganton and elsewhere had the most to fear—partly because they had the most to lose, and partly because they often represented the local Confederate leadership that both Northern troops and the many "home yankees" serving under Stoneman most resented. Slaves often contributed to the vulnerability of their masters, sometimes in proactive ways. Selina Norwood was one of several women who noted bitterly that slaves had collaborated with Union troops in either the destruction or the theft of their owners' property. She recalled of the rampage of Gillem's troops through Morganton that as "they tore everything to pieces" at her Uncle Avery's house, a "negro boy" guided them through it, apparently pointing out the location of the valuables that they stole.[60] During Stoneman's attack on Boone, a slave cost his master his life. According to at least one of several accounts, Jacob Councill was working in a field with a slave when several soldiers approached. Councill, who was too old to have rendered military service to the Confederacy, declared his "neutrality" to his attackers, but his slave contradicted, calling him "an infernal rebel." In response, the soldiers opened fire and killed the elderly man.[61]

More often, as was true throughout the South, the mere presence of Union troops in an area—or even the anticipation of their presence—led slaves to escape. Mrs. George Harper recorded in her diary that several of her family's "Negro men, Dick and others," had absconded two days before Stoneman reached Caldwell County; on the day of his arrival, about fifty more in the upper Yadkin Valley fled.[62] Calvin Cowles in Wilkesboro had to inform the eastern North Carolina owner of two slaves he had leased for the war's duration (ironically, to keep them out of harm's way) that they had escaped. "It becomes my painful duty to inform you that your Boys Nelson & James have gone off with the Yankees," Cowles wrote Rev. C. B. Reddick of Greenville, North Carolina, on April 6. "Gen. Stoneman pass[ed] through here . . . & the Boys took my Horses and one saddle & went off with them, not even bidding me good-bye." Noting that "the greater Number of Negro fellows did likewise," he assured Reddick that he "could do nothing to prevent it." The Union troops appeared so unexpectedly that they "gave no one time to run property to a secure place."[63]

Yet even more threatening to the more affluent members of these communities were the class tensions stirred up, or even ignited, by the presence of Union troops. In the same letter in which Joseph Norwood described the relief he felt at how little damage was inflicted by Stoneman's men, he wrote of a still gnawing worry: "We have been under constant apprehension about tory—or robber raids, and I have been serving on guard at town every third night, and have been as much as two weeks without taking off my clothes. We are in danger constantly." Soon after Stoneman departed Lenoir, local raiders did indeed attack the then vulnerable town, ransacking houses and threatening the women who were forced to watch the plunder.[64]

Perhaps the most striking instance of such a violent postscript to the Union troops' presence occurred in the western part of Burke County, where Robert C. Pearson's home was among several plundered by angry—and by then drunken—local raiders. Pearson, a banker and an influential official of the Western North Carolina Railroad, was not present at the time, but another member of his household described the ordeal. She began with a description of the attackers that revealed her class and cultural biases. They were "lazy and disloyal elements that inhabit our 'South Mountains' around the town of Morganton, that class of people, which you have no doubt heard of, they are an ignorant, illiterate, uncultivated set, untrue in every respect, false to their God and traitors to their country."

She went on to describe their actions: "When the 'rear guard,' the nine robbers, entered the house to plunder and pilfer, these women (the lazy class from the mountains) followed in, to reap their share of the spoils, they (the women) exceeded in number the Yanks present on that occasion, after the house had been generally robbed, . . . the mountain women were laden with everything they could carry, such as . . . clothing, bedding, even dishes, and such." With contemptuous amusement, she went on to describe the reaction of one of the women, an "old hag," when the mob discovered a wine cellar of sorts and distributed bottles of champagne among themselves. The sound of the cork popping from the first bottle they opened led to a panic. The old woman fled, declaring that "it was pizen, put there to kill them for nobody had ever seed liquor pop that way." The narrator then went on to describe the earlier behavior of these "South Mountain" women when Gillem's troops attacked Morganton. They "swarmed our streets proclaiming their 'jubilee,' and rejoicing that the Yankees had arrived." Under what she called "their pretense of great devotion to the 'Union cause,' " these "dishonest traitorous hordes of our own beautiful mountain clime" spurred the Union troops on during what she claimed were two and a half days of plundering and wholesale theft.[65]

Asheville was the next town to brace for a visit from Stoneman's raiders. Unlike in most other communities, officials there were aware that his troops were headed their way and had ample time to mount an effective defense at Swannanoa Gap, the most accessible route into Buncombe from McDowell County. Gen. James G. Martin, commander of Confederate forces in western North Carolina, ordered all troops in the area, including a full regiment of Thomas's Legion and a brigade under General Palmer's command, to converge at the gap. Moving east from Asheville, they arrived in time to cut trees and erect a barricade across the narrow pass. After two days of trying to break through, a frustrated General Gillem, then heading the Union forces, was forced to make a circuitous detour to the south. They moved through Ruther-ford, Polk, and Henderson Counties to cross the Blue Ridge through the Hickory Nut Gap and approach Asheville from the south.[66]

This was the second time in the same month that Asheville had been the target of a Union attack. But most local officials knew they were not likely to fare as well as they had three weeks earlier, when to their surprise, they had, with relative ease, routed other Federal forces moving into Buncombe County from Tennessee. In early April, just after Stoneman's raid was launched into the northwestern part of North Carolina, some 900 Ohio infantry, under the com-mand of Isaac B. Kirby, were ordered to move from Greenville, Tennessee, southward up the French Broad Valley to Asheville. On April 5, the few Confederate forces still stationed in the city, along with a number of residents home on leave, met the approaching Ohioans at Craggy, four miles north of the city (the present-day site of the University of North Carolina at Asheville). For five hours each side shot at the other, before Kirby, mistakenly believing that Confederate reinforcements had arrived on the scene after dark, ordered a hasty retreat. That so-called Battle of Asheville proved to be, according to one histo-rian, "as close to bloodless as a five-hour firefight can get," with both sides "just going through the motions."[67]

Neither local residents nor Confederate officials had any reason to expect such luck to hold in an encounter with Stoneman's men, having been alerted to their activities elsewhere in the region. Their only hope lay in the fact that by this time, the combined might of Sherman's and Grant's armies had extin-guished the last flame of effective Confederate resistance and the war would be over before the enemy approached Buncombe County. Given the time lag imposed by their detour, Gillem's forces did not reach the outskirts of Asheville until April 23, nearly a week after Johnston had surrendered to Sherman near Durham and two weeks after Lee had surrendered to Grant. Union army commander Gillem and Confederate commander Martin received news of Johnston's surrender that evening. On the morning of April 24, the men met on the southern outskirts of the city and agreed to a truce, the terms of which, according to Martin, were that the Gillem "should go through Asheville to Tenn. and that I would furnish him rations for his men and that we would observe the Truce."[68] All went according to plan, and on April 26, a much relieved Asheville citizenry watched from their windows or their yards as Gillem led nearly 3,000 soldiers in an orderly march through the town.

The most impressive accounts of subsequent events came from local women. Two stories in particular capture the dramatic and contradictory nature of these final days of uncertainty and change. Mary Taylor Brown, who lived on the road between Hendersonville and Asheville along which Gillem's forces moved, reported to her step-son that the two days between the Union army's approach and the working out of the truce were rough ones indeed for residents of that particular neighborhood. As had been the case elsewhere along Stoneman's route, the presence of Federal troops seemed to unleash the wrath of bushwhackers, looters, and other scavengers within the area. Mrs. Brown vividly recounted her terror:

> Sunday night [April 23] and Monday morning was a trying time with us.
> God grant we may never live to endure the like again[;] squads of armed
> ruffians were coming in and plundering and cursing all night long while I
> was the only one to encounter them in the house and Pa was the only one to
> contend with them at the stables, barns, corn crib and smoke house, where
> they robbed us of every thing but a little hay and few pieces of bacon. . . .
> My soul stood trembling within me lest some demon would lay violent
> hands upon my person and I might be deprived the use of the firearm I had
> concealed to use in self defense. . . . But, thank God my prayers were heard
> and I escaped untouched, tho' a thousand curses were hurled into my face
> and I was called a thousand times "a damned lying rebel."[69]

In many ways, Mrs. Brown's experience was not unlike that of many other western Carolinians, particularly during the previous year or so. What set her story apart and made it somewhat surreal were the events of the following day.

Once the truce between Generals Gillem and Martin had been reached and word spread that hostilities had, at least for the moment, ceased, W. Vance Brown, Mary's husband, invited Gillem and several of his staff to stay with them. "Little indeed was the sum of all we had to offer for the repasts of our invited guests," Mrs. Brown wrote, "but the best of our little we gave as unto friends, tho' they were all our foes." Following dinner, "the officers and men enjoyed their pipes and laughed and talked in gay good humor, feeling quite at home among such friendly rebels. . . . All gathered in a social group and found enjoyment in a game of cards, a merry joke, a song, etc around the family hearth. Maria [Vance Brown's daughter] played and sang some of her Rebel airs and the gentlemen sang some of their Union songs. Genl. Gillem had his band come up and play some beautiful old Union pieces [and] thus the hours passed" until one o'clock in the morning. In a rather understated assessment of the evening, Mrs. Brown wrote that "Monday night quite a different scene was presented from the one on Sunday."[70]

That party must have seemed to those involved a very intimate expression of the end of the war itself. But it was not to be. Katherine Polk, who lived in town, picked up Mary Brown's narrative where she left off to describe an even more curious turn of events later that day, and one that seems to have baffled most historians. The march of Gillem's troops through Asheville was for the most part orderly, though an attempt by one local soldier serving under Gillem to break ranks and escape marred the proceedings. He was shot and killed in front of Mrs. Polk and her children, and he "laid there several hours before some compassionate souls gave him burial." "This circumstance," she wrote, "made a great impression on the tender little hearts that witnessed the tragedy." Of more consequence, though, was her discovery after the troops had filed by that two of her family's slaves, both nurses, were among "several other negroes in the neighborhood [who] joined the forces & gone off with the Yankees."[71]

Despite these setbacks, Katherine Polk, like most Asheville residents, breathed a sigh of relief that these troops moved through their community so placidly and orderly compared to how they plundered their way through Boone, Salisbury, Morganton, and other towns. The next morning, April 26, Miss Polk recalled, "we all felt very secure" as the troops continued to march on toward Tennessee along the French Broad River, "having strictly regarded the rights of property." But she quickly added, "[T]hat was in the morning of an ever memorable day."[72]

Late that afternoon, the Union forces took Asheville residents completely by surprise when they turned back on the city in an undisciplined spree of looting and ransacking. Katherine Polk was on a quiet walk with friends, during which they were "discussing the affairs of the day & congratulating ourselves on its peaceful termination," when suddenly they heard galloping horses and clanking sabers. They "turned to see the meaning of it all; a troop of Yankee Cavalry in hot pursuit of three women. Pistols were fired in quick succession." Thus began two harrowing days during which Katherine and other women were chased through the streets, harassed by various groups of "ruffians," had their houses searched and looted, and in many cases, witnessed their men (in Katherine's case, her uncle) arrested and carried away by "these wretches."[73]

One explanation for this sudden reversal of policy seems to be that General Gillem, after the first march through Asheville, left his troops and proceeded quickly back to Tennessee, where his political ambitions compelled him to attend the convening of the first postwar legislative session in Nashville. Gen. Samuel B. Brown was left in charge, and he wasted no time in ordering his troops back into Asheville to do what no doubt many had had the urge to do all along—pillage this stronghold of rebellion that had proved so elusive a target of Federal forces throughout the war. According to Mary Taylor Brown, Brown alone instigated the attack. General Brown (no relation to Mary), "being one of the greatest rascals at large, disobeyed orders and cared for nothing but plunder. . . . He himself is known by the Federals to be associated with his men in robbing or having the people robbed. The officers told me so."[74]

But other explanations seem equally valid. Given Brown's predecessor's own propensities for plunder, some historians have speculated that Alvan Gillem himself authorized the return attack before he left. The official reason for this dramatic reversal, as Brown (and later Stoneman from Tennessee) explained, was that Joseph Johnston's terms of surrender to Sherman had not been accepted by the new president, Andrew Johnson, and thus the truce established on the other side of Asheville two days before was rendered invalid.[75]

Thus the town once proposed as a capital for the Southern Confederacy met as harsh a fate at Union hands as any mountain community, or, for that matter, any community within the state. James Martin, who was still in command of Confederate forces in the region, reported: "I have heard of no worse plundering [than that] in and near Asheville by General Brown—I believe no one escaped entirely."[76] Michigan troops were particularly brutal, according to local

Troops moving along the French Broad River (From Drake, Fast and Loose in Dixie*)*

citizens. Of their behavior on that first night, Cornelia Phillips Spencer wrote, "The Tenth and Eleventh Michigan regiments certainly won for themselves . . . a reputation that should damn them to everlasting fame."[77]

Brown's men captured all Confederates they encountered—thirty officers and about forty soldiers—pillaging as they went their homes and those of other prominent local officials, including those of James Martin and Judge John L. Bailey. Bailey's daughter left a harrowing account of a gang of "villainous looking men" who ransacked their house, beat her father, fired shots at him when he attempted to resist their thefts, and carried her brother away under arrest. According to Martin, far more women than men remained in town and they were treated even more roughly, especially "when the men were able to get liquor." They confiscated and destroyed all arms and armaments they could find and burned the building where the armory had operated. The following day they moved out into the surrounding countryside of Buncombe County, "carrying on their work of plunder and destruction."[78]

On Friday, April 28, Brown led his forces out of the county and on toward Tennessee, but it was a sad day for many Asheville residents since they took some thirty prisoners (mostly the Confederate officers) with them, including James Martin. Another of those prisoners was Judge Bailey's son, who had been arrested in his home two days earlier. Sarah Bailey Cain described that final encounter with this now detestable force. As she and the judge walked toward the bank building where the prisoners were held to see her brother off, she wrote, "We passed through an immense crowd of a few citizens, a great many privates, and insolent negroes in U.S. uniforms. One of these negroes called out to my father, 'How do you like this, old man?'" Because of that incident alone, she stated, "I have loathed the uniform ever since." In moving quickly to see her brother, Sarah walked under a U.S. flag that the troops had suspended from the Eagle Hotel out over the street. She was later reprimanded for having done so by other women who had walked around the square to avoid passing under what they still viewed as an enemy's emblem. She re-called seeing among the prisoners Col. James Robert Love, who turned to her father and ranted, "Judge Bailey, I have heard of Mexican treachery, but this exceeds all!"[79]

The ransacking of Asheville marked the official end of Stoneman's raid. That it concluded on such an unexpectedly hostile and destructive note, particularly after news of the war's end elsewhere reached the region, cast a pall over many western Carolinians, despite efforts of other Union officials to make amends.

Union commander William J. Palmer, who was moving through the mountains south of Asheville toward Tennessee (until ordered to move into South Carolina in an attempt to block Jefferson Davis's escape), was quick to send his regrets over Brown's actions to his Confederate counterpart. He sent a dispatch from Hickory Nut Gap to General Martin, ordering that he and all other officers arrested and en route to Knoxville be released and acknowledging that Brown should have given notice of the termination of the armistice before attacking the city.[80]

But even that two-day rampage in and around Asheville did not mark the end of fighting in western North Carolina. Early in May, Federal officials in Tennessee ordered yet another raid on Haywood County to clear the mountains of continued guerrilla activity. The 2nd North Carolina Mounted Infantry, one of the regiments of Unionist highlanders raised by George W. Kirk, again invaded the state. Commanded this time by Col. William C. Bartlett, nearly a thousand cavalrymen, now mostly New Yorkers, moved quickly to occupy Waynesville, which they did without opposition from local residents.[81]

But their raid took place just as separate Confederate forces under Gen. James Martin and Col. James R. Love had moved west from Asheville into the area and Colonel William Holland Thomas had moved east with about two hundred Indians. On May 6, a chance encounter at White Sulphur Springs, just south of Waynesville, between a company of Thomas's Legion and Bartlett's men led to a skirmish. Local historians later claimed that it was here that the "last guns of the war [were] fired by regular Confederates acting under orders." The single casualty, one of Bartlett's soldiers named James Arwood, was, according to R. T. Conley, the man who shot him, "doubtless the last man killed by regular command east of the Mississippi. I yet have his gun as a relic."[82] The Union troops, caught by surprise, quickly retreated back into Waynesville.

As Thomas's companies converged with those of Love and Martin, for a total of no more than five hundred men, they took positions along the ridges that surrounded the small town. In a creative attempt to intimidate Barlett and his troops, Thomas ordered that hundreds of bonfires be built along the ridges that night. Once the fires were lit, the Cherokees danced around them, "shattering the night with chilling war whoops." William W. Stringfield noted in his memoirs, "The bonfires and hideous yells had the desired effect." On the morning of May 7, Colonel Bartlett sent out a flag of truce, requesting a conference with Thomas. That conference led to one of more memorable moments in this sequence of events. As Stringfield described it, "Colonel Love, with several of his men, and Colonel Thomas, with 20 of his largest and most warlike looking Indians, stripped to the waist and painted and feathered off in fine style, entered the town."[83]

Thomas apparently thought his ruse the night before was successful enough to take the offensive in his meeting with Bartlett. He issued an ultimatum: either the Union commander surrender his force and immediately leave Waynesville, or "he would turn his Indians upon the Yankee regiment and have them all scalped." In the full light of day, Thomas's threats meant little to Bartlett, and James Martin soon intervened to acknowledge more realistically the situation he and his men faced in the wake of the Confederacy's collapse. He agreed to surrender all of the western North Carolina forces under his authority. In return, Bartlett—and Kirk, whose men were plundering other nearby areas— would lead their troops out of North Carolina. With these terms accepted, a ceremonial surrender was staged in Waynesville on May 9, a month to the day after Lee had surrendered to Grant. In what must have seemed a rather anti-climactic finale to the continued turbulence in the mountains during that in-terim, Martin, Thomas, Love, and other Confederate officers signed parole papers, then discharged their troops to return home.[84]

Western North Carolinians faced an unsettled future. One of the most signifi-cant sources of confusion and anxiety was the assassination of Abraham Lin-coln, which enraged Northerners and created an atmosphere in which ven-geance would be legitimized as a reaction to the war. Andrew Johnson's rise to the presidency was a particularly worrisome development to former Confeder-ates in western North Carolina. As a dedicated Unionist from East Tennessee, Johnson had long been viewed as an enemy by Confederate loyalists. The enforced repudiation of Confederate currency undermined the cash basis of the regional economy as well and insured that the standard of living would not improve measurably in the near future. The arrest of Governor Vance on May 13 and the elevation of William W. Holden, the state's leading peace proponent, to the position of provisional governor meant that the state and local governments would be disrupted in the short term. Finally, the imminent passage of the Thirteenth Amendment meant that slavery would end, and the people of west-ern North Carolina would have to adjust to a new social and economic world.

Relieved that the fighting was over, most people in western North Carolina accepted the reimposition of Federal authority without any overt sign of hostility. For Confederate army deserters, draft evaders, and open supporters of the Union, peace was particularly welcome. Even those who had remained committed to the Confederacy throughout the four-year conflict accepted its final resolution. Marcus Erwin, the editor of the *Asheville News* and a leading advocate of secession, undoubtedly spoke for most western Carolinians who had supported the fight for Southern independence when he announced in his paper as early as February that he was willing to accept reunification with the national government.[85] This concession by the Confederate leadership and its followers did not necessarily bring an end to violence in the mountains, however. The animosities that had developed over a four-year period, especially those generated in the chaos of the last few months of the war, were not as easily resolved as the larger military conflict from which they had grown.

County elites found that the positions of leadership and symbols of authority that had provided them their power base no longer existed or were being ignored by people who felt that the leadership had misled them by forcing them to suffer through this failed revolt. In a rather remarkable effort to restore some form of order to the badly disrupted mountain society through legalistic means rather than military force, all parties accepted something of an informal truce and a restoration of traditional relationships. Caldwell County issued a written agreement, which was distributed to the "leading bushwhackers." The resolutions, composed by Samuel Finley Patterson, the chairman of the county court, stipulated that "the said Military Authorities or forces be withdrawn from service; that no further effort be made to enforce the conscription law in the county; that the said recusant conscripts and others be permitted to return quietly to their homes and pursue their lawful occupations unmolested; that restitution of all captured or stolen property be made, as far as possible, by both parties and that both parties shall hereafter demean themselves as quiet, orderly citizens."[86]

Later events demonstrated that this basic understanding prevailed in most mountain communities and that the routine of daily life would resume. Patterson was satisfied that this effort to end the internal warfare within Caldwell County was effective, believing that the truce had given "the leading bushwhackers . . . great satisfaction, as well as the recusant conscripts who were in the woods."[87] Yet, even under the best of circumstances, hard feelings did not disappear and latent hostilities were just beneath the surface waiting to explode. In neighboring Wilkes, James Gwyn was less optimistic than Patterson. He noted in his diary on May 4, "We have a quiet time now, our Southern armies are disbanded, . . . and terms of peace are said to be agreed upon." But he added ominously, "All we dread here now is robbers & no doubt there will be plenty of them this summer."[88]

His fears were warranted, for a troublesome minority refused to end its aggressions. The least repentant of these outlaws operated in Gwyn's own county. A band emerged in the wake of Stoneman's raid through Wilkes (many of the members were deserters from his forces) that continued to reek havoc on prominent families in the area. The outlaws, who operated out of a two-story log cabin situated on a hilltop with a commanding view of the Yadkin River valley in Wilkes County, soon earned notoriety as the Fort Hamby gang, named for the widow who owned the house. Its leader, referred to only as Major Wade, was apparently a renegade Federal soldier whose object was the accumulation of loot and perhaps the perpetuation of violence for its own sake. The Fort Hamby gang, made up of twenty-five to thirty men, became emboldened by success and began to move beyond Wilkes to attack prominent families in Caldwell, Alexander, and Watauga Counties as well.[89]

Caldwell citizens were the first to use force to put down this continued harassment. On May 7, in response to one such raid, several former members of the home guard organized and moved across the county line to attack Fort Hamby. Catching the looters by surprise, they nearly penetrated the stronghold when Major Wade tricked them into a cease-fire, during which his men armed themselves and emerged from their "fort" firing, killing at least two of their attackers, both of whom were teenage boys. Former Confederate regulars led the next attempt to subdue the band. Veterans from several mountain and piedmont counties surrounded the fort and laid siege. Unable to take the structure by storm, the posse set fire to an outbuilding that soon started to burn the fort itself. The renegades were forced into the open; three of them were shot; the rest quickly surrendered. Major Wade made a break for freedom, and, despite the best efforts of the veteran soldiers, he escaped. His less fortunate followers (from four to eight, according to differing accounts) were tied to stakes in the ground and summarily executed. Their fort was carefully and completely razed so that it could not be used by others.[90]

Other such gangs suffered similar fates, though in less dramatic circumstances. The arrival of Federal forces, which were detachments of Sherman's cavalry, two days after the fort's destruction served to quell other terrorist activity in that area.[91] Thus, though in very different fashion from their fellow western Carolinians in Buncombe and Haywood Counties, Caldwell and Wilkes residents experienced the war's end in particularly traumatic and brutal terms.

Even more troublesome was the adjustment required of black and white western North Carolinians to the end of slavery. Throughout the war, white highlanders were reluctant to dispense with the peculiar institution. One of the major arguments of the peace movement of 1863–64 in the mountains was that only an early peace would keep slavery alive.[92] Slave trading remained brisk in the mountains in the early weeks of 1865.[93] When Jefferson Davis's administration proposed that slaves be allowed to volunteer for Confederate service late in 1864, Zebulon Vance vociferously objected in his newspaper, and there is no evidence that any of his western constituents disagreed with him.[94]

Calvin Cowles expressed greater concern over the numerous slaves he had hired out locally from owners in eastern North Carolina, where slaves were being conscripted to build fortifications. He informed one such owner, Rev. C. B. Reddick, that he found it "unreasonable for authorities to call on us both for the same slaves in Greenville [N.C.] & Wilkes Co." Cowles made it clear that his concern was primarily monetary: "I fear all the Negro men will be conscripted," he wrote at the end of February, adding, "In that event what about the hire of your boys? Would you expect for me to pay for services never rendered?"[95] A month later, his fears seem to have abated, with a not unwelcome side effect for Cowles. On March 29, he informed Reddick that the presence of a new enrollment officer in the county had brought a change in his slaves' behavior. "They've been no further trouble," he noted. "The boys are scared of conscription and are working very hard now."[96]

But just two days later Stoneman's raiders moved through Wilkes County, and Cowles was soon writing Reddick once again, this time informing him that his slaves were gone altogether.[97] The military upheaval mountain residents endured over the next month undermined whatever stability slavery had maintained during the war. It also broke down much of the highland slaveholders' resistance to change. When, on April 29, Gen. John Schofield decreed the emancipation of North Carolina's enslaved population in his general proclamation of Reconstruction, many, perhaps most, slaveholders in the region viewed it as anticlimactic. As noted earlier, Stoneman's raid had proved the single most liberating event of the war for many mountain slaves, and even the slaveholders not directly in the path of Union forces had found that they had lost much control of the slaves still with them.

Once slavery's end became a reality, white reactions ranged from bitterness and frustration to mere annoyance or complacency. After most of William Holland Thomas's fifty freed slaves departed, he declared to his wife that their absence would cause no "pecuniary injury." "If they can do without us we probably can do without them," he reasoned.[98] The Harpers of Happy Valley, who suffered one of the greatest losses of human property in the region, also seemed resigned. On April 2, Ella Harper informed her husband: "When I heard the negroes had gone I looked upon the move as the dawn of freedom to us. I would not care if every man, women & child of them would leave. It would be very hard at first to get along but we would soon live more & better than we ever did."[99] Others expressed relief at no longer having to support burdensome black dependents, given the other economic and agricultural hardships they faced in the weeks after the war's end. Katherine Polk's mother stated that "she could not possibly feed the negroes who were not absolutely necessary to the comfort of the family; they must go to their emancipators for help."[100]

On the other hand, former owners were astounded and chagrined by the assertiveness of freedmen and their families in exercising their new independence. Cornelia Henry of Buncombe County warned her husband William, who was not yet home from the war: "You have no idea how big the nigs feel. Ole Sam and Lena there is no difference, but take care for the others. Even Rose feels her freedom."[101]

One of the first actions taken by many of the newly freed persons was to leave the scene of their bondage and enjoy the liberty recently granted them. As already noted, Stoneman's troops provided a significant impetus for many slaves along their route to leave. Even in Asheville, which ultimately experienced an increase rather than a decrease in its African American population, as freedmen and women from throughout the surrounding countryside were drawn to the city, local slaveholders were not immune from the influence of Union troops. According to one report, "All of Mrs. J. W. Patton's servants left her and went with the Yankees, not a single one of all she had remained to do a thing in the house or in the kitchen. They even took her beautiful carriage and, crowding into it, drove off in full possession."[102]

Powerless to stop this movement, embittered former masters tried to convince themselves that they did not need the workers who were leaving. Cornelia Henry, for example, wrote, "The negro has gone to Tenn. now and I hope he may never come back again."[103] They expressed great disdain for the short-sightedness of such assertions of independence. "Thousands of poor deluded negroes have left their confederate homes to seek a better life and found a worse," wrote one Asheville mistress in June. "None of our servants have left us, tho' we told them to go if they wish." She went on to express the ambivalence many highlanders must have felt about the repercussions of emancipation: "I should be sorry to part with any servants, for they are to me as a part of our family and I feel attached to them as to my own children. Yet I cannot approve [of] their remaining here other than as slaves, for they will not do without the care of the white man. They will require continual watching and daily instruction in their labors." She concluded by heartily endorsing any plans that would have "the negroes all sent to Africa as soon as possible."[104]

What most distressed the former masters, however, was the willingness of their former chattel to inform on them to the occupying Union soldiers. Already feeling dishonored by the failure of Southern armies, the slaveowners deeply resented the willingness of Northern soldiers to accept the word of African Americans over that of former Confederates. One correspondent, no doubt in response to what he had heard about slaves' reaction to Stoneman's troops, wrote: "Tell Pa if he has anything of value to put away, to bury it himself where no mortal eye can see. . . . Do all your hiding yourselves, for the negroes think the yanks are their friends and will tell everything and a heap more besides. That is my experience with them and everybody else about here. The yanks treated people a heap worse where the nigs told tales on them."[105]

Fortunately for mountain residents, the former slaves represented only a small proportion of the population, and the difficult problems associated with racial adjustment could be placed in a broader context of community relations and kept in some perspective. This did not mean that the inevitable changes were more acceptable to whites or that blacks received better treatment than to those in the other parts of the state. It simply meant that race relations were part of a whole package of economic, social, political, and intellectual relationships that would have to be simultaneously renegotiated within mountain communities.

The last nine months of the Civil War in western North Carolina thoroughly disrupted the traditional society that had been constructed there. Towns, neighborhoods, and even families had been torn asunder by economic deprivation and the violence brought by both formal military organizations and ad hoc bands of terrorists. The spiraling inflation and the Confederate currency's eventual complete loss of value brought financial ruin and growing dependency for many yeoman and tenant families. Deaths on and off the battlefields removed many of the most productive members of mountain society. Slavery's demise only added to the economic and social disruption. At the same time, the traditional leaders could no longer provide guidance to the population, because the elite had so thoroughly identified itself with the failed experiment of Confederate nationhood. Traditional social structures including schools, churches, and political parties had been destroyed or altered beyond recognition.

The sense of loss overwhelmed many western Carolinians, and they were quick to place blame for the ignominious and unforeseen end to the four years of struggle they had endured. Mary Taylor Brown expressed the bitterness of many fellow mountain residents at war's end: "Many are the innocent sufferers by this cruel, cruel war. Brought about by wicked designing politicans; office seekers, robbers of the people; discharges of the government, who rather than rob gratify their unholy desires and accomplish their evil purposes, would slay ten thousand innocent people and hurl a million souls into perdition!!"[106]

Yet regardless of such pent-up anger and the natural tendency to cast blame, western Carolinians demonstrated a determination to put the war behind them and move on. Despite the chaos of recent months, highlanders retained their strong family ties, economic skills, and knowledge obtained by previous experience and education. The survival of these seemingly mundane qualities, along with a sense of both pride and resignation, provided mountain residents with considerable resilience. In the same letter in which she had earlier expressed her anger, Mary Taylor Brown wrote: "I will boldly say, I am a Southern woman! and have battled for her rights. . . . To defend the South, love prompted me to action and an undying confidence that she was right carried me onward through fire and blood." Yet, she concluded, "Now that in God's providence slavery is abolished and the states again brought into union and under the same government, I cordially respond from my heart, All is well!"[107] Upon such determination and spirit the people of North Carolina's highland region would reconstruct their world.

AFTERMATH

A Peace We Little Expected and Did Not Want

A N observer traveling through the mountains of western North Carolina in
1890 for the first time since May 1865 would have been struck by the
transformation that had taken place. First, the travel itself would have been
so much easier since railroads rather than muddy trails traversed much of the
region. Asheville was then a small city rather than a town, and most county seats
were sizable towns rather than tiny villages. Large stores carrying goods from all
parts of the nation and the world were found in almost every county. Deep in
the woods lumberjacks were harvesting the immense hardwood forests, and
growing numbers of mountaineers were employed in textile mills located along
mountain and piedmont rivers. At an increasing rate, local leaders and outside
reformers were establishing educational institutions, from mission schools to
colleges. Many locations in the mountains were actively embracing the growing
tourist and resort trade. Church membership was growing, and new churches

and other religious organizations were making their marks on the highland populace.

Reminders of the antebellum period and the destruction of the Civil War were still present, but they were not difficult to ignore by highland residents, who rushed to take advantage of the opportunities provided by the changes. The majority of western North Carolinians still lived on farms, and for most of them, the economic boom times were only a rumor. Since mountain families continued to be large, the demand for land outstripped the resources available. Farms became smaller and smaller, and they often were no longer capable of providing a subsistence for a family. At the same time, the new capitalist elite, who had profited from tourism, lumbering, the railroad, and other forms of economic development, secured legislation to further undermine small farms. In the 1880s, for example, the North Carolina legislature passed a series of fence laws that restricted the rights of farmers to graze their stock on the open woodlands of the region. Suddenly forced to feed their livestock on the decreasingly available family land, greater numbers of western North Carolina farmers faced giving up their independence and accepting tenant farmer status. Although most farmers were able to avoid the tyranny of cotton dependency and its rapid price swings that doomed other Southern farmers, they faced equally formidable obstacles in maintaining their family farming tradition.

The Civil War itself seemed remote, but there were reminders of it both in events that took place in western North Carolina and in the national trends that had not affected the region. Reconciliation of the various factions created by the war had been incomplete at best. In many ways the animosities created by the 1861–65 struggle continued with little abatement in the region's politics. Most leaders of the secession movement in the mountains, including Thomas Clingman and William Holland Thomas, found themselves in permanent political exile and were rarely elected to office again. Antisecession Confederates like Zebulon Vance were forced from power for a period, but by 1876 they had assumed control of the dominant Democratic Party in the state and the mountain region. Unionists and newly enfranchised blacks joined the Republican Party, and they struggled in an uneasy alliance to wrest control of the state and local governments from their hated opponents. Although the spirit of the war remained in politics, there was no glorification of the war, which so many highland residents recalled with painful memories. Memorial statues to Confederate soldiers were not erected in many mountain counties until the beginning of World War I.

Zebulon B. Vance, 1866 (North Carolina Division of Archives and History)

For more marginalized elements of mountain society, the impact of the war was limited and often negative. The positive racial adjustments had not followed the emancipation of African Americans in any meaningful way, and by 1890, increasingly racist whites challenged the small gains made by highland blacks. Mountain whites increasingly viewed segregation as an acceptable solution to the question of race control, as would their counterparts throughout the South. White mountain women found that their lives were dramatically changed after the war, but not to their advantage. Many were forced to farm without adult male assistance or to give up their independent household and to move in with relatives. Others found themselves and their children working in unsafe and uncomfortable textile factories as their farms failed.

Somewhat unexpectedly, western North Carolina, like other parts of Southern Appalachia, became the object of national interest. Local color writers described the rural mountaineer lifestyle in inaccurate and unflattering terms and helped to create an enduring "hillbilly" stereotype. At the same time, religious and educational reformers entered the mountain area to bring economic, social, and spiritual salvation to the local population. One result of this effort was the revival of a dying handicraft tradition that has come to be particularly associated with the mountains of western North Carolina. Tourism, too, rebounded, and the region's scenic beauty and cool climate encouraged even greater numbers of visitors to spend their summers in the mountains. This image of a traditional, even static western North Carolina endured as tremendous change transformed the region.

Of course, none of these developments was obvious to highlanders, who were attempting to reconstruct their lives in the summer and fall of 1865 and in the years that immediately followed. In part, mountain residents failed to see any change because they were constantly reminded of the immediate past. Violence related to the war continued to be a feature of mountain life. A group of renegades, known as the Adair gang, terrorized Rutherford County residents, stealing and looting. The gang even murdered a black family who sought to defend their property from the vandals. The Teague band in Haywood County and the Fort Hamby gang in Wilkes also continued their wartime depredations throughout much of the rest of 1865, as if peace had never been established.[1] As late as September 1865, Brig. Gen. Thomas A. Heath, who was stationed at the newly established Union troop headquarters of the western North Carolina district in Morganton, reported continued unrest in Madison, Yancey, Watauga and Buncombe Counties. He described that activity as mostly "depredations and crimes committed . . . by recent deserters from the Rebel Army." The degree of unrest was such that he did not even trust his junior officers to patrol alone.[2]

Personal wartime vendettas were also waged in the region. As one highlander noted, "The necessities of war left much grudges to settle in times of peace."[3] In Madison County, a laborer working on construction project at Mars Hill College bragged to fellow workers about his role as part of a home guard unit that had murdered three brothers and nearly killed their mother. Days later, the mother's brother, James Norton, approached the work site in broad daylight, announced his relationship to the laborer's victims, and shot the man. Norton was tried for murder but acquitted by jurors who found his vengeance justified. In the same county, members of the Shelton family murdered a member of the family that had provided the guide for the troops of James Keith who had committed the 1863 massacre described in Chapter 5.[4]

Other cases similar to Norton's were brought to court, though they were not always resolved peaceably. Circuit court judge Augustus S. Merrimon told of his efforts to preside over a session in Clay County as hundreds of armed men roamed the streets of Hayesville, the county seat. As the session commenced, a riot involving some eighty men broke out. Merrimon called in the sheriff and demanded that he swear in a posse of sixty armed men from all factions to maintain the peace. This expedient worked well enough that Merrimon continued to use similar tactics to bring order in other counties he served.[5]

Recognizing that both legal and extralegal revenge could poison the atmosphere in North Carolina for years to come, the state legislature passed an amnesty act in December 1866. Its purpose was to grant amnesty not only to "all officers and soldiers of either Union or Confederate armies who in the course of duty, or under the order of a superior, committed 'any homicides, felonies, or misdemeanors'" but to civilians as well. Despite efforts to challenge the legitimacy of such amnesty, the North Carolina Supreme Court determined that the act was the most effective means yet to end the vendettas and acts of private retribution. In upholding the law, the court declared it not only constitutional but essential if the judicial branch was ever going to function effectively.[6] Even without Republican attempts to overrule the amnesty law after 1868, the legal system could make little claim to either impartiality or judicial restraint in the mountains or elsewhere in the state for many years after the war.

Battles that could not be fought within the legal system were immediately transferred to the realm of politics. When the war ended, President Andrew Johnson, himself an Appalachian Unionist, appointed William W. Holden, the 1864 peace candidate, as provisional governor of North Carolina. Much to the surprise of his many opponents, Holden acted in a generally nonpartisan manner and appointed both former Unionists as well as members of the antebellum and Confederate elite to local offices. Ironically, his evenhandedness worked against him in the fall election of 1865, when he was defeated in the gubernatorial election by a former political ally, Jonathan Worth. This election returned much of the state's wartime leadership to power, as did the state legislature by electing former Confederate senator William A. Graham to the U.S. Senate. The waning statewide strength of the Unionists was further diminished when Worth was overwhelming reelected in 1866 and the legislature refused to endorse the Fourteenth Amendment.[7] Yet mountain Unionism remained quite strong. Highland voters supported Holden by a significant majority in 1865.[8] In the mountain counties, the lines drawn by the 1863 congressional and 1864 gubernatorial contests, as well as the internal warfare that continued after 1863, shaped the partisanship that emerged soon after the war.

The unwillingness of North Carolinians and other Southern elites to guarantee protection to Unionists and African Americans prompted Republicans in Congress to pass legislation in 1867 and 1868 to force radical changes in the political system of the South. Such measures reinforced the Republican Party in North Carolina—a coalition dominated by white Unionists from the piedmont and mountains, African Americans from the eastern counties, and a small number of so-called carpetbaggers, Northerners seeking political and economic opportunities. Through Radical Republicans' considerable clout at state and national levels blacks were enfranchised and much of the former Confederate leadership was excluded from the political process. A state constitutional convention in 1868 created the most democratic constitution in North Carolina's history, and in the first election held under the new order, the Republican ticket carried the mountain counties with 56 percent of the vote. William Holden became governor (this time by popular mandate rather than appointment), and Tod R. Caldwell of Morganton became his lieutenant governor.[9] In the federal elections of that same year, Republicans delivered approximately 52 percent of the mountain vote to their presidential candidate, Ulysses S. Grant.[10]

Although blacks represented a small proportion of the mountain populace, the number of Republican votes they cast was not insignificant. Many white Republicans in the western part of the state, however, found their new political alliance with African American voters distasteful. On the day of the 1868 presidential election, a minor race riot broke out in Asheville, which put many white Republicans on the defensive. The violence broke out soon after a black man was denied the right to vote by an election clerk. When he attempted to move on into the polling place anyway, he was knocked down. Accounts of what happened next vary, but apparently word of the incident spread through the streets and a fight broke out. One African American was shot and killed, and as many as eighteen other blacks were injured by a mob made up largely of angry young white men. Several arrests were made, and a trial resulted, but the violence proved to be an isolated incident. Three years later, Democrat Nicholas Woodfin, who defended the white rioters at the trial, testified before a congressional committee on race relations in Reconstruction Buncombe County: "Since that time we have had no disturbance there on any public occasion at all. Well there is more disposition to conciliate the colored vote now by both parties."[11]

Black Republican leaders in the mountains seem to have learned the importance of appearances in their efforts at political activism, even to the point of deferring to white party leaders. One group assured William Scott, a Republican congressional candidate seeking their support in 1871, that they appreciated his attentions. "We know that our state and condition are backward, yet we are not so far back as to be ungrateful for kindness," they wrote. "We will not only give you our humble support, but . . . we shall make strenuous efforts to secure that of every other colored man in the County."[12]

But the riot in Asheville emphasized just how radical an upheaval black suffrage had created in the political system. The ousted leaders, incensed that they had been replaced by their inferiors, established the Conservative Party and challenged the Republicans on their weakest point—their biracial coalition. The most effective tool the desperate Conservatives had to counter the black vote was the Ku Klux Klan. Although the Klan's presence in North Carolina was concentrated in the upper piedmont, Rutherford and Polk Counties were also strongholds of KKK activity. Buncombe County, too, saw a significant Klan presence, which was generated by Rutherford leader Randolph Shotwell, who moved to Asheville from Rutherfordton for a short time to edit the *Asheville Citizen-Times*, the Conservative newspaper. Klan violence was minimal in Buncombe County compared to that in Rutherford and other counties, but Shotwell and his followers there did attempt to intimidate the local district attorney to prevent prosecutions of Klan members for lawless activities.[13]

The much more intense activity in Rutherford and Polk Counties was probably influenced by an outbreak of Klan violence across the state line in South Carolina. When Randolph Shotwell returned to Rutherfordton in 1870, he assumed leadership of the Klan. Although he claimed to advocate a moderate approach, a number of vicious attacks on former Unionists, an assault and rape of the wife of a prominent local Republican, and the destruction of a Republican newspaper office had attracted state and federal attention. In response to these incidents, Governor Holden requested that additional federal troops be

*Blacks registering to vote in Asheville (*Harper's Weekly, *September 28, 1867)*

dispatched to North Carolina to restore order. The troops sent to Rutherford in the summer of 1871 arrested some thirty-five men, including Shotwell, who was tried and found guilty. He spent two years in a federal prison in New York. Despite these arrests, the influence of the Klan continued to spread. It was not until a group of Klansmen raped the wife of a white Republican leader that public opinion in Rutherford County turned against the terrorists.[14]

Perhaps the greatest indication of the continued strength of Unionism in the mountains was the so-called Kirk-Holden War. In 1870, Governor Holden sought a new ally in his battle against the Klan and called on George W. Kirk, the Union colonel from Tennessee who was notorious for his wartime recruitment efforts and raids through western North Carolina, to join forces with him. Kirk posted handbills in Marshall, Burnsville, and Asheville urging all of those who had served under him in the 2nd and 3rd North Carolina Mounted Infantries to return to service in order to avenge the blood of Unionists. Much to the horror of mountain Conservatives who remembered the destruction and chaos Kirk's forces had once reeked, he raised over 600 men, ranging from teenagers to elderly men. They moved quickly to the state's piedmont, where they arrested those named on a list provided by the governor—both Klan leaders and, more controversially, political critics of Holden. When federal authorities objected to this unorthodox means of repression, Holden asked Kirk to turn over his prisoners to government authorities and to disband.[15]

Although many citizens of both parties were unintimidated by the Klan's presence, the Republican share of the mountain vote declined precipitously. Serious factional splits, exacerbated by the pressure from the Klan, reduced the Republican vote in the 1870 legislative elections to 40 percent in western North Carolina, which resulted in a virtual Conservative sweep of all of the seats in the region and allowed Conservatives to control the state legislature.[16] From that position of power, they impeached William Holden for abuses associated with the suppression of the Klan, particularly his collusion with Kirk.[17] His conviction on six of eight charges in a trial presided over by Judge Augustus Merrimon of Asheville elevated mountain Republican Tod Caldwell of Morganton to the governor's chair in 1870. While western North Carolina Unionists had gained control of the governorship, the two parties were clearly little more than collections of men who would go to any extreme to gain or retain power.

The two parties in the mountains recognized that they were just carrying on the internal war of 1861–65 in another guise. Recognizing the need for thorough organization, they adopted the language and structure of military units.[18] One Republican announced at the beginning of a campaign that it was time "to throw out the skirmish forces preparatory to the gigantic struggle which must ensue later on." Party literature, broadsides, and even ballots were regarded as the "implements of war," while party newspapers were regarded as the "big guns" of the electoral battle from which "counter charges" were made against enemy attacks.[19] This organizational rigor was firmly entrenched in both Republican and Democratic Parties by the 1880 national elections, so that straight party voting could be maintained and violence minimized.

This increased discipline within the political system did not mean that campaigning was not aggressive or that attacks on the opposition were not unrelenting. In fact, mountain Democrats took full advantage of the racism of white voters to associate their local opponents with the Civil Rights Act of 1875, which permitted racially mixed schools and other public facilities.[20] Zebulon Vance's gubernatorial campaign against Thomas Settle in 1876 was particularly hard fought in the mountains, with Settle attacking Vance for sanctioning the abuse of Unionists by the Confederate army during the war.[21] In 1882, Zebulon Vance, then a U.S. senator, headed an investigating committee that spent weeks trying to document corruption among Republican revenue agents in western

North Carolina.[22] In the mid-1880s, a number of mountain Democrats, led by Richmond Pearson of Asheville, rebelled against their own party leadership for passing fence and stock laws that restricted the grazing rights of mountain farmers. The split in Democratic ranks that resulted greatly strengthened the Republicans, who evenly split the vote with their opponents.[23] The Democrats regained their advantage in the mountains by running another heavily racist campaign in 1890. They attacked the Republicans for supporting the Lodge Election Bill, which authorized the use of force to insure fair federal elections in the South.[24] Thus, the two-party political system remained vigorous in western North Carolina after the war. Although sufficient discipline was imposed by the partisan organizations to prevent sustained outbreaks of violence, no contemporary observer doubted that politics in the mountains represented the continuation of the war in another form.

A related activity provoked other memories of the war and a violent response from the mountain population as well. During the war, the Lincoln administration had passed an internal revenue bill that included among its provisions a tax on alcohol produced for human consumption. After the war, this tax was retained and mountain farmers found themselves taxed by the national government on a product that had been traditionally produced in the mountains. In the 1870s and early 1880s, federal officers raided stills in western North Carolina and elsewhere in Southern Appalachia, creating confrontations in which both moonshiners and federal officers were killed or wounded. Despite substantial corruption among the revenue agents in the western counties, public opinion in the mountains slowly swung in favor of enforcement. In the 1880s, residents of the towns and small cities in particular began to view the moonshiners as renegades who should be prosecuted rather than protected.[25] Unlike the sustained hostility that marked federal efforts to enforce changes in race laws in the mountains, federal programs to regulate and tax liquor production were finally accepted by the majority of western Carolinians.

The violent events surrounding the suppression of moonshining, combined with the significant demographic developments in western North Carolina, contributed to the emerging picture of the Southern mountaineer. Between 1860 and 1890, the population of the region more than doubled, despite the loss of life resulting from the Civil War.[26] This burgeoning growth placed great pressure on the land available for highland farms, given the size of the rural populace (fewer than one in ten people in western North Carolina lived in a town classified as "urban"). As historian Ronald Eller has pointed out, the

usual solution to this population explosion was for families to continue dividing their farms among family members. The result was a precipitous decline in
the size of the average mountain farm. In the last three decades of the nineteenth century, the number of farms in western North Carolina increased from
approximately 38,000 to more than 47,000, while total acreage actually declined slightly.[27] Smaller farms, often located on marginal land, as the pressure
of population forced the use of previously untouched ridge land, were not economically viable. Many mountain farmers found themselves unable to maintain
their independent ownership of their land. A significant number sunk into permanent tenant relationships—in contrast to the often temporary tenant agree-
ments of the antebellum period. The result was the emergence of a large group
of identifiably poor farmers and laborers throughout the region who appeared
to have little hope to escape from their impoverished situation.

Seizing upon the themes of wilderness, poverty, and violence, local color
writers used western North Carolina as one of the primary settings for the
perpetuation of the "hillbilly" stereotype. As Cratis Williams has noted, some
of the earliest of these stories used the North Carolina mountains to introduce
many of the stock characters and motifs that would populate these accounts of
Southern mountain life. Among the first of these writers was Rebecca Harding
Davis, whose writings on mountain people actually first appeared during the
war, with stories set in her own West Virginia. After the war, she wrote about
residents of the Carolina highlands, where she set the best and most widely
read of her stories, "The Rose of Carolina," and "The Yares of Black Mountain," both of which were published in national magazines in 1874 and 1875,
respectively. Davis introduced the subject of mountaineer poverty and geographical isolation in her descriptions of highland life in and around Asheville
after the war.[28]

Other fictional versions of the Carolina highlands quickly followed Davis's
and were also disseminated to a national readership. In 1877 in a story published in *Scribner's Monthly*, Frances Hodgson Burnett introduced the theme
of interpersonal violence. In "Lodusky," she used the traditional one-room
schoolhouse as the setting for a fight between two undisciplined mountain
youths to determine which of them would escort the heroine home. A year later,
Constant Fenimore Woolson brought virtually all of the elements of the stereotype together in "Up in the Blue Ridge," a story published in *Appleton's Journal*. One of the main characters was a former Confederate army officer who was
organizing resistance to the federal Internal Revenue Service. While Woolson

celebrated the sense of community shared by western Carolinians, she also emphasized the geographical isolation and war-related violence that appeared to be central to life there.[29]

Conflicting interpretations of mountaineers' Civil War experience emerged as part of this "discovery" of Appalachia by these and other writers. Along with the more negative stereotypes emerging, an ennobling and romanticized view of mountaineers was also taking shape, based on the simplistic notion that they were an all-white populace unburdened by slavery, racism, or class tensions. As early as 1872, an Ohio minister preached that "there belongs to mountain regions a moral elevation of their own. They give birth to strong, free, pure and noble races. . . . Slavery, falsehood, base compliance, luxury, belong to the plains. Freedom, truth, hardy sacrifice, simple honor, to the highlands."[30] A later chronicler explained, "The aristocratic slaveholder from his river-bottom plantation looked with scorn on the slaveless dweller among the hills; while the highlander repaid his scorn with high disdain and even hate."[31]

The corollary to this assumption that highlanders resented slaveholders as much as they did slavery was that, as Berea College president William Frost proclaimed in 1899, "when the Civil War came, . . . Appalachia America clave to the old flag." For Frost, "it was this old-fashioned loyalty which held Kentucky in the Union, made West Virginia 'secede from secession,' and performed prodigies of valor in east Tennessee, and even in the western Carolinas."[32] By the turn of the century, the idea of a monolithic Southern mountain region that was solidly antisecession and anti-Confederate was firmly in place, and the exceptionalism of this region of the South, along with the perception of its patriotism, whiteness, and frontier way of life led to the creation of "Holy Appalachia," as Allen Batteau has termed it in his recent study of the region's "invention" by outside interests.[33]

On the other hand, western Carolinians themselves interpreted their war experiences in another, equally invalid way. As historian Richard Starnes has demonstrated, the glorification of the Confederacy and its cause was perpetuated by its mountain veterans as much as those anywhere else in the South. The United Confederate Veterans had local chapters, or "camps," in most of the counties west of Asheville, and women in many of those counties formed chapters of the United Daughters of the Confederacy as well. William W. Stringfield, one of the leading proponents of postwar commemoration in the region, denied that Unionism was widespread in the mountains, declaring that the notion was a misconception propagated by outsiders. "No people were more zealous for the South," he declared in his regimental history of the 69th North Carolina, "than Western North Carolinians." He claimed that those in Haywood County, his current residence, and across the western part of the state, remained "loyal to their State, section, and nation and [were] not ashamed of their Confederate record."[34]

But as with the Unionist myths, which were indeed perpetuated from outside the region, the idea that the Carolina highlands represented a solid pro-Southern front throughout the war was the result of equally selective interpretations of that past. Western North Carolina's late-nineteenth-century leaders, who were either veterans of the war or sons of veterans, carefully perpetuated this sense of Southerness in their regimental and county histories. They made much of what was true—the initial enthusiasm with which mountain residents enlisted in Confederate service—but moved well beyond truth in portraying that enthusiasm as having been sustained for the war's duration. For example, Allen Davidson's son, Theodore Davidson of Cherokee County, told an Asheville literary club in 1905 that "the ardor with which the mountain . . . population flew to arms at the call of their respective states, and the fidelity they exhibited for the cause throughout four years of struggle, self-denial, suffering death and social destruction," was "especially true of the North Carolina Mountaineer."[35] As Richard Starnes notes, in locals' memories of the war, and the "official" and unofficial accounts that sustained those memories, "unpleasant topics such as desertion, internal dissent, and outright disloyalty were replaced by images of Confederate solidarity, bravery in battle, and devotion to duty."[36]

Nevertheless, it was the external, Unionized version of Appalachia's wartime experience that drew so much attention to the region in the decades following the war. The perceived "whiteness" and national patriotism of southern highlanders added to the region's appeal and interest to not only the authors who wrote about it but also the missionaries, educators, and social workers who participated in the "discovery" of Appalachia from the late nineteenth through the early twentieth centuries.[37]

These fictionalized accounts and many others about other sections of the mountain South convinced an educated Northern reading audience that western North Carolina and the rest of the people in the southern highlands were in great need of cultural, social, and economic assistance. Among those most influenced by these perceptions were members of the Presbyterian Board of Home Missions. They supported the establishment of the Home Industrial School for Girls near Asheville in 1877 and took over the Dorlan Institute in Hot

Springs (formerly Warm Springs) in Madison County, soon after the school was founded in 1879.[38] With these first institutions, religious organizations began to concentrate on providing to "isolated" mountain children the needed education in the social graces, economic skills, and general knowledge that would allow them to adjust to broader society. Much of the impetus for this missionary work was to reach a people who had been cut off from religious instruction. Ironically, as noted earlier, the number of formal religious organizations in the mountains was growing significantly during this period—without outside assistance. By 1890, in fact, the magnitude of formal church affiliation in the mountains had substantially surpassed that of the United States as a whole.[39]

The image of western North Carolina as an isolated region inhabited by a violent and poor people who lived a static, frontierlike existence proved hard to shake. Many authors and home mission educators, and thus the readers of their descriptions of the region, viewed the mountains as an unchanging world. This ideal of "our contemporary ancestors" or "yesterday's people" was very attractive to outsiders. But even on its own terms the stereotype did not accurately describe mountain life. These same commentators admitted that outside developments like the Civil War and the internal revenue tax were responsible for the violence that was so often attributed to an inherent primitivism.[40]

For western North Carolinians themselves, the idea that they lived in an unchanging human environment was incomprehensible. They were, for the most part, pleased with the vast change taking place in much of their region and viewed it as progress. Not only did they fully acknowledge it and recognize its beneficial effects they also would likely have agreed that the primary agent of that change was the continued construction of the Western North Carolina Railroad. The war's outbreak had halted the much anticipated line, with tracks having been laid only into the eastern part of Burke County by the spring of 1861. An effort was made to resume work during Reconstruction, and tracks were laid to Old Fort in McDowell County, but the costs of replacing facilities destroyed by the war and unstable management curtailed most construction work.[41] In 1870, the state purchased full control of the railroad and provided the necessary capital to continue construction. By 1875, the state had committed its most readily available resource to the building of the line—convict labor.

Using convict labor was a common practice in the South during this time period. Southern states hired out their prison populations as a source of revenue or capital, including state construction projects, in which they served as a source of very inexpensive labor. By 1875, there were 300 male and 16 female convicts, many of whom were African Americans, working to lay track up the steep slopes of the Swannanoa Gap. The work was slow, difficult, and very dangerous. Despite Governor Zebulon Vance's decision to increase the number of convicts working on the western road, the line did not reach the top of the Blue Ridge until 1879. In the previous four years, nine miles of track had been laid on three miles of land. Six tunnels were blasted out of the mountain, including the 1,800-foot-long Swannanoa tunnel. At least 125 convicts perished in that one location alone.[42] With this major obstacle conquered, it appeared as if the mountain region west of the Blue Ridge would receive railroad service in the near future.

In fact, there were serious delays, and the line was not completed until 1891. After it reached Asheville in 1880, the line was constructed north through Madison County and connected with railroads in Tennessee two years later. While this development provided the line with income needed to sustain its business operations, the vast majority of counties west of the Blue Ridge remained unserved. Slowly the western, or Ducktown, line advanced westward toward the Smokies, reaching Waynesville in 1883, Dillsboro in 1884, and Murphy in 1891. The work remained tragically dangerous, and dozens of convicts continued to die every year, including nineteen who drowned in a particularly egregious accident in Jackson County.[43] These main lines were quickly connected with more remote locations by feeder lines, which were constructed by businesses and communities not served by the trunk line.

Two types of businesses took particular advantage of this transportation breakthrough. One was the logging industry. Large lumber concerns in the Northeast and Midwest, having exhausted their supplies of easily available timber, sought unharvested stands of hardwoods elsewhere and were soon attracted to the mountains of North Carolina. The first cuttings, which were begun in the 1880s, had been carried out by local small enterprises that cut selectively and transported the logs to the mills by using "slash" dams on small creeks and rivers, and then shipped the timber to outside markets by rail. When major logging companies moved into the area after 1890, they found this mode of operation too inefficient and built spur railroad lines in order to exploit the timber resources directly.[44]

Tourism was the other major business in the mountains to take advantage of the improvement in transportation. The major tourist attractions, as they had been before the war, were Flat Rock and Hendersonville in Henderson County, White Sulphur Springs in Haywood County, Hot Springs in Madison County, and especially Asheville. These communities had long featured modern hotels, summer homes, and in some cases, the healing waters of mineral springs. The railroad dramatically increased the number of tourists who could reach these areas from major metropolitan areas of the South and Northeast. In addition, Asheville and the surrounding area gained a reputation as being a healthful location for sufferers of tuberculosis, and many people suffering from this dangerous disease spent extended periods in the mountains.[45] Tourism expanded rapidly during the late nineteenth century and generated considerable income to the increasing numbers of highlanders being driven off their small mountain farms.

Most of the mountain residents leaving their highland homes to find work ended up in the textile factories that were being built along the rushing streams in the mountain and piedmont counties of Tennessee, North Carolina, and South Carolina. Once again, the railroad was partially responsible for making these areas accessible to both the urban markets of the North and the workers from the mountains. The cotton mills in Lenoir, Morganton, Marion, and Rutherfordton, the larger of which had been established there as early as 1872, became major employers. Equally significant, mountain residents found that the greater number of textile factories established just to their east in the piedmont of North and South Carolina offered other opportunities. The growing pressure of population on the land and the resulting rural poverty drove many western North Carolinians off their farms and into these factories. Historian Jacquelyn Hall and her colleagues observed that "widows, female-headed households, single women, and laborers—those with the least access to the land, labor, and capital necessary for surviving in the emerging market-based economy—predominated among the first wave of migrants to Piedmont factories in the 1870s and early 1880s."[46] Mountain women who had been economically marginalized by the deaths and injuries of their husbands and male relatives during the war often found factory work to be a viable alternative to subsistence farming, which was providing them an increasingly precarious existence.

To contemporary observers in the mountains, the rapid changes that followed the railroads to western North Carolina must have seemed almost revolutionary. Growing towns and small cities, with their shops and small businesses, provided centers where even the most rural of the region's inhabitants had access to modern goods and services. The success of the lumber, tourism, and textile businesses provided alternative sources of income to a population pre-

viously sustained by traditional family farms. At the same time, social organizations like churches and schools established by both natives of the area and
outsiders provided the necessary support system to build communities in locations where wartime experiences had turned neighbors against neighbors. In
addition, the political system had matured to the point that it was able to limit
the violence associated with war-related conflicts. Proof of this growing cohesion and rejection of violence was the increasing support among the majority of
mountaineers for the officials in the Internal Revenue Service in their war
against illegal distillers.

Given these developments, how is one to judge the impact of the Civil War in
western North Carolina? For those who were adults during the 1861 to 1865
period, the war was undoubtedly the most traumatic and significant experience
of their lives. For many mountain men, participation in Confederate or Union
armies exposed them to locations and associations that they never would have
seen or experienced in their normal lifetimes. For many of the women left
behind, the fighting and the internal warfare in the mountains brought terror
and hardship that was unimagined before 1861. These traumas would scar the
survivors in a variety of ways throughout the rest of their lives. In some cases,
the strain of the war contributed to debilitating mental illness that rendered
individuals dysfunctional and thus incapable of contributing further to his or
her family, neighborhood, or region.[47] But it is important to make a distinction between the impact on individuals on the one hand and the entire region
on the other.

It is apparent that western North Carolina in 1861 was a region on the verge
of significant social and economic change. Although their enterprises were not
yet connected to the emerging Southern rail system, a large proportion of the
planters, yeoman farmers, artisans, merchants, and professionals were already
integrated into the market economy of the South. Transportation to the outside
world may have been primitive, but an extensive trade took place nevertheless.
Farm and forest products flowed north, east, and south, and manufactured
products and necessities not produced in the mountains were purchased by
general merchants located throughout the highlands and resold to their numerous customers on a cash basis. While some families sustained themselves
without having to resort to buying supplies from local stores, they were still
dependent on the craft skills of their neighbors, who were involved in this wider
distribution of goods. The expansion of slavery in the mountains is evidence of

the growth of the commercial side of the region's economy, in terms of both the surplus capital to be expended on slaves and the expanded labor base it could profitably absorb.

Despite this expansion of the mountain economy and the significant integration of the area into regional and national trade patterns, the people of western North Carolina were in danger of falling further behind their lowland neighbors. As a number of scholars have noted, the presence of a railroad was instrumental in spurring economic activity in the upland and mountain South.[48] The political and economic leadership, without regard to partisan affiliation or business interest, recognized this fact well before the war and had long pushed for rail connections to their region. The Civil War destroyed whatever opportunity there was for western North Carolina to join this national transportation system and thus stalled the economic expansion of the region by a least a decade. The importance of the railroad's impact can be seen in the burst of activity and development that took place in the 1880s and 1890s, when it finally traversed the region.

As the North Carolina mountains started to urbanize and industrialize in the 1880s, the small farm began to diminish as the basis of the mountain economy. Traditional handicrafts became less important and less practiced as a rapidly increasing number of stores began to supply manufactured items at a low cost. The individuals and households that continued to function in traditional ways came to be viewed as deficient in some way and became the subject of local color stories and the object of missions' efforts to bring them into the modern world. Observers from that time to the present have decried this destruction of a way of life. In particular, they have bemoaned the loss of community and the emergence of the more individualistic lifestyle of the modern age. The evidence presented in this study points out that this conclusion involves a misunderstanding of the traditional mountain community. The neighborhood in western North Carolina was usually an integrated economic system. Residents of an area were mutually dependent upon one another's skills to carry out the wide variety of activities in order to sustained a largely self-sufficient community. Thus, the social structure of mountains was built on economically interdependent communities. The wartime disruptions caused by the removal of vital services and the individuals who performed them confirmed just how strong these communal bonds had been.

Yet a community as envisioned by most observers included much more than an interdependent economic system. A shared system of values, membership in common institutions, and a willingness to live in harmony were also considered essential to the traditional highland lifestyle. While the subtle intimacies of such relationships are difficult to reconstruct a century and a half later, the existing evidence suggests that the settlements of western North Carolina only partially met these standards. It seems quite clear that antebellum social institutions were relatively few in number and were only beginning to mature in 1861. Kinship networks were at some level an important factor here, though it is difficult to trace their impact except in areas, such as Shelton Laurel, where extended families settled together, or among the elite of the rich river valleys east of the Blue Ridge, where families had laid early claims and persisted in the area for several generations. For many other highlanders, even this social grouping was not a major factor in their lives.

One of the few organized groups found in almost every late antebellum community was the political party. Thus it is hardly surprising that political parties served as a potent means of identity for approximately 80 percent of the white males in western North Carolina. Ironically, these groups were much more likely to divide the mountain population into factions—even splitting family members in many cases—than they were to unite it. By 1861 the traditional community in the North Carolina mountains was not yet fully formed. It was heavily dependent on kinship ties in some areas but not others and divided by partisan allegiances.

This immature social system was completely shattered by the war. The economic base of the community was destroyed as a significant proportion of the most productive farmers, craftsmen, and businessmen were taken from the region. The already inadequate transportation system became overburdened, and it virtually disintegrated. Basic items, like salt, were no longer available, and many women and children became dependent upon government assistance rather than their neighbors for their sustenance. At the same time, differing antebellum partisan loyalties often translated into intense differences during the war. Neighbors and kinsmen often found themselves shooting at each other in an internal war driven by vengeance and desperation. The incursion of Federal raiding parties and standing Confederate forces late in the war only aggravated the violence, disruption, and tensions already so infused throughout most highland home fronts. By the end of 1864, much of the mountain region was facing a critical breakdown of community on a variety of levels.

Once the war was over, most western Carolinians sought to reestablish the traditional community system as they had known it before the war. In some

cases, this proved to be impossible. Individuals who had made strong commitments during the war, such as Lawrence M. Allen in Madison County and
Zebulon Vance and Augustus Merrimon in Buncombe, found it expedient to
live elsewhere in North Carolina. Many other mountain residents discovered
that they could be safe only where their neighbors had espoused the same
wartime allegiances as they had. New political alignments emerged after the war
and often served as rallying points for neighborhoods. Some groups started
their own churches to distinguish themselves from other denominations or
sects in the mountains.[49] Since some families had divided during the war,
kinship was not always a reliable source of support.

Social institutions that had been notably weak before the war began to play a
much more prominent role in western North Carolina society. Church membership increased dramatically; by some accounts, it nearly doubled. The number
and the quality of schools grew rapidly as they became centers for social
integration. The expansion of businesses and factories offered new employment opportunities for the inhabitants of western North Carolina. In fact, the
improvement in transportation that came with the railroads encouraged the
formation of communities based on criteria other than place of residence. It is
clear, however, that the trauma of the Civil War convinced most highlanders that
some kind of social harmony was absolutely essential, and they actively and
consciously sought this type of support system. Ironically, the idea of community in the Southern mountains may have emerged as an ideal to be pursued
only after its greatest failure.

It seems fair to conclude that the legacy of the Civil War was an ambiguous
one in western North Carolina. Its immediate economic and social impact was
overwhelmingly negative, and the early postwar years saw very little improvement in the situation. Communities simply could not be reconstructed along
traditional, antebellum lines, and new allegiances and institutions had to be
forged. When economic change came with the railroads in the 1880s, these new
community institutions had greater flexibility and strength and adapted readily
to the changing circumstances. It would appear, therefore, that by destroying
the viability of the more traditional community system, the Civil War eased the
way for the modernization of western North Carolina. Perhaps the greatest
irony is that those who most ardently supported the Confederacy wanted to
prevent this kind of change at all costs.

NOTES

ABBREVIATIONS

CSAAL   Confederate States of America Armory Letterbook, Asheville, N.C., Archives
        and Records Division, Virginia State Library, Richmond, Va.
HL   Hunter Library, Special Collections, Western Carolina University, Cullowhee,
        N.C.
NCDAH   North Carolina Department of Archives and History, Raleigh, N.C.
OR   U.S. War Department, *War of the Rebellion: A Compilation of the Official Records
        of the Union and Confederate Armies*. 128 vols. Washington, D.C.: U.S. Govern-
        ment Printing Office, 1880–1901. (All citations to *OR* are to series 1, unless
        otherwise noted.)
PML   Pack Memorial Library, Asheville, N.C.
SCC   Southern Claims Commission Records—Case Files (RG 217), National Archives,
        Washington, D.C.
SHC   Southern Historical Collection, University of North Carolina, Chapel Hill, N.C.
WRPL   William R. Perkins Library, Special Collections, Duke University, Durham, N.C.

INTRODUCTION

1. Sarah J. Lenoir to Annie, July 10, 1862, Lenoir Family Papers, SHC.

2. Gale, "Recollections of Life in the Southern Confederacy," 14, 17.

3. Woodward, *Mary Chesnut's Civil War*, 342, 422–24; Woodward and Muhlenfeld, *Private Mary Chesnut*, 77–78; Henry Capers, *Life and Times of Memminger*, 370–71; Fitzsimmons, *From the Banks of the Oklawaha*, 114.

4. Malet, *Errand to the South*, 248.

5. William Holland Thomas to his wife, January 14, 1861, Thomas Papers, WRPL.

6. James W. Taylor, *Alleghania*, 1–2, 15–17.

7. Vinovskis, "Have Social Historians Lost the Civil War?" 34–35.

8. Sutherland, "Getting the 'Real War' into the Books," 200–201. See also Paludan, "Actors and Heroes," 493–99.

9. See, for example, Thomas, *Confederate State of Richmond*; Gerald Capers, *Occupied City* [New Orleans]; Walker, *Vicksburg*; Currie, *Enclave* [Vicksburg]; Maslowski, *Treason Must Be Made Odious* [Nashville]; Rosen, *Confederate Charleston*; and Dyer, *Secret Yankees* [Atlanta].

10. See, for example, Fellman, *Inside War*; Ash, *Middle Tennessee Society Transformed*; Kenzer, *Kinship and Neighborhood*; Durrill, *War of Another Kind*; Crofts, *Old Southampton*; Morgan, *Emancipation in Virginia's Tobacco Belt*; McCaslin, *Tainted Breeze*; LeeAnn Whites, *Civil War as a Crisis*; Sutherland, *Seasons of War*; Bryant, *How Curious a Land*;

Tripp, *Yankee Town, Southern City*; Dyer, *Secret Yankees*; and Rogers, *Confederate Home Front*. Forthcoming community studies of the war years include Jonathan Sarris on two north Georgia counties; Robert Tracy McKenzie on Knoxville, Tennessee; and David H. McGee on Raleigh, North Carolina.

11. The most comprehensive examinations of the impact of the Civil War on individual Appalachian communities are Dunn, *Cades Cove*, ch. 5; Paludan, *Victims*; Sarris, " 'Hellish Deeds in a Christian Land' "; Crawford, "Confederate Volunteering," "Dynamics of Mountain Unionism," "Mountain Farmers," and "Political Society"; and a forthcoming book by Martin Crawford on Ashe County, North Carolina, and one by Ralph Mann on Sandy Basin and Burkes Garden, Virginia.

For studies affirming the centrality of the war in instigating or at least accelerating a transformation of some aspect of Appalachian society, see McKinney, *Southern Mountain Republicans*, particularly ch. 2; Cunningham, *Apples on the Flood*, 100–101; Paludan, *Victims*; Salstrom, "Agricultural Origins of Economic Dependency," 272–73, 278–79; Miller, *Revenuers and Moonshiners*, 19, 41–42; and Noe, *Southwest Virginia's Railroad*, chs. 6, 7, and epilogue.

12. Lee, *Price of Nationhood*, 8.

13. John Campbell, *Southern Highlander and His Homeland*.

14. See, for instance, Escott, *Many Excellent People*, chs. 2 and 3; Durrill, *War of Another Kind*; Kruman, "Dissent in the Confederacy"; Honey, "War within the Confederacy"; Auman, "Neighbor against Neighbor" (diss.); and Bynum, *Unruly Women*. Quote from Sutherland, *Guerrillas, Unionists, and Violence*, 12.

Chapter One

1. Hamilton and Cameron, *Papers of Shotwell*, 2:280.

2. Quoted in Wellman, *Dead and Gone*, 172–73.

3. Physical descriptions of North Carolina's mountains during the mid-nineteenth century are in Avery and Boardman, "Arnold Guyot's Notes," and James W. Taylor, *Alleghania*. See also Cotton, "Appalachian North Carolina," 28–30, and Blackmun, *Western North Carolina*, 5–12.

4. Blethen and Wood, "Pioneer Experience," 67–73; Blackmun, *Western North Carolina*, 156–71; Phifer, "Slavery in Microcosm," 139–41. See also Blethen and Wood, "Appalachian Frontier and the Southern Frontier."

5. *Eighth Census, 1860: Population* (Washington, D.C.: Government Printing Office, 1864). Total based on seventeen mountain counties. See table 1.3 in Inscoe, *Mountain Masters*, 23, which includes data for all of these counties except Polk and Rutherford.

6. Sondley, *History of Buncombe County*, 1:396–98.

7. Computed from *Agriculture in the U.S. in 1860* (Washington, D.C.: Government Printing Office, 1864), 104–11. For a breakdown on mountain county farm size, see table 1.3 in Inscoe, *Mountain Masters*, 23.

8. The number of sheep slightly exceeded the number of cattle and milk cows combined in western North Carolina in 1850 and 1860. In the latter year, mountain counties had 100,563 sheep and 98,069 cattle and cows. Computed from *Agriculture in the U.S. in 1860*,

104–11. See also Goe, "Sheep and the Mountains of North Carolina," 90; McDonald and McWhiney, "Antebellum Southern Herdsman"; Hilliard, *Hog Meat and Hoecake*; MacMaster, "Cattle Trade in Western Virginia"; Inscoe, *Mountain Masters*, 14–19; and Blethen and Wood, "Pioneer Experience," 85–87.

9. T. McGimsey to Thomas Henderson, May 3, 1811, in Newsome, "Twelve North Carolina Counties," 419.

10. Lanman, *Letters from the Allegheny*, 384.

11. Olmsted, *Journey in the Back Country*, 258–59, 293. On the not-so-hidden agenda behind Olmsted's observations of the southern highlands, see Inscoe, "Olmsted in Appalachia," 181–82.

12. See, for example, Opie, "Where American History Began"; Ronald Eller, "Land and Family"; and Billings, Blee, and Swanson, "Culture, Family, and Community."

13. Among the most recent studies reflecting this new complexity are the essays in Pudup, Billings, and Waller, *Appalachia in the Making*; Dunaway, *First American Frontier*; Noe, *Southwest Virginia's Railroad*; Rasmussen, *Absentee Landowning and Exploitation*; and Hsiung, *Two Worlds in the Tennessee Mountains*.

14. Finger, "Cherokee Accommodation and Persistence," 31. See also Finger, *Eastern Band of Cherokees* and "North Carolina Cherokees"; on Thomas's role, see Godbold and Russell, *Confederate Colonel and Cherokee Chief*.

15. Finger, "Cherokee Accommodation and Persistence," provides the most recent and most succinct treatment of these issues.

16. R., "Week in the Great Smoky Mountains," 131. The writer notes the location of Quallatown as Jackson County, which it had been since that county's creation in 1851. He also cites the Indian population of the area as 1,500.

17. Dunn, *Cades Cove*, 72.

18. Bode and Ginter, *Farm Tenancy and the Census*, 116–17, 131 (table 6.1); Dunaway, *First American Frontier*, ch. 4, esp. table 4.2, p. 92. See also Dunaway, "Speculators and Settler Capitalists"; Salstrom, "Newer Appalachia"; and Robert Mitchell, *Commercialism and Frontier*, 88–89.

On antebellum tenantry elsewhere in the South, see Guion Griffin Johnson, "Landless People of Antebellum North Carolina," 23–32; Houkek and Heller, "Searching for Nineteenth-Century Farm Tenants"; Mendenhall, "Rise of Southern Tenancy"; J. William Harris, *Plain Folk and Gentry*; Orser, *Material Bases of the Postbellum Tenant Plantation*, 37–38; Lacy Ford, *Origins of Southern Radicalism*, 84–88; Bolton, *Poor Whites in the Antebellum South*; Royce, *Origins of Southern Sharecropping*; McCurry, *Masters of Small Worlds*; and Cline, " 'Something Wrong in South Carolina.' "

19. For Jackson County, see Blethen and Wood, "Pioneer Experience," 83–95; for Haywood County, see Joseph Reid, "Antebellum Southern Rental Contracts," 69–83.

20. See correspondence between Alfred W. Bell and Mary Bell, 1861–63, Bell Papers, WRPL.

21. *Eighth Census, 1860: Population*, for Burke, Buncombe, and Wilkes Counties; Guion Griffin Johnson, "Landless People of North Carolina," 23–32. Wilma Dunaway provides the most thorough statistical analysis of the variety of forms landless agricultural labor took throughout the region in *First American Frontier*, 91–108.

22. Calvin J. Cowles to Robert Maxwell, February 10, 1862, Cowles Papers, NCDAH. For

Cowles's correspondence and accounts with his tenants, see letters to and from Thornton Profitt, John Dula, David E. Horton, etc., in ibid. On the vast extent of absentee land ownership in Appalachia, see Rasmussen, *Absentee Landowning and Exploitation*, and Dunaway, "Speculators and Settler Capitalists," 52–68.

23. Joseph Reid, "Antebellum Southern Rental Contracts," 71–79.

24. Phifer, "Slavery in Microcosm," 141. For other examples of western North Carolinians who employed farm tenants, see numerous letters from A. L. Hackett and Thomas Bouchelle to Samuel F. Patterson, 1860–64, Jones and Patterson Family Papers; James C. Harper Diaries, vol. 2, 1855, and vol. 3, 1861; and various entries in Hamilton Brown Papers, all in SHC.

25. Lacy Ford, *Origins of Southern Radicalism*, 87.

26. On early settlement of slaves and slaveholders in western North Carolina, see Phifer, "Slavery in Microcosm," 138–41; Chambers, *Breed and the Pasture*, 70–72; Hickerson, *Echoes of Happy Valley*; and Walton, "Sketches of the Pioneers." On the introduction of slavery into the eighteenth-century Virginia and Kentucky mountains, see Eslinger, "Shape of Slavery on Virginia's Kentucky Frontier," and Davis-DeEulis, "Slavery on the Margins of the Virginia Frontier."

27. For these and subsequent figures, see tables 3.1, 3.2, and appendix in Inscoe, *Mountain Masters*, 60–61, 84–85, 265–66. The discrepancy is accounted for by the fact that four of the region's five largest slaveholders, who had holdings of from 80 to 174 slaves, were Burke County residents.

28. Ibid. These were Ashe, Watauga, Yancey, and Madison Counties.

29. Ibid.

30. See Patton, *Condensed History of Flat Rock*; Sadie Smathers Patton, "Fame of WNC as Major Health Resort Dates from Eighteenth Century," *Asheville Citizen*, March, 26, 1950; Marsh, *Historic Flat Rock*; Colton, *Guidebook to Scenery*; and Dykeman, *French Broad*.

31. Olmsted, *Journey in the Back Country*, 253.

32. The sample counties are Ashe, Buncombe, Burke, Cherokee, and Yancey. Data on slaveholders' occupations is drawn from a variety of sources and thus is only approximate. For a general discussion of slaveholders engaged in nonagricultural occupations, see Oakes, *Ruling Race*, 58–65.

33. Inscoe, "Mountain Masters," 143–73. See also Crawford, "Political Society," 373–90. For a discussion of the slaveholding elite in the Kentucky mountains, see Pudup, "Social Class and Economic Development," and Billings and Blee, "Agriculture and Poverty in the Kentucky Mountains."

34. For figures on increased value and number of slaves in the mountain counties, see Inscoe, *Mountain Masters*, 81–86. For broader data on Appalachia's slave population, see Stuckert, "Black Populations of Southern Appalachian"; Richard Drake, "Slavery and Antislavery in Appalachia"; Murphy, "Slavery and Freedom in Appalachia"; and several essays in Inscoe, *Appalachia in Black and White*.

35. For discussion of slaves as miners in Appalachia and the South, see Phifer, "Champagne at Brindletown"; David Williams, "Georgia's Forgotten Miners"; Starobin, *Industrial Slaves in the Old South*, 214–19; Lewis, *Coal, Iron, and Slaves*; Lewis, *Black Coal Miners in America*; Dew, *Bond of Iron*; Stealey, *Antebellum Kanawha Salt Business*; and several essays in Inscoe, *Appalachia in Black and White*.

For the use of slaves in railroad construction, see Abrams, "Western North Carolina Railroad"; Inscoe, *Mountain Masters*, 79–81; and Noe, *Southwest Virginia's Railroad*, ch. 4.

36. For classic statements of these assumptions, see John Campbell, *Southern Highlander and His Homeland*, 91; Kephart, *Our Southern Highlanders*, 382–83; and Weller, *Yesterday's People*, 88–89. Among the earliest challenges to these assumptions were Dykeman, "Appalachia in Context," and Wilhelm, "Appalachian Isolation." The most recent include the introduction and several essays in Billings, Norman, and Ledford, *Confronting Appalachian Stereotypes*.

37. See Ronald Eller, "Search for Community in Appalachia"; Beaver, *Rural Community in the Appalachian South*, 140–44; and several essays in Puglisi, *Diversity and Accommodation*, esp. Mitchell's introductory essay, " 'From the Ground Up.' "

38. Friedman, *Enclosed Garden*, 3.

39. On Happy Valley in Caldwell and Wilkes Counties, see Hickerson, *Echoes of Happy Valley*; on the Catawba River valley, Phifer, *Burke*; on Shelton Laurel, Paludan, *Victims*; on Rocky Creek, Beaver, *Rural Community in the Appalachian South*; on the Toe River valley, Deyton, "Toe River Valley to 1865"; and on the Tuckaseigee, Blethen and Wood, "Land and Family in the Tuckaseigee Valley."

40. For a good overview of this debate, see Kulikoff, "Transition to Capitalism." See also Genovese, "Yeoman Farmers in a Slaveholders' Democracy."

41. Hahn, *Roots of Southern Populism*, 36–40; Lacy Ford, *Origins of Southern Radicalism*, chs. 6 and 7. See also Lacy Ford, "Yeoman Farmers in the South Carolina Upcountry," and Weiman, "Farmers and the Market."

42. See Pudup, "Limits of Subsistence," and Salstrom, "Agricultural Origins of Economic Dependency."

43. Robert Mitchell, *Commercialism and Frontier*; Schlotterbeck, " 'Social Economy' of an Upper South Community"; Mann, "Mountain, Land, and Kin Networks"; Hsiung, "How Isolated Was Appalachia?"; Crawford, "Mountain Farmers and the Market Economy"; Salstrom, "Newer Appalachia."

44. Inscoe, "Diversity in Antebellum Mountain Life." On individual merchants in western North Carolina, see Blethen and Wood, "Trader on the Western Carolina Frontier," and Godbold and Russell, *Confederate Colonel and Cherokee Chief*, 27–35, 47–52. On similar trends elsewhere in Appalachia, see Pudup, "Town and Country in the Transformation of Appalachian Kentucky," and Hofstra and Mitchell, "Town and Country in Backcountry Virginia."

45. Inscoe, *Mountain Masters*, ch. 2. For the most systematic treatment of just how extensive such commercial conduits were in terms of the volume, variety, and "spatial organization of external trade" from the entire Southern Appalachian region, see Dunaway, *First American Frontier*, 131–45, 195–208.

46. Inscoe, "Diversity in Antebellum Mountain Life."

47. Quote from Malet, *Errand to the South*, 215. For contemporary commentary by visitors to these resorts, see Malet, *Errand to the South*, 235–37; Lanman, *Letters from the Allegheny*, 427; Featherstonaugh, *Canoe Voyage*, 2:281; Colton, *Guidebook to the Scenery*; and Buckingham, *Slave States of America*, 197.

48. Sondley, *History of Buncombe County*, 2:829; Blethen and Wood, "Trader on the

Western Carolina Frontier," 160–65; Ready, *Asheville, Land of the Sky*, 19–21. Quote is from Wolfe, *Hills Beyond*, 186.

49. For contemporary commentary on these towns, see Lanman, *Letters from the Allegheny*, 125; Newsome, "A. S. Merrimon Journal," 300–330; Avery and Boardman, "Arnold Guyot's Notes," 251–318; Colton, *Guidebook to the Scenery*, 15–22; and Disturnell, *Springs, Waterfalls, Sea-Bathing Resorts*, 137–38.

50. Burnett, "Hog Raising and Hog Driving"; Dykeman, *French Broad*, 139; Blackmun, *Western North Carolina*, 215–21; Inscoe, *Mountain Masters*, 44–48. See also MacMaster, "Cattle Trade in Western Virginia."

51. Blackmun, *Western North Carolina*, 157–59; Lambert, "Oconaluftee Valley."

52. Watson, "Squire Oldway and His Friends"; Lacy Ford, "Rednecks and Merchants"; Hahn, *Roots of Southern Populism*, 40–49.

53. S. R. Mount to William Holland Thomas, April 5, 1853, Thomas Papers, WRPL.

54. "Western North Carolina," *North Carolina Planter* 2 (1859): 323, quoted from the *Franklin Observer*.

55. Elisha Mitchell to Thomas L. Clingman, n.d., in Lanman, *Letters from the Allegheny*, 195; Konkle, *John Motley Morehead*, 244–45.

56. Inscoe, *Mountain Masters*, 165–69.

57. Ibid., 169–76. On the sectional and partisan debates on internal improvement issues in the state, see Jeffrey, "Internal Improvements and Political Parties."

58. Henretta, "Families and Farms."

59. Salstrom, "Newer Appalachia"; Salstrom, *Appalachia's Path to Dependency*.

60. Introduction to Robert Mitchell, *Appalachian Frontiers*, 3, 7. See also Robert Mitchell, " 'From the Ground Up.' "

61. Crayon, "Winter in the South," 721. For a full analysis of Crayon's (David Hunter Strother's) impact on antebellum Appalachian imagery, see Hsiung, *Two Worlds in the Tennessee Mountains*, 163–75.

CHAPTER TWO

1. *Raleigh Register*, August 12, 1842.

2. For indications of party divisions in western North Carolina between 1840 and 1860, see tables 6.1, 6.2, and 6.3 in Inscoe, *Mountain Masters*, 136–41. See also Jeffrey, *State Parties and National Politics*, for a statewide context of mountain voting patterns.

3. Jeffrey, *State Parties and National Politics*, esp. chs. 5, 7–9; Kruman, *Parties and Politics*, chs. 3–4; Pegg, *Whig Party in North Carolina*, 156–210; Norton, *Democratic Party in Ante-Bellum North Carolina*, chs. 3–5. On free suffrage, see Jeffrey, " 'Beyond Free Suffrage.' " On ad valorem taxation, see Butts, "Challenge to Planter Rule"; Butts, " 'Irrepressible Conflict' "; and William Burton, "Issue of *Ad Valorem* Taxation." For the effects of both issues on mountain politics, see Inscoe, *Mountain Masters*, 140–51.

For an analysis of the second party system across the state line, see Bergeron, *Antebellum Politics in Tennessee*, and Brashear, "Election Ground." For that across the Upper South, see Crofts, *Reluctant Confederates*, ch. 2.

4. The fullest biographical treatment of Clingman is Jeffrey, *Thomas Lanier Clingman*.

Other treatments of his antebellum political career include Jeffrey, "'Thunder from the Mountains'"; Kruman, "Clingman and the Whig Party"; and Inscoe, "Clingman, Mountain Whiggery, and the Southern Cause."

5. Thomas L. Clingman, "On the Political Aspect of the Slave Question, Delivered in the House of Representatives, December 22, 1947" and "In Defence of the South against the Aggressive Movement of the North, Delivered in the House of Representatives, January 22, 1950," both in Clingman, *Speeches and Writings*, 225, 253–54.

6. The election results gave Clingman 8,673 votes to Vance's 3,211. See *Asheville News*, August 20, 1857; quote from Wilmington paper reprinted in *Asheville News*, July 16, 1857.

7. Phifer, "Saga of a Burke County Family," pt. 3, 306–7. A blemish on W. W. Avery's record was an 1851 incident in which he had shot and killed another Democrat, Samuel Fleming of Yancey County, in the Burke County courthouse; the incident was the culmination of a long-standing feud. See Gass, "'Misfortune of a High-Minded and Honorable Gentleman.'"

8. For a discussion of John Brown and Appalachia, see Inscoe, "Race and Racism in Southern Appalachia," 109–10; Abel, *Man on Fire*, 245–48; and Warch and Fauton, *John Brown*, 53–54.

9. *Asheville News*, December 29, 1859.

10. Zebulon Vance, "To the Citizens of the Eighth Congressional District of North Carolina," February 13, 1860 (Washington, D.C.: H. Polkinhorn, 1861), 3; Clingman, "Against the Revolutionary Movement of the Anti-Slavery Party, Delivered in the Senate of the United States, January 16, 1860," in Clingman, *Speeches and Writings*, 451.

11. On more general reactions to the Harpers Ferry raid in North Carolina and the Upper South, see Howard, "John Brown's Raid"; Blaser, "North Carolina and Brown's Raid"; Kruman, *Parties and Politics*, 187–89; and Crofts, *Reluctant Confederates*, 70–72.

12. *Asheville News*, November 19, December 29, 1859; Alexander, *Here Will I Dwell*, 126; Henderson County Slave Records, NCDAH.

13. Marcus Erwin to John W. Ellis, December 22, 1959, in Tolbert, *Papers of Ellis*, 1:335.

14. *Asheville News*, December 29, 1859; Erwin to Ellis, December 22, 1859, in Tolbert, *Papers of Ellis*, 1:335–36.

15. *Asheville News*, January 29, 1857.

16. Ibid., January 19, 1860; Boykin, *North Carolina in 1861*, 185–86; Guion Griffin Johnson, *Ante-Bellum North Carolina*, 89.

17. Vance speech, March 16, 1860, quoted in Shore, *Southern Capitalists*, 71.

18. *Franklin Observer*, March 16, 1860.

19. *Asheville News*, December 29, 1859.

20. The fullest account of Avery's role in the Democratic Party in 1860 is Peterson, "W. W. Avery in Democratic National Convention." See also Dumond, *Secession Movement*, 45; Sitterson, *Secession Movement*, 162; and Hesseltine, *Three against Lincoln*.

21. Nicholas W. Woodfin to David L. Swain, May 17, 1860, Swain Papers, SHC.

22. Clingman, *Speeches and Writings*, 449–51; *Asheville News*, August 9, November 1, 1860; Sitterson, *Secession Movement*.

23. *Asheville News*, July 4, November 1, 1860; Cotton, "Appalachian North Carolina," 76; Sitterson, *Secession Movement*, 170–71.

24. J. Buxton to Ralph Buxton, June 8, 1860, Buxton Papers, SHC.

25. *Iredell Express*, October 5, 1860, quoted in Ambrose, "Critical Year," 21.

26. *Raleigh Register*, October 17, 1860; *Asheville News*, November 1, 1860; Ambrose, "Critical Year," 22.

27. *Asheville News*, November 1, 1860.

28. Sallie L. Lenoir to Rufus T. Lenoir, October 29, 1860, Lenoir Family Papers, SHC.

29. Connor, *Manual of North Carolina*, 985–86; Burnham, *Presidential Ballots*, 648–68. For statewide results, see Kruman, *Parties and Politics*, 199–200. For a breakdown of total votes and percentages in North Carolina's mountain counties, see table 9.1 in Inscoe, *Mountain Masters*, 221.

30. Clingman, *Speeches and Writings*, 514n, 515.

31. Isaac T. Avery to David L. Swain, November 16, 1860, Swain Papers, SHC. The three revolutionary battles to which Avery referred were all South Carolina encounters in which Burke County patriots took part.

32. Edward Jones Erwin to George Phifer Erwin, January 10, 1861, Erwin Papers, SHC. For more details on Erwin's conversion from Unionist to disunionist, see Inscoe, "Fatherly Advice on Secession."

33. *North Carolina Standard*, January 8, 1861.

34. Vance to William Dickson, December 11, 1860, in Johnston, *Papers of Vance*, 71; David W. Siler to Rufus S. Siler, December 7, 1860, Siler Papers, SHC.

35. *TriWeekly Standard*, January 31, February 14, 1861.

36. *Raleigh Register*, January 2, 1861, quoted in Cotton, "Appalachian North Carolina," 78.

37. *North Carolina Standard*, January 1, 1861.

38. "Speech of T. N. Crumpler, of Ashe on Federal Relations, Delivered in the House of Commons, January 10, 1861," circular published by the *Raleigh Register* (1861), NCDAH.

39. J. P. Eller to Vance, January 28, 1861, Vance Papers, NCDAH; W. W. Lenoir to Vance, January 7, 1861, in Johnston, *Papers of Vance*, 80.

40. Stringfield, "Sixty-ninth Regiment," in Walter Clark, *Histories of the Several Regiments*, 733–34. For the most comprehensive treatment of Upper South Unionism, see Crofts, *Reluctant Confederates*, chs. 5 and 6. On Unionist sentiments elsewhere within North Carolina, see Sitterson, *Secession Movement*, ch. 4; Kruman, *Parties and Politics*, ch. 8; and Honey, "War within the Confederacy."

41. Stringfield, "Sixty-ninth Regiment," 734–35.

42. The vast literature on Unionism in East Tennessee includes Hume, *Loyal Mountaineers*; Temple, *East Tennessee and the Civil War*; Mary Campbell, *Attitudes of East Tennesseans*; Fisher, *War at Every Door*; Atkins, *Parties, Politics, and Sectional Conflict*; Groce, "Mountain Rebels"; Queener, "East Tennessee Sentiment"; and Sheeler, "Development of Unionism." For one explanation for the differences in Unionist sentiment on either side of the state line, see Inscoe, "Mountain Unionism, Secession, and Regional Self-Image."

43. Quoted in Sheppard, *Cabins in the Laurel*, 65.

44. G. W. J. Moore to David W. Siler, December 21, 1861, Siler Papers, SHC.

45. Thomas to his wife, January 1, 1861, Thomas Papers, WRPL.

46. Ibid., January 14, 1861.

47. Malet, *Errand to the South*, 248. On Memminger's ties to the region, see Marsh, *Historic Flat Rock*, 14–16.

48. Thomas to his wife, January 1 and June 17, 1861, Thomas Papers, WRPL.

49. C. C. Jones to Vance, February 4, 1861, in Johnston, *Papers of Vance*, 95–96.

50. For other examples of concerns about Virginia's course of action, see Zebulon B. Vance to C. C. Jones, February 11, 1861, Vance Papers; James Gwyn to Rufus T. Lenoir, March 11, 1861, Lenoir Family Papers; and William J. Brown to Jno. Evans Brown, March 21, 1861, Morrison Papers, all in SHC.

51. "To the People of Buncombe County," February 18, 1861, broadside, in Civil War Papers, PML. For a similar argument, see W. W. Lenoir to Zebulon B. Vance, January 7, 1861, in Johnston, *Papers of Vance*, 80.

An outgrowth of this distinction made between the Upper and Lower South was an idea for the formation of a Central Confederacy, in which border states united temporarily as a separate nation in order to bring the extremists of New England and the Deep South to the bargaining table. Although the correspondence of several western Carolinians, including Zebulon Vance, indicates some interest in the idea, it was a scheme espoused largely by East Tennesseans. For more on the Central Confederacy, see Inscoe, *Mountain Masters*, 234–36, and Crofts, *Reluctant Confederates*, 109.

52. William John Brown to Jno. Evans Brown, April 15, 1861, Morrison Papers, SHC.

53. Quoted in Sitterson, *Secession Movement*, 220–21.

54. Quoted in Michael Johnson, *Toward a Patriarchal Republic*, 49–50. For the full text of Brown's "Public Letter" of December 7, 1860, see Freehling and Simpson, *Secession Debated*, 149–54.

55. On incidents of such racial tensions in western North Carolina, see Inscoe, *Mountain Masters*, 98–99, 211–12. On statewide reaction to these uprisings, see Elliott, "Nat Turner Insurrection"; Blaser, "North Carolina and Brown's Raid"; and Howard, "John Brown's Raid."

56. Brownlow, *Sketches of the Rise*, 109.

57. "David W. Siler to Fellow Citizens of Macon County," March 4, 1861, circular, in Mary Gash and Family Papers, NCDAH.

58. J. P. Eller to Vance, January 28, 1861, Johnston, *Papers of Vance*, 93.

59. Calvin J. Cowles to S. W. Roosevelt, December 10, 1860, Cowles Papers, NCDAH; Calvin C. Jones to Vance, February 4, 1861, in Johnston, *Papers of Vance*, 95.

60. Tod R. Caldwell to William A. Graham, February 11, 1861, in Hamilton and Williams, *Papers of Graham*, 4:233.

61. Burgess S. Gaither to William A. Graham, February 12, 1861, in ibid., 234.

62. S. O. Deaver to Vance, January 28, 1861; B. F. Eller to Vance, December 27, 1860; and William L. Love to Vance, February 1, 1861, all in Johnston, *Papers of Vance*, 92, 74, 94; J. M. Hamilton to Vance, January 14, 1861, Vance Papers, NCDAH.

63. S. O. Deaver to Vance, January 28, 1861, and J. P. Eller to Vance, January 28, 1861, in Johnston, *Papers of Vance*, 92–93.

64. Ammons, *Outlines of History of French Broad*, 28–29.

65. Vance to Thomas George Walton, January 19 and 22, 1861, Walton Papers, and Vance to C. C. Jones, February 11, 1861, Vance Papers, SHC; Kruman, *Parties and Politics*, 206; Crofts, *Reluctant Confederates*, ch. 8.

66. For the vote and percentages by county, see table 9.2 and map 7 in Inscoe, *Mountain Masters*, 242, 245.

67. S. F. Patterson to his son, March 16, 1861, Jones and Patterson Family Papers, SHC.

68. Vance to George N. Folk, January 9, 1861, in Johnston, *Papers of Vance*, 82.

69. Auman, "Neighbor against Neighbor" (diss.), ch. 2; see also Kruman, *Parties and Politics*, 215–19; Escott, *Many Excellent People*, 32–34; and Crofts, *Reluctant Confederates*, 144–52.

70. James Gwyn to Rufus T. Lenoir, March 11, 1861, Lenoir Family Papers, SHC; *North Carolina Standard*, March 20, 1861; Nicholas W. Woodfin to Weldon N. Edwards, April 13, 1861, Conway Collection, NCDAH. For thorough accounts of the peace conference, see Dumond, *Secession Movement*, 239–66, and Crofts, *Reluctant Confederates*, 201–14.

71. James Gwyn to Rufus T. Lenoir, March 11, 1861, Lenoir Family Papers, SHC.

72. Clingman, *Speeches and Writings*, 564.

73. "David W. Siler to Fellow Citizens of Macon County," March 4, 1861, Mary Gash and Family Papers, NCDAH.

74. W. Caleb Brown to Jno. Evans Brown, March 22, 1861, W. Vance Brown Papers, SHC.

75. S. A. Tate ("Sis") to W. W. Lenoir, April 6, 1861, Lenoir Family Papers, SHC.

76. A letter from Samuel McDowell Tate in Morganton to Edward W. Jones, April 13, 1861, Jones and Patterson Family Papers, SHC, indicated that Tate not only anticipated the attack there but also expected Confederate troops to attack Washington within a day or two.

77. "David W. Siler to Fellow Citizens of Macon County," March 4, 1861, Mary Gash and Family Papers, NCDAH.

78. Charles Manly to David L. Swain, April 22, 1861, Swain Papers, NCDAH.

79. Dowd, *Life of Zebulon B. Vance*, 441.

80. Josiah Cowles to Calvin J. Cowles, June 3, 1861, and Calvin J. Cowles to S. W. Roosevelt, May 6, 1861, both in Cowles Papers, NCDAH.

81. N. W. Woodfin, "To the Voters of Buncombe County," May 9, 1861, Civil War Papers, PML.

82. Other early secessionists elected included William Holland Thomas (Jackson County), William Hicks (Haywood), Joel E. Foster (Ashe and Alleghany), John C. McDowell (Burke), James Councill (Watauga), James H. Greenlee (McDowell), and Milton Penland (Yancey). Former conditional Unionists who ran unopposed included Edmund W. Jones (Caldwell), Allen T. Davidson (Cherokee), William M. Shipp (Henderson), Peter Eller (Wilkes), and James A. McDowell (Madison), a brother of John C. McDowell of Burke. See McCormick, *Personnel of the Conventions of 1861*.

83. Sitterson, *Secession Movement*, 245n; Jones, *Knocking at the Door*, 4–5.

84. S. W. Siler to Judson Siler, May 27, 1861, Mary Gash and Family Papers, NCDAH; Sheppard, *Cabins in the Laurel*, 65.

CHAPTER THREE

1. Mary Bryan to Louise Leventhorpe, January 8, 1861, Bryan-Leventhorpe Family Papers, and Amelia Gwyn to Sister Sallie, April 15, 1861, Lenoir Family Papers, both in SHC.

2. *Carolina Watchman*, April 23, 1861.

3. James M. Gentry to Jonathan Faw, May 6, 1861, Walter Wager Faw Papers, Tennessee State Archives, Nashville, quoted in Crawford, "Confederate Volunteering," 34.

4. Heath, "North Carolina Militia," 39–40. Heath makes his comparison by dividing the state into halves, so that his measurement of greater militia activity in the west applies to as many western piedmont counties as it does mountain counties.

5. Marcus Erwin to John W. Ellis, December 22, 1959, Ellis Papers, NCDAH.

6. Duncan J. Devan and Thomas H. Holes to Thomas J. Faison, November 25, 1860, NCDAH, cited in Iobst, "North Carolina Mobilizes," 48; Siler, "To the Fellow Citizens of Macon County," in Mary Gash and Family Papers, NCDAH.

7. Iobst, "North Carolina Mobilizes," 5–11. These efforts on Avery's part earned him respect beyond the state. Once elected to the First Confederate Congress, he was appointed chairman of its Committee on Military Affairs. See Peterson, "W. W. Avery in Democratic National Convention," 478.

8. Jonathan Worth to Charlest Beatty Mallett, December 19, 1860, in Mallett Papers, SHC, quoted in Iobst, "North Carolina Mobilizes," 11.

9. Iobst, "North Carolina Mobilizes," 7.

10. Ibid., 34; Heath, "North Carolina Militia," 74–75; *North Carolina Standard*, December 12, 1860.

11. Edmund W. Jones to S. F. Patterson, May 20, 1861, Jones and Patterson Family Papers, SHC.

12. Ashe, *History of North Carolina*, 2:603; Barrett, *Civil War in North Carolina*, 14–15.

13. Phifer, *Burke*, 320.

14. "Constitution and By-Laws of the Buncombe Riflemen, Asheville, N.C., Organized December 20th, 1859" (Asheville: Western Advocate Office, 1860), PML. Of the fourteen units incorporated by that act of February 22, 1861, the Buncombe Riflemen was the only one based in western North Carolina. See Heath, "North Carolina Militia," 62, and Iobst, "North Carolina Mobilizes," 143.

15. Clipping from scrapbook of Mrs. James Harvey Greenlee, quoted in Theodore F. Davidson, *Reminiscences and Traditions*, 24, pamphlet in PML.

16. Theodore F. Davidson, *Reminiscences and Traditions*, 23; on Joseph McDowell's acquisition of Fergeson's table service at King's Mountain, see Dugger, *War Trails of the Blue Ridge*, 56–57.

17. Robert B. Vance et al. to John W. Ellis, April 18, 1861, in Tolbert, *Papers of Ellis*, 2:624–25.

18. Quote from Josiah Cowles to Calvin J. Cowles, June 18, 1861, Cowles Papers, NCDAH. For other reactions statewide to the Bethel victory, see Iobst, "North Carolina Mobilizes," 81–83, and Barrett, *Civil War in North Carolina*, 30–31.

19. William J. Brown to Jno. Evans Brown, April 15, 1861, Theodore Davidson Morrison Papers, SHC. (Brown began this letter on April 15, but in reporting the unfolding events to his son in Australia, he continued adding to it over the next several days.)

20. Hughes, *Hendersonville in Civil War Times*, 22–23.

21. Iobst, "North Carolina Mobilizes," 86–88, 90–93; Paludan, *Victims*, 34–35; William C. Walker to John W. Ellis, July 5, 1861, and Balis M. Edney to Ellis, July 7, 1861, both in Tolbert, *Papers of Ellis*, 2:883–84, 884–85; W. C. Allen, *Annals of Haywood County*, 64–69; Godbold and Russell, *Confederate Colonel and Cherokee Chief*, 102–5.

22. Zebulon Vance, "To the Citizens of the Eighth Congressional District of North Carolina," February 13, 1861 (Washington, D.C.: H. Polkinhorn, 1861), 7; Dowd, *Life of Zebulon B. Vance*, 441–42.

23. *Carolina Watchman*, May 9, 1861; *North Carolina Standard*, May 11, 1861; N. C. Westall, "Rough and Ready Guards, Asheville's Own Company Had Interesting Career," *Asheville Times*, October 9, 1921, quoted in Jim Taylor, "Buncombe Rough and Ready Guards."

24. *Raleigh Register*, May 22, 1861, quoted in Russell, "William Holland Thomas," 336; *State Journal*, May 22, 1861.

25. Mary Gash to Addie Patton, June 5, 1861, Mary Gash and Family Papers, NCDAH.

26. William Enloe and J. Ramsey Dills to John Ellis, June 28, 1861, in Tolbert, *Papers of Ellis*, 2:874. See Turpin, "Southwestern North Carolina on Eve of the War," for more on enlistments in that corner of the state.

27. James C. Harper Diaries, vol. 3, entry for April 27, 1861 (typescript, 15), and George W. F. Harper Diaries, entries for April 27–30, 1861, both in SHC; Alexander, *Here Will I Dwell*, 127.

28. Dedmond, "Harvey Davis's Unpublished Diary," 379, 382.

29. James Gwyn Diary, vol. 4, entry for May 1, 1861, Gwyn Papers, SHC; Calvin J. Cowles to Andrew Cowles, May 1, 1861, Cowles Letter Book, NCDAH.

30. James Gwyn to Rufus T. Lenoir, May 2, 1861, Lenoir Family Papers, SHC.

31. Crawford, "Confederate Volunteering," 40–41.

32. Blackmun, *Western North Carolina*, 333; Ora L. Jones, "Transylvania County," *Asheville Citizen-Times*, February 24, 1917.

33. List of pledges, n.d. [1861], in Walton Papers, SHC.

34. Griffin, *History of Old Tryon and Rutherford*, 250–51.

35. *Rutherfordton Press*, June 5, 1861, quoted in ibid., 251.

36. William Graves to Rev. J. Rumple and the Prebyterian Committee of Concord of Missions, August 1, 1861, reproduced in McGeachy, *Confronted by Challenge*, 235–36.

37. On Presbyterian ministers who were encouraged to become chaplains in the Concord Presbytery, which included western North Carolina, see McGeachy, *Confronted by Challenge*, 239–40, and Thompson, *Presbyterians in the South*, 1:134.

38. J. A. Kimsey to "Old Father," June 3, 1861, Whitaker Papers, WRPL.

39. Graves to Rumple, August 1, 1861, McGeachy, *Confronted by Challenge*, 236.

40. James C. Harper Diaries, entries for May 15, 19, June 16, 1861, SHC, cited in McGee, "'Home and Friends,'" 367.

41. *Carolina Watchman*, August 5, 1861.

42. *Asheville News*, April 10, 12, 1862, cited in Phillip Davis, "Mountain Heritage, Mountain Promise," 82.

43. Dedmond, "Harvey Davis's Unpublished Diary," 382.

44. *Rutherfordton Press*, June 5, 1861, quoted in Griffin, *History of Old Tryon and Rutherford*, 251.

45. *Carolina Watchman*, April 23, 1861.

46. M. A. Jones to "Aunty," May 14, 1861, Jones and Patterson Family Papers, SHC.

47. Laura Norwood Journal, cited in McGee, "'Home and Friends,'" 369.

48. Patton, *Story of Henderson County*, 125.

49. Ella Harper to George W. F. Harper, July 7, 1862, George W. F. Harper Papers, SHC.

50. Norman, *Portion of My Life*, 117–18, cited in Crawford, "Confederate Volunteering," 35.

51. M. A. Jones to "Aunty," May 14, 1861, Jones and Patterson Family Papers, SHC.

52. *Asheville News*, February 1, March 14, 1862; *Hendersonville Times*, March 10, 1862.

53. Ashe, *History of North Carolina*, 2:661. The thirteen counties to which Ashe refers are the fifteen in 1860 on which this study focuses, minus Rutherford and Polk.

54. *Greensborough Patriot*, May 7, 1861.

55. *Raleigh Register*, July 9, 1861.

56. In addition to Asheville, camps were also established just outside Wilmington, in Garysburg (adjacent to Weldon), and in Danville, Virginia, as a cooperative venture involving both North Carolina and Virginia recruits. See Barrett, *Civil War in North Carolina*, 18, and Iobst, "North Carolina Mobilizes," 249–60. For the location of Camp Patton and other camps in Asheville, see Arthur, *Western North Carolina*, 602.

57. Quote from Tucker, *Zeb Vance*, 108. In addition to Camp Patton, other Confederate posts that served the Asheville area at some point over the course of the war were Camp Jeter and Camp Woodfin, and several fortifications, including one atop Stoney Hill (renamed Battery Park after the war) and another on Beaucatcher Mountain. See Arthur, *Western North Carolina*, 602, and Sondley, *History of Buncombe County*, 2:689–92.

58. Baylis M. Edney to Henry T. Clark, July 11, 26, August 4, 1861, Clark Governor's Papers, NCDAH.

59. Crawford, "Confederate Volunteering," 43–49 (see esp. tables 1, 2, 3); Jim Taylor, "Buncombe Rough and Ready Guards," 25–32. For confirmation of these trends in other parts of the Confederacy, see Reid Mitchell, *Civil War Soldiers*.

60. Quoted in Patton, *Story of Henderson County*, 125.

61. Crawford, "Confederate Volunteering," 43–49; Jim Taylor, "Buncombe Rough and Ready Guards," 25–32.

62. James Gwyn Diary, vol. 4, entry for May 1, 1861, Gwyn Papers, and James Gwyn to Rufus T. Lenoir, May 2, 1861, Lenoir Family Papers, SHC.

63. For detailed accounts of this incident, see Elizabeth McPherson, "Letters from North Carolina," 504–5, and 264–68; Dykeman, *French Broad*, 129–31; Paludan, *Victims*, 57–58; and Trotter, *Bushwhackers!* ch. 1.

64. Jones, *Knocking at the Door*, 5; Hughes, *Hendersonville in Civil War Times*, 10.

65. Balis M. Edney to John W. Ellis, May 20, 1861, Tolbert, *Papers of Ellis*, 2:766.

66. Robina Norwood to Lizzie Lenoir, September 18, 1861, Lenoir Family Papers, SHC.

67. Alfred Bell to Mary Bell, January 30, 1862, Bell Papers, WRPL.

68. For an explanation of the transfer, see Johnston, *Papers of Vance*, 103n, and Ashe, *History of North Carolina*, 631.

69. Mercer Fain to John W. Ellis, June 23, 1861, in Tolbert, *Papers of Ellis*, 2:869–70.

70. William C. Walker to John W. Ellis, July 5, 1861, in ibid., 883–84.

71. Robina Norwood to Lizzie Lenoir, September 11, 1861, Lenoir Family Papers, SHC.

72. Josiah Cowles to Calvin J. Cowles, April 19 and May 1, Cowles Letter Book, NCDAH.

73. Calvin J. Cowles to "Uncle," June 17, 1861, Cowles Letter Book, NCDAH.

74. Laura Norwood to Thomas Lenoir, May 23, 1861, Lenoir Family Papers, SHC.

75. Robina Norwood to Lizzie Lenoir, June 17, 1861, Lenoir Family Papers, SHC.

76. Ibid., September 11, 1861.

77. Robert B. Vance to Zebulon B. Vance, May 28, 1861, in Johnston, *Papers of Vance*, 103.

78. Mary Bell to Alfred W. Bell, March 5, April 28, 1862, Bell Papers, WRPL.

79. Frederick K. Black to John W. Ellis, June 17, 1861, in Tolbert, *Papers of Ellis*, 2:846.

80. Baylis Edney to John W. Ellis, May 20, 1861, in ibid., 766.

81. Crawford, "Confederate Volunteering," 46.

82. Deyton, "Toe River Valley to 1865," 460–61. In 1861, the valley was divided into separate counties, with the creation of Mitchell County (in the upper valley) and Yancey County (in the lower valley). This division was also a reflection of the political differences among residents of the valley over secession.

83. William A. Enloe and J. Ramsay Dills to John W. Ellis, June 28, 1861, in Tolbert, *Papers of Ellis*, 2:874–75. See also Russell, "William Holland Thomas," 337.

84. James W. Dobson et al. to John W. Ellis, June 11, 1861, in Tolbert, *Papers of Ellis*, 2:834.

85. Henry T. Clark to Judah P. Benjamin, November 16, 1861, in *OR* 52 (2):210.

CHAPTER FOUR

1. James W. Taylor, *Alleghania*, v, 15–16.

2. Frost, "Our Contemporary Ancestors," 313. See Chapter 11, nn. 28 and 37, for other useful analyses of the Union myth applied to Appalachia.

3. On East Tennessee Unionism, see the works listed in Chapter 2, n. 42, and Chapter 5, n. 2. The most comprehensive treatment of Unionism in piedmont North Carolina is Auman, "Neighbor against Neighbor" (diss.).

4. Hodge Mashburn (McDowell County), Disallowed Claim, SCC.

5. On the collapse of the Unionist front in the South after the attack on Fort Sumter and Lincoln's call for troops, see Degler, *Other South* 166–69, and Crofts, *Reluctant Confederates*, 334–41.

6. Temple, *Notable Men of Tennessee*, 243.

7. Jones, *Knocking at the Door*, 9–10.

8. James Gwyn to Rufus T. Lenoir, May 2, 1861, Lenoir Family Papers, SHC.

9. On the differences in the political leadership on either side of the state line before the war, see Inscoe, "Mountain Unionism, Secession, and Regional Self-Image."

10. Younce, *Adventures of a Conscript*, 4–5.

11. Quoted in Paludan, *Victims*, 64.

12. For a variety of recent work dealing with the Unionist experience in various parts of the Confederacy, see Dyer, *Secret Yankees*; Sutherland, *Guerrillas, Unionists, and Violence*; Bohannon, " 'They Had Determined to Root Us Out' "; Inscoe and McKinney, "Highland Households Divided"; Nelson, "Red Strings and Half Brothers"; and Stefanco, " 'Enemies of the Country.' "

13. The fullest account of the agency remains Klingberg, *Southern Claims Commission*.

14. Nagel, *One Nation Indivisible*, 4–9; 1861 quote by Illinois Republican Owen Lovejoy on p. 9.

15. Temple, *East Tennessee and the Civil War*, 544.

16. Hayes, *Heritage of Union County, Georgia*. On the strength of Unionism in north Georgia, see Robert Davis, "Forgotten Union Guerrilla Fighters," and Sarris, "Anatomy of an Atrocity."

17. Jones, *Knocking at the Door*, 3.

18. Ibid.

19. Paludan, *Victims*, 60.

20. Browne, *Four Years in Secessia*, 351; Kellogg, *Capture and Escape*, 165; Richardson, *Secret Service*, 444.

21. Degler, *Other South*, 100.

22. Younce, *Adventures of a Conscript*, 2–3.

23. On the differences in antislavery sentiment in the Carolina and Tennessee highlands, see Inscoe, "Mountain Unionism, Secession, and Regional Self-Image."

24. Diary entry, April 20, 1861, and letter to brother, April 1861, both in Escott, *North Carolina Yeoman*, 306, 350.

25. Jones, *Knocking at the Door*, 14. See Inscoe, *Mountain Masters*, 237–39, for other Unionist arguments based on the security of slavery.

26. Hadley, *Seven Months a Prisoner*, 180–81.

27. John Horton (Watauga County), Allowed Claim, SCC; Dugger, *War Trails of the Blue Ridge*, 203–5.

28. Crawford, "Dynamics of Mountain Unionism," 64–65. Worth, a Quaker, was a cousin of Jonathan Worth, one of North Carolina's most outspoken Unionists and a Reconstruction governor.

29. See Cowles Papers, NCDAH. See also Chapter 9 for a description of Cowles's wartime slave trading activities.

30. Jones, *Knocking at the Door*, 8.

31. Andrews, *South Since the War*, 110–12.

32. Ibid., 112.

33. Savage, *Loyal Element of North Carolina*, 4. Savage cites a Captain Hock of the Twelfth New York Cavalry as the source of this quote.

34. J. Drake, *Fast and Loose in Dixie*, 177, 117–18.

35. Parkins, *How I Escaped*, 114–15. Parkins labeled this book a novel, though it varies only slightly from his autobiographical narrative, "Between Two Flags."

36. Richardson, *Secret Service*, 451.

37. James Gwyn Diary, vol. 4, entry for September 1, 1863, and Julia P. Gwyn to her uncle, July 25, 1863, Gwyn Papers, SHC.

38. Baylis M. Edney to John W. Ellis, May 20, 1861, in Tolbert, *Papers of Ellis*, 2:766. See full discussion of the Edneyville Unionists in Chapter 3.

39. McCrary, *Transylvania Beginnings*, 46.

40. Crawford, "Dynamics of Mountain Unionism," 60. On the relationship between proximity to East Tennessee and Confederate enlistments in western North Carolina, see Chapter 3.

41. Burson, *Race for Liberty*, 105. See Arthur, *History of Watauga County*, and John Horton Allowed Claim, SCC.

42. [Lawrence Allen], *Partisan Campaigns of Allen*, 10.

43. Reuben Rice, Robert W. Arrington (Madison County), Disallowed Claims, SCC.

44. Deyton, "Toe River Valley to 1865." See also Sheppard, *Cabins in the Laurel*, ch. 4, for another account of the wartime divisions in Yancey and Mitchell Counties.

45. Dunn, *Cades Cove*, 128.

46. Hunt, "Our Escape from Camp Sorghum," 108–9.

47. Nehemiah Norton, (McDowell County) Allowed Claim, SCC.

48. Samuel Williams (Burke County), George W. Hampton (Cherokee County), and John Glass (Wilkes County), Allowed Claims, SCC. See McKinney, "Women's Role in Civil War Western North Carolina," 52–53, on the impact of such splits on wives and mothers.

49. Sidney McLean (Madison County), Allowed Claim, SCC. For other examples of such divisions among brothers, see Allowed Claims of Miles M. Sneede and A. G. Hunsucker (both Cherokee County) and the Banner family (Watauga County), in which one brother was a Confederate soldier and three joined Union companies.

50. J. Drake, *Fast and Loose in Dixie*, 140–41.

51. Stafford, *In Defense of the Flag*, 61–62.

52. Egan, *Flying, Gray-Haired Yank*, 279–82. For a fuller study of such divisions in Appalachia, see Inscoe and McKinney, "Highland Households Divided."

53. Fellman, *Inside War*, 48.

54. Jones, *Knocking at the Door*, quotes on 3, 17.

55. Josiah J. Cowles to Calvin Cowles, September 12, 1863, Cowles Papers, NCDAH. On David Worth, see Crawford, "Dynamics of Mountain Unionism," 65–67. For other examples of Unionists forced to maintain these deceptions within their communities, see Dyer, *Secret Yankees*; Stefanco, " 'Enemies of the Country' "; and Bohannan, " 'They Had Determined to Root Us Out.' "

56. Elisha Green, [son of Joseph] (Rutherford County), Disallowed Claim, SCC.

57. Elisha Blackwell (Cherokee County), Disallowed Claim, SCC.

58. Clark T. Rogers (Macon County), Disallowed Claim, SCC.

59. Burson, *Race for Liberty*, 82.

60. William Donaldson [or Donelson] (Cherokee County), Disallowed Claim, SCC. See Allowed Claims of Benjamin West (Madison County), Joshua Winkler (Watauga County), and Samuel Honeycutt (Yancey County), all of whom were forced to serve in local home guard companies.

61. Drury Weeks (Cherokee County), Disallowed Claim, SCC.

62. Thomas Burgess's widow (Burke County), Allowed Claims, SCC.

63. Harmon and Hazlehurst, "Captain Isaiah Conley's Escape," 236–37. See Langworthy, *Reminiscences of a Prisoner of War*, 53–57, for a second description of Sheriff Hamilton and his activities on behalf of Union fugitives. See Allowed Claim, SCC, of widow Mary M. Welborn, of Wilkes County, whose Unionist husband served as justice of the peace "under the rebel State government," in order to avoid Confederate conscription. He used that position "in aiding escaping Federal soldiers and Confederate deserters."

64. Younce, *Adventures of a Conscript*, 14–16.

65. Burson, *Race for Liberty*, 80.

66. J. Drake, *Fast and Loose in Dixie*, 160.

67. Dugger, *War Trails of the Blue Ridge*, 204–5.

68. Ibid., 203. For similar activity in Ashe County, see Younce, *Adventures of a Conscript*,

69. Sidney S. McLean, Allowed Claim (Madison County), SCC.

70. On other western North Carolinians who joined Union regiments, see Robert Barker Papers, McClung Collection, Lawson McGee Library, Knoxville, Tennessee, and Glenna Hicks, "Forgotten Sons," ch. 3. Although two other Union regiments had formed in coastal North Carolina in 1862 and 1863, there was no 1st North Carolina Mounted Infantry, thus making the 2nd the first unit made up of western North Carolina Unionists.

71. Chapter 5 will deal in more detail with these recruiting missions and their implications in terms of guerrilla warfare in the region.

72. Jones, *Knocking at the Door*, 35.

Chapter Five

1. Rufus Lenoir to Walter Lenoir, November 7, 1864, Lenoir Family Papers, SHC.

2. The literature on East Tennessee Unionism is extensive. Among the more recent and most sophisticated analyses of the subject are Atkins, *Parties, Politics, and Sectional Conflict*, ch. 8; Fisher, *War at Every Door*, ch. 2; Wallenstein, " 'Helping to Save the Union' "; and Groce, "Social Origins of East Tennessee's Confederate Leadership." On the differences in Unionist mobilization in East Tennessee and western North Carolina, see Inscoe, "Mountain Unionism, Secession, and Regional Self-Image."

3. Fisher, *War at Every Door*, ch. 3; Bryan, " 'Tories' amidst Rebels"; Madden, "Unionist Resistance to Confederate Occupation"; Groce, "Mountain Rebels."

4. Henry T. Clark to J. P. Benjamin, November 16, 1861, Clark Governor's Papers, NCDAH; *North Carolina Standard*, November 30, 1861; Cotton, "Appalachian North Carolina," 96; Barrett, *Civil War in North Carolina*, 197; Paludan, *Victims*, 67–68.

5. *Asheville News*, January 30, 1862.

6. Ibid., February 27, 1862. See Chapter 7 for a more in-depth discussion of Asheville's armory.

7. Marcus Erwin to Henry T. Clark, July 21, 1861, and D. O. Williams to Clark, July 28, 1861, both in Clark Governor's Papers, NCDAH.

8. Edmund W. Jones to Cousin Ursilla, April 19, 1862, Bryan-Leventhorpe Family Papers, SHC.

9. *OR* 10 (1):628–29.

10. Marcus Erwin to Henry T. Clark, April 17 and 29, 1862; J. B. Sawyer to Clark, April 21, 1862; and Clark to Erwin, April 28, 1862, Clark Letterbook, pt. 2, 305–6, Clark Governor's Papers, NCDAH; *North Carolina Standard*; Paludan, *Victims*, 67–68; Barrett, *Civil War in North Carolina*, 197.

11. *Asheville News*, May 15, 1862; Cotton, "Appalachian North Carolina," 97.

12. Russell, "William Holland Thomas," 352–54.

13. William H. Thomas to Henry T. Clark, March 14 and April 13, 1862, Clark Governor's Papers, NCDAH; Crow, *Storm in the Mountains*, 8–9.

14. Thomas to Zebulon B. Vance, November 22, 1862, in Johnston, *Papers of Vance*, 385.

15. Ibid.

16. Albert Moore, *Conscription and Conflict*, ch. 2; Memory Mitchell, *Legal Aspects of Conscription*, 11–13.

17. Douglas, "Conscription and the Writ of Habeas Corpus," 12, quoted in Cotton, "Appalachian North Carolina," 103.

18. Alex J. Cansler to [Henry T.] Clark, August 20, 1861, Clark Governor's Papers, NCDAH.

19. William W. Stringfield, "Unpublished Reminiscences," typescript, Stringfield Papers, NCDAH, 51–52.

20. Quoted in Barrett, *Civil War in North Carolina*, 184.

21. Quoted in Paludan, *Victims*, 81.

22. Anonymous letter to Vance, September 25, 1862, in Johnston, *Papers of Vance*, 227–28.

23. D. W. Siler to Vance, November 3, 1862, in Johnston, *Papers of Vance*, 302–3.

24. Hamilton and Cameron, *Papers of Shotwell*, 1:184.

25. Matthew N. Love to father, April 20, 1862, Love Papers, WRPL.

26. Norm Harrold to Jefferson Davis, January 11, [1863], quoted in full in Albert Moore, *Conscription and Conflict*, 19–21. Moore notes that Harrold's letter was never sent to Davis but was found by Union cavalrymen moving through a deserted Confederate camp on the Chowan River, near Winton, N.C.

27. Ella Harper to G. W. F. Harper, November 8, 1862, George W. F. Harper Papers, SHC.

28. Zebulon B. Vance to James A. Seddon, January 5, 1863, in Mobley, *Papers of Vance*, 2:5.

29. Coulter, *Confederate States of America*, 464; Lonn, *Desertion during the Civil War*, 36. Lonn even suggests that of the total number of Confederate officers who deserted the army, 42 percent were North Carolinians. A more recent work disputes that figure and North Carolina's status as having the highest desertion rate. See Bearman, "Desertion as Localism," 324. Other works on Civil War desertion are Tatum, *Disloyalty in the Confederacy*; Owsley, "Defeatism in the Confederacy"; and Hallock, "Role of Community in Civil War Desertion." On North Carolina desertions specifically, see Bardolph, "Inconstant Rebels"; Richard Reid, "Test Case of 'Crying Evil' "; Kruman, "Dissent in the Confederacy"; and Giuffre, "First in Flight."

30. Bearman, "Desertion as Localism," 329 (table 2). Bearman divided the state into five regions. After the mountains, the coastal region had the highest ratio of deserters to enlisted men, at 14.9 percent. The lower piedmont had the lowest, with only a 3.7 percent desertion rate.

31. James C. Taylor, "60th North Carolina Regiment," ch. 3. Taylor also offers the fullest socio-economic analysis of who did and who didn't desert within this regiment, and the factors that shaped those decisions.

32. Proclamation by Zebulon B. Vance, January 26, 1863, in Mobley, *Papers of Vance*, 2:27–29.

33. John W. Reese to Christina Reese, March 26, 1863, Reese Papers, WRPL.

34. Ibid., November 19, 1863. For an insightful discussion of Reese as an example of why some men did not desert the 60th Regiment, see James C. Taylor, "60th North Carolina Regiment," 137–40.

35. Morris, "Sixty-fourth Regiment," 659–71. See also Paludan, *Victims*, 91–93, and Trotter, *Bushwhackers!* 216–19.

36. Morris, "Sixty-fourth Regiment," 661, 664.

37. Morris rationalized that this massive desertion came just before a Confederate surrender at Cumberland Gap in August 1863, claiming that by slipping away from the field and heading home, these men were able to join other Confederate units and continue to fight. There is little evidence to indicate that many of the 64th deserters ever did so. Ibid., 663.

38. Jule Gash to Col. [?], September 1, 1863, Mary Gash and Family Papers, NCDAH.

39. Paludan's *Victims* is the fullest treatment of the Shelton Laurel massacre, but subsequent accounts provide additional details. These include Jim Taylor, "Killings on the Shelton Laurel"; James Hall, "Shelton Laurel Massacre"; and Trotter, *Bushwhackers!* 209–34.

40. [Allen], *Partisan Campaigns*, 10. Curiously, Paludan makes no mention of John Kirk in *Victims*. His role (and the conflicting accounts of the reasons for his presence in Madison County) are laid out in James Hall, "Shelton Laurel Massacre," 22, and Allen, "Partisan Campaigns."

41. The ages of the victims given here are based on Jim Taylor, "Killings on the Shelton Laurel," 9, which is a more recent and, on this part of the story, more detailed account than Paludan's in *Victims*.

42. Vance to Heth, January 21, 1863, reel 13, McKinney and McMurry, *Vance Papers*.

43. A. S. Merrimon to Vance, February 16, 24, 1863, and W. H. Bailey to Vance, February 18, 1863, both reel 16; and Vance to W. G. M. Davis, February 27, 1863, and Vance to Seddon, February 2, 1863 (quote), both reel 13, all in ibid., and *OR*, ser. 2, 5:838. On the aftermath of the massacre, see Paludan, *Victims*, ch. 5, and Jim Taylor, "Killings on the Shelton Laurel," 10–11.

44. Noe makes this case most fully in his essay, "Exterminating Savages" (quote on 109). For other treatment of this issue within Appalachia, see Dunn, *Cades Cove*, 127–41; Sarris, " 'Hellish Deeds in a Christian Land' "; Sarris, "Anatomy of an Atrocity"; and several essays by Ralph Mann on Sandy Basin, Virginia, listed in the Bibliography. On the relationship between traditional troops and guerrillas elsewhere in the South during the war, see Grimsley, *Hard Hand of War*; Neely, "Was the Civil War a Total War?"; several essays in Sutherland, *Guerrillas, Unionists, and Violence*; Bohannon, " 'They Had Determined to Root Us Out' "; Inscoe and McKinney, "Highland Households Divided"; Nelson, "Red Strings and Half Brothers"; and Stefanco, " 'Enemies of the Country.' "

45. Other treatments of the localized context of guerrilla warfare in Appalachia include Sarris, "Execution in Lumpkin County"; Mann, "Ezekiel Counts's Sand Lick Company"; Mann, "Family Group, Family Migration, and the Civil War"; and several essays in Sutherland, *Guerrillas, Unionists, and Violence*.

46. Vance to Seddon, March 21, 25, 1863, reel 16, and Seddon to Vance, April 2, 1863, reel 17, McKinney and McMurry, *Vance Papers*; Vance to Jefferson Davis, March 9, 1864, *OR* 51 (2):833. See also Jim Taylor, "Papers of Vance." On George W. Lee's activities elsewhere in Georgia, see Dyer, *Secret Yankees*, ch. 5; Sarris, " 'Hellish Deeds in a Christian Land,' " ch. 4; and Sarris, "Execution in Lumpkin County," 139–42.

47. R. F. Armfield to Vance, February 19, 1863, in *OR* 18:886–87, reprinted in Yearns and Barrett, *North Carolina Civil War Documentary*, 107–8.

48. Ibid.

49. W. G. M. Davis to Henry Heth, January 20, 1863, Letterbook, Vance Governor's Papers, 1862–63, 100–101, NCDAH.

50. Baylis M. Edney to J. A. Seddon, February 22, 1863, *OR* 51 (2):775; James A. Seddon to Vance, March 26, 1863, in Mobley, *Papers of Vance*, 2:98–99.

51. T. W. Atkins and other citizens of western North Carolina to J. A. Seddon, July 29, 1863, copy in Vance Governor's Papers, NCDAH.

52. "Petition from Citizens of Watauga County, N.C.," reproduced as part of John Horton Allowed Claim, SCC.

53. Robert B. Vance to Zebulon B. Vance, September 21, 23, 1863, reel 19, and Zebulon B. Vance to Seddon, October 1, 1863, reel 3, McKinney and McMurry, *Vance Papers*.

54. W. Murdock to Zebulon B. Vance, September 18, 1863, reel 20, ibid.

55. Deposition of William Sutton, November 2, 1886, in Isaac Montgomery Pension File, U.S. Army Pension Records, National Archives, quoted in Sarris, "'Hellish Deeds in a Christian Land,'" 144.

56. *OR* 31 (1):235; M. L. Brittain to Zebulon B. Vance, November 1, 1863, reel 20, McKinney and McMurry, *Vance Papers*; Crow, *Storm in the Mountains*, 51.

57. Athens *Southern Watchman*, November 11, 1863, quoted in Sarris, "'Hellish Deeds in a Christian Land,'" 145.

58. Savage, *Loyal Element of North Carolina*, 4. For other accounts of this network, see Burson, *Race for Liberty*, 80; Hesseltine, "Underground Railroad from Confederate Prisons"; and Inscoe, "'Moving through Deserter Country.'"

59. Shelton, "Hard Road to Travel," 938.

60. J. Drake, *Fast and Loose in Dixie*, 178–79. For similar descriptions of Unionists and outliers by other fugitives, see Richardson, *Secret Service*, 457–59; Hadley, *Seven Months a Prisoner*, 180–81; and Kellogg, *Capture and Escape*, 165.

61. Younce, *Adventures of a Conscript*, 88.

62. Report by Lt. Col. George W. Lay, September 2, 1863, in *OR*, ser. 4, 2:783–86, quoted in Auman, "Neighbor against Neighbor" (diss.), 247.

63. David Schenk Diary, entry for June 11, 1863, SHC. On disaffection in the piedmont, see Auman, "Neighbor against Neighbor" (diss.).

64. W. H. McNeil to Vance, July 19, 1863, Vance Governor's Papers, NCDAH.

65. "Bannie" to her husband, September 3, 1863, Kinyoun Papers, WRPL, quoted in Auman, "Neighbor against Neighbor," 242. For these kinds of complaints to Vance from Yadkin and Wilkes Counties, see Jim Taylor, "Papers of Vance."

66. Julia P. Gwyn to James Gwyn, July 25, 1863, and James Gwyn Diary, vol. 4, entry for September 1, 1863, Gwyn Papers, SHC.

67. Auman, "Neighbor against Neighbor" (diss.), 240–41.

68. Vance to Seddon, August 26, 1863, in *OR* 29 (1):676; Robert E. Lee to Vance (telegram), September 1, 1863, and Vance to Robert F. Hoke, September 7, 1863, both in Mobley, *Papers of Vance*, 258, 267.

69. Vance to Hoke, September 7, 1863, Vance Governor's Papers, NCDAH. The fullest account of these events are in Auman, "Neighbor against Neighbor," ch. 4.

70. Josiah J. Cowles to Calvin Cowles, September 12, 1863, Cowles Papers, NCDAH.

71. Calvin Cowles to James M. Sanders, September 27, 1863; Cowles to Vance, October 9, 1863; and Cowles to W. W. Holden, December 3, 1863, all in Letterbook K, Cowles Papers, NCDAH.

72. Auman, "Neighbor against Neighbor" (diss.), 258–60.

73. Morris, "Sixty-fourth Regiment," 667; Patton, *Condensed History of Flat Rock*, 40–42.

74. Coffin, "Murder of Andrew Johnstone." For other accounts of the murder, see Patton, *Condensed History of Flat Rock*, 42–43, and Memminger, *Historical Sketch of Flat Rock*, 15–16. Memminger was the son of Confederate secretary of war Christopher G. Memminger. On the background of Johnstone and his home, see Patton, *Story of Henderson County*, 210–11.

75. J. N. Bryson to William C. Walker, June 29, 1863, in *OR*, ser. 4, 2:732. J. N. Bryson was not related to Goldman Bryson, the Cherokee County Unionist discussed earlier in this chapter.

76. Vance to George W. Hayes, June 6, 1863, Vance Governor's Papers, NCDAH; *North Carolina Standard*, June 10, 1863.

77. Eklanah Turbyfill testimony in Evelyn McIntosh Hyatt Book [United Daughters of the Confederacy compilation of Haywood County veterans and casualties], SHC.

78. Harmon and Hazlehurst, "Captain Isaiah Conley's Escape," 236.

79. R. C. E. to Addy Patton, February 26, 1863, Mary Gash and Family Papers, NCDAH.

80. Shelton, "Hard Road to Travel," 939.

81. Walter Clark, *Histories of Several Regiments*, 3:524, 664–65; *OR* 29 (2):836–37; Trotter, *Bushwhackers!* 106.

82. Aiken, "Eightieth Regiment," 661.

83. The number of wagons captured differs considerably from source to source. Twenty-eight comes from what seems to be the most reliable source: *OR* 20 (2):395. See also Trotter, *Bushwhackers!* 103, and Godbold and Russell, *Confederate Colonel and Cherokee Chief*, 118–19.

84. See Trotter's account of this episode (*Bushwhackers!* 102–5) drawn largely from the perspective of Vance's captors in Kirk, *History of the 15th Pennsylvania*, 345–56.

85. Report of Maj. Gen. John G. Foster, February 7, 1864, *OR* 32 (1):159. See also Barrett, *Civil War in North Carolina*, 232–33; Godbold and Russell, *Confederate Colonel and Cherokee Chief*, 120; and Crow, *Storm in the Mountains*, 58–59.

86. *North Carolina Standard*, February 16, 1864; L. F. Siler to Vance, February 8, 1864, and S. V. Perkins to Vance, February 12, 1864, reel 22, McKinney and McMurry, *Vance Papers*.

87. C. D. Smith to Vance, February 15, 1864, Vance Governor's Papers, NCDAH.

88. J. W. McElroy to Vance, April 12, 1864, *OR* 53:326–27; Arthur, *Western North Carolina*, 604; *Asheville News*, April 21, 1864. The day before the raid on Burnsville, local women had staged a bread riot of sorts there. See Chapter 8 for an account of that incident.

89. Vance to Seddon, April 11, 1864, *OR* 53:325.

90. Vance to Jefferson Davis, March 4, 1864, *OR* 51 (2):832–33; William C. De Journett to Vance, May 4, 1864, reel 23, and W. P. Bynum to Vance, May 7, 1864, reel 3, both in McKinney and McMurry, *Vance Papers*; and Cotton, "Appalachian North Carolina," 118.

91. Calvin J. Cowles to Vance, November 23, 1863, in Letterbook K, Cowles Papers, NCDAH.

92. Lt. J. C. Wills to Vance, April 29, 1864, quoted in Barrett, *Civil War in North Carolina*, 241. See also C. J. Cowles to Vance, May 5, 1864; Mary Coral to Vance, May 10, 1864; and James Callery to Vance, May 23, 1864, all reel 23, McKinney and McMurry, *Vance Papers*.

93. The discussion below draws on several different accounts of Kirk's raid, including Arthur, *Western North Carolina*, 604–8; Barrett, *Civil War in North Carolina*, 233–37; Trotter, *Bushwhackers!* ch. 10; and Dewey Williams, *Civil War Camp in North Carolina*.

94. Trotter, *Bushwhackers!* 98–99. It had been on such a recruiting trip into Madison County in October 1863 that Confederate cavalry stationed in Marshall had moved on Kirk's men at Warm Springs but were repelled, and their leader, Col. John W. Woodfin, a younger brother of Nicholas and one of Asheville's most prominent citizens, was killed. Woodfin had been a mentor to Zebulon Vance, which made news of his death a particularly hard blow to the governor.

95. For several accounts of the raid from both Union and Confederate officials, see *OR* 39 (1):232–37, and Blackston McDaniel to Andrew Johnson, July 7, 1864, in Graf and Haskins, *Papers of Johnson*, 7:19–21. For a detailed reminiscence of the skirmish at Winding Stairs by a Confederate participant, see Dugger, *War Trails of the Blue Ridge*, 126–33.

For other reactions by local citizens, see George Harper to Walter W. Lenoir, July 11, 1864, George W. F. Harper Papers; Walton, "Sketches of the Pioneers in Burke County History," 22e, typescript in Thomas George Walton Papers; George Phifer Erwin to his sister Sallie, July 1, 10, 1864, Erwin Papers; and testimony of Calloway Horton (one of the conscripts captured at Camp Vance who volunteered to join Kirk's regiment), ca. 1897, Confederate Papers, all in SHC.

96. Report of Col. John B. Palmer, Asheville, July 4, 1864, in *OR* 39 (1):235.

97. Calvin J. Cowles to J. L. Pennington, July 4, 1864, and Cowles to W. W. Holden, July 14, 1864, both in Letterbook L, Cowles Papers, NCDAH.

98. Vance to Breckinridge, August 7, 1864, *OR* 42 (3):1183–84; see also *OR*, ser. 4, 3:816.

99. Vance to Seddon, December 13, 1864, reel 13, McKinney and McMurry, *Vance Papers*; *OR* 42 (3):1253. For an example of the complaints registered by local residents against Thomas, see C. D. Smith to Vance, November 20, 1864, reel 26, McKinney and McMurry, *Vance Papers*.

100. *OR* 39 (1):854; Godbold and Russell, *Confederate Colonel and Cherokee Chief*, 124–25.

101. Vance to Vaughn, December 17, 1864, reel 13, McKinney and McMurry, *Vance Papers*.

Chapter Six

1. See Escott and Crow, "Social Order and Violent Disorder," 373–402, and Beringer et al., *Why the South Lost the Civil War*.

2. See Kruman, *Parties and Politics*; Escott, *Many Excellent People*; Inscoe, *Mountain Masters*; and Jeffrey, *State Parties and National Politics*.

3. See Jeffrey, "'Thunder from the Mountains'"; Kruman, "Clingman and the Whig Party"; and Inscoe, "Clingman, Mountain Whiggery, and the Southern Cause."

4. Marcus Erwin to Henry T. Clark, July 21, 1861; Alex J. Cansler to Clark, August 20, 1861; and James Wagg to [Clark], August 31, 1861, Clark Governor's Papers, NCDAH; Baylis M. Edney to John W. Ellis, May 20, 1861, in Tolbert, *Papers of Ellis*, 2:765–66; Inscoe, *Mountain Masters*, 250–55.

5. James McPherson, *Battle Cry of Freedom*, 430; Thomas, *Confederate Nation*, 152–53.

6. Thomas, *Confederate Nation*, 153.

7. Auman, "Neighbor against Neighbor" (diss.), 97–101.

8. Marcus Erwin to Henry T. Clark, April 29, 1862, Clark Governor's Papers, NCDAH.

9. Anonymous to Zebulon B. Vance, September 25, 1862, reel 15, McKinney and McMurry, *Vance Papers*.

10. *Asheville News*, August 21, July 17, 1862.

11. S. M. Collins to Zebulon B. Vance, June 6, 1863, reel 18, McKinney and McMurry, *Vance Papers*.

12. David W. Siler to Zebulon B. Vance, November 3, 1863, reel 13, McKinney and McMurry, *Vance Papers*; Johnston, *Papers of Vance*, 302.

13. Moses Wilkerson to Henry T. Clark, July 18, 1862, Clark Governor's Papers, NCDAH.

14. Henry T. Clark to George W. Randolph, August 4, 1862, Letterbook, Clark Governor's Papers, NCDAH; see also *OR* 51 (2):706–8.

15. J. W. McElroy to Zebulon B. Vance, December 26, 1862, reel 15, and S. A. Dean to Vance, March 19, 1864, reel 22, McKinney and McMurry, *Vance Papers*.

16. Zebulon B. Vance to John Letcher, January 27, 1863, and S. Bassett French to Vance, January 30, 1863, reel 13, McKinney and McMurry, *Vance Papers*.

17. Jas. M. Grant to Zebulon B. Vance, February 26, 1963, reel 16, and A. T. Davidson to Vance, May 5, 1863, reel 3, McKinney and McMurry, *Vance Papers*.

18. Marcus Erwin to Zebulon B. Vance, March 22, 1863, reel 16, and Vance to Jas. A. Seddon, March 25, 1863, reel 13, McKinney and McMurry, *Vance Papers*.

19. Zebulon B. Vance to Jefferson Davis, November 12, 1862, and James A. Seddon to Vance, March 26, 1863, reel 13, McKinney and McMurry, *Vance Papers*; *OR*, ser. 4, 2:247–48.

20. Zebulon B. Vance to James A. Seddon, April 11, 1864, and Seddon to Vance, April 23, July 6, 1864, reel 13, McKinney and McMurry, *Vance Papers*.

21. *Daily Progress*, June 18, 1863; Yates, *Confederacy and Zeb Vance*, 46.

22. Fayetteville *Observer*, April 20, 1863.

23. Yates, *Confederacy and Zeb Vance*, 55.

24. James McPherson, *Battle Cry of Freedom*, 611–12.

25. Jo[h]n D. Hyman to Zebulon B. Vance, March 19, 1864, reel 3, McKinney and McMurry, *Vance Papers*; *North Carolina Standard*, November 20, 1863.

26. James A. Patton to Zebulon B. Vance, April 21, 1863, reel 7, McKinney and McMurry, *Vance Papers*.

27. Cotton, "Appalachian North Carolina," 125.

28. *North Carolina Standard*, June 8, 12, 1861; William Harris, *William Woods Holden*, 109.

29. William Harris, *William Woods Holden*, 111–12.

30. Zebulon B. Vance to Harriett E. Vance, May 18, [1861], reel 1, McKinney and McMurry, *Vance Papers*.

31. William Harris, *William Woods Holden*, 112.

32. William Holland Thomas to Henry T. Clark, October 17, 1861, Clark Governor's Papers, NCDAH.

33. Godbold and Russell, *Confederate Colonel and Cherokee Chief*, 97–99.

34. A. T. Davidson to John M. Davidson, November 27, 1861, Davidson Papers, SHC.

35. *North Carolina Standard*, December 11, 1861.

36. Ibid., February 19, 1862; Fayetteville *Observer*, February 6, 1862.

37. *Raleigh Register*, April 5, 1862; *North Carolina Standard*, April 9, 1862; *State Journal*, April 16, June 4, 18, 1862; Tucker, *Zeb Vance*, 151–52; Fayetteville *Observer*, May 15, 1862.

38. Fayetteville *Observer*, June 19, 1862.

39. William Harris, *William Woods Holden*, 118–19.

40. Henry M. Earle to Henry T. Clark, March 8, 1862, Clark Governor's Papers, NCDAH.

41. *Raleigh Register*, July 12, 1862.

42. Kruman, *Parties and Politics*, 137–40.

43. *North Carolina Standard*, November 25, 1862; *State Journal*, November 27, 1862.

44. *Raleigh Register*, December 6, 1862; *North Carolina Standard*, August 16, November 21, 25, 1862; *Raleigh Register*, September 24, December 6, 1862; *Asheville News*, November 27, 1862; *State Journal*, November 29, 1862; *People's Press*, December 12, 1862; *Daily Progress*, December 22, 1862.

45. Paludan, *Victims*, 104–8. See Chapter 5 for a full account of the Shelton Laurel massacre.

46. Jas. M. Grant to Zebulon B. Vance, February 26, 1863, reel 16, McKinney and McMurry, *Vance Papers*.

47. A. T. Davidson to Zebulon B. Vance, March 11, 23, 1863, reel 3, McKinney and McMurry, *Vance Papers*.

48. Ibid., March 23, 1863.

49. John D. Hyman to Zebulon B. Vance, May 25, 1863, reel 3, McKinney and McMurry, *Vance Papers*.

50. J. D. Hyman to Zebulon B. Vance, April 30, 1863, and A. T. Davidson to Zebulon B. Vance, March 23, 1863, reel 3, McKinney and McMurry, *Vance Papers*.

51. L. S. Gash to Zebulon B. Vance, June 1, 1863, reel 3, McKinney and McMurry, *Vance Papers*.

52. *Daily Progress*, April 3, 15, 1863.

53. *North Carolina Standard*, July 17, 1863.

54. *Daily Progress*, July 21, 1863.

55. [Robert B. Vance] to Zebulon B. Vance, August 24, 1863, reel 3, McKinney and McMurry, *Vance Papers*.

56. Auman, "Neighbor against Neighbor" (diss.), 246–49.

57. *North Carolina Standard*, August 4, 14, 21, 28, 1863.

58. Ibid., August 21, 28, 1863.

59. Ibid., August 28, 1863.

60. William Harris, *William Woods Holden*, 137–38.

61. *North Carolina Standard*, July 28, 1863.

62. W. Murdock to Zebulon B. Vance, August 12, 1863, and F. W. Johnston to Vance, August 14, 1863, reel 19, McKinney and McMurry, *Vance Papers*.

63. T. Davis to Zebulon B. Vance, September 1, 1863, reel 19, McKinney and McMurry, *Vance Papers*.

64. L. S. Gash to Zebulon B. Vance, September 7, 11, 1863, and Wm. Dedman to Vance, September 13, 1863, reel 19, McKinney and McMurry, *Vance Papers*.

65. Zebulon B. Vance, Proclamation, September 7, 1863, reel 13, McKinney and Mc-Murry, *Vance Papers*; *Daily Progress*, September 8, 1863.

66. William Harris, *William Woods Holden*, 138–40.

67. *North Carolina Standard*, October 13, 1863.

68. Ibid.

69. Ibid.

70. Ibid.

71. Ibid., November 6, 1863.

72. *Daily Conservative*, July 5, 1864.

73. *Daily Progress*, October 5, 1864.

74. A. S. Merrimon to Zebulon B. Vance, September 21, 1863, reel 3, and W. Murdock to Vance, September 18, 1863, reel 19, McKinney and McMurry, *Vance Papers*. See Chapter 5 for a more complete account of the raid on Waynesville.

75. *North Carolina Standard*, November 3, 10, 17, 27, 1863.

76. Warner and Yearns, *Biographical Directory of Confederate Congress*, 153–54.

77. *North Carolina Standard*, January 12, February 9, 1864; *Daily Progress*, February 2, 13, 1864; J. B. Carpenter to Zebulon B. Vance, February 3, 1864, reel 22, McKinney and McMurry, *Vance Papers*.

78. Z. B. Vance to Jefferson Davis, December 30, 1863, reel 13, McKinney and McMurry, *Vance Papers*; *OR* 51 (2):807.

79. W. E. Blanton to [Zebulon B. Vance], January 16, 1864, reel 21, McKinney and McMurry, *Vance Papers*.

80. John D. Hyman to Zebulon B. Vance, January 30, 1864, reel 3, McKinney and McMurry, *Vance Papers*.

81. Marcus Erwin to Zebulon B. Vance, January 26, 1864, reel 3, McKinney and Mc-Murry, *Vance Papers*.

82. T. L. Clingman to Zebulon B. Vance, February 18, 1864, reel 3, McKinney and McMurry, *Vance Papers*.

83. *Daily Conservative*, April 16, 1864.

84. *North Carolina Standard*, March 3, 1864.

85. Ibid., May 24, 1864.

86. Jesse M. Frank to Jesse Hedrick, April 2, 1864, Siler Family Papers, privately held.

87. Yates, "Governor Vance and the Peace Movement," 102.

88. *Daily Conservative*, April 27, 1864.

89. Ibid., May 23, 24, 25, July 2, 4, 1864; Richard Reid, "Holden and 'Disloyalty' in the Civil War," 39.

90. Auman and Scarboro, "Heroes of America." See Noe, "Red String Scare," on the movement in southwest Virginia, and McGee, " 'On the Edge of a Crater,' " on its presence in Raleigh.

91. *North Carolina Standard*, June 29, 1864.

92. Lerner, "Inflation in the Confederacy," 172. See Chapter 7 for a fuller discussion of the currency crisis's impact on western North Carolina.

93. Oates, *With Malice toward None*, 423–31; *OR* 39 (1):236–37.

94. *North Carolina Standard*, June 17, 1864.

95. *Daily Progress*, July 18, 1864; Yates, "Governor Vance and the Peace Movement," 111.

96. S. B. Erwin to Zebulon B. Vance, August 6, [18]64, reel 3, McKinney and McMurry, *Vance Papers*.

97. Fayetteville *Observer*, December 8, 15, 1864.

98. Ibid., December 1, 1864.

99. Yates, "Governor Vance and the End of War," 320.

100. *Daily Progress*, January 31, February 25, 1865.

101. *OR* 49 (1):1034–35.

102. Chapter 10 provides a full account of Stoneman's Raid.

Chapter Seven

1. Elizabeth Watson to James Watson, October 29, 1861, James Watson Papers, HL.

2. William F. Jones to Samuel F. Patterson, June 23, 1863; E. Bryan to Patterson, October 13, 1862; and S. T. Jones to Patterson, October 22, 1862, Jones and Patterson Family Papers, SHC; Calvin J. Cowles to Andrew Cowles, June 25, 1862, Cowles Papers, NCDAH; Ella R. Harper to G. W. F. Harper, November 8, 18, 1862, and George W. F. Harper Papers, SHC; *North Carolina Standard*, November 18, 1862.

3. D. W. Siler to Zebulon B. Vance, November 5, 1862, reel 13, McKinney and McMurry, *Vance Papers*.

4. Mary C. Williams et al. to Vance, January 27, 1864, and James Bailey to Vance, January 25, 1863, reel 16, ibid.; Mary Sibbitt to [Henry T. Clark], January 28, 1862, Clark Governor's Papers, NCDAH.

5. Tyre York et al. to Vance, October 12, 1862, reel 15, McKinney and McMurry, *Vance Papers*.

6. James Gwyn to Joseph C. Norwood, February 12, 1862, Gwyn Papers, SHC. See also Montreville Patton to Zebulon B. Vance, October 12, 1863, reel 20; C. D. Smith to Vance, October 21, 1863, reel 3; A. D. Childs et al. to Vance, November 29, 1863, reel 20; and S. J. Westall to Vance, January 17, 1864, reel 21, McKinney and McMurry, *Vance Papers*; and *North Carolina Standard*, May 31, November 14, 1864.

7. [Niece] to Lizzie Lenoir, December 26, 1862, Lenoir Family Papers, SHC.

8. Maryann Arrowood to Zebulon B. Vance, November 26, 1863, reel 20, and Margaret E. Love to Vance, May 10, 1864, reel 23, McKinney and McMurry, *Vance Papers*.

9. James A. Seddon to Zebulon B. Vance, April 23, 1864, reel 13, ibid.

10. Ella Harper to her husband, George, November 18, 1862, George W. F. Harper Papers, SHC.

11. Deyton, "Toe River Valley to 1865," 463. On such efforts elsewhere in North Carolina, see J. Kent Coward, "The Community in Crisis," in Max Williams, *History of Jackson County*, 439; Escott, "Poverty and Governmental Aid for the Poor"; and Entrekin, "Poor Relief in North Carolina." On efforts elsewhere in the Confederacy, see Massey, "Food and Drink Shortages"; Massey, *Ersatz in the Confederacy*, chs. 3 and 4; and Escott, " 'Cry of the Sufferers.' "

12. "List of Indigent Volunters Wifes in Wallins Laurel District," Madison County, May 25, 1863, in Miscellaneous Records, Madison County, NCDAH.

13. "A Census Report of the Names & Numbers of the Igedent [*sic*] Wives of Soldiers . . . in Capt. Geo. W. Brown's District, May 9, 1863," Hackett Collection, NCDAH.

14. N. N. Davidson to William Walker, April 30, 1864, Walker Papers, HL.

15. Joseph C. Norwood to Walter Lenoir, November 17, 1863, Lenoir Family Papers, SHC.

16. Calvin J. Cowles to Josiah J. Cowles, November 23, December 19, 1863, Letterbook K, Calvin J. Cowles Papers, NCDAH. As Chapter 8 will demonstrate, by the war's last year those women so deprived sometimes took matters into their own hands through collective and drastic measures to feed themselves and their children.

17. *Eighth Census of the United States, 1860: Agriculture*, 105–7, 109–11.

18. H. and H. J. Spicer to Calvin J. Cowles, January 26, 1863, Cowles Papers, NCDAH.

19. Wright, *Old South, New South*, 30–31; Blethen and Wood, "Pioneer Experience," 77.

20. D. C. Shoop to Zebulon B. Vance, March 24, 1864, reel 24, and W. M. Crisp et al. to Vance, May 14, 1863, reel 17, McKinney and McMurry, *Vance Papers*. For similar pleas, most in the form of community or neighborhood petitions to the governor, see William Adkins, Statement, n.d., and R. F. Callaway et al. to Vance, November 11, 1863, reel 15; W. Joiner et al. to Vance, March 31, 1863, reel 16; Hirum Green et al. to Vance, May 16, 1863, reel 17; J. J. Neal et al. to Vance, June 4, 1863, reel 18; Jno. H. Addington to Vance, March 31, 1864, reel 22; and Cynthia McDaniel et al. to Vance, n.d., reel 26, all ibid.

21. John A. Coxey et al. to Zebulon B. Vance, March 24, 1864, reel 26; R. E. A. Love to Vance, April 22, 1864, reel 23; and L. S. Gash to Vance, June 1, 1863, reel 18, all ibid.

22. Jas. Eller et al. to Zebulon B. Vance, November 8, 1862, reel 15; E. Morgan et al. to Vance, October 17, 1863, reel 20; N. A. Powell to Vance, September 15, 1864, reel 24; V. Ripley et al. to Vance, October 3, 1864, E. J. Alston et al. to Vance, October 24, 1864, and Wiley T. Walker et al. to Vance, November 1, 1862, reel 25, all ibid.

23. Elizabeth Conley et al. to Zebulon B. Vance, July 10, 1863, reel 18, ibid.; see also Benjamin Deboard et al. to Vance, October 20, 1863, reel 20, ibid.

24. S. H. Miller to Zebulon B. Vance, March 23, 1863, reel 16; Moses Young et al., statement, June 1, 1863, Thomas Baker et al. to Vance, July 1, 1863, and B. C. Lankford to Vance, July 18, 1863, all reel 18, all ibid.

25. N. W. Woodfin to Zebulon B. Vance, October 1, 1863, reel 20, ibid.

26. Thomas Atkinson to Zebulon B. Vance, November 27, 1863, reel 20; N. Brown to Vance, January 6, 1864, reel 21; J. J. Erwin to Vance, February 1, 1864, and [W.] Murdock to Vance, February 7, 1864, reel 3; J. A. Reagan to Vance, February 15, 1865, and R. V. Welch to Vance, February 20, 1864, reel 22; and J. M. Warren to Vance, March 15, 1865, reel 26, all ibid.

27. A. W. Cumming to Zebulon B. Vance, April 14, 1863, reel 17; R. T. Walker to Vance, March 2, 1865, reel 4; Wm. Lankford to Vance, April 14, 1863, reel 17; and A. T. Summey to Vance, May 20, 1863, reel 7, all ibid.

28. Joseph Cathey to H. E. Drummond, February 27, 1863, Cathey Papers, NCDAH; William L. Henry to Zebulon B. Vance, May 16, 1864, reel 23, McKinney and McMurry, *Vance Papers*. Some British historians maintain that scholars can identify capitalist modernization in an area by locating a demand for consumer goods. See Levine, "Consumer Goods and Capitalist Modernization."

29. Crawford, "Mountain Farmers and the Market Economy."

30. [Mrs.] H. T. McLelland to Zebulon B. Vance, February 22, 1863, reel 16, and John Lono to Vance, n.d., reel 26, McKinney and McMurry, *Vance Papers*.

31. Alfred W. Bell to Zebulon B. Vance, February 23, 1863, ibid.

32. William W. England to Alexander England, December 7, 1862, England Family Papers, NCDAH.

33. Rothenberg, "Market and Massachusetts Farmers," 305.

34. Phillip Davis, "Mountain Heritage, Mountain Promise," 135.

35. Zebulon B. Vance, Proclamation, April 13, 1863, reel 13, McKinney and McMurry, *Vance Papers*.

36. Alfred W. Bell to Zebulon B. Vance, February 23, 1863, ibid.

37. Wm. L. Henry to H. T. Clark, July 22, 1861, Clark Governor's Papers, NCDAH.

38. Floyd, "Asheville Armory and Rifle," 21.

39. Ibid., 22.

40. William R. Young to Zebulon B. Vance, November 13, 1862, Johnston, *Papers of Vance*, 341–44.

41. *North Carolina Standard*, January 29, 1862; Floyd, "Asheville Armory and Rifle," 22.

42. Downer's entire report is reproduced in Floyd, "Asheville Armory and Rifle," 22–23.

43. Floyd, "Asheville Armory and Rifle," 23.

44. Blethen and Wood, "Land and Family in the Tuckaseigee Valley," 6.

45. "Estimate of Funds for the Asheville Armory for the First Quarter, 1863," and "Estimate of Funds for the Asheville Armory for the Second Quarter, 1863," CSAAL, 80.

46. B. Sloan to J. Gorgas, April 15, 1863, CSAAL, 80.

47. "Small Arms: Confederate Long Arms," in *Encyclopedia of the Confederacy*, 4:1455.

48. B. Sloan to E. Clayton, December 31, 1862, and January 13, 1863, CSAAL, 9 and 18; Floyd, "Asheville Armory and Rifle," 21–23.

49. B. Sloan to R. W. Pulliam, December 29, 1862, and B. Sloan, Order No. 15, February 16, 1863, CSAAL, 7 and 46.

50. B. Sloan to Peter Mallett, January 2, 4, and 8, 1863; B. Sloan, Order No. 11, January 15, 1863; and Sloan Order, January 22, 1863, all in CSAAL, 10–11, 13–15, 23, and 27–28.

51. B. Sloan to J. Gorgas, May 25, 1863, and "Rates of Wages, June 1863," CSAAL, 96 and 126.

52. B. Sloan to Jas. H. Burton, January 3, 1863; B. Sloan to J. Gorgas, February 4, 1863; and other entries, all in CSAAL, 12, 35, 71, 148, and 155.

53. B. Sloan to Peter Mallett, April 27, 1863, and B. Sloan to editor of *Asheville News*, March 21, 1863, CSAAL, 87 and 70.

54. Runaway slave advertisements in the *Asheville News* (July 17, October 4, 1862, for example) indicated that the escaped slaves were from eastern North Carolina towns, such as New Bern and Fayetteville. For a fuller account of slaves moved into western North Carolina during the war, see Chapter 9.

55. B. Sloan to W. F. M. Galbraith, January 14 and 19, 1863, CSAAL, 19 and 25.

56. B. Sloan, Order, February 21, 1863, CSAAL, 51.

57. The *Asheville News* reported that Unionists "are threatening to pay Asheville a visit, and have been expected for several days" (quoted in *Daily Progress*, January 19, 1863). See Chapter 5 for a full account of the raid on Marshall.

58. B. Sloan to J. Gorgas, January 10 and June 24, 1863, CSAAL, 17 and 110.

59. Ibid., September 14, 1863, CSAAL, 147–48.

60. *North Carolina Standard*, August 4, 21, 28, 1863.

61. C. C. McPhail to W. S. Downer, December 2, 1863, and B. Sloan, Order No. 11, January 15, 1863, CSAAL, 220 and 23.

62. B. Sloan to Peter Mallett, September 10, 1863, and C. C. McPhail to McKinna and Patton, October 17, 1863, CSAAL, 145–47 and 176.

63. B. Sloan, Memorandum, February 11, 1863, and B. Sloan to J. Gorgas, February 7, 1863, CSAAL, 41 and 38.

64. B. Sloan to McKean Johnson, January 29, 1863, and C. C. McPhail to C. B. Brank, October 15, 1863, CSAAL, 30 and 173.

65. B. Sloan to W. Hughes, February 18, 1863, and B. Sloan to S. S. McClanahan, April 29, 1863, CSAAL, 48 and 88–89.

66. A. S. Merrimon to Zebulon B. Vance, September 7, 16, 18, 1863; J. W. McElroy to Vance, September 10, 1863; R. W. Pulliam et al. to Vance, September 16, 1863; and W. Murdock to Vance, September 18 and 20, 1863, all reel 19, McKinney and McMurry, *Vance Papers*.

67. B. Sloan to J. Gorgas, September 5, 1863, and B. Sloan to Peter Mallet, September 10, 1863, CSAAL, 143 and 145–47.

68. J. Gorgas to C. C. McPhail, November 4 and 26, 1863; C. C. McPhail to R. B. Vance, November 24, 1863; and [Robert B.] Vance Special Order, November 24, 1863, all in CSAAL, 192, 208, and 201–3.

69. Compiled from reports titled "Estimates of Funds for the Asheville Armory," CSAAL, 29, 80, 123, and 185.

70. Compiled from reports titled "Balance of Money Due," CSAAL, 37, 55, 91, 100, 125, 139, and 212.

71. B. Sloan to J. Gorgas, April 15, 1863, CSAAL, 82–83.

72. Wm. L. Henry to Zebulon B. Vance, May 16, 1864, reel 23, McKinney and McMurry, *Vance Papers*.

73. Information on the Bells' prewar lives comes from the inventory description of the Bell Papers, WRPL. Their entry into the ranks of slaveholders is traced in Chapter 9.

74. Mary Bell to Alfred Bell, June 13, 1862, April 15, December 16, 1864, ibid.

75. Ibid., April 15, 1864.

76. Ibid., December 16, 1864.

77. C. G. Memminger to Zebulon B. Vance, June 30, 1864, reel 3, McKinney and McMurry, *Vance Papers*.

78. Gale, "Life in the Southern Confederacy."

79. *Asheville News*, November 3, 1864.

CHAPTER EIGHT

1. *North Carolina Standard*, August 19, 1863.

2. Faust, "Alters of Sacrifice," 1228. See also Faust, *Mothers of Invention*.

3. Escott, *Many Excellent People*, ch. 3; Fellman, *Inside War*, ch. 5; Rable, *Civil Wars*; Clinton, *Tara Revisited*.

4. Scott, *Southern Lady*, ch. 4. See Anglin, "Lives on the Margin."

5. Manarin and Jordan, *North Carolina Troops*, 535; Arthur, *History of Watauga County*, 160–61. For a full but undocumented account of the Blalocks' story, see Trotter, *Bushwhackers!* ch. 14.

6. Albert Siler to Josey Siler, July 10, 1862, Siler Papers, WRPL.

7. Fellman, *Inside War*, 193.

8. Claim of Louisa Stiles, SCC.

9. Lizzie Lenoir to Rufus Lenoir, September 21, 1862, Lenoir Family Papers.

10. Arthur, *Western North Carolina*, 616.

11. William Church et al. to Zebulon B. Vance, June 9, 1864, reel 23, McKinney and McMurry, *Vance Papers*.

12. Inscoe, " 'Moving through Deserter Country' "; Trotter, *Bushwhackers!* 188–94, 199–200; Mary E. Welborn and Margaret Williams, Allowed Claims, SCC.

13. J. Drake, *Fast and Loose in Dixie*, 148–50.

14. Shelton, "Hard Road to Travel."

15. Hunt, "Our Escape from Camp Sorghum," 113.

16. Poem by "militant unionist" [probably from Taylorsville], n.d., Vance Governor's Papers, NCDAH, quoted in Auman, "Neighbor against Neighbor" (diss.), 291.

17. Mann, "Guerrilla Warfare and Gender Roles." See also Dunn, *Cades Cove*, ch. 5, esp. 135–38, for other examples of how mountain women served in partnership with their husbands in defending their homes from enemy forces.

18. Parkins, *How I Escaped*, 617. See Chapter 4, note 36.

19. Cornelia Henry to William Lewis Henry, n.d., Robert Henry Papers, PML. On George W. Kirk's attack that sent William Henry into hiding, see "Historic Scrap of 1865," typescript in R. T. Underwood Reminiscences, WRPL.

20. Sheppard, *Cabins in the Laurel*, 64.

21. Paludan, *Victims*, 96.

22. James Hall, "Shelton Laurel Massacre," 23.

23. For Allen's own account of that incident, see Allen, "Partisan Campaigns of Colonel Lawrence M. Allen," 10, printed pamphlet in Davidson Papers, NCDAH.

24. *OR*, ser. 4, 2:732.

25. Tom Gash to Charlie Slagle, November 27, 1864, Siler Papers, SHC.

26. Freel, *Unto the Hills*, 139–40, includes the first version of Tatham's story. Curiously, the second version also comes from Freel, *Our Heritage*, 227. Chapters 20–22 of *Unto the Hills* include several other stories of the harassment and torture of Cherokee County women by Union raiders and bushwhackers.

27. Claim of Thomas S. Runnion, SCC.

28. J. Keener to Zebulon B. Vance, April 3, 1863, reel 3, McKinney and McMurry, *Vance Papers*.

29. Tyre York to Zebulon B. Vance, May 5, 1864, and James M. Morris to Vance, April 27, 1864, reel 23, McKinney and McMurry, *Vance Papers*.

30. Freel, "Story of Life of Margaret Walker during the Civil War." For a fuller, but more fictionally embellished account, see Freel, *Unto the Hills*, 154–61.

31. Mary Bell to Alfred Bell, February 19, 1864, and Alfred to Mary Bell, March 17, 1864, Bell Papers, WRPL.

32. J. W. McElroy to Zebulon B. Vance, April 12, 1864, in *OR* 1:326–27. On riots elsewhere, see Friedman, *Enclosed Garden*, 102–4; Escott, "Moral Economy of the Crowd"; Chesson, "Harlots or Heroines?" 131–46, 172–74; and Bynum, "War within a War," 43–49.

33. Lizzie Lenoir to "Sade" [Sarah J.] Lenoir, January 22, 1865, Lenoir Family Papers, SHC.

34. Ibid. The reference to distillers refers to resentment by many people late in the war that much of the corn being raised was turned into liquid form, thus contributing to—or failing to alleviate—the region's ongoing food shortages.

35. J. K. Baldwin et al. to Zebulon B. Vance, September 27, 1862, reel 15, McKinney and McMurry, *Vance Papers*; *North Carolina Standard*, November 20, 1863.

36. See McGee, " 'Home and Friends,' " for a discussion of the impact of ministers and their sermons on female congregants. See also Silver, *Confederate Morale and Church Propaganda*, 25–32.

37. Minutes, September 3, 1864, Silver Creek Primitive Baptist Association Minute Books, SHC. See also Friedman, *Enclosed Garden*, ch. 5.

38. Jesse Sentell et al. to Zebulon B. Vance, August 16, 1863, reel 19; A. Glaty et al. to Vance, October 21, 1864, reel 25; and Amos Hildebrand et al. to Vance, reel 26, McKinney and McMurry, *Vance Papers*; Fayetteville *Observer*, April 9, 1863.

39. Hattie Deaver to [?], April 1, 1861, and Sallie to Addie Patton, July 19, 1861, Mary Gash and Family Papers, NCDAH.

40. A. W. Cummings to Zebulon B. Vance, April 14, 1863, reel 17, McKinney and McMurry, *Vance Papers*.

41. Margaret E. Love to Zebulon B. Vance, May 10, 1864, reel 23, ibid.

42. Cornelia Henry to her son "Pinck" and to her sister Dora, both December 27, 1864, Robert Henry Papers, PML.

43. Mary Middleton Orr, "The Experiences of a Soldier's Wife in the Civil War," in McCrary, *Transylvania Beginnings*, 297–305.

44. Wilkeson, *Recollections of a Private Soldier*, 232–33, quoted in Paludan, *Victims*, 23.

45. Gale, "Life in the Southern Confederacy," 13, 17.

46. Anglin, "Lives on the Margin," 190–96.

47. Mary to Alfred Bell, November 13, 1861, Bell Papers, WRPL.

48. Alfred to Mary Bell, January 30, 1862; Mary to Alfred Bell, April 4, 1862, Bell Papers, WRPL. For an expanded version of her activity during the war, see Inscoe, "Coping in Confederate Appalachia."

49. Mary to Alfred Bell, August 26, 1862, Bell Papers, WRPL.

50. Ibid., July 8, 1864. "My darkies" is a reference to the most dramatic aspect of Mary's new independence: she purchased a slave family in March 1864. See Chapter 9 for a full account of that purchase and the circumstances leading up to it.

51. Ibid., April 22, 1864.

52. Ibid., June 5 and July 8, 1864.

53. For a discussion of other women throughout the Confederacy who succeeded and even thrived in rising to the challenges posed by the war, see Scott, *Southern Lady*, ch. 4. See also Rable, *Civil Wars*, and Faust, *Mothers of Invention*.

54. McGee, " 'Home and Friends,' " 366–72.

55. On the gunboat subscription campaign among women in Caldwell, Buncombe, and

Macon Counties, respectively, see Ella Harper to George W. F. Harper, May 30, 1862, and George W. F. Harper Papers, SHC; *Asheville News*, April 10, July 10, 1862; and Mary to Alfred Bell, May 22, 1862, Bell Papers, WRPL.

56. Alfred to Mary Bell, April 22, 1864, Bell Papers, WRPL.

57. McGee, "'Home and Friends,'" drawn from Ella Harper to George W. F. Harper, May 4 and 11, 1863, and Ella Harper diary, entries from March to May 1864, George F. W. Harper Papers, SHC.

58. Mary to Alfred Bell, May 22, 1862. Faust, "Altars of Sacrifice," 1206–7.

59. Anonymous to Zebulon B. Vance, January 5, 1864, reel 21, McKinney and McMurry, *Vance Papers*.

Chapter Nine

1. Calvin J. Cowles to William W. Holden, October 9, 1861, Cowles Papers, NCDAH.

2. *North Carolina Standard*, October 16, 1861.

3. Fletcher, *Ashe County*, 88; Shepherd, *Heritage of Ashe County*; Arthur, *Western North Carolina*, 165; and Crawford, "Political Society," 383. The authors are grateful to Crawford for his clarification and interpretation of these events.

4. Zebulon B. Vance to John Evans Brown, n.d., reproduced under the title "Conditions Just after the War," in *Confederate Veteran* 39 (June 1931): 215–17. Vance went on to detail the losses suffered by the Avery and Patton families. The other three slaveholders killed in the area were John W. Woodfin, William Waightstill Avery, and Andrew Johnstone. The circumstances of their deaths are described in Chapter 5.

5. Among the best treatments of the new economic demands and opportunities for slave labor during the Civil War include Mohr, *On the Threshold of Freedom*; Morgan, *Emancipation in Virginia's Tobacco Belt*, ch. 5; and Berlin, *Freedom*, vol. 1, ch. 9. None of the above makes any reference to an active slave trade unrelated to Confederate military or industrial demands. The only references made to a more conventional slave trade among civilians during the war years were to areas outside the Confederacy, in Kentucky and Missouri. See Berlin, *Freedom*, 1:453, 494–95.

6. On more serious racial incidents in the early days of the war elsewhere in North Carolina and the South, see Schneider, "Institution of Slavery in North Carolina," 135–37; Wish, "Slave Disloyalty under the Confederacy"; and Robinson, "In the Shadow of Old John Brown." On legislation passed in reaction to such activity in North Carolina, see Nelson, "Some Aspects of Negro Life," 146–47.

7. Nelson, "Some Aspects of Negro Life," 145–47; quote from *North Carolina Standard*, February 5, 1861.

8. Avery and Erwin circular, quoted in Sitterson, *Secession Movement*, 220–21. William Vance Brown to John Evans Brown, April 15, 1861, Morrison Papers, SHC.

9. Joseph E. Brown Public Letter, December 7, 1860, reproduced in Freehling and Simpson, *Secession Debated*, 145–59.

10. For one example, see *Asheville News*, January 8, 1862.

11. The actual percentages of slave populations in North Carolina's mountain counties varied greatly—from Burke County, with more than a fourth of its residents slaves in 1860, to

Madison and Watauga Counties, with slaves making up a mere 3.6 and 2 percent, respectively, of their populations. For demographic shifts and fluctuations in the profitability of slaves in the region, see Inscoe, *Mountain Masters*, 82–86.

12. See Inscoe, *Mountain Masters*, 76–81, 89–92, for a discussion of antebellum slave hiring practices among western North Carolinians.

13. Vance to Jefferson Davis, October 25, 1862, in Johnston, *Papers of Vance*, 277.

14. Massey, "Confederate Refugees in North Carolina," 177–82; Woodward, *Mary Chesnut's Civil War*, 343, 422–24; Henry Capers, *Life and Times of Memminger*, 370–71.

15. Gale, "Life in the Southern Confederacy," 18. On the Polks' Louisiana slaveholdings, see Polk, *Leonidas Polk, Bishop and General*, 1:182–83.

16. Vance quoted in Nelson, "Some Aspects of Negro Life," 157. Confederate order quoted in Wish, "Slavery Disloyalty under the Confederacy," 442. On the movement of coastal slaves to inland and highland areas, see Nelson, "Some Aspects of Negro Life," 157–59; Morgan, *Emancipation in Virginia's Tobacco Belt*, 112–13; Mohr, *On the Threshold of Freedom*, ch. 4; Mohr, "Slavery and Class Tensions," 68–72; and Durrill, *War of Another Kind*, ch. 2.

17. N. W. Woodfin to David L. Swain, May 12, 1862, Walter Clark Papers, NCDAH. For examples of advertisements, see various issues of *Asheville News*, *North Carolina Standard*, and *State Journal*, December 1861 and March 1862.

18. W. H. Thomas to Vance, November 22, 1862, in Johnston, *Papers of Vance*, 385–86.

19. Calvin J. Cowles to brother Andrew, March 5, 1862, and Cowles to E. Foster, January 9, 1863, both in Letterbook K, Cowles Papers, NCDAH.

20. Calvin J. Cowles to brother Andrew, June 9, June 25, July 8, 1862, January 30, 1863, ibid.; Cowles to his wife, April 5, 1863, in Cowles Papers, SHC.

21. See, for example, Cowles's letters to owners in Hyde, Wake, and Pitt Counties; to D. C. Murray, September 10, October 10, 1863; to brother Andrew, September 15, 1863; to Rev. C. B. Reddick, February 25 and April 6, 1865; and to sister Mary, November 28, 1862, all in Letterbook K, NCDAH.

22. A. T. Davidson to John Davidson, February 3, 1863, Davidson Family Papers, Atlanta History Center.

23. W. W. Lenoir to Joseph Norwood, May 3, 1863, Lenoir Family Papers, SHC; William Pickens to Vance, March 2, 1863, Vance Governor's Papers, NCDAH.

24. O. P. Gardner suit, Rutherford County Slave Records, NCDAH; slave contracts, 1861–65, Corpening Family Papers, WRPL. (There is no 1865 contract for the second woman.) John Cimprich provides the most comprehensive analysis of slave prices in relation to inflation rates for 1861–63 in *Slavery's End in Tennessee*, 15–17. See also Nelson, "Some Aspects of Negro Life," 163–64.

25. Calvin to Mary Cowles, May 21, 1863, Letterbook K, Cowles Papers, NCDAH. See also bill of sale of Ashe County slave to Petersburg, Va., buyer, October 20, 1864, in Ashe County Slave Records, NCDAH.

26. Laura Norwood to Thomas I. Lenoir, May 23, 1861, Lenoir Family Papers, SHC.

27. W. W. [Walter] Lenoir to Rufus Lenoir, July 8, 1861, ibid.

28. Ibid., April 14, 1862.

29. Ibid.

30. Ibid., April 19, 1858. (This letter is reprinted in Hickerson, *Echoes of Happy Valley*, 53.)

31. William A. Lenoir to William Lenoir, October 16, 1835, Lenoir Family Papers, SHC; Shrader, "William Lenoir," 208; Harper, *Fort Defiance and the General*, 75.

32. James Gwyn to Rufus Lenoir, May 15, 1861, Lenoir Family Papers, SHC.

33. W. W. Lenoir to Thomas I. Lenoir, February 25, 1863, and James Gwyn to Rufus Lenoir, January 12, 1863, ibid.

34. W. W. Lenoir to Joseph Norwood, May 3, 1863, and James Gwyn to Rufus Lenoir, February 9, 1863, ibid.

35. W. W. Lenoir to Mother, May 17, 1863, ibid.

36. See, in addition to letters in notes 32–35, above, A. C. Hargrove to Thomas I. Lenoir, February 13, 1863; Thomas C. Norwood to Thomas Lenoir, March 9, 1863; W. W. Lenoir to Rufus Lenoir, August 17, 1863; and W. W. Lenoir to Aunt Sade, March 27, 1864, all ibid.

37. For slave population figures for these and other western North Carolina counties, see Inscoe, *Mountain Masters*, 60–61 (table 3.1), 84–85 (table 3.2). On Macon County slaves, see also Sutton, *Heritage of Macon County*, 46–48.

38. The basic source for this discussion of the Bells is the wartime correspondence between Alfred and Mary Bell in the Alfred W. Bell Papers, WRPL. For fuller treatments of their situation, see Inscoe, "Coping in Confederate Appalachia" and "The 1864 Slave Purchases of Mary Bell."

39. Alfred to Mary Bell, December 9, 1862, Bell Papers, WRPL.

40. Ibid., March 17, 1864, and Mary to Alfred Bell, March 11, 1864, Bell Papers, WRPL.

41. Mary to Alfred Bell, March 11, 1864, ibid. For the description of the sale by Alfred's brother Benjamin, see Benjamin's letter of March 11, 1864, Bell Papers, WRPL.

42. Alfred to Mary Bell, March 31, April 8, 1864, ibid.

43. Mary to Alfred Bell, July 8, November 17, 1864, ibid.

44. Ibid., November 24, 1864.

45. Mary Taylor Brown to John Evans Brown, June 20, 1865, W. Vance Brown Papers, SHC.

46. J. Jarratt to Vance, October 12, 1864, Vance Governor's Papers, NCDAH. See also Moser, "Reaction in North Carolina."

47. Vance's speech in Boston before Andrew Post No. 15 of the Grand Army, December 8, 1886, quoted in Dowd, *Life of Zebulon B. Vance*, 447–48.

48. John H. Phillips to "Cousin," October 13, 1862, Love Papers, WRPL.

49. D. W. Siler to Vance, November 3, 1862, in Johnston, *Papers of Vance*, 303.

50. L. S. Gash to Vance, June 1, 1863, Vance Governor's Papers, NCDAH.

51. Walter to Rufus Lenoir, July 23, 1863, Lenoir Family Papers, SHC.

52. Ibid.

53. W. W. Lenoir to Sade Lenoir, March 27, 1864, ibid.

54. Rufus Lenoir to Walter Lenoir, December 12, 1864, ibid.

55. Estate settlement, February 4, 1865, ibid.

56. Mary Cowles to Calvin J. Cowles, February 9, 1865, Cowles Papers, NCDAH.

57. Rufus L. Patterson to his father, December 8, 1864, Jones and Patterson Family Papers, SHC.

58. Ibid.

59. See, for example, Parkins, *How I Escaped*, 113–16; Burson, *Race for Liberty*, 79; Browne, *Four Years in Secessia*, 470; and Gilmore, *Adrift in Dixie*, 118–23. For an overview of slave encounters with such fugitives, see Inscoe, " 'Moving through Deserter Country.' "

60. Bliss, *Prison Life of James M. Fales*, 55–56.

61. Newlin, *Account of the Escape of Six Soldiers*, 56; Richardson, *Secret Service*, 444.

62. Richardson, *Secret Service*, 445.

63. Browne, *Four Years in Secessia*, 368.

64. Egan, *Flying Gray-Haired Yank*, 272–73.

65. Alonzo Cooper, *In and Out of Rebel Prisons*, 197–99.

66. Parkins, *How I Escaped*, 118.

67. Burson, *Race for Liberty*, 79–82.

68. From a 1973 interview with Louise L. Mobley of Burke County, recorded in Fleming, "Out of Bondage," 110.

69. Chambers, *Breed and the Pasture*, 48–50.

70. Freel, *Unto the Hills*, 132–33, 145–46.

71. Jones, *Knocking at the Door*, 9.

Chapter Ten

1. Vance to David L. Swain, September 22, 1864, reel 3, McKinney and McMurry, *Vance Papers*.

2. Ibid.

3. McGee, " 'Home and Friends,' " 384.

4. Gale, "Life in the Southern Confederacy." On the impact of sermons on Confederate women, see Faust, *Mothers of Invention*, 191–95.

5. A. T. Summey to Zebulon B. Vance, August 31, 1864, reel 7, McKinney and McMurry, *Papers of Vance*.

6. Rufus L. Patterson to L. M. Fries, February 6, 1865, Patterson Family Papers, NCDAH; Escott, *Many Excellent People*, 78; McGee, " 'Home and Friends,' " 383.

7. Ironically, their moves put both families directly in the path of Stoneman's raiders later in the spring, as is discussed later in this chapter. See Spencer, *Last Ninety Days of the War*, 214–15, and Van Noppen, "Significance of Stoneman's Last Raid," 163–64, 501.

8. John Roberts to Vance, October 6, 1864, and Jacob Siler to Vance, October 31, 1864, reel 25; Augustus S. Merrimon to Vance, January 25, 1865, reel 26; and Joshua Roberts to Vance, February 17, 1865, reel 4, McKinney and McMurry, *Papers of Vance*.

9. Minutes, September 3, 1864, Silver Creek Primitive Baptist Association Minute Books, SHC.

10. G. W. Howell to Vance, October 17, 1864, reel 25, McKinney and McMurry, *Papers of Vance*.

11. Ann M. Alexander to Vance, January 5, 1865, reel 7, ibid.

12. See Inscoe, "1864 Slave Purchases of Mary Bell" and "Mountain Masters as Confederate Opportunists."

13. *Asheville News*, November 3, 1864.

14. A. M. Powell to Vance, December 9, 1864, reel 25, McKinney and McMurry, *Papers of Vance*.

15. Robert H. Cowan to Vance, December 10, 1864, reel 25, ibid.

16. R. C. Washburn to Vance, January 31, 1865, reel 26; and J. K. Blankenship to Vance, November 11, 1864, and O. L. Erwin to Vance, October 21, 1864, reel 25, ibid.

17. N. A. Powell to Vance, September 15, 1864, reel 24; A. Glaty et al. to Vance, October 21, 1864, and E. J. Alston et al. to Vance, October 24, 1864, reel 25; and Wm. Weaver et al. to James A. Seddon, February 1, 1865, and E. C. Bartlett to Vance, February 6, 1865, reel 26, ibid.

18. V. Ripley et al. to Vance, October 3, 1864, and James D. Hyman to Vance, October 14, 1864, reel 25, ibid.

19. Wiley T. Walker et al. to Vance, November 1, 1864, and James Calloway to Vance, December 27, 1864, reel 25; and Amos Hildebrand et al. to Vance, January 2, 1865, reel 26, ibid.

20. Augustus S. Merrimon to Vance, November 28, 1864, reel 25, and A. Mitchell to Vance, September 17, 1864, reel 24, ibid.

21. Tod R. Caldwell et al. to Vance, February 4, 1865, reel 26, ibid.

22. James Sloan to Vance, January 17, 1865, reel 26, ibid.

23. E. R. Norton to Vance, September 27, 1864, reel 24, and I. W. Hennega to Vance, February 17, 1865, reel 4, ibid.

24. Escott, *Many Excellent People*, 57–58; Escott, "Poverty and Government Aid for the Poor." See Chapter 7 for a detailed account of local relief efforts earlier in the war.

25. See Paludan, *Victims*, 22–23, and J. Kent Coward, "The Community in Crisis," in Max Williams, *History of Jackson County*, 438.

26. Mont[reville] Patton to Vance, September 29, 1864, reel 3, and J. L. Henry to [Vance], September 30, 1864, reel 24, McKinney and McMurry, *Papers of Vance*.

27. Margaret Walker statement [October 1864], Walker Papers, HL. For more on her role in the incident, see Chapter 8.

28. Ibid.

29. E. Cranor to Vance, November 12, 1864, reel 25, McKinney and McMurry, *Papers of Vance*.

30. W. H. McNeil to Vance, November 19, 1864, reel 25, ibid.

31. E. Cranor to Vance, November 12, 1864, ibid.

32. *North Carolina Standard*, February 10, 1865.

33. T. Davis to Vance, February 14, 1865, reel 4, McKinney and McMurry, *Papers of Vance*.

34. J. M. Lyle to Laura Lyle, November 21, 1864, Lyle-Siler Family Papers, SHC.

35. Henry Diary, entries from September 28 to October 26, 1864 (quote from latter entry), Robert Henry Papers, PML.

36. T. G. Craft to Vance, February 25, 1865, reel 4, McKinney and McMurry, Papers of Vance; *North Carolina Standard*, February 25, 1865.

37. W. Murdock to Vance, December 9, 1864, reel 25, McKinney and McMurry, *Papers of Vance*.

38. W. E. Earle to Geo. Little, January 11, 1865, reel 26, ibid.

39. J. L. Henry to Vance, January 13, 1865; Montreville Patton to Vance, February 13, 1865, both in reel 4, ibid.

40. George Tait to Vance, February 13, 1865, reel 26, ibid.; *OR* 47 (2):1178.

41. R. V. Blackstock to Vance, February 27, 1865, reel 4, McKinney and McMurry, *Papers of Vance.*

42. *OR* 49 (1):1034. Such activity was not limited to troops stationed in the mountains. A Confederate officer defending Kinston from Sherman's approach in eastern North Carolina reported that one entire company of mountain men had deserted en masse in late February 1865. See A. H. Baird to Vance, February 25, 1865, reel 4, McKinney and McMurry, *Papers of Vance.*

43. Stringfield, "Sixty-ninth Regiment," 758. Stringfield mistakenly dates this attack as March, rather than February. See Trotter, *Bushwhackers!* 238.

44. W. C. Allen, *Annals of Haywood County*, 81–82; Stringfield, "Sixty-ninth Regiment," 758.

45. Stringfield, "Memoirs of the Civil War," May 10, 1901. For a condensed published version of this document, see W. C. Allen, *Annals of Haywood County*, 86–92. See also Crow, *Storm in the Mountains*, 121–23.

46. The most thorough treatment of Stoneman's Raid is found in the four-part series: Van Noppen, "Significance of Stoneman's Last Raid." These articles were later compiled into a pamphlet, *Stoneman's Last Raid.* References here are made to the *NCHR* articles. Other major published sources on the raid include Arthur, *Western North Carolina*, ch. 9; Spencer, *Last Ninety Days of the War*; and Trotter, *Bushwhackers!* pt. 5.

47. Van Noppen, "Significance of Stoneman's Last Raid," 34. See page 40 for a breakdown of the men, by county, serving in Kirk's 3rd North Carolina Mounted Infantry from western North Carolina.

48. The fullest account of the skirmish in Boone comes from Arthur, *History of Watauga County*, 176–80. See also Van Noppen, "Significance of Stoneman's Last Raid," 36–39, and Trotter, *Bushwhackers!* 254–56.

49. Van Noppen, "Significance of Stoneman's Last Raid," 38.

50. Joseph C. Norwood to Walter W. Lenoir, April 2, 1865, in Hickerson, *Echoes of Happy Valley*, 104.

51. Van Noppen, "Significance of Stoneman's Last Raid," 150.

52. James Gwyn Diary, vol. 4, entry for April 1, 1865, Gwyn Papers, SHC.

53. William H. Palmer to Frank H. Jackson, in Kirk, *History of the 15th Pennsylvania*, 729, quoted in Van Noppen, "Significance of Stoneman's Last Raid," 154–55, and Hickerson, *Echoes of Happy Valley*, 105. On the role of Masonry as a bond between Northerners and Southerners who encountered one another in this area, see Escott, "Clinton A. Cilley," 413–15.

54. Kirk, *History of the 15th Pennsylvania*, 538; Van Noppen, "Significance of Stoneman's Last Raid," 164–65.

55. Van Noppen, "Significance of Stoneman's Last Raid"; Barrett, *Civil War in North Carolina*, 356–59.

56. Spencer, *Last Ninety Days of the War*, 214–15.

57. Laura Norwood to Walter Gwyn, April 25, 1865, Gwyn Papers, SHC.

58. For two firsthand accounts of the clash at Rocky Ford, see Capt. W. L. Twitty to A. C. Avery, April 7, 1896, in Avery Papers, SHC (Twitty mistakenly reported that skirmish took place across from the John's River, rather than the Catawba), and Beall, "Notes on Stone-

man's Raid." See also Van Noppen, "Significance of Stoneman's Last Raid," 507–8, and Phifer, *Burke*, 326–27.

59. Beall, "Notes on Stoneman's Raid."

60. Selina L. Norwood, quoted in ibid., cited in Van Noppen, "Significance of Stoneman's Last Raid," 508.

61. Trotter, *Bushwhackers!* 235. Another version of the story identified Councill's slave as a woman (see Arthur, *History of Watauga County*, 177–78), while others make no mention of a slave at all.

62. Mrs. George W. F. Harper Diary, entries for March 26, 28, 1865, quoted in Van Noppen, "Significance of Stoneman's Last Raid," 149.

63. Calvin J. Cowles to C. B. Reddick, April 6, 1865, Cowles Papers, NCDAH.

64. Ella Harper Diary, April 17, 1865, George W. F. Harper Papers, SHC; Trotter, *Bushwhackers!* 281–82.

65. Beall, "Notes of Stoneman's Raid in Burke County." Ina Van Noppen, who cites Beall's narrative extensively in "Significance of Stoneman's Last Raid," notes that although the authorship is attributed to Beall, this description was obviously provided by a woman in the Pearson household. See Van Noppen, "Significance of Stoneman's Last Raid," 508 n. 228.

66. *OR* 49 (1):335.

67. Trotter, *Bushwhackers!* ch. 26, quote on 294; McCoy, "Battle of Asheville"; Sondley, *History of Buncombe County*, 2:693–95.

68. J. G. Martin to Cornelia Phillips Spencer, June 11, 1866, quoted in Van Noppen, "Significance of Stoneman's Last Raid," 516. Van Noppen dispels the common assumption that Martin and Gillem had been classmates at West Point, to which many attributed their opportunity for cordial talks on Asheville's outskirts. Accounts vary too as to whether Gillem learned of Johnston's surrender from Martin or was informed by his own sources.

69. Mary Taylor Brown to John Evans Brown, June 20, 1865, W. Vance Brown Papers, SHC. This is an extraordinary thirty-six-page letter that Mrs. Brown wrote to her new stepson in Australia. (She had married his father, W. Vance Brown, the year before.) The quote appears on page 8 of the letter.

70. Ibid., 9–10.

71. Gale, "Life in the Southern Confederacy," 50.

72. Ibid., 52.

73. Ibid., 52–55.

74. Mary Taylor Brown to John Evans Brown, June 20, 1865, W. Vance Brown Papers, SHC.

75. Ibid., 11; Van Noppen, "Significance of Stoneman's Last Raid," 520–21; Trotter, *Bushwhackers!* 286–87.

76. James Martin to Cornelia Phillips Spencer, June 11, 1866, Swain Papers, SHC, quoted in Van Noppen, "Significance of Stoneman's Last Raid," 521.

77. Spencer, *Last Ninety Days of the War*, 231–33.

78. Martin to Spencer, June 11, 1866, and Cain, "Last Days of the War in Asheville," quoted in Van Noppen, "Significance of Stoneman's Last Raid," 522–23; Barrett, *Civil War in North Carolina*, 364–65; Arthur, *Western North Carolina*, 620. Katherine Polk Gale provided detailed descriptions of violent attacks made on men and women in several promi-

nent households, including that of James W. Patton and her own. See Gale, "Life in the Southern Confederacy," 12–16.

79. Cain, "Last Days of the War," 523. Curiously, this is almost the only source that mentions the presence of black troops among those who attacked and occupied Asheville.

80. Wm. J. Palmer to J. G. Martin, April 28, 1865, reproduced in full in Arthur, *Western North Carolina*, 620–21.

81. The most complete historical accounts of the events that took place near Waynesville are found in Crow, *Storm in the Mountains*, 135–40, and Trotter, *Bushwhackers!* ch. 27.

82. Conley, "Last Gun of the War," typescript of letter to the *Atlanta Constitution*, July 12, 1892, in which Conley took issue with another letter writer who had claimed that the last shots of the war had been fired at Macon, Georgia, between April 20 and 30. See also R. T. Underwood Reminiscences, n.d., WRPL. Underwood, a veteran of the Thomas's Legion 1st Regiment, wrote a seven-page report that confirms Conley's account of the skirmish and subsequent surrender at White Sulphur Springs.

83. Stringfield, "Memoirs of the Civil War," 75, copies in both HL, and Stringfield Papers, McClung Collection, Lawson McGee Library, Knoxville, Tennessee; Crow, *Storm in the Mountains*, 138–39.

84. Although he is mistaken as to the dates of these events, W. C. Allen provides a full account of the surrender in his *Annals of Haywood County*, 82–85 (quote on 84).

85. *Daily Progress*, February 25, 1865; *North Carolina Standard*, February 28, 1865.

86. Resolution by Caldwell County Court, April 22, 1865, quoted in Escott, *Many Excellent People*, 79. Paul Escott discusses similar efforts made in Randolph County (see 79–80).

87. Samuel Finley Patterson to Rufus Lenoir Patterson, June 2, 1865, Patterson Family Papers, SHC, quoted in Escott, *Many Excellent People*, 80.

88. James Gwyn Diary, vol. 4, entry for May 4, 1865, Gwyn Papers, SHC.

89. H. A. Eller, "Recollections of Bushwhacker Rule," 1–2; Flowers, "History of Fort Hamby."

90. H. A. Eller, "Recollections of Bushwhacker Rule," 6–7; Flowers, "History of Fort Hamby." There are considerable discrepancies in accounts of Fort Hamby. See, for example, Trotter, *Bushwhackers!* ch. 28.

91. Trotter, *Bushwhackers!* 312.

92. John D. Hyman to Zebulon B. Vance, January 30, 1864, reel 3, McKinney and McMurry, *Vance Papers*; *North Carolina Standard*, February 17, 1865.

93. See Calvin J. Cowles to sister Mary, February 9, 1865, Cowles Papers, NCDAH; Inscoe, "Slave Purchases of Mary Bell."

94. *Daily Conservative*, January 2, 1865; *Daily Progress*, February 12, 1865.

95. Calvin J. Cowles to Rev. C. B. Reddick, February 28, 1865, Cowles Papers, NCDAH.

96. Ibid., March 29, 1865.

97. Ibid., April 6, 1865. See the fuller discussion of this letter earlier in this chapter.

98. William Holland Thomas to Sallie Thomas, November 4, 1865, Thomas Papers, WRPL, quoted in Godbold and Russell, *Confederate Colonel and Cherokee Chief*, 130.

99. Ella Harper to Geo. W. F. Harper, April 2, 1865, George W. F. Harper Papers, SHC.

100. Gale, "Life in the Southern Confederacy," 58.

101. Cornelia Henry to William Henry, May 27, 1865, Robert Henry Papers, PML.

102. Mary Taylor Brown to John Evans Brown, June 20, 1865, 18–19, W. Vance Brown Papers, SHC.

103. Cornelia Henry to William Henry, May 27, 1865, Robert Henry Papers, PML.

104. Mary Taylor Brown to John Evans Brown, June 20, 1865, 19–20, W. Vance Brown Papers, SHC.

105. Cornelia Henry to Dora and Matt Henry, June 4, 1865, Robert Henry Papers, PML.

106. Mary Taylor Brown to John Evans Brown, June 20, 1865, 24, W. Vance Brown Papers, SHC.

107. Ibid., 31.

Chapter Eleven

1. Blackmun, *Western North Carolina*, 359; Cornelia Henry to William Henry, May 27, 1865, Robert Henry Papers, PML.

2. Thomas R. Heath to Col. C. A. Cilley, September 3, 1865, [C-3093], Library of Congress, Washington, D.C.

3. Statement by Col. V. S. Lusk of Asheville, reproduced in McKinney, "Klan in the Southern Mountains"; quote on 92.

4. Wellman, *Kingdom of Madison*, 88–92; Paludan, *Victims*, 21–23.

5. Van Noppen and Van Noppen, *Western North Carolina*, 15.

6. Paludan, *Victims*, 109–10.

7. On these developments at the state level, see Hamilton, *Reconstruction in North Carolina*, 106–206; Olsen, "North Carolina," 161–63; Escott, *Many Excellent People*, 92–112; and William Harris, *William Woods Holden*, 156–206.

8. Cotton, "Appalachian North Carolina," 171.

9. Computed from Matthews, *North Carolina Votes*, 9–106.

10. Ibid., 114–211.

11. Olson, "Race Relations in Asheville," 153–56; quote on 156.

12. Alexander Gates et al. to William L. Scott, May 31, 1871, Scott Papers, WRPL. See McKinney, "Southern Mountain Republicans and the Negro," for the broader context of race and politics in postwar Appalachia.

13. McKinney, "Klan in the Mountains," 91–92.

14. Asheville *Pioneer*, June 22, July 6, November 9, 30, 1871; Trelease, *White Terror*, 340.

15. Hamilton, *Reconstruction in North Carolina*, 482–533; Trelease, *White Terror*, 215–17.

16. Hoffman, "Republican Party in North Carolina," 81–82; [New York] *Tribune Almanac and Political Register* (1872), 69.

17. Harris, *William Woods Holden*, 278–309.

18. Asheville *Pioneer*, November 7, 1874. For an overview of this process, see McKinney, "Mountain Republican Party-Army."

19. M. N. Corbett to Thomas Settle III; W. S. Newton to Thomas Settle Jr., September 5, 1874; M. M. Shofner III to Settle, October 1894; and J. A. Byerly to Settle, November 7, 1892, all in Thomas Settle Jr. and Thomas Settle III Papers, SHC.

20. McKinney, *Southern Mountain Republicans*, 49.

21. Charlotte *Democrat*, July 31, 1876.

22. U.S. Senate, "Testimony before the Senate Special Committee."

23. Asheville *Advance*, June 14, 1885, September 19, 1886.

24. McKinney, *Southern Mountain Republicans*, 136–37.

25. Miller, *Revenuers and Moonshiners*, 106, 127–65.

26. Belcher, "Population Growth and Characteristics," 38.

27. Ronald Eller, *Miners, Millhands, and Mountaineers*. For analysis of these issues at a community level, that of Beech Creek, Kentucky, from 1850–1910, see Blee and Billings, *Road to Poverty* and "Agriculture and Poverty in the Kentucky Mountains."

28. Cratis Williams, "Southern Mountaineer in Fact and Fiction," 119; Noe, " 'Deadened Color and Colder Horror,' " 76–77. Noe demonstrates how these two stories, particularly the latter, had much to do with the emergence of the myth of the region as having been predominantly Unionist during the war.

29. Cratis Williams, "Southern Mountaineer in Fact and Fiction," 121–22.

30. Goodrich, *Mountain Homespun*, 13.

31. Samuel Wilson, *Southern Mountaineers*, 57.

32. Frost, "Our Contemporary Ancestors," 313–14.

33. Ibid., 314; Batteau, *Invention of Appalachia*, 78.

34. Stringfield, "Sixty-ninth Regiment," 734, quoted in Starnes, " 'Stirring Strains of Dixie,' " 257. Starnes's study of the Lost Cause in Haywood County is the most thorough treatment of these themes. For the development of similar phenomena across the state line in the north Georgia mountains, see Andrew, "Martial Spirit, Christian Virtue, and the Lost Cause"; Sarris, " 'Hellish Deeds in a Christian Land,' " ch. 5; and Robert Davis, "Memoirs of a Partisan War."

35. Theodore Davidson, "Carolina Mountaineer," 84–85, quoted in full in Inscoe, *Mountain Masters*, 262.

36. Starnes, " 'Stirring Strains of Dixie,' " 259.

37. The literature on the postwar "discovery" of Appalachia continues to grow. See especially, Shapiro, *Appalachia on Our Mind*, 86–97; Klotter, "Black South and White Appalachia"; Noe, "Toward the Myth of Unionist Appalachia"; Noe, "Deadened Color and Colder Horror"; Silber, *Romance of Reunion*, 143–58; Silber, " 'What Does America Need So Much As Americans?' "; Inscoe, "Race and Racism in Southern Appalachia," 108–13; Batteau, *Invention of Appalachia*, 74–85; and Shannon Wilson, "Lincoln's Sons and Daughters."

38. Shapiro, *Appalachia on Our Mind*, 54–55; Van Noppen and Van Noppen, *Western North Carolina*, ch. 7.

39. U.S. Dept. of the Interior, *Report on the Statistics of Churches*, 74; see also Van Noppen and Van Noppen, *Western North Carolina*, ch. 3.

40. See Waller, "Feuding in Appalachia," and Batteau, *Invention of Appalachia*, for discussions of the origin of violence as part of Appalachian stereotyping.

41. Trelease, *North Carolina Railroad*, 92, 224, 292–93, 299.

42. Abrams, "Western North Carolina Railroad," 29–44.

43. Ibid., 53–62. Williams, *History of Jackson County*, 199–200. The convicts drowned when the scow on which they were crossing the Tuckaseigee River to their worksite capsized.

44. See Lambert, "Logging in the Great Smokies," 351–53, and Ronald Eller, *Miners, Millhands, and Mountaineers*, 87–91.

45. Van Noppen and Van Noppen, *Western North Carolina*, 378–82, 388–89; Bishir, Southern, and Martin, *Guide to Historic Architecture*, 36–41.

46. Jacquelyn Hall, *Like a Family*, 33.

47. Paludan, *Victims*, 132; Godbold and Russell, *Confederate Colonel and Cherokee Chief*, 121, 132–33.

48. Ronald Eller, *Miners, Millhands, and Mountaineers*, 65–85; Trelease, *North Carolina Railroad*; Lacy Ford, *Origins of Southern Radicalism*, 236–38; Wright, *Old South, New South*, 39–42; Hahn, "Unmaking of Southern Yeomanry," 187.

49. Dorgan, *Giving Glory to God*, 31–32; Van Noppen and Van Noppen, *Western North Carolina*, ch. 3.

BIBLIOGRAPHY

PRIMARY SOURCES

Manuscripts

Ann Arbor, Mich.
  William L. Clements Library, University of
    Michigan
    Schoff Collection
Asheville, N.C.
  Pack Memorial Library
    Civil War Papers
    Robert Henry Papers
    [William Lewis] Henry Diary
    William Holland Thomas Papers
Atlanta, Ga.
  Atlanta History Center
    Davidson Family Papers
    William H. Parkins Papers
Chapel Hill, N.C.
  Southern Historical Collection, University
    of North Carolina
    A. C. Avery Papers
    Hamilton Brown Papers
    W. Vance Brown Papers
    Bryan-Leventhorpe Family Papers
    Ralph Potts Buxton Papers
    Tod R. Caldwell Papers
    David Miller Carter Papers
    Confederate Papers
    Calvin J. Cowles Papers
    John Mitchell Davidson Papers
    William G. Dickson Papers
    George Phifer Erwin Papers
    J. B. Gaither Papers
    Gale and Polk Family Papers
    Thomas Jefferson Green Papers
    James Gwyn Papers
    George W. F. Harper Diaries
    James C. Harper Diaries
    William A. Hoke Papers
    Jones and Patterson Papers
    E. M. Law Papers

    Lenoir Family Papers
    Lyle-Siler Family Papers
    Charles Beatty Mallett Papers
    Theodore Davidson Morrison Papers
    Lindsay Patterson Papers
    James W. Patton Papers
    David Schenk Diary
    Thomas Settle Jr. and Thomas Settle III
      Papers
    John McKee Sharpe Papers
    Jacob Siler Papers
    Silver Creek Primitive Baptist
      Association Minute Books
    David L. Swain Papers
    Zebulon Baird Vance Papers
    Thomas George Walton Papers
Cullowhee, N.C.
  Special Collections, Hunter Library,
    Western Carolina University
    Beal-Siler Family Papers
    D. D. Benedict Papers
    Absalom Joshua Burum Diary
    Joseph Cathey and Cathey Family
      Papers
    A. T. Davidson Papers
    Edmonston-Kelly Family Papers
    Fain Family Papers
    Hampton-Patterson Families Papers
    William Walker Stringfield Papers
    James W. Terrell Papers
    William Holland Thomas Papers
    William Walker Papers
    James Watson Papers
    James W. Wilson Papers
Durham, N.C.
  Special Collections, William R. Perkins
    Library, Duke University
    Alfred W. Bell Papers

Corpening Family Papers
John Hendricks Kinyoun Papers
Thomas Lenoir Papers
Matthew N. Love Papers
John W. Reese Papers
William Lafayette Scott Papers
Albert Siler Papers
William Holland Thomas Papers
R. T. Underwood Reminiscences
Zebulon Baird Vance Papers
James Whitaker Papers
Knoxville, Tennessee
  McClung Collection, Lawson McGee
    Library
  Robert B. Barker Papers
  W. W. Stringfield Papers
Raleigh, N.C.
  North Carolina Department of Archives
    and History
    Col. Joseph Cathey Papers
    Henry T. Clark Governor's Papers
    Katherine Clark Pendleton Conway
      Collection
    Walter Clark Papers
    Calvin J. Cowles Papers
    Allen T. and Theodore F. Davidson
      Papers
    John W. Ellis Governor's Papers
    Alexander England Family Papers
    Mary Gash and Family Papers
    James Gordon Hackett Collection
    Daniel Harvey Hill Papers
    Paul E. Hubbell Papers
    Evelyn McIntosh Hyatt Papers

Miscellaneous Records
  Cherokee County
  Henderson County
  McDowell County
  Madison County
  Yancey County
Patterson Family Papers
Slave Records
  Ashe County
  Henderson County
  Rutherford County
William W. Stringfield Papers
David L. Swain Papers
Zebulon Baird Vance Papers
Zebulon B. Vance Governor's Papers
Stephen Whitaker Papers
W. N. Whitaker Diary
Richmond, Va.
  Archives and Records Division, Virginia
    State Library
  Confederate States of America Armory
    Letterbook, Asheville, N.C.
Washington, D.C.
  Library of Congress
    Robert B. Vance Papers
  National Archives
    Confederate Military Records,
      Department of East Tennessee (RG
      109)
    Records of U.S. Army Continental
      Commands, District of East
      Tennessee (RG 393)
    Southern Claims Commission
      Records—Case Files (RG 217)

Newspapers

Asheville *Advance*
Asheville News
Asheville *Pioneer*
Asheville *Spectator*
Atlanta *Daily Intelligencer*
Carolina Watchman (Salisbury)
Charlotte *Democrat*
Daily Conservative (Raleigh)
Daily Progress (Raleigh)
Fayetteville *Observer*
Franklin Observer

Greensborough Patriot
Hendersonville Times
Iredell Express
Knoxville Whig
Louisville *Courier-Journal*
North Carolina Standard
People's Press (Salem)
Raleigh Register
Rutherfordton Press
State Journal (Raleigh)
TriWeekly Standard (Raleigh)

Unpublished Typescripts

Beall, R. L. "Notes on Stoneman's Raid in Burke County and the Town of Morganton" (1866). David L. Swain Papers, Southern Historical Collection, University of North Carolina at Chapel Hill.

Cain, Sarah Jane Bailey. "The Last Days of the War in Asheville." Archibald Henderson Papers, Southern Historical Collection, University of North Carolina at Chapel Hill.

Coffin, Eleanor Johnstone. "The Murder of Andrew Johnstone." Civil War Collection, Special Collections, University of Tennessee, Knoxville.

Conley, Capt. Isaiah. "Account of Captain Conley's Escape from Prison." Manuscript Dept., Library of Congress, Washington, D.C.

Conley, R. T. "The Last Gun of the War." Evelyn McIntosh Hyatt Papers, N.C. Department of Archives and History, Raleigh.

Davis, Charles G. "Army Life and Prison Experiences of Major Charles G. Davis." Special Collections, University of Tennessee, Knoxville.

Eller, H. A. "Recollections of Bushwhacker Rule in Western North Carolina, 1864–1865." Paul E. Hubbell Papers, N.C. Department of Archives and History, Raleigh.

Flowers, Robert L. "History of Fort Hamby: Its Capture and Destruction." A. C. Avery Papers, Southern Historical Collection, University of North Carolina at Chapel Hill.

Freel, Margaret Walker. "Story of the Life of Margaret Walker during the Civil War." William Walker Papers, Special Collections, Hunter Library, Western Carolina University, Cullowhee, N.C.

Gale, Katherine Polk. "Life in the Southern Confederacy, 1861–1865." Leonidas Polk Papers, Southern Historical Collection, University of North Carolina at Chapel Hill.

Harper, Emma L. "A Woman's Experiences in the War between the States as Described in Stoneman's Raid." North Carolina Collection, University of North Carolina at Chapel Hill.

Matthews, Mrs. A. "A Partial Record of the Life, Ancestry, and War Experiences of W. C. Sales." Southern Historical Collection, University of North Carolina at Chapel Hill.

McTeer, Will A. "Among Loyal Mountaineers." Civil War Collection, Special Collections, University of Tennessee, Knoxville.

Orr, Mary Middleton. "The Experiences of a Soldier's Wife in the Civil War." Privately owned.

Parkins, William H. "Between Two Flags; or The Story of the War by a Refugee" (1885). Atlanta History Center, Atlanta, Ga.

Stringfield, W. W. "Memoirs of the Civil War." Special Collections, Hunter Library, Western Carolina University, Cullowhee, N.C.

Walton, Thomas G. "Sketches of the Pioneers in Burke County History." Southern Historical Collection, University of North Carolina at Chapel Hill.

Published Primary Documents

Aiken, R. R. "Eightieth Regiment." In *Histories of the Several Regiments and Battalions from North Carolina in the Great War, 1861–1865*. Vol. 4, edited by Walter Clark, 117–28. Greensboro, N.C.: Nash Brothers, 1901.

[Allen, Lawrence M.] *Partisan Campaigns of Col. Lawrence M. Allen*. Raleigh: Edwards and Broughton, 1894.

Andrews, Sidney. *The South Since the War, as Shown by Fourteen Weeks of Travel and Observation in Georgia and the Carolinas*. Boston: Ticknor and Fields, 1866.

Ash, Stephen V., ed. *Secessionists and Other Scoundrels: Selections from Parson Brownlow's Book*. Baton Rouge: Louisiana University Press, 1999.

Avery, Myron H., and Kenneth S. Boardman, eds. "Arnold Guyot's Notes on the Geography of the Mountain District of Western North Carolina." *North Carolina Historical Review* 15 (July 1938): 251–318.

Bailey, Lloyd, ed. *News from Yancey: Articles from Area Newspapers, 1840–1900*. Burnsville, N.C.: Yancey Graphics, 1983.

Berlin, Ira, et al., eds. *Freedom: A Documentary History of Emancipation, 1861–1867*. Series 1. Cambridge: Cambridge University Press, 1985–.

Bliss, George N., ed. *The Prison Life of Lieut. James M. Fales*. Providence, R.I.: N. Bangs, Williams and Co., 1882.

Browne, Junius Henry. *Four Years in Secessia: Within and Beyond the Union Lines: Embracing a Great Variety of Facts, Incidents, and Romance of the War*. Hartford, Conn.: O. D. Case and Co., 1865.

Brownlow, William G. *Sketches of the Rise, Progress, and Decline of Secession*. Philadelphia: George W. Childs, 1862.

Buckingham, James S. *The Slave States of America*. Vol. 2. London: Fisher, Son and Co., 1842.

Burson, William. *A Race for Liberty: or My Capture, My Imprisonment, and My Escape*. Wellsville, Ohio: W. G. Foster, 1867.

Clark, Walter, ed. *Histories of the Several Regiments and Battalions from North Carolina in the Great War, 1861–1865*. Vols. 3 and 4. Goldsboro, N.C.: Nash Brothers, 1901.

Clarke, F. W. "A Trip to North Carolina." *Appalachia* 2 (June 1879).

Clingman, Thomas L. *Selections from the Speeches and Writings of Hon. Thomas L. Clingman of North Carolina, with Additions and Explanatory Notes*. Raleigh: John Nichols, 1887.

Colton, Henry E. *Guidebook to the Scenery of Western North Carolina*. Asheville, N.C.: Western Advocate Office, 1860.

Cooper, Alonzo. *In and Out of Rebel Prisons*. Oswego, N.Y.: R. J. Oliphant, 1888.

Crayon, Porte [David Hunter Strother]. "A Winter in the South." *Harper's New Monthly Magazine* 15–16 (October 1857–May 1858).

Crow, Vernon H., ed. " 'The Justness of Our Cause': The Civil War Diaries of William W. Stringfield." *Publications of the East Tennessee Historical Society* 56–57 (1980/1981).

Davidson, Allen T. "Reminiscences of Western North Carolina." *The Lyceum* 1 (January, April, May 1891).

Davidson, Theodore F. "The Carolina Mountaineer: The Highest Type of American Character." In *First Annual Transactions of the Pen and Plate Club of Asheville, N.C.* Asheville, N.C.: Hackney and Mole, 1905.

Davis, Robert S., Jr., ed. "Memoirs of a Partisan War: Sion Darnell Remembers North Georgia, 1861–1865." *Georgia Historical Quarterly* 80 (Spring 1996): 93–116.

DeBow, James D. B. *The Interest in Slavery of the Southern Non-Slaveholder*. Charleston: Evans and Cogswell, 1860.

Dedmond, Francis B., ed. "Harvey Davis's Unpublished Civil War Diary and the Story of Company D of the First North Carolina Cavalry." *Appalachian Journal* 13 (Summer 1986): 368–407.

Dimock, George. "A Trip to Mt. Mitchell in North Carolina." *Appalachia* 1 (June 1877).

Disturnell, John. *Springs, Waterfalls, Sea-Bathing Resorts and Mountain Scenery: Of the United States and Canada*. New York: J. Disturnell, 1855.

Drake, J. Madison. *Fast and Loose in Dixie*. New York: Authors' Publishing Co., 1880.

Egan, Michael. *The Flying Gray-Haired Yank; or The Adventures of a Volunteer*. New York: Business Mirror, 1863.

Ellis, Daniel. *The Thrilling Adventures of Daniel Ellis: The Great Union Guide of East Tennessee . . .* New York: Harper and Bros., 1867.

Escott, Paul D., ed. *North Carolina Yeoman: The Diary of Basil Armstrong Thomasson, 1853–1862*. Athens: University of Georgia Press, 1997.

Featherstonaugh, George W. *A Canoe Voyage Up the Minnay Sotor*. 2 vols. London: R. Bentley, 1847.

Freehling, William W., and Craig Simpson, eds. *Secession Debated: Georgia's Showdown in 1860*. New York: Oxford University Press, 1992.

Frost, William G. "Our Contemporary Ancestors in the Southern Mountains." *Atlantic Monthly* 83 (March 1899): 311–19.

Gilmore, James R. *Adrift in Dixie: or a Yankee Officer Among the Rebels*. New York: Carlton Publishers, 1866.

Glazier, Willard. *The Capture, the Prison Pen, and the Escape, Giving a Complete History of Prison Life in the South*. Hartford, Conn.: H. E. Goodwin, 1868.

Goe, J. S. "Sheep and the Mountains of North Carolina." *North Carolina Planter* 3 (March 1860): 88–94.

Graf, Leroy, and Ralph Haskins, eds. *The Papers of Andrew Johnson*. 7 vols. Knoxville: University of Tennessee Press, 1967–.

Hadley, J. V. *Seven Months a Prisoner*. New York: Charles Scribner's Sons, 1898.

Hamilton, J. G. deRoulhac, and Rebecca Cameron, eds. *The Papers of Randolph Abbott Shotwell*. 3 vols. Raleigh: North Carolina Historical Commission, 1929–36.

Hamilton, J. G. deRoulhac, and Max R. Williams, eds. *The Papers of William A. Graham*. 5 vols. Raleigh: North Carolina Division of Archives and History, 1957–73.

Harmon, George D., and Edith Blackburn Hazlehurst, eds. "Captain Isaiah Conley's Escape from a Southern Prison, 1864." *Western Pennsylvania Historical Magazine* 47 (April 1964).

Harper, George W. F. *Reminiscences of Caldwell County, N.C. in the Great War of 1861–1865*. Lenoir, N.C.: Privately printed, 1913.

Hesseltine, William B., ed. *Three against Lincoln: Murat Halstead Reports the Caucuses of 1860*. Baton Rouge: Louisiana State University Press, 1960.

Hickerson, Thomas Felix, ed. *Echoes of Happy Valley: Letters and Diaries, Family Life in the South, Civil War History*. Durham, N.C.: Privately printed, 1962.

Hume, Thomas. *The Loyal Mountaineers of Tennessee*. Knoxville: Ogden Press, 1888.

Hundley, Daniel R. *Social Relations in Our Southern States*. New York: Henry B. Price, 1860.

Hunt, Charles O. "Our Escape from Camp Sorghum," *War Records Read before the Commandry of the State of Maine*. Vol. 1. Portland, Maine: Thurston Print, 1918.

Huntington, J. H. "Reports of the Councillors for the Autumn: Natural History." *Appalachia* 2 (May 1881).

Johnston, Frontis W., ed. *The Papers of Zebulon Baird Vance, 1843–1862*. Vol. 1. Raleigh: North Carolina Department of Archives and History, 1963.

Jones, Alexander H. *Knocking at the Door: His Course Before the War, During the War, and After the War*. Washington, D.C.: McGill and Wetherow, 1866.

Kellogg, John Azor. *Capture and Escape: A Narrative of Army and Prison Life*. Original Papers, No. 2. Madison: Wisconsin Historical Commission, 1908.

Kirk, Charles E., ed. *The History of the 15th Pennsylvania Volunteer Cavalry*. Philadelphia: Historical Committee of the 15th Pennsylvania Cavalry, 1906.

Langworthy, Daniel W. *Reminiscences of a Prisoner of War and His Escape*. Minneapolis: Bryant Printing Co., 1915.

Lanman, Charles. *Letters from the Allegheny Mountains*. New York: G. P. Putnam, 1849.

McKinney, Gordon B., and Richard M. McMurry, eds. *The Papers of Zebulon Baird Vance*. Frederick, Md.: University Publications of America, 1987. Microfilm, 39 reels.

McPherson, Elizabeth G., ed. "Letters from North Carolina to Andrew Johnson." *North Carolina Historical Review* 28 (October 1951) and 29 (April 1952).

Malet, William W. *An Errand to the South in the Summer of 1862*. London: R. Bentley, 1863.

Matthews, Donald R., ed. *North Carolina Votes: General Election Returns by County*. Chapel Hill: University of North Carolina Press, 1962.

Mobley, Joe A., ed. *The Papers of Zebulon Baird Vance, 1863*. Vol. 2. Raleigh: North Carolina Division of Archives and History, 1995.

Morris, B. T. "Sixty-fourth Regiment." In *Histories of the Several Regiments and Battalions from North Carolina in the Great War, 1861–1865*. Vol. 3, edited by Walter Clark, 659–71. Greensboro, N.C.: Nash Brothers, 1901.

Newlin, William Henry. *An Account of the Escape of Six Federal Soldiers from Danville, Virginia . . . in the Winter of 1862–64*. Cincinnati: Western Methodist Book Concern Print, 1886.

Newsome, A. R., ed. "A. S. Merrimon Journal, 1853–54." *North Carolina Historical Review* 8 (July 1931): 300–330.

Norman, William M. *A Portion of My Life: Being a Short and Imperfect History Written While a Prisoner of War on Johnson's Island, 1864*. Winston-Salem, N.C.: John F. Blair, 1959.

Olmsted, Frederick Law. *A Journey in the Back Country in the Winter of 1853–1854*. New York: Mason Bros., 1860. Reprint, New York: G. P. Putnam, 1907.

Parkins, W. H. *How I Escaped*. New York: Home Publishing Co., 1889.

R. "A Week in the Great Smoky Mountains." *Southern Literary Messenger* 31 (August 1860): 121–31.

Rawick, George P., ed. *The American Slave: A Composite Autobiography*. Vol. 14, *North Carolina Narratives*. Westport, Conn.: Greenwood Press, 1972.

Richardson, Albert D. *The Secret Service, the Field, the Dungeon, and the Escape*. Hartford, Conn.: American Publishing Co., 1865.

Savage, James W. *The Loyal Element of North Carolina during the War*. Omaha: Loyal Legion, 1886.

Shelton, W. H. "A Hard Road to Travel Out of Dixie." *Century Magazine* 40 (October 1890).

Speer, Allen Paul, ed. *Voices from Cemetery Hill: The Civil War Diary, Reports, and Letters of Colonel William Henry Asbury Speer, 1861–1864*. Johnson City, Tenn.: Overmountain Press, 1997.

Spencer, Cornelia Phillips. *The Last Ninety Days of the War in North Carolina*. New York: Watchman Publishing Co., 1866.

Stafford, David W. *In Defense of the Flag: A True War Story*. Kalamazoo, Mich.: Ihling Bros. and Everard, 1903.

Stringfield, William W. "Sixty-ninth Regiment." In *Histories of the Several Regiments and Battalions from North Carolina in the Great War, 1861–1865*. Vol. 3, edited by Walter Clark, 732–41. Greensboro, N.C.: Nash Brothers, 1901.

Taylor, James W. *Alleghania: A Geographical and Statistical Memoir*. St. Paul, Minn.: James Davenport Publishing, 1862.

Taylor, Michael W., ed. *The Cry Is War, War, War: The Civil War Correspondence of Lts. Burwell Thomas Cotton and George Job Huntley, 34th Regiment North Carolina Troops*. Dayton, Ohio: Morningside Press, 1994.

Temple, Oliver P. *East Tennessee and the Civil War*. c1899. Reprint, New York: Books for Libraries Press, 1971.

———. *Notable Men of Tennessee, from 1833 to 1875: Their Times and Their Contemporaries*. New York: Cosmopolitan Press, 1912.

Tolbert, Noble J., ed. *The Papers of John Willis Ellis*. 2 vols. Raleigh: North Carolina Division
    of Archives and History, 1964.
U.S. Department of the Interior. *Report on the Interior: Report on the Statistics of Churches of
    the United States at the Eleventh Census, 1890*. Washington, D.C.: Government Printing
    Office, 1894.
U.S. Department of War. *The War of the Rebellion: A Compilation of the Official Records of the
    Union and Confederate Armies*. 128 vols. Washington, D.C.: U.S. Government Printing
    Office, 1880–1901.
U.S. Senate, "Testimony before the Senate Special Committee to Investigate the Administration
    of the Collection of Internal Revenue in the Sixth District of North Carolina." *Senate
    Miscellaneous Documents* 166, 47th Cong., 1st sess., 1882.
Wilkeson, Frank. *Recollections of a Private Soldier*. New York: Putnam, 1887.
Woodward, C. Vann., ed. *Mary Chesnut's Civil War*. New Haven: Yale University Press, 1981.
Woodward, C. Vann, and Elisabeth Muhlenfeld, eds. *The Private Mary Chesnut: The
    Unpublished Civil War Diaries*. New York: Oxford University Press, 1984.
Yearns, W. Buck, and John C. Barrett, eds. *North Carolina Civil War Documentary*. Chapel
    Hill: University of North Carolina Press, 1980.
Younce, W. H. *The Adventures of a Conscript*. Cincinnati, Ohio: Editor Publishing Co., 1901.

Secondary Sources

. Books

Abel, Jules. *Man on Fire: John Brown and the Cause of Liberty*. New York: Macmillan, 1971.
Alexander, Nancy. *Here Will I Dwell: The Story of Caldwell County*. Lenoir, N.C.: Privately
    printed, 1956.
Allen, W. C. *Annals of Haywood County*. 1935. Reprint, Spartanburg, S.C.: Reprint Co., 1977.
Ammons, John. *Outlines of History of the French Broad Association and Mars Hill College*.
    Raleigh: Broughton and Edwards, n.d.
Anderson, Mrs. John Huske. *North Carolina Women of the Confederacy*. Fayetteville: N.C.
    Division of the United Daughters of the Confederacy, 1926.
Arthur, John Preston. *A History of Watauga County, North Carolina*. Richmond: Everett
    Waddey Co., 1915.
——. *Western North Carolina: A History, 1730–1913*. Raleigh, N.C.: Edwards and Broughton,
    1914.
Ash, Stephen V. *Middle Tennessee Society Transformed, 1860–1870: War and Peace in the Upper
    South*. Baton Rouge: Louisiana State University Press, 1988.
——. *When the Yankees Came: Conflict and Chaos in the Occupied South, 1861–1865*. Chapel
    Hill: University of North Carolina Press, 1995.
Ashe, Samuel A'Court. *History of North Carolina*. 2 vols. Raleigh: Broughton and Edwards,
    1925.
Atkins, Jonathan M. *Parties, Politics, and the Sectional Conflict in Tennessee, 1832–1861*.
    Knoxville: University of Tennessee Press, 1997.
Bailey, Fred A. *Class and Tennessee's Confederate Generation*. Chapel Hill: University of North
    Carolina Press, 1987.
Barney, William L. *The Road to Secession: A New Perspective on the Old South*. New York:
    Praeger, 1972.

Barrett, John G. *The Civil War in North Carolina*. Chapel Hill: University of North Carolina Press, 1963.

———. *North Carolina as a Civil War Battleground, 1861–1865*. Raleigh: North Carolina Department of Archives and History, 1960.

———. *Sherman's March through North Carolina*. Chapel Hill: University of North Carolina Press, 1956.

Batteau, Allen. *The Invention of Appalachia*. Tucson: University of Arizona Press, 1990.

Beaver, Patricia D. *Rural Community in the Appalachian South*. Lexington: University Press of Kentucky, 1986.

Bender, Thomas. *Community and Social Change in America*. Baltimore: Johns Hopkins University Press, 1978.

Bergeron, Paul H. *Antebellum Politics in Tennessee*. Lexington: University Press of Kentucky, 1982.

Bernstein, Iver. *The New York City Draft Riots: Their Significance for American Society and Politics in the Age of the Civil War*. New York: Oxford University Press, 1990.

Beringer, Richard E., Herman Hattaway, Archer Jones, and William N. Still Jr. *Why the South Lost the Civil War*. Athens: University of Georgia Press, 1986.

Billings, Dwight B., Gurney Norman, and Katherine Ledford, eds. *Confronting Appalachian Stereotypes: Back Talk from an American Region*. Lexington: University Press of Kentucky, 1999.

Bisher, Catherine W., Michael T. Southern, and Jennifer F. Martin. *A Guide to the Historic Architecture of Western North Carolina*. Chapel Hill: University of North Carolina Press, 1999.

Blackmun, Ora. *Western North Carolina: Its Mountains and Its People to 1880*. Boone, N.C.: Appalachian Consortium Press, 1977.

Blee, Kathleen B., and Dwight B. Billings. *The Road to Poverty: The Making of Wealth and Hardship in Appalachia*. New York: Cambridge University Press, 1999.

Bode, Frederick A., and Donald E. Ginter. *Farm Tenancy and the Census in Antebellum Appalachia*. Athens: University of Georgia Press, 1986.

Bolton, Charles C. *Poor Whites in the Antebellum South: Tenants and Laborers in Central North Carolina and Northeast Mississippi*. Durham, N.C.: Duke University Press, 1994.

Boney, F. N. *Southerners All*. Macon, Ga.: Mercer University Press, 1984.

Boykin, James H. *North Carolina in 1861*. New York: Bookman Associates, 1961.

Bragg, William Harris. *Joe Brown's Army: The Georgia State Line, 1862–1865*. Macon, Ga.: Mercer University Press, 1987.

Brewer, Alberta, and Carson Brewer. *Valley So Wild: A Folk History*. Knoxville: East Tennessee Historical Society, 1975.

Browder, Nathaniel C. *The Cherokee Indians and Those Who Came After: Notes for a History of Cherokee County, North Carolina, 1835–1860*. Hayesville, N.C.: Privately printed, 1973.

Bryant, Jonathan M. *How Curious a Land: Conflict and Change in Greene County, Georgia, 1850–1885*. Chapel Hill: University of North Carolina Press, 1996.

Burnham, W. Dean. *Presidential Ballots, 1836–1892*. Baltimore: Johns Hopkins University Press, 1955.

Burton, Orville V., and Robert C. McMath Jr., eds. *Class, Conflict, and Consensus: Antebellum Southern Community Studies*. Westport, Conn.: Greenwood Press, 1982.

Butler, Lindley S., and Alan D. Watson, eds. *The North Carolina Experience: An Interpretive and Documentary History*. Chapel Hill: University of North Carolina Press, 1984.

Bynum, Victoria. *Unruly Women: The Politics of Social and Sexual Control in the Old South*. Chapel Hill: University of North Carolina Press, 1992.

Campbell, John C. *The Southern Highlander and His Homeland*. New York: Russell Sage
    Foundation, 1921.
Campbell, Mary E. R. *Attitudes of East Tennesseans toward the Union, 1846–1861*. New York:
    Vantage Press, 1961.
Capers, Gerald M. *Occupied City: New Orleans under the Federals, 1862–1865*. Lexington:
    University Press of Kentucky, 1965.
Capers, Henry D. *The Life and Times of C. G. Memminger*. Richmond: Everett Waddey Co.,
    1893.
Casstevens, Frances H. *The Civil War and Yadkin County, North Carolina: A History*.
    Jefferson, N.C.: McFarland and Co., 1997.
Cathey, Cornelius O. *Agricultural Developments in North Carolina, 1783–1860*. Chapel Hill:
    University of North Carolina Press, 1956.
Cecil-Fronsman, Bill. *Common Whites: Class and Culture in Antebellum North Carolina*.
    Lexington: University Press of Kentucky, 1992.
Censer, Jane Turner. *North Carolina Planters and Their Children, 1800–1860*. Baton Rouge:
    Louisiana State University Press, 1984.
Chambers, Joseph Lenoir. *The Breed and the Pasture*. Charlotte, N.C.: Stone and Barringer,
    1910.
Cimprich, John. *Slavery's End in Tennessee, 1861–1865*. Tuscaloosa: University of Alabama
    Press, 1985.
Clinton, Catherine. *The Plantation Mistress: Woman's World in the Old South*. New York:
    Pantheon Books, 1982.
——. *Tara Revisited: Women, War, and the Plantation Legend*. New York: Abbeville Press,
    1995.
Clinton, Catherine, and Nina Silber, eds. *Divided Houses: Gender and the Civil War*. New York:
    Oxford University Press, 1992.
Connor, R. D. W., ed. *A Manual of North Carolina*. Raleigh, N.C.: E. M. Uzell, 1913.
Cooper, Horton. *History of Avery County, North Carolina*. Asheville, N.C.: Biltmore Press,
    1964.
Cooper, William J., Jr. *Liberty and Slavery: Southern Politics to 1860*. New York: Knopf, 1983.
Coulter, E. Merton. *The Confederate States of America, 1861–1865*. Baton Rouge: Louisiana
    State University Press, 1950.
Cox, A. B. *Foot Prints on the Sands of Time: A History of South-western Virginia and North-
    western North Carolina*. Sparta, N.C.: Star Publishing Co., 1900.
Crass, David Colin, et al. *The Southern Colonial Backcountry: Interdisciplinary Perspectives on
    Frontier Communities*. Knoxville: University of Tennessee Press, 1998.
Crawford, Martin. *Passages of War: Ashe County, North Carolina, from the 1850s to the 1870s*.
    Charlottesville: University of Press of Virginia, 2000.
Crofts, Daniel W. *Old Southampton: Politics and Society in a Virginia County, 1834–1869*.
    Charlottesville: University Press of Virginia, 1992.
——. *Reluctant Confederates: Upper South Unionists in the Secession Crisis*. Chapel Hill:
    University of North Carolina Press, 1989.
Crow, Vernon H. *Storm in the Mountains: Thomas' Confederate Legion of Cherokee Indians and
    Mountaineers*. Cherokee, N.C.: Press of the Museum of the Cherokee Indian, 1982.
Culpepper, Marilyn Mayer. *Trials and Triumphs: The Women of the American Civil War*. East
    Lansing: Michigan State University Press, 1991.
Cunningham, Rodger. *Apples on the Flood: The Southern Mountain Experience*. Knoxville:
    University of Tennessee Press, 1987.

Current, Richard Nelson. *Lincoln's Loyalists: Union Soldiers from the Confederacy*. Boston: Northeastern University Press, 1992.

Currie, James T. *Enclave: Vicksburg and Her Plantations, 1863–1870*. Jackson: University Press of Mississippi, 1980.

Davidson, Theodore F. *Reminiscences and Traditions of Western North Carolina*. Asheville, N.C.: Service Printing Co., 1928.

Degler, Carl N. *The Other South: Southern Dissenters in the Nineteenth Century*. New York: Harper and Row, 1974.

Dew, Charles B. *Bond of Iron: Master and Slave at Buffalo Forge*. New York: W. W. Norton, 1994.

Dorgan, Howard. *Giving Glory to God in Appalachia: Worship Practices of Six Baptist Sub-Denominations*. Knoxville: University of Tennessee Press, 1988.

Dowd, Clement. *The Life of Zebulon B. Vance*. Charlotte, N.C.: Observer Printing and Publishing, 1897.

Dugger, Shepherd M. *War Trails of the Blue Ridge*. Banner Elk, N.C.: Privately printed, 1932.

Dumond, Dwight L. *The Secession Movement, 1860–1861*. New York: Macmillan, 1931.

Dunaway, Wilma A. *The First American Frontier: Transition to Capitalism in Southern Appalachia, 1700–1860*. Chapel Hill: University of North Carolina Press, 1996.

Dunn, Durwood. *An Abolitionist in the Appalachian South: Ezekiel Birdseye on Slavery, Capitalism, and Separate Statehood in East Tennessee, 1841–1846*. Knoxville: University of Tennessee Press, 1997.

——. *Cades Cove: The Life and Death of a Southern Mountain Community, 1818–1937*. Knoxville: University of Tennessee Press, 1988.

Durrill, Wayne K. *War of Another Kind: A Southern Community in the Great Rebellion*. New York: Oxford University Press, 1990.

Dyer, Thomas G. *Secret Yankees: The Unionist Circle in Confederate Atlanta*. Baltimore: Johns Hopkins University Press, 1999.

Dykeman, Wilma. *The French Broad*. New York: Rinehart and Co., 1955.

Eaton, Clement. *The Freedom-of-Thought Struggle in the Old South*. New York: Harper and Row, 1964.

Eller, Ronald D. *Miners, Millhands, and Mountaineers: Industrialization of the Appalachian South, 1880–1930*. Knoxville: University of Tennessee Press, 1982.

Escott, Paul D. *After Secession: Jefferson Davis and the Failure of Confederate Nationalism*. Baton Rouge: Louisiana State University Press, 1978.

——. *Many Excellent People: Power and Privilege in North Carolina, 1850–1900*. Chapel Hill: University of North Carolina Press, 1985.

Fain, James T. *A Partial History of Henderson County*. New York: Arno Press, 1980.

Faust, Drew Gilpin. *The Creation of Confederate Nationalism: Ideology and Identity in the Civil War South*. Baton Rouge: Louisiana State University Press, 1988.

——. *Mothers of Invention: Women of the Slaveholding South in the American Civil War*. Chapel Hill: University of North Carolina Press, 1996.

——, ed. *The Ideology of Slavery: Proslavery Thought in the Antebellum South, 1830–1860*. Baton Rouge: Louisiana State University Press, 1981.

Fellman, Michael. *Inside War: The Guerrilla Conflict in Missouri during the American Civil War*. New York: Oxford University Press, 1989.

Finger, John R. *The Eastern Band of Cherokees, 1819–1900*. Knoxville: University of Tennessee Press, 1984.

Fisher, Noel C. *War at Every Door: Partisan Politics and Guerrilla Violence in East Tennessee, 1860–1869*. Chapel Hill: University of North Carolina Press, 1997.

Fitzsimmons, Frank L. *From the Banks of the Oklawaha*. Hendersonville, N.C.: Golden Glow Publishing Co., 1976.

Fletcher, Arthur L. *Ashe County: A History*. Jefferson, N.C.: Asheve County Research Assocation, 1963.

Ford, Lacy K. *Origins of Southern Radicalism: The South Carolina Upcountry, 1800–1860*. New York: Oxford University Press, 1988.

Ford, Thomas R., ed. *The Southern Appalachian Region: A Survey*. Lexington: University of Kentucky Press, 1962.

Fossett, Mildred B. *History of McDowell County*. Marion, N.C.: McDowell County American Revolution Bicentennial Commission, 1976.

Freel, Margaret Walker. *Our Heritage: The People of Cherokee County, North Carolina*. Asheville, N.C.: Miller Printing Co., 1956.

——. *Unto the Hills*. Andrews, N.C.: Privately printed, 1976.

Friedman, Jean E. *The Enclosed Garden: Women and Community in the Evangelical South, 1830–1900*. Chapel Hill: University of North Carolina Press, 1985.

Godbold, E. Stanly, and Mattie U. Russell. *Confederate Colonel and Cherokee Chief: The Life of William Holland Thomas*. Knoxville: University of Tennessee Press, 1990.

Goodrich, Frances Louisa. *Mountain Homespun*. Knoxville: University of Tennessee Press, 1989.

Greene, Gary Franklin. *A Brief History of the Black Presence in Henderson County, North Carolina*. Asheville, N.C.: Biltmore Press, 1996.

Griffin, Clarence W. *The History of Old Tryon and Rutherford Counties, 1730–1930*. Asheville, N.C.: Miller Printing Co., 1937.

Grimsley, Mark. *The Hard Hand of War: Union Military Policy toward Southern Civilians, 1861–1865*. Cambridge: Cambridge University Press, 1996.

Hahn, Steven. *The Roots of Southern Populism: Yeomen Farmers and the Transformation of the Georgia Upcountry, 1850–1890*. New York: Oxford University Press, 1983.

Hahn, Steven, and Jonathan Prude, eds. *The Countryside in the Age of Capitalist Transformation: Essays in the Social History of Rural America*. Chapel Hill: University of North Carolina Press, 1985.

Hall, Jacquelyn Dowd, et al. *Like a Family: The Making of a Southern Cotton Mill World*. Chapel Hill: University of North Carolina Press, 1987.

Hamilton, J. G. de Roulhac. *Reconstruction in North Carolina*. Gloucester, Mass.: Peter Smith, 1964.

Harper, Margaret E. *Fort Defiance and the General*. Hickory, N.C.: Clay Printing Co., 1976.

Harris, J. William. *Plain Folk and Gentry in a Slave Society: White Liberty and Black Slavery in Augusta's Hinterlands*. Middleton, Conn.: Wesleyan University Press, 1985.

Harris, William C. *William Woods Holden: Firebrand of North Carolina Politics*. Baton Rouge: Louisiana State University Press, 1987.

Hayes, Johnson J. *The Land of Wilkes*. Wilkesboro, N.C.: Wilkes County Historical Society, 1962.

——. *The Heritage of Union County, Georgia*. Vol. 1. Waynesville, N.C.: Wadsworth Publishing Co., 1994.

Hesseltine, William B. *Civil War Prisons: A Study in War Psychology*. Columbus: Ohio State University Press, 1930.

Hicks, George L. *Appalachian Valley*. New York: Holt, Rinehart and Winston, 1976.

Higgins, Jody, ed. *Common Times: Written and Pictorial History of Yancey County*. Burnsville, N.C.: Yancey Graphics, 1981.

Hill, Daniel Harvey. *A History of North Carolina in the War between the States*. 2 vols. Raleigh: Edwards and Broughton, 1926.

Hilliard, Sam B. *Hog Meat and Hoecake: Food Supply in the Old South, 1840–1860*. Carbondale: Southern Illinois University Press, 1972.

Hollingsworth, J. C. *History of Surry County*. Greensboro, N.C.: W. H. Fisher Co., 1935.

Hsiung, David C. *Two Worlds in the Tennessee Mountains: Exploring the Origins of Appalachian Stereotypes*. Lexington: University Press of Kentucky, 1997.

Hughes, N. Colin. *Hendersonville in Civil War Times*. Hendersonville, N.C.: Privately published, 1936.

Hyde, Samuel C., Jr., ed. *Plain Folk of the South Revisited*. Baton Rouge: Louisiana State University Press, 1997.

Inscoe, John C. *Mountain Masters: Slavery and the Sectional Crisis in Western North Carolina*. Knoxville: University of Tennessee Press, 1989.

——, ed. *Appalachia in Black and White: Race Relations in the Nineteenth Century Mountain South*. Lexington: University Press of Kentucky, forthcoming.

Jeffrey, Thomas E. *State Parties and National Politics: North Carolina, 1815–1861*. Athens: University of Georgia Press, 1989.

——. *Thomas Lanier Clingman: "Fire Eater" from the Carolina Mountains*. Athens: University of Georgia Press, 1998.

Johnson, Guion Griffin. *Ante-Bellum North Carolina: A Social History*. Chapel Hill: University of North Carolina Press, 1937.

Johnson, Michael P. *Toward a Patriarchal Republic: The Secession of Georgia*. Baton Rouge: Louisiana State University Press, 1977.

Kenzer, Robert C. *Kinship and Neighborhood in a Southern Community: Orange County, North Carolina, 1849–1881*. Knoxville: University of Tennessee Press, 1987.

Kephart, Horace. *Our Southern Highlanders: A Narrative of Adventure in the Southern Appalachians and a Study of Life among the Mountaineers*. New York: Macmillan, 1936.

Klingberg, Frank W. *The Southern Claims Commission*. Berkeley: University of California Press, 1955.

Konkle, Burton A. *John Motley Morehead and the Development of North Carolina, 1796–1966*. Philadelphia: William J. Campbell, 1922.

Kruman, Marc W. *Parties and Politics in North Carolina, 1836–1865*. Baton Rouge: Louisiana State University Press, 1983.

Lee, Jean B. *The Price of Nationhood: The American Revolution in Charles County*. New York: W. W. Norton, 1994.

Lewis, Ronald L. *Black Coal Miners in America: Race, Class, and Community Conflict, 1780–1980*. Lexington: University Press of Kentucky, 1987.

——. *Coal, Iron, and Slaves: Industrial Slavery in Maryland and Virginia, 1715–1865*. Westport, Conn.: Greenwood Press, 1979.

Lonn, Ella. *Desertion during the Civil War*. New York: Century Co., 1928.

——. *Salt as a Factor in the Confederacy*. Tuscaloosa: University of Alabama Press, 1965.

McCaslin, Richard B. *Portraits of Conflict: A Photographic History of North Carolina in the Civil War*. Fayetteville: University of Arkansas Press, 1997.

——. *Tainted Breeze: The Great Hanging at Gainesville, Texas, 1862*. Baton Rouge: Louisiana State University Press, 1994.

McCormick, James M. *Personnel of the Conventions of 1861*. Chapel Hill: James Sprunt Spruill Historical Studies, No. 1, 1900.

McCoy, George W. *The Battle of Asheville*. Asheville, N.C.: Buncombe County Confederate Centennial Committee, 1965.

McCrary, Mary Jane. *Transylvania Beginnings: A History*. Easley, S.C.: Southern Historical
      Press, 1984.
McCurry, Stephanie. *Masters of Small Worlds: Yeoman Households, Gender Relations, and the
      Political Culture of the Antebellum South Carolina Low Country*. New York: Oxford
      University Press, 1995.
McGeachy, Neill R. *Confronted by Challenge: A History of the Presbytery of Concord, 1795–1973*.
      Concord, N.C.: Delmar Co., 1985.
McKenzie, Robert Tracy. *One South or Many? Plantation Belt and Upcountry in Civil War Era
      Tennessee*. New York: Cambridge University Press, 1994.
McKinney, Gordon B. *Southern Mountain Republicans, 1865–1900: Politics and the
      Appalachian Community*. Chapel Hill: University of North Carolina Press, 1978.
McPherson, James M. *Battle Cry of Freedom: The Civil War Era*. New York: Ballantine Books,
      1988.
——. *For Cause and Comrades: Why Men Fought in the Civil War*. New York: Oxford
      University Press, 1997.
Manarin, Louis H., and Weymouth T. Jordan. *North Carolina Troops, 1861–1865: A Roster*. Vol.
      7. Raleigh: North Carolina Division of Archives and History, 1966–.
Marsh, Blanch. *Historic Flat Rock*. Asheville, N.C.: Biltmore Press, 1961.
Maslowski, Peter. *Treason Must Be Made Odious: Military Occupation and Wartime
      Reconstruction in Nashville, Tennessee, 1862–1865*. Millwood, N.Y.: KTO Press, 1978.
Massey, Mary Elizabeth. *Bonnet Brigades*. New York: Knopf, 1966.
——. *Ersatz in the Confederacy*. Baton Rouge: Louisiana State University Press, 1952.
Medford, Clark. *The Early History of Haywood County*. Waynesville, N.C.: Privately printed,
      1961.
Memminger, Edward Read. *An Historical Sketch of Flat Rock*. Asheville, N.C.: Stephens Press,
      1954.
Miller, Wilbur R. *Revenuers and Moonshiners: Enforcing Federal Liquor Law in the Mountain
      South, 1865–1900*. Chapel Hill: University of North Carolina Press, 1991.
Mills, Gary B. *Southern Loyalists in the Civil War: The Southern Claims Commission, A
      Composite Directory of Case Files Created by the U.S. Commissioner of Claims, 1871–1880*.
      Baltimore, Md.: Genealogical Publishing Co., 1994.
Mitchell, Memory F. *Legal Aspects of Conscription and Exemption in North Carolina, 1861–
      1865*. Chapel Hill: University of North Carolina Press, 1965.
Mitchell, Reid. *Civil War Soldiers*. New York: Viking Press, 1988.
——. *The Vacant Chair: The Northern Soldier Leaves Home*. New York: Oxford University
      Press, 1993.
Mitchell, Robert D., ed. *Appalachian Frontiers: Settlement, Society, and Development in the
      Preindustrial Era*. Lexington: University Press of Kentucky, 1990.
——. *Commercialism and Frontier: Perspectives on the Early Shenandoah Valley*. Charlottesville:
      University Press of Virginia, 1977.
Mohr, Clarence L. *On the Threshold of Freedom: Masters and Slaves in Civil War Georgia*.
      Athens: University of Georgia Press, 1986.
Moore, Albert Burton. *Conscription and Conflict in the Confederacy*. New York: Macmillan,
      1924.
Morgan, Lynda J. *Emancipation in Virginia's Tobacco Belt, 1850–1870*. Athens: University of
      Georgia Press, 1992.
Morton, Patricia, ed. *Discovering the Women in Slavery: Emancipating Perpsectives on the
      American Past*. Athens: University of Georgia Press, 1996.

Mull, J. Alex, and Gordon Boger. *Recollections of the Catawba Valley*. Boone, N.C.: Appalachian Consortium Press, 1983.

Nagel, Paul C. *One Nation Indivisible: The Union in American Thought, 1776–1861*. New York: Oxford University Press, 1964.

Noe, Kenneth W. *Southwest Virginia's Railroad: Modernization and the Sectional Crisis*. Urbana: University of Illinois Press, 1994.

Noe, Kenneth W., and Shannon H. Wilson, eds. *The Civil War in Appalachia: Collected Essays*. Knoxville: University of Tennessee Press, 1997.

Norton, Clarence C. *The Democratic Party in Ante-Bellum North Carolina, 1835–1861*. Chapel Hill: University of North Carolina Press, 1930.

Oakes, James. *The Ruling Race: A History of American Slaveholders*. New York: Knopf, 1982.

Oates, Stephen B. *With Malice toward None: The Life of Abraham Lincoln*. New York: Harper and Row, 1977.

Orser, Charles E., Jr. *Material Bases of the Postbellum Tenant Plantation*. Athens: University of Georgia Press, 1988.

Otto, John Solomon. *Southern Agriculture during the Civil War Era, 1860–1880*. Westport, Conn.: Greenwood Press, 1994.

Owens, Harry P., and James J. Cooke, eds. *The Old South in the Crucible of War*. Jackson: University of Mississippi Press, 1983.

Paludan, Phillip Shaw. *Victims: A True Story of the Civil War*. Knoxville: University of Tennessee Press, 1981.

Patton, Sadie Smathers. *A Condensed History of Flat Rock, the Little Charleson of the Mountains*. Asheville, N.C.: Church Printing Co., n.d.

——. *The Kingdom of the Happy Land*. Asheville, N.C.: Stephens Press, 1957.

——. *The Story of Henderson County*. Asheville, N.C.: Miller Printing, 1947.

Pearsall, Marion. *Little Smoky Ridge: The Natural History of a Southern Appalachian Neighborhood*. Tuscaloosa: University of Alabama Press, 1959.

Pegg, Herbert D. *The Whig Party in North Carolina*. Chapel Hill: Colonial Press, 1968.

Phifer, Edward W. *Burke: The History of a North Carolina County, 1777–1920*. Morganton, N.C.: Privately published, 1977.

Polk, William M. *Leonidas Polk, Bishop and General*. New York: Longmans, Green, and Co., 1915.

Potter, David M. *The Impending Crisis, 1848–1861*. New York: Harper and Row, 1976.

Powers, Elizabeth D., and Mark E. Hannah. *Cataloochee: Lost Settlement of the Smokies*. Charleston, S.C.: Powers-Hannah Publishers, 1982.

Price, R. E. *Rutherford County: Economic and Social*. Chapel Hill: University of North Carolina Press, 1918.

Pudup, Mary Beth, Dwight Billings, and Altina L. Waller, eds. *Appalachia in the Making: The Mountain South in the Nineteenth Century*. Chapel Hill: University of North Carolina Press, 1996.

Puglisi, Michael J., ed. *Diversity and Accommodation: Essays on the Cultural Composition of the Virginia Frontier*. Knoxville: University of Tennessee Press, 1997.

Rable, George. *Civil Wars: Women and the Crisis of Southern Nationalism*. Urbana: University of Illinois Press, 1989.

Ramage, James A. *Rebel Raider: The Life of John Hunt Morgan*. Lexington: University Press of Kentucky, 1986.

Ramsdell, Charles W. *Behind the Lines in the Southern Confederacy*. New York: Greenwood Press, 1944.

Rasmussen, Barbara. *Absentee Landowning and Exploitation in West Virginia, 1760–1920*. Lexington: University Press of Kentucky, 1994.

Ready, Milton. *Asheville, Land of the Sky: An Illustrated History*. Northridge, Calif.: Windsor Publications, 1986.

Rogers, William Warren, Jr. *Confederate Home Front: Montgomery during the Civil War*. Tuscaloosa: University of Alabama Press, 1999.

Rosen, Robert N. *Confederate Charleston: An Illustrated History of the City and People during the Civil War*. Columbia: University of South Carolina Press, 1994.

Royce, Edward. *The Origins of Southern Sharecropping*. Philadelphia: Temple University Press, 1993.

Royster, Charles. *The Destructive War: William Tecumseh Sherman, Stonewall Jackson, and the Americans*. New York: Vintage Books, 1991.

Salstrom, Paul. *Appalachia's Path to Dependency: Rethinking a Region's Economic History, 1790–1940*. Lexington: University Press of Kentucky, 1994.

Scott, Anne Firor. *The Southern Lady: From Pedestal to Politics, 1830–1930*. Chicago: University of Chicago Press, 1970.

Shapiro, Henry D. *Appalachia on Our Mind: The Southern Mountains and Mountaineers in the American Consciousness, 1870–1920*. Chapel Hill: University of North Carolina Press, 1978.

Shepherd, Ruth W., ed. *The Heritage of Ashe County, North Carolina*. Winston-Salem, N.C.: Hunter Publishing Co., 1984.

Sheppard, Muriel E. *Cabins in the Laurel*. Chapel Hill: University of North Carolina Press, 1935.

Shore, Laurence. *Southern Capitalists: The Ideological Leadership of an Elite, 1832–1885*. Chapel Hill: University of North Carolina Press, 1986.

Silber, Nina. *The Romance of Reunion: Northerners and the South, 1865–1900*. Chapel Hill: University of North Carolina Press, 1993.

Silver, James W. *Confederate Morale and Church Propaganda*. Tuscaloosa: University of Alabama Press, 1957.

Sitterson, J. Carlyle. *The Secession Movement in North Carolina*. Chapel Hill: University of North Carolina Press, 1939.

Smathers, George H. *The History of Land Titles in Western North Carolina*. Asheville, N.C.: Miller Printing Co., 1938.

Smith, C. D. *A Brief History of Macon County*. Franklin, N.C.: Privately printed, 1891.

Snay, Mitchell. *Gospel of Disunion: Religion and Separatism in the Antebellum South*. Chapel Hill: University of North Carolina Press, 1993.

Sondley, F. A. *A History of Buncombe County, North Carolina*. 2 vols. Asheville, N.C.: Advocate Printing Co., 1930.

Starobin, Robert S. *Industrial Slaves in the Old South*. New York: Oxford University Press, 1970.

Stealey, John E., III. *The Antebellum Kanawha Salt Business and Western Markets*. Lexington: University Press of Kentucky, 1993.

Sutherland, Daniel E. *Seasons of War: The Ordeal of a Confederate Community, 1861–1865*. New York: Free Press, 1995.

———, ed. *Guerrillas, Unionists, and Violence on the Confederate Home Front*. Fayetteville: University of Arkansas Press, 1999.

Sutton, Jessie, ed. *The Heritage of Macon County, North Carolina*. Winston-Salem, N.C.: Hunter Publishing Co., 1987.

Tatum, Georgia Lee. *Disloyalty in the Confederacy*. Chapel Hill: University of North Carolina Press, 1934.

Taylor, Rosser H. *Slaveholding in North Carolina: An Economic View*. Chapel Hill: University of North Carolina Press, 1926.

Thomas, Emory M. *The Confederacy as Revolutionary Experience*. Englewood Cliffs, N.J.: Prentice-Hall, 1971.

——. *The Confederate Nation, 1861–1865*. New York: Harper and Row, 1979.

——. *The Confederate State of Richmond: A Biography of the Capital*. Austin: University of Texas Press, 1971.

Thompson, Ernest Trice. *Presbyterians in the South, 1607–1861*. 2 vols. Richmond, Va.: John Knox Press, 1963.

Trelease, Allen W. *The North Carolina Railroad, 1849–1871, and the Modernization of North Carolina*. Chapel Hill: University of North Carolina Press, 1991.

——. *White Terror: The Ku Klux Klan Conspiracy and Southern Reconstruction*. New York: Harper and Row, 1971.

Tripp, Steven Elliott. *Yankee Town, Southern City: Race and Class Relations in Civil War Lynchburg*. New York: New York University Press, 1997.

Trotter, William R. *Bushwhackers! The Mountains*. Vol. 2 of *The Civil War in North Carolina*. Greensboro, N.C.: Signal Research, 1988.

Tucker, Glenn. *Zeb Vance: Champion of Personal Freedom*. Indianapolis: Bobbs-Merrill, 1965.

Van Noppen, Ina W. *Stoneman's Last Raid*. Raleigh: N.C. State University Printing Office, 1966.

Van Noppen, Ina W., and John J. Van Noppen. *Western North Carolina since the Civil War*. Boone, N.C.: Appalachian Consortium Press, 1973.

Vinovskis, Maris A., ed. *Toward a Social History of the American Civil War: Exploratory Essays*. New York: Cambridge University Press, 1990.

Walker, Peter F. *Vicksburg: A People at War, 1860–1865*. Chapel Hill: University of North Carolina Press, 1960.

Waller, Altina L. *Feud: Hatfields, McCoys, and Social Change in Appalachia, 1860–1900*. Chapel Hill: University of North Carolina Press, 1988.

Warch, Richard, and Jonathan F. Fauton, eds. *John Brown*. Englewood Cliffs, N.J.: Prentice-Hall, 1973.

Ward, Doris Cline, ed. *The Heritage of Old Buncombe County*. Vol. 1. Winston-Salem, N.C.: Hunter Publishing Co., 1981.

Warner, Ezra J., and W. Buck Yearns. *Biographical Directory of the Confederate Congress*. Baton Rouge: Louisiana State University Press, 1975.

Weller, Jack. *Yesterday's People: Life in Contemporary Appalachia*. Lexington: University Press of Kentucky, 1965.

Wellman, Manly Wade. *Dead and Gone: Classic Crimes of North Carolina*. Chapel Hill: University of North Carolina Press, 1954.

——. *The Kingdom of Madison: A Southern Mountain Fastness and Its People*. Chapel Hill: University of North Carolina Press, 1973.

White, M. L. *A History of the Life of Amos Owens*. Rutherfordton, N.C.: Privately printed, 1901.

Whites, LeeAnn. *The Civil War as a Crisis in Gender: Augusta, Georgia, 1860–1890*. Athens: University of Georgia Press, 1995.

Wiley, Bell I. *The Plain People of the Confederacy*. Baton Rouge: Louisiana State University Press, 1943

Williams, David. *The Georgia Gold Rush: Twenty-niners, Cherokees, and Gold Fever*. Columbia: University of South Carolina Press, 1993.

Williams, Dewey E. *A Civil War Camp in North Carolina: Burke County's Camp Vance.*
     Morganton, N.C.: Privately printed, 1977.
Williams, Max R., ed. *The History of Jackson County.* Sylva, N.C.: Jackson County Historical
     Association, 1987.
Wilson, Samuel T. *The Southern Mountaineers.* New York: J. J. Little and Ives, 1914.
Wolfe, Thomas. *The Hills Beyond.* New York, 1935. Reprint, New York: New American Library,
     1982.
Wright, Gavin. *Old South, New South: Revolutions in the Southern Economy since the Civil War.*
     New York: Basic Books, 1986.
Yates, Richard E. *The Confederacy and Zeb Vance.* Tuscaloosa, Ala.: Confederate Publishing,
     1958.

Articles and Essays

Andrew, Rod, Jr. "Martial Spirit, Christian Values, and the Lost Cause: Military Education at
     North Georgia College, 1871–1915." *Georgia Historical Quarterly* 79 (Fall 1996): 486–505.
Anglin, Mary K. "Lives on the Margin: Rediscovering the Women of Antebellum Western North
     Carolina." In *Appalachia in the Making: The Mountain South in the Nineteenth Century,*
     edited by Mary Beth Pudup, Dwight B. Billings, and Altina L. Waller, 185–209. Chapel
     Hill: University of North Carolina Press, 1995.
Ash, Stephen V. "Poor Whites in the Occupied South, 1861–1865." *Journal of Southern History*
     58 (February 1991): 39–62.
Auman, William T. "Neighbor against Neighbor: The Inner Civil War in the Randolph County
     Area of Confederate North Carolina." *North Carolina Historical Review* 61 (January
     1984): 59–92.
Auman, William T., and David D. Scarboro. "The Heroes of America in Civil War North
     Carolina." *North Carolina Historical Review* 58 (October 1981): 327–63.
Baker, Robin E. "Class Conflict and Political Upheaval: The Transformation of North Carolina
     Politics during the Civil War." *North Carolina Historical Review* 59 (April 1992): 148–78.
Bardolph, Richard. "Confederate Dilemma: North Carolina Troops and the Deserter Problem."
     Parts 1 and 2. *North Carolina Historical Review* 66 (January 1989): 61–86; 67 (April
     1989): 179–210.
———. "Inconstant Rebels: Desertion of North Carolina Troops in the Civil War." *North
     Carolina Historical Review* 41 (April 1964): 163–89.
Bearman, Peter S. "Desertion as Localism: Army Unit Solidarity and Group Norms in the U.S.
     Civil War." *Social Forces* 70 (December 1991): 321–42.
Belcher, John C. "Population Growth and Characteristics." In *The Southern Appalachian
     Region: A Survey,* edited by Thomas R. Ford, 37–53. Lexington: University Press of
     Kentucky, 1962.
Billings, Dwight B. "(Re)Introducing Appalachia: Talking Back to Stereotypes." Introduction to
     Confronting Appalachian Stereotypes: Back Talk from an American Region, edited by
     Dwight B. Billings, Gurney Norman, and Katherine Ledford, 3–20. Lexington: University
     Press of Kentucky, 1999.
Billings, Dwight B., and Kathleen M. Blee. "Agriculture and Poverty in the Kentucky
     Mountains: Beech Creek, 1850–1910." In *Appalachia in the Making: The Mountain South
     in the Nineteenth Century,* edited by Mary Beth Pudup, Dwight B. Billings, and Altina L.
     Waller, 233–69. Chapel Hill: University of North Carolina Press, 1995.
———. "Appalachian Inequality in the Nineteenth Century: The Case of Beech Creek, Kentucky."
     Journal of the Appalachian Studies Association 4 (1992): 113–23.

Billings, Dwight B., Kathleen M. Blee, and Louis Swanson. "Culture, Family, and Community in Preindustrial Appalachia." *Appalachian Journal* 13 (Winter 1986): 154–70.

Blaser, Kent. "North Carolina and John Brown's Raid." *Civil War History* 24 (December 1978): 295–320.

Blethen, H. Tyler, and Curtis W. Wood. "The Antebellum Iron Industry in Western North Carolina." *Journal of Appalachian Studies Association* 4 (1992): 79–87.

——. "The Appalachian Frontier and the Southern Frontier: A Comparative Perspective." *Journal of the Appalachian Studies Assocation* 3 (1991): 36–47.

——. "The Pioneer Experience to 1851." In *The History of Jackson County*, edited by Max R. Williams, 67–100. Sylva, N.C.: Jackson County Historical Society, 1987.

——. "A Trader on the Western North Carolina Frontier." In *Appalachian Frontiers: Settlement, Society, and Development in the Preindustrial Era*, edited by Robert D. Mitchell, 150–65. Lexington: University Press of Kentucky, 1990.

Boyd, William K. "North Carolina on the Eve of Secession." *Annual Report of the American Historical Association for the Year 1910* (Washington, D.C.: AHA, 1912): 165–77.

Bryan, Charles F., Jr. "'Tories' amidst Rebels: Confederate Occupation of East Tennessee, 1861–1863." *East Tennessee Historical Society's Publications* 60 (1988): 3–22.

Burnett, Edmund C. "Hog Raising and Hog Driving in the Region of the French Broad River." *Agricultural History* 20 (April 1946): 86–103.

Butts, Donald C. "The "Irrepressible Conflict': Slave Taxation and North Carolina's Gubernatorial Election of 1860." *North Carolina Historical Review* 58 (January 1981): 44–66.

Bynum, Victoria. "War within a War: Women's Participation in the Revolt of the North Carolina Piedmont, 1863–1865." *Frontiers* 9 (1987): 43–49.

Carlton, David L. "The Revolution from Above: The National Market and the Beginnings of Industrialization in North Carolina." *Journal of American History* 87 (September 1990): 450–54.

Chesson, Michael. "Harlots or Heroines? A New Look at the Richmond Bread Riots." *Virginia Magazine of History and Biography* 92 (April 1984): 131–75.

Clark, Ernest James, Jr. "Aspects of the North Carolina Slave Code, 1815–1869." *North Carolina Historical Review* 39 (Spring 1962): 148–64.

Clinton, Catherine. "Sex and the Sectional Crisis." In *Taking Off the White Gloves: Southern Women and Women Historians*, edited by Michele Gillespie and Catherine Clinton, 43–63. Columbia: University of Missouri Press, 1998.

Crawford, Martin. "Confederate Volunteering and Enlistment in Ashe County, North Carolina." *Civil War History* 37 (March 1991): 29–50.

——. "The Dynamics of Mountain Unionism: Federal Volunteers of Ashe County, North Carolina." In *The Civil War in Appalachia: Collected Essays*, edited by Kenneth W. Noe and Shannon H. Wilson, 55–78. Knoxville: University of Tennessee Press, 1997.

——. "Mountain Farmers and the Market Economy: Ashe County during the 1850s." *North Carolina Historical Review* 72 (October 1994): 430–50.

——. "Political Society in a Southern Mountain Community: Ashe County, North Carolina, 1850–1861." *Journal of Southern History* 55 (August 1989): 373–90.

Crofts, Daniel W. "The Union Party of 1861 and the Secession Crisis." *Perspectives in American History* 9 (1978–79): 327–76.

Davis, Robert S., Jr. "Forgotten Union Guerrilla Fighters in the North Georgia Mountains." *North Georgia Journal* 5 (Summer 1988): 28–33.

Davis-DeEulis, Marilyn. "Slavery on the Margins of the Virginia Frontier: African American Literacy in Western Kanawha and Cabell Counties, 1795–1840." In *Diversity and*

Accommodation: Essays on the Cultural Composition of the Virginia Frontier, edited by
Michael J. Puglisi, 194–212. Knoxville: University of Tennessee Press, 1997.

Deyton, Jason B. "The Toe River Valley to 1865." *North Carolina Historical Review* 24
(October 1947): 423–66.

Dodge, David. "The Cave Dwellers of the Confederacy." *Atlantic Monthly* 68 (October 1891).

Douglas, Clarence D. "Conscription and the Writ of Habeas Corpus in North Carolina during
the Civil War." *Trinity College Historical Society Historical Papers* 14 (1922): 129–42.

Drake, Richard B. "Slavery and Antislavery in Appalachia." *Appalachia Heritage* 14 (Winter
1986): 25–33.

——. "Southern Appalachia and the South: A Region within a Section." *Journal of the
Appalachian Studies Association* 3 (1991): 18–27.

Dunaway, Wilma A. "Diaspora, Death, and Sexual Exploitation: Slave Families at Risk in the
Mountain South." *Appalachian Journal* 26 (Winter 1999): 128–49.

——. "Speculators and Settler Capitalists: Unthinking the Mythology about Appalachian
Landholding, 1790–1860." In *Appalachia in the Making: The Mountain South in the
Nineteenth Century*, edited by Mary Beth Pudup, Dwight B. Billings, and Atlina L. Waller,
50–75. Chapel Hill: University of North Carolina Press, 1995.

Dykeman, Wilma. "Appalachia in Context." In *An Appalachia Symposium*, edited by J. W.
Williamson, 28–42. Boone, N.C.: Appalachian Consortium Press, 1977.

Eaton, Clement. "Slave Hiring in the Upper South: A Step toward Freedom." *Mississippi Valley
Historical Review* 46 (March 1960): 107–14.

Eller, Ronald D. "Class, Conflict, and Modernization in the Appalachian South." *Appalachian
Journal* 10 (Winter 1983): 183–86.

——. "Land and Family: An Historical View of Preindustrial Appalachia." *Appalachian Journal*
13 (Winter 1986): 154–70.

——. "The Search for Community in Appalachia." In *Contemporary Appalachia: In Search of a
Usable Past*, edited by Carl Ross. 1–19. Boone, N.C.: Appalachian Consortium Press,
1987.

Elliott, Robert N. "The Nat Turner Insurrection as Reported in the North Carolina Press."
North Carolina Historical Review 38 (January 1961): 1–18.

Escott, Paul D. "Clinton A. Cilley, Yankee War Hero in the Postwar South: A Study in the
Compatibility of Regional Values." *North Carolina Historical Review* 68 (October 1991):
404–26.

——. " 'The Cry of the Sufferers': The Problem of Welfare in the Confederacy." *Civil War
History* 23 (September 1977): 228–40.

——. "The Failure of Confederate Nationalism: The Old South's Class System in the Crucible
of War." In *The Old South in the Crucible of War*, edited by Harry P. Owens and James J.
Cooke, 15–28. Jackson: University of Mississippi Press, 1983.

——. "The Moral Economy of the Crowd in Confederate North Carolina." *Maryland Historian*
13 (Summer 1982): 1–17.

——. "Poverty and Governmental Aid for the Poor in Confederate North Carolina." *North
Carolina Historical Review* 61 (October 1984): 462–80.

Escott, Paul D., and Jeffrey J. Crow, "The Social Order and Violent Disorder: An Analysis of
North Carolina in the Revolution and the Civil War." *Journal of Southern History* 52
(August 1986): 373–402.

Eslinger, Ellen. "The Shape of Slavery on Virginia's Kentucky Frontier, 1775–1800." In
Diversity and Accommodation: Essays on the Cultural Composition of the Virginia Frontier,
edited by Michael J. Puglisi, 172–93. Knoxville: University of Tennessee Press, 1997.

Faust, Drew Gilpin. "Altars of Sacrifice: Confederate Women and the Narratives of War." *Journal of American History* 76 (March 1990): 1200–1228.

——. "'Trying to Do a Man's Business': Slavery, Violence and Gender in the American Civil War." *Gender and History* 4 (Summer 1992): 192–208.

Fellman, Michael. "Women and Guerrilla Warfare." In *Divided Houses: Gender and the Civil War*, edited by Catherine Clinton and Nina Silber, 147–65. New York: Oxford University Press, 1992.

Finger, John R. "Cherokee Accommodation and Persistence in the Southern Appalachians." In *Appalachia in the Making: The Mountain South in the Nineteenth Century*, edited by Mary Beth Pudup, Dwight B. Billings, and Altina L. Waller, 25–49. Chapel Hill: University of North Carolina Press, 1995.

——. "The North Carolina Cherokees, 1838–1866: Traditionalism, Progressivism, and the Affirmation of State Citizenship." *Journal of Cherokee Studies* 5 (Spring 1980): 17–29.

Floyd, William B. "The Asheville Armory and Rifle." *Bulletin of the American Society of Arms Collectors* 44 (1981): 21–23.

Ford, Lacy K. "Rednecks and Merchants: Economic Development and Social Tensions in the South Carolina Upcountry, 1865–1900." *Journal of American History* 71 (September 1984): 294–318.

——. "Yeoman Farmers in the South Carolina Upcountry: Changing Production Patterns in the Late Antebellum Period." *Agricultural History* 60 (Fall 1986): 17–37.

Fox-Genovese, Elizabeth. "Women in Agriculture during the Nineteenth Century." In *Agriculture and National Development: Views on the Nineteenth Century*, edited by Lou Ferleger, 267–301. Ames: Iowa State University Press, 1990.

Gass, W. Conrad. "'The Misfortune of a High-Minded and Honorable Gentleman': W. W. Avery and the Southern Code of Honor." *North Carolina Historical Review* 61 (Summer 1979): 278–97.

Genovese, Eugene D. "Yeoman Farmers in a Slaveholders' Democracy." *Agricultural History* 49 (April 1975): 331–42.

Green, Fletcher M. "Democracy in the Old South." *Journal of Southern History* 12 (February 1946): 3–23.

Groce, W. Todd. "The Social Origins of East Tennessee's Confederate Leadership." In *The Civil War in Appalachia: Collected Essays*, edited by Kenneth W. Noe and Shannon H. Wilson, 30–55. Knoxville: University of Tennessee Press, 1997.

Hahn, Steven. "The Unmaking of the Southern Yeomanry: The Transformation of the Georgia Upcountry, 1860–1890." In *The Countryside in the Age of Capitalist Transformation: Essays in the Social History of Rural America*, edited by Steven Hahn and Jonathan Prude, 182–98. Chapel Hill: University of North Carolina Press, 1985.

Hall, James O. "The Shelton Laurel Massacre: Murder in the North Carolina Mountains." *Blue & Gray* (February 1991): 20–26.

Hall, Van Beck. "The Politics of Appalachian Virginia, 1790–1830." In *Appalachian Frontiers: Settlement, Society, and Development in the Preindustrial Era*, edited by Robert D. Mitchell, 166–86. Lexington: University Press of Kentucky, 1991.

Hallock, Judith Lee. "The Role of Community in Civil War Desertion." *Civil War History* 29 (June 1983): 123–34.

Henretta, James A. "Families and Farms: *Mentalite* in Pre-Industrial America." *William & Mary Quarterly*, 3rd ser., 35 (January 1978): 3–32.

Hesseltine, William B. "The Propaganda Literature of Confederate Prisons." *Journal of Southern History* 1 (February 1935): 22–40.

——. "The Underground Railroad from Confederate Prisons to East Tennessee." *East Tennessee Historical Society Publications* 2 (1930): 55–69.

Hofstra, Warren R., and Robert D. Mitchell. "Town and Country in Backcountry Virginia: Winchester and the Shenandoah Valley, 1730–1800." *Journal of Southern History* 59 (August 1993): 619–46.

Honey, Michael K. "The War within the Confederacy: White Unionists of North Carolina." *Prologue* (Summer 1986): 75–93.

Houkek, John T., and Charles F. Heller Jr. "Searching for Nineteenth-Century Farm Tenants." *Historical Methods* (Spring 1986).

Howard, Victor B. "John Brown's Raid at Harpers Ferry and the Sectional Crisis in North Carolina." *North Carolina Historical Review* 55 (October 1978): 396–420.

Hsiung, David C. "How Isolated Was Appalachia? Upper East Tennessee, 1780–1835." *Appalachian Journal* 14 (Summer 1989): 336–49.

——. " 'Seeing' Early Appalachian Communities through the Lens of History, Geography, and Sociology." In *The Southern Colonial Backcountry: Interdisciplinary Perspectives on Frontier Communities*, edited by David Colin Crass et al., 42–58. Knoxville: University of Tennessee Press, 1998.

Inscoe, John C. "Coping in Confederate Appalachia: Portrait of a Mountain Woman and Her Community at War." *North Carolina Historical Review* 59 (October 1992): 388–413.

——. "Diversity in Antebellum Mountain Life: The Towns of Western North Carolina." In *The Many Faces of Appalachia: Proceedings of the 7th Annual Appalachian Studies Conference*, edited by Sam Gray, 153–68. Boone, N.C.: Appalachia Consortium Press, 1985.

——. "The 1864 Slave Purchases of Mary Bell: The Civil War's Empowerment of an Appalachian Woman." In *Discovering the Women in Slavery: Emancipating Perspectives on the American Past*, 61–81. Athens: University of Georgia Press, 1996.

——. "Fatherly Advice on Secession: Edward Jones Erwin's Letters to His Son at Davidson College, 1860–1861." *American Presbyterians* 69 (Summer 1991): 97–109.

——. "Mountain Masters: Slaveholding in Western North Carolina." *North Carolina Historical Review* 61 (April 1984): 143–73.

——. "Mountain Masters as Confederate Opportunists: The Profitability of Slavery in Western North Carolina, 1861–1865." *Slavery & Abolition* 16 (April 1995): 85–110.

——. "Mountain Unionism, Secession, and Regional Self-Image: The Contrasting Cases of Western North Carolina and East Tennessee." In *Looking South: Chapters in the Story of an American Region*, edited by Winfred B. Moore Jr. and Joseph F. Tripp, 115–32. Westport, Conn.: Greenwood Press, 1989.

——. " 'Moving through Deserter Country': Fugitive Accounts of the Inner Civil War in Southern Appalachia." In *The Civil War in Appalachia: Collected Essays*, edited by Kenneth W. Noe and Shannon H. Wilson, 159–86. Knoxville: University of Tennessee Press, 1997.

——. "Olmsted in Appalachia: A Connecticut Yankee Encounters Slavery and Racism in the Southern Highlands, 1954." *Slavery & Abolition* 9 (September 1988): 171–82.

——. "Race and Racism in Southern Appalachia: Myths, Realities, and Ambiguities." In *Appalachia in the Making: The Mountain South in the Nineteenth Century*, edited by Mary Beth Pudup, Dwight B. Billings, and Altina L. Waller, 103–31. Chapel Hill: University of North Carolina Press, 1995.

——. "Thomas Clingman, Mountain Whiggery, and the Southern Cause." *Civil War History* 33 (March 1987): 42–62.

Jeffrey, Thomas E. " 'Beyond Free Suffrage': North Carolina Parties and the Convention Movement of the 1850s." *North Carolina Historical Review* 62 (October 1985): 387–419.

——. "County Divisions: A Forgotten Issue in Antebellum North Carolina Politics." Parts 1 and 2. *North Carolina Historical Review* 65 (July 1988): 314–54; (October 1988): 469–91.

——. "Internal Improvements and Political Parties in Antebellum North Carolina." *North Carolina Historical Review* 55 (April 1978): 11–56.

——. "National Issues, Local Interests, and the Transformation of Antebellum North Carolina Politics." *Journal of Southern History* 50 (February 1984): 43–74.

——. " 'Thunder from the Mountains': Thomas Lanier Clingman and the End of Whig Supremacy in North Carolina." *North Carolina Historical Review* 56 (October 1979): 366–95.

Johnson, Guion Griffis. "The Landless People of Antebellum North Carolina." *Carolina Comments* (January 1983): 23–32.

Klotter, James C. "The Black South and White Appalachia." *Journal of American History* 66 (March 1980).

Kruman, Marc W. "Dissent in the Confederacy: The North Carolina Experience." *Civil War History* 27 (December 1981): 293–311.

——. "Thomas L. Clingman and the Whig Party: A Reconsideration." *North Carolina Historical Review* 64 (January 1987): 1–17.

Kulikoff, Allan J. "The Transition to Capitalism in Rural America." *William & Mary Quarterly*, 3rd ser. (January 1989).

Lambert, Robert S. "Logging the Great Smokies, 1880–1930." *Tennessee Historical Quarterly* 21 (December 1961): 350–63.

——. "The Oconaluftee Valley, 1800–1860: A Study of the Sources for Mountain History." *North Carolina Historical Review* 35 (October 1958): 415–26.

Lerner, Eugene M. "Inflation in the Confederacy." In *Studies in the Quantity Theory of Money*, edited by Milton Friedman, 160–78. Chicago: University of Chicago Press, 1956.

Levine, David. "Consumer Goods and Capitalist Modernization." *Journal of Interdisciplinary History* 22 (Summer 1991): 67–77.

Lewis, Ronald L. "Beyond Isolation and Homogeneity: Diversity and the History of Appalachia." In *Confronting Appalachian Stereotypes: Back Talk from an American Region*, edited by Dwight B. Billings, Gurney Norman, and Katherine Ledford, 21–43. Lexington: University Press of Kentucky, 1999.

McDonald, Forrest, and Grady McWhiney. "The Antebellum Southern Herdsman: A Reinterpretation." *Journal of Southern History* 41 (May 1975): 147–66.

McGee, David H. " 'Home and Friends': Kinship, Community, and Elite Women in Caldwell County, North Carolina, during the Civil War." *North Carolina Historical Review* 74 (October 1997): 363–88.

McKaughan, Joshua. " 'Few Were the Hearts . . . That Did Not Swell with Devotion': Community and Confederate Service in Rowan County, North Carolina, 1861–1862." *North Carolina Historical Review* 73 (April 1996): 156–83.

McKenzie, Robert Tracy. "Wealth and Income: The Preindustrial Structure of East Tennessee in 1860." *Appalachian Journal* 21 (Spring 1994): 260–79.

McKinney, Gordon B. "The Blair Committee Investigation of 1883: Industrialization in the Southern Mountains." *Appalachian Journal* 26 (Winter 1999): 150–66.

——. "Economy and Community in Western North Carolina, 1860–1865." In *Appalachia in the Making: The Mountain South in the Nineteenth Century*, edited by Mary Beth Pudup, Dwight Billings, and Altina L. Waller, 163–84. Chapel Hill: University of North Carolina Press, 1995.

——. "The Klan in the Southern Mountains: The Lusk-Shotwell Controversy." *Appalachian Journal* 8 (Winter 1981): 89–104.

——. "The Mountain Republican Party-Army." *Tennessee Historical Quarterly* 32 (Summer 1973): 124–39.

——. "The Political Uses of Appalachain Identity after the Civil War." *Appalachian Journal* 7 (Spring 1980): 200–209.

——. "Preindustrial Jackson County and Economic Development." *Journal of the Appalachian Studies Association* 2 (1990): 1–10.

——. "Premature Industrialization in Appalachia: The Asheville Armory, 1862–1863." In *The Civil War in Appalachia: Collected Essays*, edited by Kenneth W. Noe and Shannon H. Wilson, 227–41. Knoxville: University of Tennessee Press, 1997.

——. "Southern Mountain Republicans and the Negro, 1865–1900." *Journal of Southern History* 41 (November 1975): 493–516.

——. "Women's Role in Civil War Western North Carolina." *North Carolina Historical Review* 69 (January 1992): 37–56.

——. "Zebulon Vance and His Reconstruction of the Civil War in North Carolina." *North Carolina Historical Review* 75 (January 1998): 69–85.

MacMaster, Richard K. "The Cattle Trade in Western Virginia, 1760–1830." In *Appalachian Frontiers: Settlement, Society, and Development in the Preindustrial Era*, edited by Robert D. Mitchell, 127–49. Lexington: University Press of Kentucky, 1991.

Madden, David. "Unionist Resistance to Confederate Occupation: The Bridge Burners of East Tennessee." *East Tennessee Historical Society Papers* 52–53 (1980–81): 22–39.

Maggard, Sally Ward. "Class and Gender: New Theoretical Priorities in Appalachian Studies." In *The Impact of Institutions in Appalachia: Proceedings of the Appalachian Studies Eighth Annual Conference*, edited by Jim Lloyd and Anne G. Campbell, 100–113. Boone, N.C.: Appalachian Consortium Press, 1986.

——. "Will the Real Daisy Mae Please Stand Up? A Methodological Essay on Gender Analysis in Appalachian Research." *Appalachian Journal* 21 (1994): 136–50.

Mann, Ralph. "Diversity in the Antebellum Appalachian South: Four Farm Communities in Tazewell County, Virginia." In *Appalachia in the Making: The Mountain South in the Nineteenth Century*, edited by Mary Beth Pudup, Dwight B. Billings, and Altina L. Waller, 132–62. Chapel Hill: University of North Carolina Press, 1995.

——. "Ezekiel Counts's Sand Lick Company: Civil War and Localism in the Mountain South." In *The Civil War in Appalachia: Collected Essays*, edited by Kenneth W. Noe and Shannon H. Wilson, 78–103. Knoxville: University of Tennessee Press, 1997.

——. "Family Group, Family Migration, and the Civil War in the Sandy Basin of Virginia." *Appalachian Journal* 19 (Summer 1992): 374–92.

——. "Guerrilla Warfare and Gender Roles: Sandy Basin, Virginia as a Test Case." *Journal of the Appalachian Studies Association* 5 (1993): 59–66.

——. "Mountain, Land, and Kin Networks: Burkes Garden, Virginia, in the 1840s and 1850s." *Journal of Southern History* 58 (August 1992): 411–34.

Massey, Mary Elizabeth. "Confederate Refugees in North Carolina." *North Carolina Historical Review* 40 (April 1963): 158–82.

——. "The Food and Drink Shortages on the Confederate Homefront." *North Carolina Historical Review* 26 (July 1949): 306–34.

Mendenhall, M. S. "The Rise of Southern Tenancy." *Yale Review* 27 (1937): 110–29.

Merrill, Michael. "Cash Is Good to Eat: Self-Sufficiency and Exchange in the Rural Economy of the United States." *Radical History Review* 3 (Winter 1977): 42–71.

Mitchell, Robert D. " 'From the Ground Up': Space, Place, and Diversity in Frontier Studies." In *Diversity and Accommodation: Essays on the Cultural Composition of the Virginia*

Frontier, edited by Michael J. Puglisi, 23–52. Knoxville: University of Tennessee Press, 1997.

Mohr, Clarence L. "Slavery and Class Tensions in Confederate Georgia." *Gulf Coast Historical Review* 4 (Spring 1989): 58–72.

Moore, James Tice. "Secession and the States: A Review Essay." *Virginia Magazine of History Biography* 94 (January 1986): 60–76.

Moser, Harold D. "Reaction in North Carolina to the Emancipation Proclamation." *North Carolina Historical Review* 44 (Winter 1967): 53–71.

Murphy, James B. "Slavery and Freedom in Appalachia: Kentucky as a Demographic Case Study." *Register of the Kentucky Historical Society* 80 (Spring 1982): 151–69.

Neely, Mark E., Jr. "Was the Civil War a Total War?" *Civil War History* 37 (March 1991): 5–28.

Nelson, B. H. "Some Aspects of Negro Life in North Carolina during the Civil War." *North Carolina Historical Review* 25 (April 1948): 143–66.

Newsome, A. R., ed. "Twelve North Carolina Counties in 1810–1811." *North Carolina Historical Review* 5 (October 1928): 413–46.

Noe, Kenneth W. "Appalachia's Civil War Genesis: Southwest Virginia as Depicted by Northern and European Writers, 1825–1865." *West Virginia History* 50 (July 1991): 91–108.

——. "'Deadened Color and Colder Horror': Rebecca Harding Davis and the Myth of Unionist Appalachia." In *Confronting Appalachian Stereotypes: Back Talk from an American Region*, edited by Dwight B. Billings, Gurney Norman, and Katherine Ledford, 67–84. Lexington: University Press of Kentucky, 1999.

——. "Exterminating Savages: The Union Army and Mountain Guerrillas in Southern West Virginia, 1861–1862." In *The Civil War in Appalachia: Collected Essays*, edited by Kenneth W. Noe and Shannon H. Wilson, 104–30. Knoxville: University of Tennessee Press, 1997.

——. "Red String Scare: Civil War Southwest Virginia and the Heroes of America." *North Carolina Historical Review* 69 (July 1992): 301–22.

——. "Southwest Virginia's Iron Road to Secession: A Reappraisal of Civil War Appalachia." *Appalachian Heritage* 17 (Spring 1989): 31–35.

——. "Toward the Myth of Unionist Appalachia, 1865–1883." *Journal of the Appalachian Studies Association* 6 (1994): 73–80.

Olsen, Otto H. "North Carolina: An Incongruous Presence." In *Reconstruction and Redemption in the South*, edited by Otto H. Olsen, 62–85. Baton Rouge: Louisiana State University Press, 1980.

Olson, Eric J. "Race Relations in Asheville, North Carolina: Three Incidents, 1868–1906." In *The Appalachian Experience: Proceedings of the 6th Annual Appalachian Studies Conference*, edited by Barry M. Buxton, 153–66. Boone, N.C.: Appalachian Consortium Press, 1983.

Opie, John. "Where American History Began: Appalachia and the Small Independent Family Farm." In *Appalachia/America: Proceedings of the 1980 Appalachian Studies Conference*, edited by Wilson Somerville, 58–67. Boone, N.C.: Appalachian Consortium Press, 1981.

Otto, John Solomon. "Southern 'Plain Folk' Agriculture: A Reconsideration." *Plantation Society in the Americas* 2 (April 1983): 29–36.

Owsley, Frank L. "Defeatism in the Confederacy." *North Carolina Historical Review* 3 (July 1926): 446–56.

Paludan, Phillip S. "Actors and Heroes: The 'New Social and Economic History' and the Civil War." *Reviews in American History* 18 (December 1980): 493–99.

Parish, Peter. "The Edges of Slavery in the Old South: or Do the Exceptions Prove the Rule?" *Slavery & Abolition* 4 (September 1983): 106–25.

Peterson, Owen M. "W. W. Avery in the Democratic National Convention of 1860." *North Carolina Historical Review* 31 (October 1954): 463–78.

Phifer, Edward W., Jr. "Champagne at Brindletown: The Story of the Burke County Gold Rush, 1829–1833." *North Carolina Historical Review* 40 (October 1962): 489–500.

——. "Saga of a Burke County Family [Averys]." Parts 1–3. *North Carolina Historical Review* 39 (Winter, Spring, Summer 1962): 1–17, 140–47, 305–24.

——. "Slavery in Microcosm: Burke County, North Carolina." *Journal of Southern History* 28 (May 1962): 137–65.

Pudup, Mary Beth. "The Limits of Subsistence: Agriculture and Industry in Central Appalachia." *Agricultural History* 64 (Winter 1990): 61–89.

——. "Social Class and Economic Development in Southeastern Kentucky, 1820–1880." In *Appalachian Frontiers: Settlement, Society, and Development in the Preindustrial Era*, edited by Robert D. Mitchell, 235–60. Lexington: University Press of Kentucky, 1991.

——. "Town and Country in the Transformation of Appalachian Kentucky." In *Appalachia in the Making: The Mountain South in the Nineteenth Century*, edited by Dwight B. Billings, Mary Beth Pudup, and Altina L. Waller, 270–96. Chapel Hill: University of North Carolina Press, 1995.

Queener, Verton M. "East Tennessee Sentiment and the Secession Movement, November 1860– June 1861." *East Tennessee Historical Society's Publications* 20 (1948): 59–83.

Rable, George. "Missing in Action: Women of the Confederacy." In *Divided Houses: Gender and the Civil War*, edited by Catherine Clinton and Nina Silber, 134–44. New York: Oxford University Press, 1992.

Ready, Milton. "Forgotten Sisters: Mountain Women in the South." In *Southern Appalachia and the South*, edited by John C. Inscoe. Vol. 3 of *The Journal of the Appalachian Studies Association* (1991): 61–67.

Reid, Joseph D., Jr. "Antebellum Southern Rental Contracts." *Explorations in Economic History* 13 (1976): 69–83.

Reid, Richard. "A Test Case of 'Crying Evil': Desertion among North Carolina Troops during the Civil War." *North Carolina Historical Review* 58 (July 1981): 234–62.

——. "William W. Holden and 'Disloyalty' in the Civil War." *Canadian Journal of History* 20 (April 1985): 44–67.

Roberts, A. S. "The Peace Movement in North Carolina." *Mississippi Valley Historical Review* 11 (September 1924).

Robinson, Armstead L. "In the Shadow of Old John Brown: Insurrection, Anxiety, and Confederate Mobility, 1861–1863." *Journal of Negro History* 65 (Fall 1980): 279–97.

Rothenberg, Winifred B. "The Market and Massachusetts Farmers, 1705–1855." *Journal of Economic History* 41 (1981): 290–313.

Rubin, Julius. "The Limits of Agricultural Progress in the Nineteenth-Century South." *Agricultural History* 49 (April 1975): 362–73.

Salstrom, Paul. "The Agricultural Origins of Economic Dependency in Appalachia, 1840– 1880." In *Appalachian Frontiers: Settlement, Society, and Development in the Preindustrial Era*, edited by Robert D. Mitchell, 261–83. Lexington: University Press of Kentucky, 1991.

——. "Newer Appalachia as One of America's Last Frontiers." In *Appalachia in the Making: The Mountain South in the Nineteenth Century*, edited by Dwight B. Billings, Mary Beth Pudup, and Altina L. Waller, 76–102. Chapel Hill: University of North Carolina Press, 1995.

——. "Subsistence-Barter-and-Borrow Systems: An Approach to West Virginia's Economic History." *West Virginia History* 51 (1992): 45–53.

Sarris, Jonathan D. "Anatomy of an Atrocity: The Madden Branch Massacre and Guerrilla

Warfare in North Georgia, 1861–1865." *Georgia Historical Quarterly* 77 (Winter 1993): 679–710.

———. "An Execution in Lumpkin County: Localized Loyalties in North Georgia's Civil War." In *The Civil War in Appalachia: Collected Essays*, edited by Kenneth W. Noe and Shannon H. Wilson, 131–57. Knoxville: University of Tennessee Press, 1997.

Schlotterbeck, John T. "The 'Social Economy' of an Upper South Community: Orange and Greene Counties, Virginia, 1815–1860." In *Class, Conflict, and Consensus: Antebellum Southern Community Studies*, edited by Orville V. Burton and Robert C. McMath Jr. 3–28. Westport, Conn.: Greenwood Press, 1982.

Shanks, Henry T. "Disloyalty to the Confederacy in Southwestern Virginia." *North Carolina Historical Review* 21 (1944): 118–35.

Sheeler, J. Reuben. "The Development of Unionism in East Tennessee." *Journal of Negro History* 29 (April 1944): 166–203.

Silber, Nina. " 'What Does America Need So Much As Americans?': Race and Northern Reconciliation with Southern Appalachia." In *Appalachia in Black and White: Race Relations in the Nineteenth Century Mountain South*, edited by John C. Inscoe. Lexington: University Press of Kentucky, forthcoming.

Smith, Mary Shannon. "Union Sentiment in North Carolina during the Civil War." In *Proceedings of the Sixteenth Annual Session of the State Literary and Historical Association of North Carolina*, 50–64. Raleigh: Edwards and Broughton, 1916.

Starnes, Richard. " 'The Stirring Strains of Dixie': The Civil War and Southern Identity in Haywood County, North Carolina." *North Carolina Historical Review* 74 (July 1997): 237–59.

Stealey, John Edmund, III. "Slavery and the Western Virginia Salt Industry." *Journal of Negro History* 59 (April 1974): 105–31.

Stuckert, Robert P. "Black Populations of the Southern Appalachian Mountains." *Phylon* 48 (June 1987): 141–51.

Sutherland, Daniel E. "Getting the 'Real War' into the Books." *Virginia Magazine of History and Biography* 98 (April 1990): 193–220.

———. "Introduction to War: The Civilians of Culpeper County, Virginia." *Civil War History* 37 (June 1991): 120–36.

Taylor, Jim. "The Killings on the Shelton Laurel." *Company Front* (Newsletter for Society for Historical Preservation of the 26th North Carolina Troops, Inc.) (August/September 1989): 5–13.

———, ed. "The Papers of Zebulon B. Vance: Destruction of Civilian Property and Abuse by Authority by Confederate Troops in North Carolina." *Company Front* (1992): 42–60.

Thornton, J. Mills, III. "The Ethic of Subsistence and the Origins of Southern Secession." *Tennessee Historical Quarterly* 48 (Summer 1989): 67–85.

Trelease, Allen W. "The Passive Voice: The State and the North Carolina Railroad, 1849–1871." *North Carolina Historical Review* 61 (April 1983): 174–204.

Van Noppen, Ina W. "The Significance of Stoneman's Last Raid." *North Carolina Historical Review* 38 (January 1961): 19–44; (April 1961): 149–72; (July 1961): 341–61; (October 1961): 500–526.

Vinovskis, Maris. "Have Social Historians Lost the Civil War? Some Preliminary Demographic Speculations." *Journal of American History* 76 (June 1989): 34–58.

Wallenstein, Peter. " 'Helping to Save the Union': The Social Origins, Wartime Experiences, and Military Impact of White Union Troops from East Tennessee." In *The Civil War in Appalachia: Collected Essays*, edited by Kenneth W. Noe and Shannon H. Wilson, 1–29. Knoxville: University of Tennessee Press, 1997.

Waller, Altina L. "Feuding in Appalachia: The Evolution of a Cultural Stereotype." In *Appalachia in the Making: The Mountain South in the Nineteenth Century*, edited by Dwight B. Billings, Mary Beth Pudup, and Altina L. Waller, 347–76. Chapel Hill: University of North Carolina Press, 1995.

Walton, Brian G. "Elections to the United States Senate in North Carolina, 1835–1861." *North Carolina Historical Review* 53 (April 1976): 168–92.

Watson, Harry L. "Conflict and Collaboration: Yeomen, Slaveholders, and Politics in the Antebellum South." *Social History* 10 (October 1985): 273–98.

———. "Squire Oldway and His Friends: Opposition to Internal Improvements in Antebellum North Carolina." *North Carolina Historical Review* 45 (April 1977): 105–19.

Weiman, Robert. "Farmers and the Market in Antebellum America: A View from the Georgia Upcountry." *Journal of Economic History* 47 (September 1987): 627–48.

Wilhelm, Gene, Jr. "Appalachian Isolation: Fact or Fiction?" In *An Appalachian Symposium*, edited by J. W. Williamson. Boone, N.C.: Appalachian Consortium Press, 1977.

Williams, Cratis D. "The Southern Mountaineer in Fact and Fiction." *Appalachian Journal* 3 (Autumn 1975 and Winter 1976): 8–61, 100–162.

Williams, David. "Georgia's Forgotten Miners: African-Americans and and the Georgia Gold Rush." *Georgia Historical Quarterly* 75 (Spring 1991): 76–89.

Wilson, Shannon H. "Lincoln's Sons and Daughters: Berea College, Lincoln Memorial University, and the Myth of Unionist Appalachia, 1866–1910." In *The Civil War in Appalachia: Collected Essays*, edited by Kenneth W. Noe and Shannon H. Wilson, 242–64. Knoxville: University of Tennessee Press, 1997.

Winters, Donald L. "'Plain Folk' of the Old South Reexamined: Economic Diversity in Tennessee." *Journal of Southern History* 53 (August 1987): 565–86.

Wish, Harvey. "Slave Disloyalty under the Confederacy." *Journal of Negro History* 23 (October 1938): 435–50.

Woodson, Carter G. "Freedom and Slavery in Appalachian America." *Journal of Negro History* 1 (April 1916): 132–50.

Yates, Richard E. "Governor Vance and the End of the War in North Carolina." *North Carolina Historical Review* 18 (October 1941): 315–38.

———. "Governor Vance and the Peace Movement." *North Carolina Historical Review* 17 (April 1940): 94–118.

Theses, Dissertations, and Unpublished Papers

Abrams, William J., Jr. "The Western North Carolina Railroad, 1855–1894." M.A. thesis, Western Carolina University, 1976.

Ambrose, Robert Paul. "A Critical Year (April 1860–April 1861): A Study in Unionist Sentiment in Western North Carolina during the Culminating Year of the Secession Movement." M.A. thesis, University of North Carolina at Greensboro, 1975.

Auman, William Thomas. "Neighbor against Neighbor: The Inner Civil War in the Central Counties of Confederate North Carolina." Ph.D. dissertation, University of North Carolina at Chapel Hill, 1988.

Blethen, H. Tyler, and Curtis Wood. "Land and Family in the Tuckaseigee Valley, 1800–1850." Paper delivered at Appalachian Studies conference, Boone, N.C., March 1986.

Bohannon, Keith C. "'They Had Determined to Root Us Out': Dual Memoirs by a Unionist Couple in Blue Ridge Georgia." Paper delivered at conference, "Families at War: Loyalty and Conflict in the Civil War South," Richmond, Va., April 1998.

Brashear, Charles Craig. "Election Ground: Place, Politics, and Partisanship in East Tennessee's Second Party System." Ph.D. dissertation, University of Georgia, 1999.

Bryan, Charles Faulkner. "The Civil War in East Tennessee: A Social Political, and Economic Study." Ph.D. dissertation, University of Tennessee, Knoxville, 1978.

Burton, William Franklin, Jr. "The Issue of *Ad Valorem* Taxation in Ante-Bellum North Carolina." M.A. thesis, University of North Carolina at Chapel Hill, 1940.

Butts, Donald C. "A Challenge to Planter Rule: The Controversy over the Ad Valorem Taxation of Slaves in North Carolina, 1858–1862." Ph.D. dissertation, Duke University, 1978.

Cline, Lori Ann. " 'Something Wrong in South Carolina': Antebellum Agricultural Tenancy and Primitive Accumulation in Three Districts." M.A. thesis, University of Georgia, 1996.

Cotton, William D. "Appalachian North Carolina: A Political Study, 1860–1889." Ph.D. dissertation, University of North Carolina at Chapel Hill, 1954.

Davis, Phillip G. "Mountain Heritage, Mountain Promise under Siege: The Origin and Devastation of Confederate Sympathy in the North Carolina Mountains during the Civil War." M.A. thesis, Wake Forest University, 1994.

Dunaway, Wilma A. "The Incorporation of Southern Appalachia into the Capitalist World Economy, 1790–1860." Ph.D. dissertation, University of Tennessee, Knoxville, 1994.

Eller, Ronald D. "The Search for Community in Appalachia." Keynote address, Ninth Appalachian Studies Conference, Boone, N.C., March 1986.

Emerson, William E. "Problems in Regionalism and Command: Civil War Desertion in the Twenty-fourth and Twenty-fifth Regiments of North Carolina Troops." Unpublished seminar paper.

Entrekin, William F., Jr. "Poor Relief in North Carolina in the Confederacy." M.A. thesis, Duke University, 1947.

Fleming, John E. "Out of Bondage: The Adjustment of Burke County Negroes after the Civil War, 1865–1890." Ph.D. dissertation, Howard University, 1974.

Gilbert, Clarence N. "The Public Career of Thomas L. Clingman." M.A. thesis, University of North Carolina at Chapel Hill, 1946.

Giuffre, Katherine Anne. "First in Flight: Desertion as Politics in the North Carolina Army." M.A. thesis, University of North Carolina at Chapel Hill, 1991.

Gray, Sam, and Theda Perdue. "Appalachia as the Promised Land: A Freedmen's Commune in Henderson County, North Carolina, 1870–1920." Unpublished paper presented at American Anthropological Association meeting, 1979.

Groce, W. Todd. "Mountain Rebels: East Tennessee Confederates and the Civil War." Ph.D. dissertation, University of Tennessee, Knoxville, 1993.

Heath, Raymond A., Jr. "The North Carolina Militia on the Eve of the Civil War." M.A. thesis, University of North Carolina at Chapel Hill, 1974.

Hicks, Glenna. "The Forgotton Sons: North Carolinians in the Union Army." M.A. thesis, Appalachian State University, 1968.

Hoffman, Richard L. "The Republican Party in North Carolina, 1867–1871." M.A. thesis, University of North Carolina, 1960.

Inscoe, John C., and Gordon B. McKinney. "Highland Households Divided: Familial Deceptions, Diversions, and Divisions in Southern Appalachia's Inner Civil War." Paper delivered at conference, "Families at War: Loyalty and Conflict in the Civil War South," Richmond, Va., April 1998.

Iobst, Richard. "North Carolina Mobilizes: Nine Crucial Months, December 1860–August 1861." Ph.D. dissertation, University of North Carolina at Chapel Hill, 1968.

Jolley, Daniel Wayne. "The Ku Klux Klan in Rutherford County, 1870–1871." M.A. thesis, University of North Carolina at Chapel Hill, 1994.

McGee, David H. " 'On the Edge of a Crater': The Transformation of Raleigh, North Carolina, in the Civil War Era." Ph.D. dissertation, University of Georgia, 2000.

McKinney, Gordon B. "Moonshiners, Law Enforcement, and Violence: Legitimacy and Community in Western North Carolina, 1862–1882." Paper delivered at Southern Historical Association meeting, New Orleans, November 1995.

Nelson, Scott. "Red Strings and Half Brothers: Civil War in Alamance County, North Carolina." Paper delivered at conference, "Families at War: Loyalty and Conflict in the Civil War South," Richmond, Va., April 1998.

Ritt, Arnold. "The Escape of Federal Prisoners through East Tennessee, 1861–1865." M.A. thesis, University of Tennessee, 1965.

Russell, Mattie. "William Holland Thomas: White Chief of the Cherokees." Ph.D. dissertation, Duke University, 1956.

Sarris, Jonathan D. " 'Hellish Deeds in a Christian Land': Southern Mountain Communities at War, 1861–1865." Ph.D. dissertation, University of Georgia, 1998.

Schneider, Tracy W. "The Institution of Slavery in North Carolina, 1860–1865." Ph.D. dissertation, Duke University, 1979.

Shay, John M. "The Anti-Slavery Movement in North Carolina." Ph.D. dissertation, Princeton University, 1970.

Shinoda, Yasuko I. "Land and Slaves in North Carolina in 1860." Ph.D. dissertation, University of North Carolina at Chapel Hill, 1971.

Shirley, Franklin R. "The Rhetoric of Zebulon B. Vance: Tar Heel Spokesman." Ph.D. dissertation, University of Florida, 1985.

Shrader, Richard A. "William Lenoir, 1751–1839." Ph.D. dissertation, University of North Carolina at Chapel Hill, 1976.

Starnes, Richard Dale. " 'Rule of the Rebs': White Supremacy, the Lost Cause, and the White Social Memory in Reconstruction North Carolina, 1865–1871." M.A. thesis, Western Carolina University, 1994.

Stefanco, Carolyn. " 'Enemies of the Country': Northern-Born Women in the Confederate South." Paper delivered at conference, "Families at War: Loyalty and Conflict in the Civil War South," Richmond, Va., April 1998.

Taylor, James Carlisle. "The Buncombe Rough and Ready Guards: A Social and Military Profile." Seminar Paper, Western Carolina University, 1991.

——. "The 60th North Carolina Regiment: A Case Study of Enlistment and Desertion in Western North Carolina during the Civil War." M.A. thesis, Western Carolina University, 1996.

Turpin, Walter. "Southwestern North Carolina on the Eve of the Civil War." Seminar paper, University of North Carolina at Chapel Hill, 1981.

Whelan, Paul A. "Unconventional Warfare in East Tennessee, 1861–1865." M.A. thesis, University of Tennessee, Knoxville, 1963.

Williams, Cratis D. "The Southern Mountaineer in Fact and Fiction." Ph.D. dissertation, New York University, 1961.

Wood, Curtis W., Jr. "Antebellum Mercantile Activity as Illustrated by the R. G. Dun Collection." Unpublished paper, 1992.

INDEX

Abolitionists, Northern, 36, 223
Adair gang, 269
Ad valorem taxation. *See* Taxation, ad valorem
Agricultural production, wartime, 167–68, 170, 174–75, 181–83, 185, 202–4
Alcohol, tax on, 275. *See also* Revenue agents
Alleghany County, N.C., 191, 196
Allen, Lawrence, 65, 116, 118–20, 121, 195, 285
Andersonville prison, 229
Andrews, Sidney, 91
Anglin, Mary, 202
Appalachia, discovery of, 276, 277–79
Armfield, R. F., 121
Armory. *See* Asheville Armory
Army of Northern Virginia, 161
Arrowood, Maryann, 169
Arwood, James, 258
Ashe, Samuel A'Court, 73–74
Ashe County, N.C., 15, 45, 86; Confederate enlistments from, 69, 75
Asheville, N.C., 5, 8, 32, 63, 179, 202, 233, 266, 281; battle of, 252; black troops in, 257; freedmen in, 263–64; industry in, 183; prisoners taken from, 257; race riot in, 271–72; settlement of, 23–24; Stoneman's raid on, 254–57; training camps in, 74, 78; Union attack on, 108, 252; Union threat to, 182; women in, 36, 202, 254, 257
Asheville Armory, 108, 176–83; slave labor at, 179; Union threat to, 123
Asheville Mutual Insurance Company, 210
Athens, Ga., 22, 123
Athens, Tenn., 99
Atkins, Thomas W., 122
Atlanta, Ga., 150, 163
Augusta, Ga., 22
Avery, Hamilton, 229–30
Avery, Isaac, 43, 230
Avery, William Waightstill, 34, 38–39, 43, 49, 61–62, 230; death of, 135

Bailey, John L., 256
Balsam Mountains, 13
Baltimore, Md., 38, 48
Banner, Lewis, 90
Banner, Napoleon, 102–3
Banner Elk, N.C., 103
Barnett, Emmaline, 170
Barter economy, 171, 184–85
Bartlett, William C., 258–59
Batteau, Allen, 277
Bearman, Peter, 114
Bell, Alfred W., 17, 79, 175–76, 184–85, 196–97, 202–4; and slaves, 218–22
Bell, John, 39–41, 42, 147
Bell, Mary, 79, 184–85, 196–97, 202–6; and slaves, 218–22
Benjamin, Judah, 81
Big Bethel, battle of, 64
Black Mountains, 13
Blacksmiths, 172, 236
Blackwell, Elisha, 99
Blake, Frederick, 79
Blanton, W. E., 159
Blaylock, Keith, 189
Blaylock, Malinda, 189, 190
Blue Ridge Mountains, 13
Boone, Daniel, 29
Boone, N.C., 9, 21, 25, 94, 134; Stoneman's raid on, 244, 250
Bower, George, 208–9
Bragg, Braxton, 123
Bragg, Thomas, 27
Brandy, 134, 171, 175. *See also* Distilleries
Bread riots, 197
Breckinridge, John C., 38, 42, 137
Bridge burners, East Tennessee, 107
Brown, John, 35, 42, 50, 61
Brown, Joseph E., 49–50, 162, 210
Brown, Mary Taylor, 222, 253–54, 255, 265
Brown, Samuel B., 255
Brown, William J., 49

Brown, William Vance, 210, 254

Browne, Junius, 228

Brownlow, William "Parson," 46, 50, 86, 106

Brown Mountain, 135

Bryan, J. A. Q., 126–27, 128–29

Bryan, Mary, 59

Bryan, Rufus, 154

Bryson, Goldman, 123

Bryson, J. N., 129

Bull Run, battle of, 64

Buncombe County, N.C., 17, 49, 51, 174; Confederate enlistments from, 75; home guard, 123; militia, 109, 142; Stoneman's raid on, 253, 257; troops stationed in, 107; women in, 71

Buncombe Riflemen, 36, 63, 65

Buncombe Rough and Readies, 79

Buncombe Turnpike, 25

Burgwyn, Henry King, Jr., 69

Burke County, N.C., 17, 27, 32, 33, 43, 49, 51; Confederate enlistments from, 69; distilleries in, 237; slaves in, 18, 229–30; Stoneman's raid on, 248–50, 251; women in, 172

Burke Rifles, 63

Burnett, Frances Hodgson, 276

Burnside, Ambrose, 103, 122, 145, 182

Burnsville, N.C., 9, 25, 51; Union attack on, 133, 197–98; women's raid in, 197–98

Burnt Chimney, N.C., 69

Burson, William, 100, 102, 229

Bushwhackers, 105, 117, 124–25, 238

Buxton, Rev. John, 40

Cades Cove, Tenn., 16, 95

Cagle, Leonard, 180

Cain, Sarah Bailey, 257

Caldwell, Tod R., 51, 57, 271, 274

Caldwell County, N.C., 41, 51, 96, 108–9; bushwhackers in, 125–28, 260; Confederate enlistments from, 68; Confederate troops in, 133–34; deserters in, 125; poor relief in, 169–70; Stoneman's raid on, 244, 245, 247, 248; Unionists in, 88; violence in, 105; women in, 204–5

Caldwell Rough and Ready Boys, 68, 72

California: admission to Union, 34

Campbell, John C., 10

Camp Patton, 74

Camp Sorghum, 95, 227

Camp Vance: Kirk's raid on, 134–36, 163, 230, 248

Camp Woodfin, 71

Cashiers, N.C., 193

Catawba River, 9, 13, 14, 20

Cathey, Joseph, 21

Cavalry, Confederate, 196, 241–42

Charleston, S.C., 18, 22, 27, 38, 213, 214–15; Democratic convention in, 38, 40; slaves from, 213, 214–15, 220

Chattahoochee River, 25

Chattanooga, Tenn., 7

Cherokee County, N.C., 15, 77, 120, 132; Confederate raid on, 143; Confederate troops in, 150; poor relief in, 170; Unionist raid on, 196; Unionists in, 101; women in, 187, 191

Cherokee Indians, 15–16, 110, 123, 132, 147, 243; as part of Thomas's Legion, 65–66; surrender of, 258–59

Cherokee Indian territory, 13, 15–16, 132

Chesnut, Mary, 6, 201, 211

Chickamauga, battle of, 157

Church, Harrison, 239

Churches, 198–99, 205; and departing troops, 70–71; postwar, 266–67, 285

Civil liberties, 160–61

Civil Rights Act of 1875, 274

Clark, Henry T., 74, 81, 107, 110, 111, 140, 143, 169, 176

Class, socio-economic, 13, 15, 20, 91, 167, 188–89; and women, 201–2, 206

Clay, Henry, 31

Clay County, N.C., 70, 234, 270

Clayton, Ephiram, 176, 178

Clergy. See Ministers

Cleveland, Tenn., 99

Clingman, Thomas, 26, 30–35, 38, 40, 43, 49, 51, 55, 65, 139, 145, 159, 267

Cloth-making, 173–74

Coleman, David, 51, 65

Columbia, S.C., 22, 27, 182, 243; Confederate prison in, 92, 124, 227

Columbus, N.C., 112

Community, 20, 22–23, 27–29, 284–85

Confederate army, 140, 241–42

Confederate Congress, 111, 140, 158, 164

Confederate Ordnance Bureau, 176–77

Confederate Party, 147, 149–50, 157–59, 161–62

Conley, R. T., 258

Conscription, 111–15, 121–22, 133–34, 138–39, 153, 157; in East Tennessee, 114; exemptions from, 142, 144–45, 168–69, 176, 236

Conscription Act, 111, 113, 140

Conservative Party, 147–50, 151–54, 159–61; postwar, 272

Constitutional Union Party, 39–40

Convict labor, 279–80

Corn supply, 134, 169–71, 182, 185, 198

Corpening, Joseph, 214

Cotton mills. *See* Textile factories

Councill, Jordan, 21, 250

County seats, in western N.C., 8, 23, 25

Cowles, Calvin, 18, 26, 50, 56, 68, 78, 91, 98, 127–28, 136, 170–71, 213, 215, 239, 250, 261

Cowles, Josiah, 56, 78, 98

Cowles, Mary, 225

Crab Creek, N.C., 94

Craggy, N.C., 252

Cranberry, N.C., 102

Cranor, Edward, 239

Crawford, Martin, 69, 75, 94

Crittenden Compromise, 52

Crumpler, Thomas, 45, 65, 69

Currency, Confederate, 162, 170, 171–72, 184, 186, 214, 219, 238, 264. *See also* Inflation, wartime

Danville, Va., 227

Davidson, Allen, 146–47, 150–51, 156–57, 213, 278

Davidson, Francis M., 132

Davidson, Samuel, 14

Davidson, Theodore, 278

Davidson, William, 14

Davis, Harvey, 68, 71

Davis, Jefferson, 6, 51, 110, 112, 113, 144, 146, 160, 241, 258, 261; and peace movement, 158–59, 162, 164

Davis, Rebecca Harding, 276

Dedman, William, 155–56, 163

Deep Creek, battle of, 132

Degler, Carl, 89

Democratic convention, 1860, 38

Democratic Party, 31–34, 40, 150, 267, 274–75

Deserters and desertion, 102, 113–14, 125–28, 133, 143, 161, 168, 171, 240; in Madison County, 116–17; in North Carolina, 114–15; and peace movement, 155; slave aid to, 228

Dillsboro, N.C., 280

Disaffection, in western N.C., 113

Distilleries, 174, 237, 275, 282. *See also* Brandy

Donaldson, William, 101

Dorlan Institute, 278–79

Douglas, Stephen A., 38, 40, 42

Dowell, Roda, 170

Downer, W. S., 177

Drake, J. Madison, 88, 96, 125, 192

Ducktown, Tenn., 280

Dugger, G. W., 102

Dugger, Shepherd, 102–3

Dunaway, Wilma, 16

Dunn, Durwood, 16, 95

Durham, N.C., 253

Eagle Hotel (Asheville), 257

Early, Jubal, 232

East Tennessee, 7, 29, 83–84, 223, 247; Federal occupation of, 103, 122; threat to western N.C. from, 107, 110, 196, 233; Unionism in, 45–46, 94, 106; Unionists in, 94, 106

East Tennessee, Confederate Department of, 118

East Tennessee, Federal District of, 243

Economic development, in western N.C., 282–84

Edney, Baylis M., 74, 121, 151, 156

Edneyville, N.C., 76, 80, 94

Egan, Michael, 97, 228

Elections, congressional: 1841, 32; 1857, 34; 1863, 153, 155–58; 1866, 271

Elections, gubernatorial: 1862, 147, 148–49; 1864, 161–63; 1865, 270–71; 1866, 271; 1868, 271; 1870, 274; 1876, 274

Elections, presidential: 1860, 38–42, 147; 1868, 271

Eller, J. P., 45

Eller, Ronald, 275

Ellis, John B., 36, 61, 63, 74, 76, 76–77, 80–81, 139, 146, 205

Emancipation of slaves, 224, 254, 261, 263–64, 268

Emancipation Proclamation, 145, 222–23

England, Alexander, 171

Enlistments, Confederate, in western N.C., 62–63, 74–77

Episcopalians, 71

Erwin, Edward Jones, 43

Erwin, Marcus, 36, 37–38, 40, 49, 61–62, 107, 109, 151, 156–57, 159, 210, 260

Erwin, O. L., 236

Escape narratives, Union, 88–89, 92–94, 124–25, 191–92, 226–29

Escott, Paul D., 238

Fagg, John A., 62

Fain, Mercer, 77

Family structure: impact of war on, 167–68

Farms and farming, in western N.C., 12, 14, 15, 21, 27–28, 181; postwar, 267, 275–76; wartime, 167–68. *See also* Tenantry

Faust, Drew Gilpin, 188, 206

Fellman, Michael, 97, 190

Fergeson, Major, 64

Finger, John, 16

Flat Rock, N.C., 6, 9, 19, 23, 25, 47, 90, 185, 201, 280; bushwhackers in, 128–29; slaves in, 211

Folk, George N., 68

Food supply, wartime, 133–34, 169–71, 174, 181, 183, 198, 236, 237

Ford, Lacy, 21

Forks of the Pigeon, 21

Fort Defiance, 215, 217–18

Fort Fisher, capture of, 164, 235, 241

Fort Hamby gang, 261, 269

Fort Hatteras, 146

Fort Sumter, attack on, 56, 60, 63, 84, 233

Fortune, William, 240

Fourteenth Amendment, 271

Frank, Jesse M., 161

Franklin, N.C., 9, 21, 25, 26, 37, 81, 100, 176, 184, 203; Confederate enlistments from, 66, 112; Union attack on, 197; women in, 205

Free blacks, 49, 210. *See also* Emancipation of slaves

Freel, Margaret Walker, 230

Free suffrage, 31

French Broad River valley, 5, 9, 13, 14, 24, 108, 109, 240, 252, 254

Friedman, Jean, 20

Frost, William, 83, 277

Fry, David, 107, 109

Fugitives, Union, 88–89, 92–94, 96–97, 102, 124–26, 130–31, 191–92, 226–29. *See also* Refugees

Gaither, Burgess, 41–42

Galbraith, W. F. M., 179

Gash, Julius, 117

Gash, Leander, 152, 156, 172, 223

Gatlinburg, Tenn., 132

Gentry, James, 60

Georgia, 22, 25; markets, 48, 214; secession of, 47

Georgia, north, 7, 8, 16, 49–50; raid on western N.C. from, 120, 150

Gettysburg, battle of, 152, 224

Gillem, Alvan C., 244, 245, 249–50, 253–55

Gordon, James Byron, 65

Gorgas, Josiah, 177–78, 182

Government aid. *See* Poor relief

Graham, William A., 146, 148–49, 271

Grain production, 14–15, 168, 170, 175, 184–85. *See also* Agricultural production, wartime; Corn supply

Grant, Alexander, 240

Grant, Henry, 97

Grant, Ulysses S., 243, 271

Graves, William, 70

Great Smokies, 13

Green, Joseph, 98–99

Greenville, S.C., 22, 25

Greenville, Tenn., 25, 117, 252

Guerrilla warfare, 105–6, 114, 116–31, 136–38, 238, 239–40; impact on women, 189

Gwyn, Amelia, 59

Gwyn, James, 53, 68, 75, 85, 168, 217, 247, 260–61

Gwyn, Julia, 126

Hahn, Steven, 21

Hall, Jacquelyn, 281

Hamilton, Joseph, 94

Hamptonville, N.C., 198

Handicrafts, 283

Happy Valley, 20, 59, 247, 263
Harper, Ella, 73, 114, 205–6, 250, 263
Harper, George, 73, 205
Harper, James, 21
Harper family, slaves of, 263
Harpers Ferry, raid on, 35–36,42, 61, 63.
  See also Brown, John
Harris, Isham G., 81
Harrold, Norm, 113
Hayesville, N.C., 270
Haywood County, N.C., 16, 99, 100, 194;
  Confederate enlistments from, 66, 70;
  home guard, 172; militia, 191; Union attack
  on, 109, 242–43, 244, 258; veterans in, 278;
  women in, 200
Haywood Invincibles, 78
Haywood Sharpshooters, 77
Heath, Raymond, 61
Heath, Thomas A., 269
Henderson County, N.C., 6, 79, 236, 240;
  bushwhackers in, 128–29; Confederate
  enlistments from, 75; conscription and,
  144; peace meeting in, 154; poor relief in,
  199; Unionists in, 76
Hendersonville, N.C., 9, 19, 23, 25, 64, 76,
  97, 253, 280; slaves in, 211; women in,
  72–73
Henretta, James, 27
Henry, Cornelia, 194, 200, 240, 263–64
Henry, James L., 132
Henry, William L., 176, 194
Heroes of America, 137, 162
Heth, Henry, 118, 120
Hickerson, Thomas, 247
Hickory Nut Gap, 25, 252, 258
Hicks, William, 199
Hillbilly stereotype, 269, 276
Hiwassee River, 14, 16, 109
Hog cholera, 167
Hogs, 14–15, 22, 25, 170, 185
Hoke, Robert F., 127–28
Holden, William W., 127, 146, 147–48, 149,
  152–54, 156, 158, 160, 171, 208–9; as gover-
  nor, 259, 270, 272
Hollingsworth family, 90
Holston Conference Female College, 199
Home guard, 101, 104, 126, 129–31, 135, 172,
  194, 195, 197, 236. *See also* Militias

Home Industrial School for Girls, 278–79
Home manufactures, 37
Home missions, 278–79
Hominy Creek, N.C., 234
Horton, John, 90
Hot Springs, N.C., 278–79, 280
Hunter, Archibald, 21
Hyatt, Elisha P., 172
Hyman, John D., 151, 156–57

Industrialism, in western N.C., 10, 175,
  177–83, 283
Inflation, wartime, 175, 264. *See also* Cur-
  rency, Confederate
Ingram, John, 219
Internal improvements, 25–26, 172–73
Internal Revenue Service, 282
Iron, pig, 102–3, 180, 181

Jackson, Andrew, 31
Jackson, Stonewall, 93
Jackson County, N.C., 16, 17, 37, 80, 108, 151;
  Confederate enlistments from, 66–67, 70;
  Union attack on, 132, 242–43
Jeff Davis Mountain Rifles, 69
Jefferson, N.C., 9, 102, 208
John Letcher, 143
Johnson, Andrew, 86, 88, 106, 255, 259, 270
Johnston, Joseph E., 162, 244; surrender to
  Sherman, 253, 255
Johnston, William, 147
Johnstone, Andrew, death of, 128–29
Jones, Alexander H., 57, 76, 85, 88, 90, 91,
  97, 154, 156, 230–31
Jones, Ann, 72
Jones, Calvin, 51
Jones, Edmund, 108
Jones, Mary Ann, 73
Junaluska Zouaves, 65

Keith, James, 116, 118–20, 195, 270
Kentucky, 7, 8, 117, 160
Key, David M., 109
King, A. A., 177
Kings Mountain, 43, 64
Kinship networks, in western N.C., 14, 284
Kinston, N.C., 99, 216
Kirby, Isaac B., 252

Kirk, George W., 103–4, 134–36, 194, 242, 258, 273
Kirk, John, 118
Kirk's raid on western N.C., 134–36, 194, 229–30, 242–43, 258
Kirk-Holden War, 273
Knoxville, Tenn., 7, 27, 50, 99, 104, 117, 212; Confederate attack on, 131; Union occupation of, 103, 122, 145, 157, 182
Knoxville Whig, 46, 106
Ku Klux Klan, 272–74

Lane, Joseph, 38, 40
Lanman, Charles, 15
Laurel Mountains, 94, 106–7, 110
Laurel Valley, 109, 117–18, 124. *See also* Shelton Laurel
Lawson, Elizabeth, 175
Leach, James T., 158, 164
Lee, George W., 120, 143
Lee, Jean, 10
Lee, Robert E., 140, 162, 244; sends troops to western N.C., 127; surrender at Appomattox, 98, 243, 259
Lenoir, Elizabeth (Lizzie), 205
Lenoir, Rufus, 105, 125–26, 215–17, 224–25
Lenoir, Sarah, 5, 9, 41, 72
Lenoir, Thomas, 17, 78, 215–16
Lenoir, W. W., 45
Lenoir, Walter, 105, 215–18, 224–25, 244
Lenoir, William, 17, 56
Lenoir, N.C., 8, 21, 23, 44, 51, 96, 205–6, 233; Stoneman's raid on, 244, 248, 251
Lillard, Jennie, 94
Lincoln, Abraham, 44, 222–23; assassination of, 259; call for troops, 56, 60, 62, 84, 106, 139; election of, 39, 41–43, 50, 231; inaugural address of, 53, 55; and peace movement, 241; reelection, l864, 162–63; views of Appalachia, 6–7
Linville River, 17
Little Tennessee River, 109
Livestock, 14–15, 22, 25, 26, 170–71, 185
Lodge election bill, 275
Logan, George W., 154–57, 158–59, 164
Logging industry, 280
Longstreet, James, 131; troops in East Tennessee, 131, 133

Loudon, Tenn., 129
Love, Dillard, 219
Love, James R., 242–43, 257, 258–59
Love, Matthew, 113
Love, Robert, 65, 172
Love, William L., 100, 151, 156
Lyle, James M., 100
Lytle, Millington, 142

McClellan, George B., 232
McDowell, Joseph, 64, 115
McDowell County, N.C., 59, 95, 167; Stoneman's raid on, 252
McElroy, John, 65, 133, 143
McGee, David, 205
McKinna and Orr, 180
McLean, Sidney, 96
Macon County, N.C., 15, 17, 37, 44, 46, 55, 61, 77, 79, 99, 189; bushwhackers in, 195; conscripts in, 142; home guard, 197; slaves in, 218–19; Unionists in, 81, 97
McPhail, C. C., 180, 182
Madison County, N.C., 44, 45, 51, 76, 238; Confederate enlistments from, 65; Confederate raid on, 143; deserters in, 115, 116–17; militia, 142; poor relief in, 169–70; postwar violence in, 269–70; railroad in, 280; Unionists in, 103, 107
Manly, Charles, 56
Mann, Ralph, 193
Manufacturing, in western N.C., 47
Marion, N.C., 163
Market economy, in western N.C., 20–21, 21–23, 25–26, 37, 48, 171, 172–73, 183, 282–83
Marshall, N.C., 9, 25, 76, 94, 116, 118; peace meeting in, 164; Unionist raid on, 180, 195
Mars Hill College, 269
Martin, James G., 164, 252, 254, 255–56, 257, 258
Memminger, Christopher, 6, 47, 90, 185, 211
Memorials, Confederate, 267, 277–78
Merchants, in western N.C., 21–22, 48, 175, 214, 235, 282
Merrimon, Augustus, 62, 120, 150, 234, 236, 270, 274, 285

Mexican War, 30, 88
Militias, 36, 61, 109, 112, 121, 140, 176. *See also* Home guard
Millers, 172
Mineral resources, in western N.C., 26, 281
Mining: copper, 19, 26; gold, 19
Ministers, 198–99, 233; and departing troops, 70–71
Mitchell, Elisha, 26
Mitchell, Ellen, 69, 71
Mitchell, Robert, 21, 28, 71
Mitchell County, N.C., 58, 95, 229; Kirk's raid on, 136
Money. *See* Currency, Confederate
Moonshine. *See* Distilleries
Moore, Barnett, 17
Morehead, John Motley, 26
Morganton, N.C., 5, 8, 17, 23, 27, 101, 234; Kirk's raid on, 135–36; Stoneman's raid on, 248–50, 251; women in, 251
Morris, B. T., 117, 121
Morrow, Elizabeth, 205
Mulberry, N.C., 93
Murphy, N.C., 25, 123, 280

Nagel, Paul, 87
Nantahala River valley, 14, 15, 81
Nelson, Thomas R. R., 86, 106
Newport, Tenn., 242–43
New River, 13, 109
Noe, Kenneth, 121
Nolen, H. W., 175–76
Nolichucky Valley, 193
Norman, Letitia, 73
Norman, William, 73
North, Nehemiah, 95
North Carolina Mounted Infantry: 2nd, 94, 103, 135, 258, 273; 3rd, 104, 135, 244, 273
North Carolina regiments: 1st, 63, 64; 21st, 127; 25th, 113; 26th, 189; 32nd, 134; 56th, 127, 133–34, 136; 58th, 102; 60th, 115; 62nd, 131; 64th, 116–20, 128, 131, 143; 69th, 241–42, 278
North Carolina Supreme Court, 161, 270
North Fork, Ashe County, 90, 94; Unionism in, 80
Norwood, Joseph C., 170, 244, 251
Norwood, Laura, 72, 248

Norwood, Robina, 77
Norwood, Selina, 250

Oconaluftee River, 14, 25, 110
Old Fort, N.C., 279
Olmsted, Frederick Law, 15, 19
Orr, Mary, 200
Outliers. *See* Bushwhackers

Paint Rock, 108
Palmer, John B., 136, 137, 250, 252
Palmer, William J., 247, 258
Paludan, Phillip, 118
Parker, Cynthia, 191
Parker, James H., 191
Parker, W. F., 108
Parkins, William H., 93, 229
Patterson, Rufus, 225–26, 234, 245, 247
Patterson, Samuel F., 52, 260
Patton, James, 21
Patton, Montreville, 57
Patton, William, 236
Peace conference, Washington, D.C., 52–53, 241
Peace meetings, in western N.C., 153
Peace movement, 153–54, 158, 163–64, 224
Pearson, Richmond, 144, 275
Pearson, Robert, 251
Pennington, J. L., 152–53
Pigeon River, 13
Pillow, Gideon J., 121, 143
Politics, postwar, 271–74
Polk, Katherine, 5, 9, 185, 201–2, 204, 211, 254–55
Polk, Leonidas, 5, 7, 185; and slaves, 211, 263
Polk County, N.C., 44, 51, 61, 168; bushwhackers in, 240; conscripts in, 142; Ku Klux Klan in, 272; militia, 112
Ponder, John, 234
Pool, John, 163
Poor relief, 169–71, 197, 237–38
Population, in western N.C., 14, 275
Presbyterian Board of Home Missions, 278–79
Primitive Baptists, 199, 234
Prisoners, escaped. *See* Fugitives
Pulliam, Robert W., 176–78

Quallatown, N.C., 16, 21, 132

Race riot, Ashville, 271–72
Railroad construction, 20, 27, 31–32, 279–80;
    slave labor and, 213
Railroads, 173, 235, 266, 280–81, 285
Raleigh, N.C., 45
Rankin, Jesse, 233
Ray, John Henry, 242
Ray, Montrevail, 133
Reconstruction, in western N.C., 270–74
Reddick, C. B., 250, 261
Red Strings. *See* Heroes of America
Reems Creek, 153–54
Reese, John W., 115
Refugees, 196, 200–201, 226, 234. *See also*
    Fugitives
Reid, Salina, 205
Republican Party, 41, 267, 271, 274–75
Republicans, Radical, 271
Revenue agents, 274–75, 282
Revolutionary War, 10, 13, 43, 64, 88
Richardson, Albert, 89, 227
Richmond, Va., 6, 48; bread riot, 197
Rifle factory. *See* Asheville Armory
Rivers, in western N.C., 13–14, 25, 109
Rocky Ford, 249
Rogers, Clark, 99–100
Rosecrans, William, 122
Rothenberg, Winifred B., 171
Rough and Ready Guards, 65
Runnion, Thomas, 196
Rutherford County, N.C., 12, 44, 98, 240;
    Confederate enlistments from, 69; con-
    scripts in, 142; home guard, 206; Ku Klux
    Klan in, 272–73; peace meeting in, 154;
    postwar violence in, 269; women in,
    69–70, 72, 206
Rutherfordton, N.C., 23, 59, 112, 272; women
    in, 69–70
Rutherfordton Riflemen, 69, 71

Salem, N.C., 234; Stoneman's raid on, 247–48
Salisbury, N.C., 27, 60, 65, 169–71; Confed-
    erate prison in, 90, 92, 124, 134, 162, 227;
    Kirk's raid on, 135; prison in, 244, 249;
    Stoneman's raid on, 244, 248
Salstrom, Paul, 28

Salt, 99, 180, 235; raid, 185, 243; scarcity of,
    166–67, 171, 173, 175, 235–36, 284
Saltville, Va., 173, 235, 243
Saluda Gap, 25
Sandy Basin, Va, 193
Savannah, Ga., 22, 213, 214
Schofield, John, 103, 134, 261
Schools, 199, 278–79, 285
Scott, William, 272
Secession, North Carolina's, 42–58, 85
Secession convention, North Carolina,
    50–52, 57, 93, 145–46
Second party system, in western N.C., 31–32
Seddon, James A., 114, 120, 122, 126, 133, 144
Semmes, Thomas J., 211
Sermons. *See* Ministers
Settle, Thomas, 274
Settlement patterns, in western N.C., 13, 14,
    23, 28
Seward, William H., 241
Shelton, David, 120
Shelton, Roderick, 88
Shelton, W. H., 131
Shelton, William, 88
Shelton Laurel, N.C., 8, 20, 88, 185, 284;
    massacre at, 117–20, 150, 195; postwar vio-
    lence in, 270; women from, 118–19, 195
Shenandoah Valley, Va., 7, 21, 163
Sheridan, Philip, 233
Sherman, William T., 233
Sherman's march, 164, 241, 243
Shoes and shoemakers, 172, 175, 236
Shotwell, Randolph, 12, 14, 113, 272
Siler, David W., 44, 50, 55, 61, 112–13, 167,
    223
Siler, Jacob, 234
Siler, Jesse, 21
Silver Creek District (Baptist), 199, 234
Slaveholders, South Carolina, 212
Slaveholders, in western N.C., 17–20, 209
Slavery, 17–20; abolition of, 224, 231, 259;
    profitability of, 19; in secession crisis,
    48–50; and Unionism, 89
Slaves: arming of, 222, 224, 250, 261; disci-
    pline of, 225–26, 229–30; emancipation
    of (*see* Emancipation of slaves); hiring
    of, 17–20, 179, 211–14, 235, 261; labor of,
    18–20, 282; prices of, 214, 221, 225; and

Stoneman's raid, 250, 254, 261–62; and Union troops, 264; wartime labor of, 183–84, 211–12

Slave trade, wartime, 209–13, 217–22, 235, 261

Sloan, Benjamin, 177–78, 180–81, 182

Smith, C. D., 132

Smith, E. Kirby, 109, 110

Social structure. *See* Class, socio-economic

Soco Gap, battle of, 242–43

South Carolina, 21, 243; markets, 25, 48, 214–15; secession of, 42–43, 46; tourists from, 23–24

Southern Claims Commission, 87, 94–96, 98, 100–101, 191

South Mountains, 251

Sparta, N.C., 191

Spartanburg, S.C., 22

Spencer, Cornelia Phillips, 256

Stafford, David, 96–97

Starnes, Richard, 277–78

Statesville, N.C., 41, 234; Stoneman's raid on, 248

Stiles, Louisa, 191

Stills. *See* Distilleries

Stock laws, 275

Stokes County, N.C., 112

Stoneman, George, 243–45, 249

Stoneman's raid, 164, 243–52, 261–62; map of, 246

Stringfield, W. W., 111, 237, 242–43, 258–59

Strother, David Hunter, 29

Suddereth, Abraham, 230

Suffrage, black, 271–72

Surry County, N.C., 32, 73

Sutherland, Daniel, 7

Swain, David L., 212, 232

Swannanoa Gap, 14, 252, 280

Swannanoa River, 13, 14, 24

Sylva, N.C., 9

Tait, George, 241–42

Tate, Sam McDowell, 248

Tate, Sarah, 56

Tatham, Ann, 195

Taxation, 49, 151, 153, 158, 238, 275; ad valorem, 31, 38

Tax-in-kind. *See* Taxation

Taylor, Jim, 75, 115

Teachers, 199, 236

Teague band, 269

Temple, Oliver, 85, 88

Tenantry, in western N.C., 12, 16–18, 20, 171–75, 184, 202, 267, 276

Tennessee National Guard, 123

Textile factories, 281

Thirteenth Amendment, 259

Thomas, William Holland, 6, 15–16, 21, 26, 43, 46–47, 55, 65, 67, 109, 110–11, 132–33, 146–47, 212, 258, 267

Thomas's Legion, 110, 123, 131, 132, 137, 237, 242–43, 252; surrender of, 258–59

Thomasson, Basil Armstrong, 89–90

Toe River valley, 13, 20, 95; Unionism in, 80

Tourism, in western N.C., 23–24, 269, 280–81

Towns, in western N.C., 22–25. *See also* County seats

Transportation, 181, 282. *See also* Internal improvements; Railroads

Transylvania County, N.C., 94, 95, 101, 171, 173, 200, 240; Confederate enlistments from, 69; Unionists in, 130–31

Trap Hill, N.C., 93, 126–27, 229

Tredegar Iron Works, 62, 177

Troops, postwar, in western N.C., 272–73

Tuckaseigee River, 14, 17, 20

Turbyfill, Elkanah, 130

Unaka Mountains, 13

Union army: attacks on western N.C., 242

Union County, Ga., 88

Unionists, 193, 277; in East Tennessee, 83–86, 88; escape to East Tennessee, 124; as militants, 125–28; postwar, 271–74; in secession crisis, 44–46, 51–52, 84–85; in western N.C., 60, 76, 84–104, 271; wives of, 170–71; women, 96, 190, 193

Union troops: from N.C., 104

United Confederate Veterans, 277

United Daughters of the Confederacy, 277–78

Valleytown, N.C., 195

Vance, Harriett E., 234, 248

Vance, Robert B., 64, 78–79, 107, 122, 131–32, 137, 151, 153, 156; capture of, 132

Vance, Zebulon B., 34–35, 37, 41, 45, 48, 51,

65, 110, 120, 133, 137–38, 145, 146, 209, 232, 234, 261, 268, 285; arrest of, 259; and conscription, 114, 144; and deserters, 115, 143, 161; gubernatorial candidate, 148–49; orders to home guards, 129–30; and peace movement, 154, 158–59; postwar career, 274–75; on secession, 44, 52–53, 56; and Shelton Laurel massacre, 120; and slavery, 211–12, 211–12, 222–23; speaking tour, in western N.C., 161

Vaughn, John C., 134, 137

Veterans, Confederate, 277–78

Vicksburg, battle of, 152

Vinovskis, Maris, 7

Violence, postwar, in western N.C., 261–62, 269–70, 279

Virginia: Stoneman's raid on, 248; western, 8

Wade, Major, 261

Walker, Margaret, 196, 239

Walker, William C., 65, 77, 170; death of, 196, 238–39

Walton, Thomas George, 69, 135, 248–49

Ward, Johnson, 112

Warm Springs, N.C., 19, 23, 182

Watauga County, N.C., 94, 102, 107, 122; Confederate enlistments from, 68; Confederate troops in, 134, 137; George Kirk's raid on, 135; Stoneman's raid on, 244

Watauga Rangers, 71

Watson, Elizabeth, 166–67

Watson, James, 166

Waynesville, N.C., 9, 19, 23, 70, 77, 100, 280; Confederate surrender at, 258–59; Union attack on, 123, 157, 242–43, 258

Webster, N.C., 70

Weeks, Drury, 101

Western Military District of N.C., 122, 131, 135–36

Western North Carolina Railroad, 27, 32, 134–35, 212, 235, 251, 279

West Virginia, 83, 92, 276, 277

Whig Party, 31–34, 40, 146

Whiskey. *See* Distilleries

White Sulphur Springs, 258, 280

Whitson, George, 176–77

Wilkesboro, N.C., 8, 17, 23, 41, 68, 93; rally in, 68, 75–76, 85; Vance visit to, 160

Wilkes County, N.C., 51, 68, 98, 100–101, 163, 168; bushwhackers in, 125–28, 239, 260–61; Confederate troops in, 133–34; deserters in, 102, 127; home guard, 195; poor relief in, 170; postwar violence in, 269; slaves in, 227, 229; Stoneman's raid on, 247, 261; Unionists in, 93; violence in, 105; women in, 191

Williams, Cratis, 276

Wills, J. C., 134

Wilmington, Charlotte, and Rutherford Railroad, 235

Wilmot Proviso, 34

Wilson Creek, 125

Winding Stairs, 135

Wise, Henry A., 36

Wolfe, Thomas, 24

Women, 187–207, 257, 284; appeals to governor, 169, 206; and departing troops, 70–73; and deserters, 114, 126; as factory workers, 281; and home front, 78; poor relief to, 169–71; postwar status, 268–69; raids for food, 197–98; as refugees, 200–201; torture of, 118–19, 194–95, 240; Unionists, 93, 96, 190, 193

Woodfin, Nicholas, 37, 39–40, 53, 57, 63–64, 65, 173, 212, 214, 272

Wool production, 173, 186

Woolson, Constant F., 276–77

Worth, David, 90, 97

Worth, Jonathan, 61–62, 149, 162, 270

Writs of habeas corpus, 144; suspension of, 160–61

Yadkin County, N.C., 90, 198; bushwhackers in, 125–28; militia, 121

Yadkin River valley, 13, 14, 250

Yadkinville, N.C., skirmish at, 121, 122

Yancey County, N.C., 31, 51, 64, 95, 242; Confederate raid on, 143; women's raid, 197–98; women in, 202

Yeomen, in western N.C., 21–23, 28, 175. *See also* Tenantry

Younce, W. H., 89, 101